Possible Worlds Theory and Contemporary Narratology

Frontiers of Narrative   SERIES EDITOR
Jesse E. Matz, *Kenyon College*

Possible Worlds Theory and Contemporary Narratology

EDITED BY ALICE BELL AND
MARIE-LAURE RYAN

University of Nebraska Press | Lincoln and London

Portions of chapter 1 were previously published in
"How to Reach Fictional Worlds," in *Fiction and Art:
Explorations in Contemporary Theory*, ed. Ananta
Ch. Suka (London: Bloomsbury Academic, an
imprint of Bloomsbury Publishing Plc., 2015),
219–27. Used with permission.

An earlier version of chapter 7 was published as
"Zeit und Possible Worlds Theory: Eskapismus in
'mögliche Zeiten' in Jack London's *The Star Rover*,"
in *Zeiten erzählen: Ansätze—Aspekte—Analysen*,
ed. Antonius Weixler and Lukas Werner (Berlin:
de Gruyter, 2015), 53–77. Used with permission.

Library of Congress Cataloging-in-Publication Data
Names: Bell, Alice, 1979– editor. | Ryan, Marie-
Laure, 1946– editor. Title: Possible worlds theory
and contemporary narratology / edited by Alice
Bell and Marie-Laure Ryan. Description: Lincoln:
University of Nebraska Press, [2019] | Series:
Frontiers of narrative | Includes bibliographical
references and index.
Identifiers: LCCN 2018011949
ISBN 9780803294998 (cloth: alk. paper)
ISBN 9781496213051 (epub)
ISBN 9781496213068 (mobi)
ISBN 9781496213075 (pdf)
Subjects: LCSH: Fantasy fiction—History and
criticism. | Narration (Rhetoric)
Classification: LCC PN3435 .P67 2019 |
DDC 809.38766—dc23
LC record available at https://lccn.loc.gov/2018011949

Set in Minion Pro by Mikala R. Kolander.

We dedicate this book to Lubomír Doležel
(October 3, 1922–January 28, 2017)

Contents

Illustrations

Tables

Introduction

Possible Worlds Theory Revisited

MARIE-LAURE RYAN AND ALICE BELL

When PW theory made its first forays into literary theory in the mid-1970s, literary studies were almost completely dominated by a conception of language that the philosopher Jaakko Hintikka labeled "language as the universal medium": "By the conception of language as the universal medium, I mean the idea that we cannot in the last analysis escape our language and as it were look at it and its logic from the outside. As a consequence, the semantics of our language is inexpressible, and cannot be theorized about in language" (1988, 53). As representatives of language as the universal medium, Hintikka had in mind logicians who recognize the existence of only one world, such as Gottlob Frege, early Bertrand Russell, Ludwig Wittgenstein, and Willard Van Orman Quine, but he also mentioned Heidegger, who conceived language not in logical terms but in poetic terms as the sacred guardian of Being. Yet Hintikka was clearly referring to the logicians when he further wrote: "One of the most important consequences of the view of language as universal medium is the uniqueness of our language and of its interpretation. All that language is good for in this view is to enable us to talk about this world. We cannot use language to talk about other possible worlds" (54).

As Thomas Martin (2004) has shown, the implications of the idea of "language as universal medium" reach far beyond the brand of logic represented by one-world philosophers: they also underlie the structuralist belief, further developed by New Criticism, poststructuralism, and deconstruction (schools to which we will globally refer as "textualist"), in the centrality of language for human cognition. Not only is there only one world, but this world is made of language, and we cannot escape from what Fredric Jameson (1975) called the "prison-house of language." Crucial to the universal medium view of language is Ferdinand de Saussure's claim that the meaning of words is not determined by their relations to objects in the world but rather by their relations to the other elements of the system, so that in language "there are only differences without positive terms" (1966, 120). The radical interpretation of "language as the universal medium" has far-reaching implications for literary studies. If semantics cannot be theorized in language, this means that the meaning of literary texts cannot be paraphrased and that interpretation is necessarily a betrayal. If the value of words is entirely determined by their neighbors in the system, this means that literary texts cannot be about things in the world (or things in an imaginary world); they must be about language itself. The only mode of reading respectful of literary meaning consists of tracing the "play of language," a play consisting of the internal relations between the elements of the textual system. Finally, if what we regard as reality is in fact a construct of language, the question of truth and reference becomes void. No distinction can be made between truth-seeking and fictional texts, for, as Roland Barthes claimed, "The fact can only have a linguistic existence" (1981, 16–17).

Hintikka's alternative to the conception of language as universal medium is language as calculus. According to this view, which takes the term *calculus* in a broader sense than differential or integral calculus, "you can so to speak stop your language and step off. In less metaphoric terms, you can discuss the semantics of your language and even vary systematically its interpretation. The term 'language as calculus' is not calculated to indicate that in this view language would be a meaningless *jeu de caractères*—this is not the idea at all. Rather, the operative word highlights the thesis that language is freely re-interpretable like a calculus" (1988, 54). Hintikka's characterization rests on two central points: (1) far from being prisoners of language, we can look at it from the outside and analyze it through a metalanguage (which can be language itself); (2) we can interpret statements made in language with respect to various fields of reference or universes of discourse. If we call these fields "worlds," point 2 presupposes the existence of multiple worlds with respect to which the truth of propositions can be evaluated. A given proposition—such as "dragons exist"—may thus be false in one world and true in another.

For literary and narrative theory, the rejection of the conception of language as universal medium in favor of language as calculus is nothing less than a paradigm change, though the doctrine of language as universal medium retained its hegemony for quite some time after the first steps of pw theory into literary territory. The new paradigm means that the question of fiction, long taken for granted, suddenly becomes worthy of attention. It also means the rehabilitation of the question of truth and reference with respect to fiction, a question that was either undecidable, heretical, or too easily resolved in a one-world model. If the one world is made of language (as in poststructuralism), we cannot get out of it, and the question of truth or falsity becomes irrelevant, since it takes an external point of view to evaluate propositions. On the other hand, if the one world is a language-independent reality, and no other world exists, all propositions about imaginary entities become automatically false or indeterminate, since they do not refer to anything. In a many-worlds ontology, fictional texts can be associated with worlds, these worlds can be imagined on the basis of all the propositions presented as true by the text, and it is possible to distinguish true statements about the members of particular fictional worlds, such as "Emma Bovary was a dissatisfied country doctor's wife," from false ones, such as "Emma Bovary was a paragon of marital fidelity."

But the evaluation of statements about fictional worlds and characters is not the primary reason of philosophers for postulating a many-worlds ontology; it is at best an added bonus, a lucky side effect for literary theory. The concept of possible worlds was first proposed by Gottfried Wilhelm Leibniz in his *Théodicée* to defend God's act of creation: when God created the world, he considered all possible worlds and chose the best of them to be actualized, even though this "best possible world" contains evil. This suggests that possibilities obey combinatorial and causal laws that even God must observe. The revival of the notion of possible worlds in twentieth-century analytic philosophy has, however, little to do with Leibniz. For philosophers such as Saul Kripke, David Lewis, Jaakko Hintikka, Alvin Plantinga, and others, the postulation of many worlds serves the purpose of formulating the semantics of the modal operators of possibility, necessity, and impossibility, which form the so-called alethic system.

To justify the postulation of multiple worlds, Lewis invoked our intuitive, prephilosophical belief that "things could be different from what they are." While things are how they are in only one way, they could be different in many different ways; this intuition justifies the postulation of one actual world (AW) and of many (perhaps an infinity) of nonactual or alternate possible worlds (APWs or PWs) where things are different. In addition to the contrast between one actual world and many merely possible ones, modal logic uses a concept of accessibility. Saul Kripke proposed a model structure (known as M-model) for modal logic that Michael J. Loux describes in the following way:

> An M-model is an ordered triple (G,K,R), where K is a set of objects, G is one of the objects belonging to K, and R is a relation defined over the members of K. Intuitively, Kripke tells us, we are to think of K as the set of all possible worlds; G is to be thought of as the actual world; and R represents a relation which Kripke calls *relative possibility* and others *accessibility*. Intuitively, we are to understand this relation in such a way that a world, W, is possible relative or accessible to a world, W', just in case every situation that obtains in W is possible in W'. . . . To get an M-model structure, the specification is subject to just one restriction: the relation of accessibility has to be reflexive; it has to be the case that every world is accessible to or possible relative to itself. (1979, 21, emphasis original)

The reflexivity of the relation of accessibility means that the actual world is also a possible world, despite its ontological difference from all others. Whether the relation is transitive or symmetrical depends on the system, for there are variations within PW theory.[1]

Within such a model, necessity and possibility can be logically defined by quantifying over the notion of world: necessity becomes "For all worlds, p (universal quantifier)," possibility becomes "For some world, p (existential quantifier)," and impossibility is expressed by the negation of the formula for possibility. Other operators have been shown to function in ways similar to the alethic system: those of the deontic system (permitted, obligatory, forbidden), of the epistemic system (believed, known, ignored), and of the axiological system (indifferent, good, bad).

Another important application of PW theory to semantic logic is the evaluation of counterfactual statements of the type "If Napoleon had won the battle of Waterloo, he would not have been exiled to Saint Helena." These statements allude to states of affairs that only take place in PWs (here: Napoleon wins the battle of Waterloo), yet as a whole they are uttered to make statements about AW. A sports fan may, for instance, use a counterfactual to express how close his team came to winning the game ("if the ref had not been blind . . .") and, by implication, how unlucky it was. Lewis's definitions of the truth conditions of counterfactuals can be informally paraphrased as follows: Imagine the set A of worlds where the antecedent holds and the consequent is true. Imagine the set B of worlds where the antecedent is true and the consequent is false. If the world that differs the least, on balance, from AW belongs to set A, the counterfactual is true; otherwise, it is false.[2] The lack of fixed criteria for measuring the overall similarity of a world to AW could be regarded as a defect of the formula, but this defect may be a blessing in disguise, because it explains why people often disagree about the truth value of a specific counterfactual statement. Just ask the fan of the other team!

A third benefit of a many-worlds ontology is its ability to provide a formal account of meaning. Can different expressions have the same meaning at all? A Saussurian conception of language as system of differences would answer this question negatively, but a PW account will say that two expressions have the same meaning when they have the same extension in all possible worlds. "The evening star" does not have the same meaning as "the morning star" because there are worlds where a different celestial object is the first to appear in the evening and the last to fade in the morning, rather than both being the planet Venus, but "a bachelor" has the same meaning as "an unmarried man" because these two expressions pick the same set of objects in all PWs. PW theory also proposes an explanation of entailment: "One statement *entails* a second just in case every world at which the first is true is a world at which the second is true" (Bricker 2008, 120).

A problematic issue with the idea of possible worlds is what lies beyond the horizon of the possible. Are there "impossible worlds," and if so, what are they? If we associate possibility with respect of the laws of logic (non-contradiction and excluded middle),[3] impossible worlds could be defined as collections of values for propositions that defy these laws. But are such collections still worlds, or are they just that—incoherent collections of truth values that do not allow inferences (by virtue of the principle that if a system of propositions contains one contradiction, everything and its negation become true in it)? If we deny incoherent collections of propositions the status of world, and if we associate "possibility" with logical coherence, then all entities that are "worlds" are logically coherent and therefore possible worlds. Then the label PW theory would rest on a redundancy (Bricker 2008). However, if we vary the notion of possibility, for instance, by interpreting it as observance of the laws of physics, then a world can be physically impossible but logically possible, and the redundancy is avoided: there are impossible worlds that still fulfill the basic conditions of worldness. This is a significant bonus for scholars of narrative media, as we shall see later. However, these scholars still face the problem of what to call the semantic domain of texts that present collections of mutually incompatible world fragments. "Logically impossible worlds" is an oxymoron if worldness is associated with logical coherence.

As we have already seen, the primary reason for the postulation of a many-worlds ontology is the development of logical notations that capture truth conditions for certain types of sentences. Within this well-defined project, however, there is room for a variety of interpretations of what possible worlds are made of and of what distinguishes AW from its merely possible satellites. Two interpretations of possibility and actuality dominate the field, both of which have yielded significant results for modal logic: actualism and modal realism.

Actualism comes in many versions. In the most radical, called by Robert M. Adams "hard actualism," everything that exists is actual, and there is no such thing as "merely possible worlds" (1979, 203). For Adams, "there could have been things that do not actually exist," but "there *are* no things that do not exist in the actual world" (1981, 7, emphasis original). In this perspective, PWs could be regarded as fictions conceived within AW that are concerned with how AW could have been.

In a less radical version of actualism, known as "possibilism" or "soft actualism" (Adams 1979, 203), entities that are merely possible do exist, but they are not instantiated, and therefore they are not actual. If one accepts this view, answers to the question "what are PWs made of?" vary: they consist of states of affairs expressed by propositions; they are matrices of truth values for propositions that differ from the matrix that describes the actual world (a position that opens the question of the mode of existence of propositions); they are different combinations of the entities found in the actual world (so that no PW can contain dragons, a serious problem for narrative applications).[4]

Alternatively (and this returns to the hard actualism position), possible worlds could be purely mental constructs. This interpretation seems the most intuitive for literary scholars: Aren't the worlds projected by fictional texts products of the mind of an author? Aren't dreams, predictions, and hypotheses world-constructing activities that originate in mental events? Nicholas Rescher has proposed an analysis of the ontological status of the possible that supports the idea of its mental origin. In the case of actual existence there is a dualism, so that the state of affairs "dogs have tails" can be distinguished from the thought that dogs have tails, but with non-existent possibilities such as "dogs have horns" there is only the thought (Rescher 1988, 168–69). Yet it is significant that Rescher does not connect possibilities to possible worlds in his essay. The mind can contemplate individual possibilities, but it cannot construct a complete possible world that attributes a truth value to every proposition. If completeness is regarded as a constitutive property of possible worlds, as it is for most PW philosophers, the "worldness" of the mental conception of possibility is questionable. On the other hand, if PWS are indeed complete, this means that their totality is beyond the grasp of the human mind. But the same can be said of our experience of the actual world.

The other dominant interpretation of possibility and actuality is David Lewis's modal realism. According to modal realism, there is no ontological distinction between the actual world and merely possible ones: both kinds are made of the same substance, that is, of material things and events. As Lewis writes,

> Our actual world is only one world among others. We call it actual not because it differs in kind from all the rest but because it is the world we inhabit. The inhabitants of other worlds may truly call their own world actual, if they mean by "actual" what we do; for the meaning we give to "actual" is such that it refers at any world *i* to the world *i* itself. "Actual" is indexical, like "I" or "here," or "now": it depends for its reference on the circumstances of utterance, to wit the world where the utterance is located. (1979, 184)

Modal realism may appear ontologically extravagant in its claim that possible worlds exist objectively, but Lewis cleverly contours the objection by distinguishing qualitative from quantitative parsimony. The postulation of PWS transgresses the principle of Occam's razor, which calls for qualitative parsimony, but once PWS are postulated, as they are in both actualism and modal realism, it does not really matter whether there are only a few or zillions of them. The indexical account of actuality is particularly appealing in an age that questions the centrality of any culture or identity or even of the human race, since the notion of indexicality allows every possible world to function as actual world, this is to say, as the center of a particular system of reality.

From a strictly philosophical point of view, the superiority of particular conceptions of actuality and possibility is not a matter of making claims about the organization of the cosmos but rather a matter of the ability of those conceptions to support and expand modal logic.[5] For instance, Lewis's modal realism is considered by many philosophers a violation of commonsense beliefs, but its elegance in dealing with modal logic is widely recognized.[6] In this perspective, if a conception of the nature of pws provides a basis for interesting proofs and semantic explanations, is it worthy of consideration? If it does not provide such a basis, it can be ignored. Most philosophical developments in pw theory since the seventies (e.g., Divers 2002; Nolan 2002) have been extremely technical contributions to modal logic, and they are not particularly useful for literary and narrative theory, because logic interprets language on the level of sentences and propositions, while literary and narrative theories do so on the level of texts. Narrative theory, in addition, is not limited to language-based storytelling. Since narratologists are not doing philosophy, and since philosophers do not agree on a pure essence of possible worlds anyway, some degree of adaptation (call it metaphorization if you want) is unavoidable. If it weren't for their intrinsic interdisciplinary adaptability, convincingly demonstrated in the Nobel symposium "Possible Worlds in Humanities, Arts and Sciences," held in 1986, pws would be confined to the relative obscurity of formal logic, the most esoteric domain of philosophy.

This is not to say that any use of the term *world* or even *possible world* in scholarly discourse is indebted to pw theory. Critics have long spoken of "the world of author such and such" in a rather loose way without asking what makes a world a world. The notion of "storyworld" that is currently gaining traction in narratology can be analyzed in terms of pw, but it remains operative without this connection. For a line of kinship to be maintained with philosophy, the three components of Kripke's M-model must be made relevant: an ontology made of multiple worlds; the designation of one and only one of these worlds as actual; and the postulation of accessibility relations between worlds. Transgressions of this ontological model can be discussed as long as they take it as the point of reference.

Possible Worlds Approaches to Literature and Narrative: A Very Short History

The following survey of landmarks in possible worlds approaches to literature and narrative will be kept to a strict minimum, leaving a more substantial discussion of some of the problems involved for the sections devoted to specific domains.

The first literary scholar to take notice of the philosophical concept of PW and to adapt it to literary issues was Thomas Pavel in his 1975 article "Possible Worlds in Literary Semantics," later expanded in his 1986 book, *Fictional Worlds*. In this article, Pavel argued against the "moratorium" imposed on questions of truth and reference by textualist literary schools. He argued that in creating a fictional world (whether this world is or isn't technically a PW), the literary text imposes its own laws on this world and defines a new horizon of possibilities. The reader must consequently adopt a new ontological perspective with respect to what exists and does not exist. "In this precise sense," writes Pavel, "one can say that literary worlds are autonomous" (1986, 175). Pavel also argued against a "segregationist" attitude toward fictional worlds that divides texts into statements that are either true or false in AW in favor of an integrationist position that regards all the propositions asserted by the text as true in the fictional world. The domain of reference for truth assignment thus shifts from AW to the world created by the text. But Pavel also warns against erecting a rigid boundary between fictional worlds and the AW, because such a boundary would prevent fictions from providing insights about our world and deprive literature of any existential, ethical, and political value. In a later article, Pavel revealed that what attracted him to PW theory was the opportunity to overcome the reigning formalism of the time and to rehabilitate content so as to read literature as the expression of human concerns: "We are trying to capture the entwining of characters in a system of values and norms, to experience their desires in a homeopathic way, and to foresee what they plan to do" (2010, 312).[7] In a PW approach, characters are no longer collections of semes, as structuralism described them, but imaginary human beings who just happen to reside in other worlds. By opening the question of concern for characters, Pavel anticipates the cognitive turn of the twenty-first century and implicitly demonstrates its compatibility with PW theory.

The next landmark is David Lewis's 1978 article "Truth in Fiction." Theoretical accounts of fictionality can do two different things: they can offer a formal definition of fiction, or they can provide guidelines for its interpretation. Lewis's article does both. Lewis's definition, like that of several other philosophical accounts (e.g., Searle 1975; Walton 1990; Currie 1990), is based on the notion of pretense: "The storyteller purports to be telling the truth about matters whereof he has knowledge. He purports to be talking about characters who are known to him, and whom he refers to, typically, by means of ordinary proper names. But his story is fiction, he is not really doing these things" (1978, 40). So what is he doing? He is doubling himself: "Here at our world we have a fiction f, told in an act a of storytelling; at some other world we have an act a' of telling the truth about known matters of fact; the stories told in a and a' match word for word, and the words have the same meaning" (40). Lewis does not specify who does the two acts of storytelling, but narratology has an easy answer: a is the act of the author, a' the act of a narrator.

For fictional worlds to stimulate the imagination, their construction must go far beyond the propositions explicitly asserted by the text and their strict logical implications. To explain how we can make either true or false statements about fictional worlds, Lewis offers an explanation adapted from his analysis of counterfactuals, though he does not assimilate fictions with counterfactuals: fictions are told as true of a PW, but (as our imaginary sports fan has shown) counterfactuals make statements about the actual world.[8] "A sentence of the form 'in the fiction f, [Ψ]' is non-vacuously true iff some world where f is told as known fact and Ψ is true differs less from our actual world, on balance, than does any other world where f is told as known fact and Ψ is not true. It is vacuously true iff there are no possible worlds where f is told as known fact" (Lewis 1978, 42). Note that Lewis speaks of "some world where f is told as known fact," not of "the world." By allowing fictions to be compatible with several PWs, he makes room for variable ways to imagine and interpret fictional worlds.

The work of Lubomír Doležel, starting in 1976 as a series of articles that led to his 1998 book, *Heterocosmica*, adopts the notion of PW with reservations in order to maintain a distinction between the ontological completeness of PW postulated by logicians and the incompleteness of fictional worlds. Doležel shows that because it is impossible to imagine a world in all its properties, fictional texts present areas of radical indeterminacy, and the play between blank and filled areas, specified and unspecified information, is an integral part of literary meaning. Doležel also adapts Frege's distinction between sense and reference into a contrast between an "intensional" narrative world, made of all the meanings conveyed by the text, and an "extensional" narrative world, made of all the entities that objectively exist in the fictional world. For instance, "Hamlet" and "the Prince of Denmark" carry different intensional meanings, but they refer to the same individual in the extensional narrative world. Finally, Doležel proposes a taxonomy of plots based on the different systems of modal logic: alethic plots, such as fairy tales and the fantastic, centered on the different abilities of different types of characters; deontic plots, such as tragedies, centered on the notions of obligation, violation, and permission; epistemic plots, such as mystery stories, based on the acquisition of knowledge; and axiological plots, such as quest narratives, based on the acquisition of desirable objects and the avoidance of a bad fate. In *Heterocosmica* Doležel anticipates the current interest in phenomena of transfictionality (cf. Saint-Gelais 2011) by distinguishing three types of intertextual relations between texts that develop the same or similar narrative material: expansion (telling new stories that take place in the same world), displacement (constructing an "essentially different version of the protoworld, redesigning its structure and reinventing the story" [1998, 207]), and transposition (moving the plot to a different spatial or historical setting representing a different world).

In 1977 Lucia Vaina published a short article, "Les mondes possibles du texte," that exercised a strong influence on the work of Umberto Eco and later of Marie-Laure Ryan. This article, which remains on a highly abstract level, describes textual worlds as complete states of affairs and narratives as successions of such states mediated by events. Vaina also suggests a self-embedding property of textual worlds, so that the semantic domain of texts can contain a number of subworlds created by the mental activity of the characters, such as believing and wishing.

Utilizing PW in *The Role of the Reader* (1984), Eco regards narrative texts not as representations of a single world but as universes made of a constellation of possible worlds. A literary text, he writes, is *"a machine for producing possible worlds* (of the *fabula*, of the characters within the *fabula*, and of the reader outside the *fabula*)" (246, emphasis original). He distinguishes the world imagined by the author, which corresponds to all the states of the *fabula*; the worlds imagined, believed, wished, and so on by the characters; and the possible worlds imagined, believed, or wished by a so-called Model Reader. A text, claims Eco, can tell three different stories: (1) the story that happens to the characters, (2) the story of what happens to a naive reader, and (3) the story of what happens to the story as text—a story deciphered by the critical reader. Numbers 1 and 2 often fall together, but they are distinguished when texts trick the reader into making false assumptions.

The next landmark is Doreen Maître's *Literature and Possible Worlds* (1983). Developing the concept of accessibility from modal logic, she distinguishes four semantic types of fictional worlds, based on their distance from the actual world, and thus begins the development of what was to become "Genre Theory" in PW theory (see the section "Genre Theory" below). In particular, she distinguishes between (1) "works that include accounts of actual historical events" (79), such as romans à clef, romanced biographies, or "true fiction," such as Truman Capote's *In Cold Blood*; (2) "works that deal with states of affairs which could be actual" (79), such as realist and naturalistic novels; (3) "works in which there is an oscillation between could-be-actual and never-could-be-actual worlds" (79), such as Henry James's *The Turn of the Screw*, which maintains ambiguity between a natural and a supernatural explanation of events; and (4) "works that deal with states of affairs which could never be actual," such as fairy tales, fables, and the brand of the fantastic represented by *The Lord of the Rings* or, a more recent example, *Harry Potter*.

Marie-Laure Ryan's 1991 book, *Possible Worlds, Artificial Intelligence and Narrative Theory*, develops several of the issues discussed so far: she turns Lewis's counterfactual analysis of truth in fiction into a guideline for interpretation that she calls the "principle of minimal departure" (see section "Theory of Fiction"); she refines Maître's typology by proposing different types of accessibility relations (see section "Genre Theory"); and she develops Eco's narrative semantics into a comprehensive model of fictional universes (see section "Narrative Semantics"). She also investigates the usefulness of PW theory for artificial intelligence by discussing several computer programs for automated story generation that organize information into domains corresponding to the beliefs, goals, and plans of characters, in addition to generating actual narrative events.

Ruth Ronen's 1994 book, *Possible Worlds in Literary Theory*, offers a useful and sophisticated survey of the philosophical notion of PW, but her main purpose is to criticize the use of the term by literary scholars: "First, literary theory gives insufficient account of the philosophical sources of thinking about possible worlds, and second, in the process of transferring possible worlds to the literary domain, the concept loses its original meaning and becomes a diffuse metaphor. . . . The result is a naïve adaptation or an inadvertent metaphorization of a concept whose original (philosophical and literary) nonfigurative significance is far from self-evident" (7). Ronen's criticism is certainly justified for some literary-critical adoptions of the PW concept, but if using the PW model for purposes other than modal logic is necessarily metaphorical, and if metaphorical use means misuse, the PW approach to narrative will be killed in the egg, together with all other interdisciplinary adaptations. In the second part of the book, Ronen defends a largely textualist conception of fictional worlds that distinguishes them from PWs on two counts: (1) they are radically incomplete because they are limited to the information provided by the text (plus its logical implications); and (2) they can be impossible.

In the late nineties and after the turn of the century, purely theoretical work inspired by PW theory becomes rarer compared to practical applications such as Nancy Traill's *Possible Worlds of the Fantastic: The Rise of the Paranormal in Fiction* (1996), Elena Semino's *Language and World Creation in Poems and Other Texts* (1997), Alice Bell's *The Possible Worlds of Hypertext Fiction* (2010), and Lubomír Doležel's *Possible Worlds of Fiction and History* (2010). More recently, PW theory also found some, albeit limited, traction in film (e.g., Buckland 2004; Uhl 2013), drama (e.g., Swift 2016), and sound studies (e.g., Voegelin 2014). Among the more theoretical contributions of this period, the following deserve special mention.

First, Thomas Martin's *Poiesis and Possible Worlds: A Study in Modality and Literary Theory* (2004) discusses the deep-reaching implications for literary theory of Jaakko Hintikka's distinction between language as universal medium and language as calculus. Metaphor provides Martin with the litmus test for the possibility of creative language play. He shows that under a conception of language as universal medium, where the meaning of words depends entirely on their relations to other words, figurative language cannot be distinguished from literal use. Many advocates of textualism insist indeed on the fundamental metaphoricity of language, but they could just as well call this metaphoricity literalness. If we are spoken by language, rather than speaking it, there is no room for distance and for play. But under Hintikka's conception of language as calculus, which allows users to distinguish the various meanings of words and to vary both their reference and their interpretation, we can deliberately extend the applicability of a word or phrase, for instance, by calling a man a lion, thereby creating what Hintikka calls "world lines" between previously unrelated individuals or sets of individuals. These lines can extend across possible worlds when we use fictional individuals as the vehicle of meaning, for instance, by calling John a Scrooge. If the essence of literature resides in creative play with language, Martin argues, then the conception of language that provides the best account of metaphor is also the best suited for literature in general.

Though the first scholars to apply pw theory to literature were of European origin, it was only in 2010 that the notion of pw made its official debut in France with the collection *La théorie littéraire des mondes possibles*, edited by Françoise Lavocat. One of the strong points of this collection is the investigation of the strategies of world creation in older literatures, from antiquity to the Renaissance and the Baroque period. But some of the contributions advocate a distanciation from the philosophical tradition in favor of a freer application of the notion of world (Lavocat 2010, 9).

The eastern European connection of pw theory is covered in Bohumil Fořt's *An Introduction to Fictional Worlds Theory* (2016). In this book, Fořt provides a most useful account of the philosophical notion of possible worlds, enriching the discussion of the Anglo-American tradition with contributions and critiques from Czech philosophers whose work deserves to be better known in the West. He shows that far from creating consensus, even among logicians, the nature of possible worlds is a widely debated issue. In the second part of the book, he moves to fictional worlds, which he regards as ontologically different from both the actual world and the possible worlds of logic on the basis of their incompleteness and because they contain only a limited number of existents—those mentioned by the text. Despite insisting on the difference between possible worlds and fictional worlds, Fořt titles the second part of his book "Fictional Worlds as Possible Worlds." In this section, he reviews and critically discusses the main issues of a possible world approach to fiction, such as impossible worlds, accessibility relations, completeness, characters with historical counterparts, narrative modalities, and minimal departure. He gives special attention to the concepts proposed by Doležel, such as authentication, the contrast between extensional and intensional fictional worlds, and "literary transduction," that is, the intertextual relations between worlds mentioned in our discussion of Doležel's work. The last section situates the PW approach with respect to the Prague school of linguistics and aesthetics. Fořt shows that this school was mostly preoccupied with the nature of literariness, but as we try to demonstrate in this book, the PW model is applicable to nonliterary and nonfictional narratives, as well as to texts of popular culture. Insofar as the model explains how users experience storyworlds, its importance is more semantic and cognitive than strictly aesthetic.

Several relatively recent developments taking place, respectively, in theory, culture, and technology suggest indeed that the field of application of PW theory stretches far beyond literary theory. The theoretical development is the expansion of narratology into a project that spans every medium capable of storytelling, such as film, drama, comics, painting, and videogames. These media are as amenable to PW theory as was literature. The cultural development is an increased interest in fantastic worlds (Wolf 2012; Saler 2012), leading to their transmedia expansion and to the rise of a participatory fan culture (Jenkins 2006) such as writing fan fiction or dressing up as fictional characters in cosplay events. The technological development, finally, is the creation of interactive computer games and online worlds that enable users to inhabit these worlds through an avatar and in some cases (such as *Second Life*) to contribute to their creation. Through Lewis's modal realism and indexical conception of actuality, PW theory is particularly well suited to account for the experience of transporting oneself into imaginary worlds, whether textual, visual, or digital, and to explain how life in these worlds can become, for some of their members, more real than RL (real life).

In the next sections, we review the major narrative contributions of PW theory in terms of its areas of application.

Theory of Fiction

While many PW-inspired literary theorists have written about fiction (e.g., Pavel, Doležel, Eco, Ryan, Ronen), the only formal, explicit definition that relies on the notion of PW is the one that was proposed by Lewis in "Truth in Fiction": a fiction is a story told as true of a world (or worlds) other than AW.[9] Here we examine some of the implications of this definition.

If a fictional story is "told as true," this means that fictional discourse takes an assertive form and does not bear overt marks of irreality. In other words, fiction denies its own status as fiction. It could be objected that fictionality is openly flagged by formulae such as "once upon a time" and "there was and there was not" or by the paratextual genre indicator "a novel" that appears on the book's title page, or outside the text proper. Moreover, there are what Dorrit Cohn (1999) called "signposts of fictionality," that is, narrative devices that suggest the fictionality of texts. Fictional stories are hardly ever told in the same way as factual ones, and fictionality can usually be detected in a blind test. But these so-called signposts, or indices, do not openly state unreality, and they do not invalidate the claim that fiction is "told as true." As for the overt formulae mentioned above, they function as general prefixes for the whole text, but once the fictional status of the narrative has been established, it is pushed to the background of the user's consciousness, and attention is shifted to the states of affairs asserted by the text.

If we couple Lewis's conception of fiction as discourse that denies its own status as fiction with his indexical conception of actuality, we can describe the experience of fiction as a playful relocation of the user to the PW where the story is told as true. Through this relocation—or recentering, as Ryan (1991) calls it—users regard the fictional world as actual in make-believe, which means as existing independently of the text, even though they know that, from the point of view of the actual world, the fictional world is created by the text. The idea of recentering into fictional worlds explains why readers, spectators, or players can regard fictional characters as (fictionally) real people and why they can experience emotions toward these characters, rather than regarding them as purely textual constructs.

By adapting his analysis of truth conditions for counterfactual statements to the case of truth in fiction, Lewis complements his definition of fiction as "story told as true of a world other than AW" with a guideline for imagining and interpreting fictional worlds. This guideline can be summarized as "in imagining fictional worlds, do not make gratuitous changes from the actual world." Ryan generalized this guideline into what she calls "the principle of minimal departure." According to this principle, we construe fictional worlds as conforming as far as possible to our representation of AW. In other words, we do not make gratuitous changes: if a text speaks of a winged horse, we imagine an entity presenting all the properties of actual horses but being able to fly. Yet we do not imagine this horse as breathing fire unless specified by the text. When the text clashes with our experience of reality, the text has the last word.

Lewis's counterfactual approach to fiction not only explains the possibility of making true or false statements about fictional worlds but also explains the possibility of deriving from fiction interpretations whose range of truth extends to the actual world, such as morals. In other words, counterfactual reasoning demonstrates how we can actually *learn* from fiction. Daniel Dohrn (2009) explains this didactic potential by asking readers to consider Cleanth Brooks's interpretation of William Faulkner's *The Sound and the Fury*: "Jason Compson betrays his family members, because individuals no longer sustained by familial and cultural unity are alienated and lost in private worlds" (Brooks quoted by Dohrn, 40). This interpretation can be turned into a truth for the actual world by the following counterfactual sentence: "If an individual in the real world behaved like Jason Compson, then he would do so because he is no longer sustained by familial and cultural unity (etc.)." Or, more generally: "Loss of support by familial and cultural unity leads to behaviors similar to Jason's." Q.E.D.

Yet Lewis's definition of fiction as stories "told as true" of another world is not without its own problems. First, as Lewis (1983) observed in "Postscript to 'Truth in Fiction,'" not all fictions are told as known fact. He mentions an Australian folk song, "The Ballad of the Flash Stockman," in which Ugly Dave, the speaker in the fictional world, tells a tall tale and brags about lying. Should one then postulate an embedded fictional world where the story is told as true, Ugly Dave pretending to be its narrator? Second, the formula could be accused of a narrative bias: there are texts such as Beckett's trilogy *Molloy, Malone Dies*, and *The Unnamable*, and Dostoevsky's *Notes from the Underground* in which the narrator (or, rather, utterer) in the fictional world does not tell a story as known fact but rather rambles on and on. Such texts are clearly fictional, since the discourse is uttered by an individuated speaking instance distinct from the author, but they are not narrative (or only marginally so), since what matters in these texts is not what happens in a world but the expression of a subjectivity.[10] This problem could be solved by the following revision of Lewis's formula: "Here at our world w_1 we have a fiction f, told in an act *a* of world-making; at some other world w2 we have an act *a'* of making statements within and about w2 and/or other worlds; the discourses uttered in *a* and *a'* match word for word, and the words have the same meaning." This suggestion would also take care of unreliable narrators. Third, there are texts that cannot be told as true of any possible world because they contain logical contradictions. Could one say that they are told about impossible worlds? For Lewis, the assumption that "there are impossible possible worlds as well as the possible possible worlds" is not to be taken seriously (1978, 46). If a fiction cannot be true of any PW, then everything becomes vacuously true in it, and this fiction cannot yield valid interpretations, much less interpretations that encompass AW, except (as Dohrn [2009, 42] also observes) for metatextual statements about artistic possibility.

Narrative Semantics

While a PW-inspired theory of fiction is based on the relations between the actual world and the textual world, a PW-inspired narrative semantics looks at the internal organization of narrative worlds. It is therefore indifferent to the distinction between fiction and nonfiction. The term *narrative world* (or *storyworld*), however, hides the true ontological structure of a text, because just as PW theory postulates a plurality of worlds, so does its application to narrative texts. Storyworlds are therefore entire modal universes consisting of multiple worlds. Moreover, the opposition between one actual world and several merely possible worlds that one finds in our native system of reality reappears within narrative universes, so that users who "recenter" themselves in imagination to a narrative universe (a precondition for immersion) will land in a new actual world. This actual world contains narrative facts comprising both static properties mentioned in descriptions and world-changing events mentioned in the more properly narrative parts. Just like real-world events, narrative events cannot be properly understood without taking into consideration a background of virtual events that could have taken place instead, leading to different states of affairs. For instance, when people plan an action, they must consider (1) what will happen if the action is taken and succeeds; (2) what will happen if the action is taken and fails; and (3) what will happen if no action is taken and events follow their predicable course.[11]

The first narratologists to recognize the narrative importance of virtual events were not PW-inspired literary scholars but French structuralists. In *Grammaire du Décaméron* (1969), Tzvetan Todorov established a catalog of modal operators for narrative events that haven't yet happened: the *obligatory* mode for the social duties of characters; the *conditional* mode for personal obligations due to a contract (if you do *p*, I will do *q*); the *optative* mode for desires and goals; and the *predictive* mode for anticipated events (46–49). In *Logique du récit* (1972), Claude Bremond distinguished descriptive statements of facts from modalized statements, which "anticipate the hypothesis of a future event, of a virtual action" (86). He diagrammed plot as possibility trees representing all the courses of action faced by characters at crucial moments in their life.

A narrative plot is not a single state of affairs; it is a succession of actually occurring events leading to changed states of affairs. But as suggested above, states of affairs consist of more than objectively occurring facts; they also include the modalized propositions that define the state of mind of characters. In *Possible Worlds* (1991) Ryan describes storyworlds as modal universes consisting of an actual world, a realm of narrative facts, which she calls the textual actual world (TAW), surrounded by the private worlds of characters (textual possible worlds, or TPWs). Among these private worlds, the belief world stands apart for its representational nature: it reflects not only the characters' beliefs about TAW but also the characters' beliefs about other characters' private worlds, which may contain beliefs about the original characters' beliefs. PW theory thus accounts efficiently for theory of mind and its recursive embedding, whose limits can only be set by the limits of the human mind. Other private worlds, such as the wish world and the obligation world, are static models of an ideal state of TAW. Insofar as they are unrealized in TAW, they motivate characters to take action, and they are one of the two motors that propel the plot forward, the other being purely accidental happenings. Goals actively pursued by characters, as well as the plans leading to the fulfillment of those goals, are held in a third kind of private world. Finally, characters may form purely imaginary worlds or, rather, universes, such as dreams, fantasies, or fictions, that lead recursively into new systems of reality centered around their own AW. Through these imaginary constructs, narrative universes acquire distinct ontological levels.

In Ryan's model, plot, or narrative action, consists of the movement of worlds within narrative universes. When changes occur in TAW, they may affect its relations to the model worlds of characters, bringing these worlds closer to or farther from fulfillment. Since the wish worlds or obligation worlds of different characters may contain conflicting requirements, the solution of one character's problems may cause conflict for another character, motivating this other character to take action. Because of antagonistic relations between characters, conflict is hardly ever completely eliminated from narrative universes, but narratives typically end when the conflicts in the main character's domain are resolved or when this character is no longer in a position to work toward the resolution of those conflicts.

Genre Theory

While narrative semantics seeks to analyze the relationships between worlds in a textual universe, PW theory has also been invoked to account for the different *kinds* of worlds found in literature. This has led to the development of typologies of fictional worlds and of what we might also call genre theory. The PW approach to genre relies on the notion of accessibility relation as a means to classify fictional worlds according to how far they represent possibility, or impossibility, in the actual world.

As we have noted above, Maître's (1983) *Literature and Possible Worlds* represents one of the founding pieces of scholarship in the area of genre theory. Traill (1991; cf. 1996) further develops PW for its application to the supernatural and the fantastic (and thus Maître's latter two categories) by proposing a new typology of the fantastic. She challenges what she calls Todorov's "influential" but "narrow conception" (1991, 196, 197) of the fantastic in which he defines the fantastic as a genre located between the "uncanny" and the "marvelous" and where there is some ambiguity as to whether the events described are "natural" or "supernatural." That is, the fantastic occurs where the reader is uncertain about whether the events are natural or supernatural (see Todorov 1975). Traill uses PW theory to distinguish between texts that utilize four different modes: (1) the "authenticated mode" (e.g., Jonathan Swift's *Gulliver's Travels*), in which both natural and supernatural realms are presented in a text as "uncontested, unambiguous fictional 'facts'" (199); (2) the "ambiguous mode" (e.g., Henry James's *The Turn of the Screw*), in which there is some ambiguity about the ontological status of the supernatural because "the narrator ... does not fully authenticate it" (200); (3) the "disauthenticated mode" (e.g., Lewis Carroll's *Alice's Adventures in Wonderland*), in which the constructed supernatural domain is "ultimately disauthenticated [as a dream] and a natural causation assigned to the events" (201); and (4) the "paranormal mode," which she subdivides into "epistemic," "psychological," and "philosophical," in which the supernatural is an inevitable part of the natural so that they are "no longer mutually exclusive" (202). While she does not give this example herself, we might categorize the spontaneous combustion of Mr. Krook in Charles Dickens's *Bleak House* and many works of magical realism as utilizing this mode.

Traill's first three categories refine Todorov's structuralist approach to the fantastic, while her fourth expands the study of the fantastic to include texts that describe phenomena of questionable existence. Traill stresses that her modes should not be used to define works of fiction, because a work of literature could adopt multiple modes. However, her typology represents an important step in genre theory, first, because she uses the epistemic qualities of a text as a means of determining the ontological status of its fictional world, and second, because she shows how the ontological status of elements in a fictional world can be both culturally and historically relative.

Also recognizing the culturally dependent nature of possibility, Ryan (1991) offers a comprehensive and more refined typology of fictional worlds that accommodates all kinds of fictional worlds as opposed to only those of the fantastic. Utilizing the concept of accessibility relations from modal logic but also recognizing that the "logical interpretation of accessibility relation is not sufficient for a theory of fictional genres" (32), Ryan proposes nine types of accessibility against which a fictional world can be assessed. These are (1) identity of properties; (2) identity of inventory; (3) compatibility of inventory; (4) chronological compatibility; (5) physical compatibility; (6) taxonomic compatibility; (7) logical compatibility; (8) analytical compatibility; and (9) linguistic capability. Each attribute can be used to ascertain the compatibility between a fictional world and the actual world. For example, works of nonfiction will be (or at least attempt to be) compatible across all categories because nonfiction attempts to represent the actual world accurately. Conversely, the worlds of science fiction may share some compatibility with the inventory of the actual world, but they will also be somewhat or completely taxonomically incompatible because they will contain natural species and manufactured objects that do not exist in the actual world. Ryan's typology can thus be used to define particular genres because it assesses characteristics of worlds relative to typical attributes of genres (e.g., talking frogs, which contravene the actual world's biological inventory, can appear in fairy tales but not in nonfiction).

Significantly, Ryan's typology of accessibility relations includes the category of logical compatibility, which assesses fictional worlds relative to the laws of noncontradiction and excluded middle. While modal logic denies the status of world to sets of propositions that contravene these fundamental laws, literary applications of PW theory have to accommodate logical impossibilities because, as we show in the subsequent two sections, they occasionally appear in the semantic domain of fictional texts.

Narrative Themes and Structures

At least three types of themes (or narrative structures) can be associated with PW theory: counterfactual history, forking-path narratives, and many-worlds cosmologies.[12] This is not to say that the authors of these narratives are necessarily influenced by PW theory nor that PW theory has a monopoly on these themes; the claim, rather, is that the themes in question can be regarded as natural outgrowths of the kinds of problems that form the concerns of PW theory.

As Doležel (2010) has argued, counterfactual history comes in two forms: nonfictional and fictional. By demonstrating that counterfactuals can have a truth value in the actual world, Lewis laid down the logical foundation for the study of "what could have been" to become a serious project from which we can learn something about history. Counterfactual history typically focuses on strategic moments when the future of the world seems to be at stake, as opposed to routine events that could go one way or the other without important consequences. Its favorite subjects are therefore events whose outcome fits an either/or pattern, such as battles, elections, or assassinations of heads of state, all of which can be determined by small causes with disproportionately large effects.[13] Rather than viewing history as a steady progression leading to predictable developments, as does, for instance, a Marxist perspective, counterfactual history endorses a turbulent vision of time where dramatic decision points alternate with calm segments. Once a branch has been taken at a decision point, the historian assumes that it can be followed in a determinate and therefore predictable way. Thus, when debating what would have happened if Napoleon had won the battle of Waterloo, counterfactual history cannot invoke events of low probability taking place after the decision point, such as Napoleon being kidnapped by the British a few days later, because it would give too much imaginative freedom to the historian. History, after all, should not be fiction, despite the blurring of the borderline caused by the consideration of imaginary situations.

Openly fictional forms of counterfactual history are much more tolerant of unlikely events causing radical changes, because in fiction an interesting plot takes precedence over didactic value. Within fiction, counterfactual history ranges from the examination of reasonably probable alternative courses of events, such as Philip Roth's *The Plot against America*, which places invented characters in a world where Charles Lindbergh beats Franklin Roosevelt for the U.S. presidency in World War II, strikes an alliance with Hitler's Germany, and takes oppressive measures against Jews, to wildly imaginative use of historical figures, such as Philip II of Spain marrying Elizabeth I of England, Cervantes writing Kafka's "Metamorphosis," and Christopher Columbus traveling east on camel back to meet the Great Khan, as in Carlos Fuentes's *Terra Nostra*. But how do we know that these characters are counterparts of historical individuals in a different world rather than unrelated homonyms? PW theory explains such possibilities through Kripke's causal theory of names. In this theory, proper names do not stand for clusters of properties but designate certain individuals in each possible world through an original act of baptism, and their reference is independent of the changes of properties that the individuals (or their counterparts) undergo in each possible world.

While counterfactual history narrates one branch of possibility and refers only implicitly to the branch taken by actual events, forking-path narratives develop several possible story lines out of a common situation, generating several possible worlds that split from each other. This type of narrative (represented by films such as *Sliding Doors*, *Run Lola Run*, and *The Butterfly Effect*) illustrates a basic mental operation that we have all performed, that of asking what would have become of us if a certain small, random event had not occurred or if we had made another decision in a certain situation. The famous butterfly that flutters its wings in China affects not only the weather in Patagonia but also our own lives.

David Bordwell has suggested that forking-path movies are not necessarily interpreted as manifestations of a cosmology made of parallel, equally existing worlds (à la David Lewis); rather, spectators tend to regard the last branch as representing what actually happened and the others as mental constructs of the characters or as possible scripts considered by the author: "Instead of calling these 'forking-path' plots, we might better describe them as *multiple-draft* narratives, with the last version presenting itself as the fullest, most satisfying revision" (2002, 102).

Genuine manifestations of a Lewisian cosmology occur in science fiction narratives inspired by the so-called many-worlds interpretation of quantum mechanics. According to this interpretation, proposed in the 1950s by Hugh Everett III, when an observer opens the box where Schrödinger's cat was subjected to a nuclear reaction that puts the poor feline in a superposition of states, this observer does not cause the cat to be either dead or alive; rather, the nuclear reaction leads to a splitting of worlds that instantiate all the possibilities predicted by Schrödinger's equation. In one of these worlds the cat is dead, in another he is alive, and the observer discovers the cat to be either dead or alive depending on what world he belongs to. This interpretation is admittedly far from being widely accepted in physics, but Max Tegmark, one of its main proponents, has invoked David Lewis's modal realism in its support. The many-worlds cosmology has provided a rich source of inspiration for science fiction writers such as John Wyndham, Ursula K. Le Guin, Frederik Pohl, Greg Bear, and Larry Niven because of the strange situations and endless quid pro quos that can arise when characters travel from world to world and meet their counterparts (Ryan 2006b).

Postmodernist and Ontologically Transgressive Worlds

As the preceding section has shown, counterfactual historical fictions and forking-path narratives play with ontological structures without necessarily creating logical impossibilities. Likewise, texts that present a multiworld universe create scenarios that radically challenge predominant theories of actual world physics, but they do not contravene logic. Many texts associated with postmodernist and otherwise ontologically transgressive worlds do, however, play with logical (im)possibility. Since pw theory is fundamentally concerned with the relationship between worlds, it is especially effective for accounting for the way that some texts play, often self-reflexively, with ontological structures. It thus offers some very effective apparatus for tackling texts that play with the logical or physical composition of worlds. As William Ashline remarks, "Not only is the transgression of taxonomic and physical norms possible in fiction, but in the development of so-called 'postmodernist fiction,' the once sacred laws of logic have been opened to violation as well" (1995, 215).

Most prolific within the genre of postmodernist fiction, fictional worlds can imaginatively subvert the laws of the actual world and/or self-reflexively undermine the world-building capacity of a text. As Brian McHale notes, postmodernist fiction's "formal strategies implicitly raise issues of the mode of being of fictional worlds, and their inhabitants, and/or reflect on the plurality and diversity of worlds, whether 'real,' possible, fictional, or what-have-you" (1992, 147; cf. 1987). McHale and others (e.g., Ashline 1995; Hutcheon 1998) have shown that common postmodernist strategies include internal narrative contradictions (e.g., Robert Coover's "The Babysitter") and/or a refusal to definitively close a narrative (e.g., John Fowles's *The French Lieutenant's Woman*); the metaleptic collapsing of boundaries between diegetic levels either inside a storyworld (e.g., Woody Allen's "The Kugelmass Episode") or across the actual-to-storyworld boundary (e.g., the transformation of the reader addressed in Italo Calvino's *If on a Winter's Night a Traveler* into a character); the reversal of the direction of time (e.g., Martin Amis's *Time Arrow*); fictional characters being conscious of being fictional (e.g., Luigi Pirandello's *Six Characters in Search of an Author*); and the migration of characters between worlds (e.g., Gilbert Sorrentino's *Mulligan Stew*). Irrespective of the device deployed, postmodernist fictions contravene logic by playing with or violating the boundaries between worlds.

The inherent ontological play at work in postmodernist fiction has meant that PW theory, or at least particular concepts from it, is often deployed to analyze, theorize, or categorize postmodern texts (e.g., McHale 1987; Ryan 1991; Punday 1997; Ashline 1995). Importantly, the application of PW theory to texts that play with ontology does not mean that this form of scholarship is completely different from other applications of PW theory; the logical contradictions that are found in many postmodernist texts are an important component of genre theory, and many applications of PW theory to postmodernist texts represent a form of narrative semantics. However, as Ryan points out, postmodernist fiction "thematiz[es] the concerns of PWT and . . . turn[s] its concepts into formal structures" (1992, 548). It is perhaps not surprising, therefore, that postmodernist texts have been analyzed using a PW framework.

Representing an additional site of ontological peculiarity, PW theory has also been used to analyze ontological impossibilities in texts outside of postmodernist fiction. PW theory forms the basis of Jan Alber's approach to unnatural narratives, which, while heavily focused on postmodernist fiction, includes all texts that contain "physically, logically, and humanly impossible scenarios and events" (2016, 14; cf. 2011). Showing the range of creative possibilities for impossibility in fiction from Old English to contemporary literature, Alber outlines various "reading strategies that help us make sense of different kinds of impossibility" (32), seeing them as a welcoming challenge that "stretch[es] the limits of human cognition" (32).

Importantly, while PW theory is also often used in the investigation of particular kinds of ontologically transgressive texts, it has also been used to investigate particular narrative devices that, while associated with postmodernist fiction, are certainly not restricted to them. Alice Bell and Jan Alber, for example, use counterpart theory and transworld identity—key components of PW theory—to analyze metalepsis (cf. Bell 2016). They conclude that in addition to providing the necessary conceptual framework for understanding the ontological mechanics of the device, the application of PW theory also allows "the analysis to . . . more accurately account for the defamiliarizing effects that [metalepses] have on readers" (Bell and Alber 2012, 186; cf. Bell 2014). The application of PW theory to logically and physically impossible scenarios within or outside of postmodernism represents an important area of development. It extends the theory well beyond its logical roots and provides an almost irresistible test bed for the examination of narrative structures. Moreover, it has developed PW theory as a cognitive approach that can account for texts across genres and literary periods.

Digital Media

If counterfactual historical fiction, forking-path narratives, and multiworld universes can be seen to thematize the concerns of PW theory, and postmodernist fictions challenge them, then the worlds created by digital texts are perhaps the actualization of PWs, not least because of the capacity for computer games to create three-dimensional worlds that can be explored by a player's avatar. Indeed, digital media have made worlds accessible to their readers/players/users, if not corporeally, at least as active participants and no longer as "non-voting members" of the fictional world, as Pavel (1986, 85) describes reader participation in literary fiction.

PW theory forms the basis of Ryan's (2001, 2015) approach to immersion in digital media. More specifically, Ryan shows how recentering, a concept developed as part of her 1991 PW approach (and explained above), is the basic condition for immersive reading. Immersion in any media, she suggests, is created via three forms of involvement with narrative: spatial immersion, the response to setting; temporal immersion, the response to story; and emotional immersion, the response to character. In digital media, interactivity also plays a part—either it enhances immersion or it blocks it. Applying this framework to the worlds created in hypertext, electronic poetry, interactive drama, digital art installations, computer games, and multiuser online worlds such as *Second Life*, Ryan questions whether interactivity is beneficial to the narrative experience, and she proposes structural models that allow choice without threatening narrative coherence.

In addition to providing an account of immersion, Ryan (2006a, 141–42) has shown how fundamental concepts from PW theory, such as counterpart relations and parallel worlds, can be applied to model the structure and content of digital worlds. She also suggests that PW theory can be used as a way "to deal with the fragmentation and occasional inconsistency of hypertext" (Ryan 2015, 199).

Several theorists have applied and developed Ryan's PW work in the context of digital media. Within game studies, Jesper Juul (2014) and Jan Van Looy (2005) apply the principle of minimal departure and the concept of recentering, respectively, to account for the player's relationship to and within the gameworld. Recognizing that many Storyspace hypertext fictions in particular utilize the self-reflexive strategies often used in postmodernist print fiction,[14] Alice Bell's *The Possible Worlds of Hypertext Fiction* develops Ryan's PW framework for its application to this kind of digital literary text. She shows that since readers are required to participate in the construction of hypertexts, often choosing from a number of different possibilities, they become aware of their active role in the fiction-making process. Moreover, because readers of Storyspace hypertexts experience different events, different versions of events, or a different ordering of events, depending upon the path they choose to take, the narrative structure of the texts further foregrounds the artificiality of the text. In addition to the branching structure that the Storyspace software facilitates, Bell shows that many Storyspace hypertexts also contain additional self-reflexive features, such as second-person address and metafictional uses of intertextuality, that draw further attention to their artificiality. Showing how PW theory can be harnessed to effectively analyze the complex ontological mechanics at work in these texts, Bell provides an account of the way that hypertexts play with world boundaries and structures.

As the preceding discussion shows, most applications of PW theory to digital texts represent a form of narrative semantics. While much scholarship in this area takes Ryan's PW model as the point of departure, Daniel Punday (2014) utilizes Doležel's distinction between "intensional" and "extensional" narrative worlds to account for the graphical user interface (GUI) in digital fiction. Using examples from interactive fiction and literary hypertext, he shows the dexterity and enormous potential that PW theory provides in the context of digital worlds scholarship.

The articles in this volume make headway into some of the potential futures of PW theory. In part 1, "Theoretical Perspectives of Possible Worlds," each essay interrogates an underdeveloped or unresolved theoretical issue within the field.

Lubomír Doležel, whose pioneering work in establishing the PW approach to literature is documented in this introduction, passed away in January 2017. We are honored to present one of his very last articles as the opening chapter of this book. "Porfyry's Tree for the Concept of Fictional Worlds" is an intellectual game reminiscent of a labyrinth or of a Choose Your Own Adventures narrative: the goal is to reach fictional worlds by navigating a decision tree made of binary oppositions. If you choose the correct branches, you will reach fictional worlds. If you do not, you may get lost in the quagmires of language as universal medium and of antirealism; your stubborn adherence to a one-world ontology may lead you right past fictional worlds; you may have to deny the importance of fiction for our understanding of the actual world; you could be forced to reject any distinction between fact and fiction; and you may crash into the rock of ontologically complete PWs. While Doležel's choices maneuver around these obstacles, one can wonder if other choices could lead to viable conceptions of fictional worlds. The game thus challenges the reader to examine and define her own position at every decision point. By following Doležel's proposed itinerary, she will learn a lot about the philosophical debates that underlie PW theory and its literary applications.

Long used in an informal way by literary critics, the term *world* (and, more particularly, *storyworld*) has recently gained traction as the designation of what narrative texts display to the mind of the reader and spectator, but for all its newly found prominence, it remains relatively undertheorized. In chapter 2, "From Possible Worlds to Storyworlds: On the Worldness of Narrative Representation," Marie-Laure Ryan interrogates storyworlds from the perspective of PW theory. Starting from a definition of storyworlds as totalities that encompass space, time, and individual existents who undergo transformations as the result of events, she examines them in terms of the following variables: (1) distance from the actual world, a criterion that raises the question of how far we have to travel from the world made familiar to us by life experience for the notion of "world" to become inapplicable; (2) size, a variable that leads from the small worlds of micronarratives to the large worlds of transmedia franchises; and (3) ontological completeness, a variable that leads from worlds assumed to share the ontological status of the actual world, despite the incompleteness of their representations, to worlds (or quasi worlds) that present ontological gaps that cannot be filled by what Ryan has called the principle of minimal departure. The contrast between complete and incomplete worlds is illustrated by readings of Racine's *Phèdre* as an example of a classical play and of Samuel Beckett's *Waiting for Godot* as an example of the theater of the absurd. Taking a stand against theories that do away with storyworld, Ryan suggests that the concept is theoretically necessary for the following reasons: (1) it provides the surrounding environment required for immersion; (2) it justifies the practice of transfictionality; (3) it encourages a mode of reading based on imagining, visualizing, and mentally simulating the action rather than being limited to the propositional content of sentences; and (4) because "worldness" can be realized to different degrees, it allows variations in the mode of representation and ontological status of fictional entities rather than reducing all fictions to a uniform model.

One of the most important contributions that possible worlds theory has made to literary studies has been demonstrating the role that alternatives play in narrative dynamics. In "Interface Ontologies: On the Possible, Virtual, and Hypothetical in Fiction," Marina Grishakova contributes to this field of investigation by providing a systematic approach to the alternative voices that can be found in a text. Grishakova reminds us that alternate possible worlds can be created by narrative devices inside the text (such as the narrator giving readers access to the private wishes or expectations of a character) and also readers' inferences or expectations generated by their existing knowledge of what is likely to happen as a generic convention. However, she argues that the narrational style of many modernist and postmodernist texts makes it more difficult for readers to distinguish ontologically between the actual and virtual components of the narrative. In previous work, Grishakova has developed the concept of "virtual voice" to account for forms of narration in which the current narrator's voice is infiltrated or inflected by another narrative agent's voice (that of the narrator or a character). In this chapter, Grishakova develops this category further to show how the juxtaposition of virtual and actual voices in narration is integral to a reader's understanding of and relationship to the fictional world. While alternative worlds generate a range of hypothetical plots, virtual voices create discursive effects by bringing in alternative perspectives. In Vladimir Nabokov's *Lolita*, virtual and actual voices are merged so as to create ambiguity about the moral stance of the narrator; in Margaret Atwood's *The Blind Assassin* (2000) the ontological status of virtual and actual voices is reversed to create a twist at the end of the novel. Ultimately, virtual voices almost always create ontological ambiguity, requiring that the reader make judgments about what is likely or probable as opposed to what is possible or impossible.

The three essays in part 2, "Possible Worlds and Cognition," investigate the ways that readers cognitively process different kinds of fictional worlds. While "postclassical" narratology has always been concerned with the way that narrative experiences are created in readers' minds, in recent years narratology has taken a more explicit "cognitive turn" by engaging with research from areas such as cognitive psychology, neuroscience, and cognitive linguistics. In "Ungrounding Fictional Worlds: An Enactivist Perspective on the 'Worldlikeness' of Fiction," Marco Caracciolo demonstrates how insights from the enactivist theory of cognition can be synthesized with PW theory in order to better account for what he defines as the "worldlikeness" of a fictional text: readers' experience of a fictional world that, in one way or another, reflects their experience of reality. Caracciolo argues that the narratological application of PW theory has been limited by its logical roots. It has thus paid less attention than it could to the experiential and embodied nature of storyworld construction. Analyzing the world-building strategies at work in Jonathan Lethem's *Girl in Landscape*, Caracciolo shows how current PW conceptions of fictional worlds need to be modified in order to accommodate the way that narratives gradually unfold and thus explain the temporal dynamics of fictional worlds. He also shows that the "worldlikeness" of fiction is driven by the experiential relevance of a fictional text.

As the introduction to this volume has shown, PW theory is often used as a tool for exploring the complex narrative universes created by postmodernist fiction either to model the unusual ontological configurations created by the texts or to explain the way that readers assimilate them. In the second essay in this part, "Postmodern Play with Worlds: The Case of *At Swim-Two-Birds*," Michelle Wang shows how PW theory can account for both. Wang argues that readers of all kinds of texts seek to resolve any cognitive disorientation that readers experience. Postmodernist texts, however, place particularly strong demands on readers because these texts create worlds that often significantly depart from our knowledge or experience of the actual world. Drawing on Ryan's typology of accessibility relations, Wang suggests that readers expect that a fictional world will resemble the actual world unless told otherwise (as per the "principle of minimal departure") but that they also expect that particular kinds of texts, including postmodernist fiction, will reframe or refashion readers' knowledge of the actual world; in these cases, the "principle of maximal departure" is deployed. Importantly, the application of the principle of maximal departure does not stop readers from drawing on their knowledge of the actual world. Rather, three factors influence readers' expectations: at which point in the text, how frequently, and in what ways do the departures from the actual world take place. Minimal departure is likely to be assumed when deviations occur later in a text, when they are less frequent, when they are not explicitly signaled in the text, and when the departures are less radical in nature (e.g., "identity of properties" rather than "logical compatibility"). Maximal departure, on the other hand, is more likely to be assumed when departures happen earlier in the text, when departures are more frequent, when they are explicitly signaled, and when they are more radical in nature. Applying the revised PW model to Flann O'Brien's *At Swim-Two-Birds*, Wang shows how several different interpretations of the text's ontological structure can be reached. She concludes that postmodernist texts invite readers to "play" with the texts' "game-like structures" and shows how PW theory offers an elegant means of accounting for that experience.

Like Wang, Jan Alber also uses PW theory to analyze narratives that contradict our knowledge and experience of the actual world, but he utilizes embodied cognition as a means of explaining how we process them. In "Logical Contradictions, Possible Worlds Theory, and the Embodied Mind," Alber argues that while logical contradictions certainly challenge our real-world experience, readers are able—and in fact strive—to make sense of them. Thus while some theorists maintain that contradictions result in unthinkable or "empty" worlds, Alber shows that they can and do manifest in a range of narrative fictions, and an approach is therefore needed to more accurately account for readers' responses to them. Drawing on enactivist theory in particular, Alber suggests that readers go through a two-stage process when they encounter logical contradictions in narrative. First, they experience an initial instinctive bodily response to the logical peculiarities that serves as "protointerpretation." They then try to make sense of this felt response by drawing on both their knowledge of the text and their experience of the actual world; this second stage of interpretation is both cerebral and emotional. Demonstrating the dexterity of his approach, Alber analyzes three texts that utilize logical contradictions in relation to three different aspects of narrative: a logically contradictory narrator in Alice Sebold's novel *The Lovely Bones*; contradictory endings in B. S. Johnson's short story "Broad Thoughts from a Home"; and contradictory temporalities in Robert A. Heinlein's short story "All You Zombies." Profiling the two-stage response process that he experiences in relation to these cognitively demanding texts, he shows that logical contradictions in narrative do not disable our interpretative capabilities. Rather, these extremely unusual and unfamiliar worlds provoke a strong emotional response in readers that will inevitably lead to a search for meaning within them.

Clearly, in a fictional world, things can be different from what they are in the real world in many ways. The essays in part 3, "Possible Worlds and Literary Genres," profile the ways in which PW theory can be used to understand fantastical, speculative, and physically impossible fictional scenarios and thus worlds that in some ways resemble but ultimately radically depart from common (Western) conceptions of the actual world. Space and time, the two basic abstract categories, according to Kant, form the preconditions of human experience. But can they really differ from what they are in AW while still being recognizable as space and time? Fictions that allow time travel, reverse the direction of time, present it as elastic, make days repeatable, or allow the past to be changed answer this question positively, at least for time. Christoph Bartsch's "Escape into Alternative Worlds and Time(s) in Jack London's *The Star Rover*" presents an original variation on this theme. To describe the experience of a hero named Darrell Standing who lives multiple lives in different bodies, Bartsch adopts David Lewis's distinction between external time and personal time: external time could be identified with the "empirical" time of TAW (called by Bartsch TAT, "textual actual time"), while personal time is bound to an individual ("character's time"). The two times normally coincide, but they become disjointed when Standing, a prisoner on death row strapped in a jacket that prevents movement, "escapes" into the life of one of his avatars. When this occurs, the personal time experienced by the hero far exceeds the length of the external time spent by his body in the restraining jacket. But TAT does not disappear entirely, because the various lives are situated in objective history, and Standing's earlier manifestations are unaware of his later incarnations, while the later incarnations are aware of the earlier ones. In Bartsch's reading, the text maintains the kind of hesitation regarded by Tzvetan Todorov as the trademark of the fantastic: on the one hand, Standing's other lives could be hallucinations due to the inhuman conditions to which he is subjected in prison (this seems to be a standard interpretation of the novel); on the other hand, Standing's travels to alternate worlds (or is it to other lives in the same world?) could occur objectively. The rich analysis to which Bartsch subjects this little-known but fascinating text demonstrates the versatility of the PW approach and its ability to deal with the temporal dimension of storyworlds.

In "'As Many Worlds as Original Artists': Possible Worlds Theory and the Literature of Fantasy," Thomas Martin asks why the fantastic, a genre enthusiastically adopted by contemporary audiences, has remained for a long time neglected or, worse, despised by literary critics. He attributes this attitude to a so-called realistic and pseudoscientific bias in narrative aesthetics and literary studies, a bias that favors Saussure over Peirce,

Joyce over Borges, Derrida over Eco. But as the references to Saussure and Derrida suggest, textualism and its cult of the signifier could also be held responsible: most of the critics who rejected the work of Tolkien did so on the grounds that it was poorly written. A true work of literary art, it was implied, should draw attention to language and not to the process of world creation. W. H. Auden's response to Tolkien's *The Lord of the Rings* ("Mr. Tolkien's world may not be the same as our own") sounds nowadays self-evident, but as long as the value of invention was only recognized on the level of *écriture*, its significance eluded critics. Martin argues that PW theory holds the key to the theoretical and aesthetic recognition of fantasy and that PW theorists have so far been too modest in promoting this potential. Whereas a one-world ontology would regard fantastic worlds as manifestations of the impossible, a many-worlds system that situates its worlds at various degrees of distance from the actual world regards the fantastic as an exploration of the richness of the possible. As Martin suggests (quoting Auden), the art of world creation does not reside in making a world plausible or verisimilar—two concepts of realism that take the actual world as implicit reference—but in making it believable by building "a world of intelligible law" where "the reader's sense of the credible is never violated." It is in the pursuit of this "intelligible law," which makes fantastic worlds autonomous with respect to reality, that Tolkien spent fifty years creating the encyclopedia of Middle Earth. Aristotle defined the task of the poet as representing what could happen according to probability and necessity (*Poetics* 5.5); in fantasy, authors show what could be and could happen according to probabilities and necessities of their own making. This is what makes their worlds believable.

Mattison Schuknecht's "The Best/Worst of All Possible Worlds? Utopia, Dystopia, and Possible Worlds Theory" debunks a few myths about utopia and dystopia and then relies on the PW model to construct a positive theory of these genres. Rejecting the view that they are necessarily concerned with social organization (there are solitary utopias too) or that they are always set in the future, Schuknecht uses two forms of the PW approach to define utopias and dystopias: the world-external, outlined by Ryan, which defines fictional genres in terms of accessibility relations from the actual world, and the world-internal, proposed by Doležel, which analyzes plots in terms of the modalities that are put into play. Schuknecht proposes to add a new significant accessibility relation to Ryan's system, a/meliorate, which covers both utopias and dystopias. In order to distinguish the two, he turns to the deontic modality, arguing that conflicts involving the permitted, prohibited, and obligatory are minimized in utopias and maximized in dystopias. The last question addressed in the chapter concerns the recent eclipse of utopian fiction in favor of dystopian. Rejecting social and historical theories that attribute the disappearance of utopias to the sorry state of the world, Schuknecht invokes a purely narratological explanation: narrative appeal (or tellability) relies on conflict, and there is plenty of it in dystopias, but in a utopia everybody's desires are satisfied, and there is consequently no room for conflict. Texts such as Plato's *Republic* and Thomas More's *Utopia*, which describe realized utopias, are didactic texts rather than entertaining narratives. It is only when utopias are in the process of being built or are threatened from the outside that they provide suitable narrative material.

Part 4, "Possible Worlds and Digital Media," explores the way that PW theory can be used to explore the digital and also the way that the digital can inform PW theory. One of the earliest and most significant forms of digital writing—hypertext—was developed before the web. This meant that the publication methods for hypertext fiction resembled those of print: a publisher produced, sold, and distributed works of fiction; readers received a literary artefact packaged as a work of fiction. Once web use exploded in the mid-1990s, publication methods changed: hypertext fiction became available to read in the same online space as works of nonfiction. Alice Bell investigates the ontological ambiguity at work in some web-based fiction in her chapter "Digital Fictionality: Possible Worlds Theory, Ontology, and Hyperlinks." In particular, she shows that external hyperlinks, which lead to websites beyond the fictional work, provide a medium-specific and thus unique means of playing with the boundary between fiction and reality. Analyzing three web-based fictions that exhibit three forms of ontological play—what Bell defines as ontological flickering, ontological refreshment, and ontological merging—she modifies Ryan's account of fictional recentering to account for the reader's interaction with and understanding of the ontology of these digital texts. She shows that external hyperlinks can be used to increase immersion and/or intensify self-reflexivity, but the creation of such narrative experiences is not the sole purpose of these texts. Instead, she argues that while the texts utilize self-reflexive techniques associated with postmodernist print fiction, the ontological mechanics at work in these particular digital fictions are used for a more contemporary thematic purpose. She concludes that the three digital fictions she analyzes should be seen as part of a broader post-postmodern cultural trend in which sincerity forms a more central part.

The capacity for digital media to create three-dimensional audiovisual spaces makes the deployment of "world" terminology especially appealing. In "Possible Worlds, Virtual Worlds" Françoise Lavocat investigates the ontological status of worlds created by digital media and explores the extent to which PW theory can be applied in this context. Distinguishing between the worlds built by multiplayer spaces (e.g., metaverses such as *Second Life* and MMORPGS such as *World of Warcraft*) and single-player videogames (e.g., *Grand Theft Auto*), she argues that digital media create worlds that utilize medium-specific modalities. In terms of alethic modality, Lavocat suggests that virtual worlds have a "magical" quality: for example, avatars can die and come back to life in videogames; entire cities can be effortlessly built in *Second Life*. In terms of epistemic modality, not only must players/users know the rules governing a particular world, but they must also deploy and refine their knowledge of digital technology in order to operate within it. Multiplayer and single-player worlds differ with respect to deontic modality, Lavocat suggests. In *Second Life* users must adhere to rules and policies within the virtual world, but those restrictions also extend out to the jurisdiction of the actual world (e.g., users should not extort money within the virtual world because this has consequences in the real world). In single-player videogames, however, there is no ontological leak to the actual world, and players' actions within the gameworld relate to that domain only. Similarly, Lavocat shows that the axiological system of *Second Life* is different from that of a single-player videogame. For example, while users' moral choices in the former potentially impact directly on other users in the actual world, users' actions on a character in a single-player videogame are more likely to indirectly affect users' sense of actual world morality, if those actions have any effect at all.

Within digital media scholarship, theorists must adapt to the fast-changing landscape of technological developments in the field. This includes developing, debating, and updating different manifestations and associated conceptualizations of texts. In the early twenty-first century, Lev Manovich proposed the metaphor of narrative as database to account for the way that digital artifacts are fragmented (i.e., stored as bits of code) and coherent (i.e., executed as connected bits of code). In "Rereading Manovich's Algorithm: Genre and Use in Possible Worlds Theory," Daniel Punday revisits Manovich's theory by exploring its relationship to possible worlds theory and, in particular, its account of fictional world ontology. He thus uses concepts developed in the context of new media to show how they relate to the PW theorization of fictional texts more generally. First, Punday argues that the concept of the "interface" can be used to categorize a particular manifestation of a fictional world and, further, that separating out the interface from the world it presents is particularly important for narrative worlds that are represented more than once (i.e., in different books or across different media). Punday then shows how several PW models can be seen to resemble the "database" structure that is so important to Manovich's approach. The structure of a single TAW surrounded by alternative TPWs proposed by Ryan represents a collection of states that can, in principle, be combined in different ways. When readers read a particular text, they consider how characters' wishes and fears (TPWs) relate to and interact with the TAW. While this is not a direct or uncomplicated relation, Punday also suggests that Doležel's account of extensional and intensional narrative worlds can be seen as embodying a database structure: an extensional world exists as a collection of objects—like a database—and in the associated intensional world, entities are configured to produce a particular state of affairs, though the reader experiences the intensional world first via a text and extracts information out of that text to imagine the associated extensional world. Utilizing the database metaphor, Punday then shows how Manovich's concept of the "algorithm" can be used to understand the way readers approach and ultimately process texts. For Manovich, algorithms are a way of representing the way that readers or players understand the logic of texts as they read/play them. Punday suggests that the algorithm can also be used to understand how readers make sense of genre: readers access particular information and perform particular steps depending on the genre of the text that they are reading.

Finally, in the postface Thomas Pavel critically responds to the volume. Taken as a whole, the articles in this book systematically outline the theoretical underpinnings of the possible worlds approach, provide updated methods of analyzing fictional narrative, and profile those methods via the analysis of a range of different texts, including utopian/dystopian literature, science fiction, fantasy, digital narratives, and postmodernist fiction. Through the variety of its contributions, *Possible Worlds Theory and Contemporary Narratology* demonstrates the vitality and versatility of one of the most vibrant strands of contemporary narrative theory and shows why PW theory has played a decisive role in postclassical narratology.

Notes

1. Note a certain circularity in the association of accessibility with possibility: a world is possible with respect to another if it is accessible from it, but it is accessible if it is possible.

2. Lewis's analysis does not work for all counterfactuals. For instance, the often heard type "If O.J. is innocent, then I am a monkey's uncle" is used to express the impossibility of the antecedent rather than the feasibility of the consequent: it is only in a world as absurd as one where I am a monkey's uncle that O. J. Simpson can be innocent of his ex-wife's murder.

3. In logic, the law of noncontradiction states that the proposition p AND ~p is false. This means that a particular state and its negation cannot occur in the same world; it is impossible for something to happen and not happen. The Law of Excluded Middle states that the proposition p OR ~p is true. This means that something either happens or does not happen; an in-between state of it both happening and not happening is impossible.

4. Dragons could, however, be regarded as novel combinations of properties of real-world entities, such as wings, lizard-like bodies, breathing, and fire.

5. David Lewis may be an exception: the confessional tone of his presentation of modal realism, anchored by multiple appearances of "I believe," suggests a strong personal commitment to this model.

6. This elegance resides in the fact that Lewis can account for modal statements without recognizing "primitive modalities," that is, without using the logical notation □ for necessity and ◊ for possibility.

7. Our translation. The original reads: "Nous nous efforçons de saisir l'imbrication des personnages dans un ensemble de biens et de normes, d'éprouver de manière homéopathique leurs désirs et de prévoir ce qu'ils se proposent d'entreprendre."

8. We quote this version of the analysis rather than Lewis's final version, which accounts for divergences between the cultural beliefs of the author's and reader's world by replacing "our actual world" with "one of the collective belief worlds of the community of origin of f" because it is much more readable. Lewis regards the beliefs of the author's world as dominant; thus, if people believed in witches in the late sixteenth century, then statements

about witches compatible with Shakespeare's text can be regarded as true of *Macbeth*.

9. Ryan (1991) offers a definition of fiction, but it is strongly inspired by Lewis and by Searle. She adds to their accounts the notion of recentering.

10. A cognitive movement in narratology (e.g., Herman 2009; Fludernik 1996) regards the representation of lived experience as more essential to narrative than the representation of a sequence of causally related events. For these scholars, Beckett's trilogy is more narrative than a fairy tale that does not probe into the characters' subjectivity. Note, however, that the revision of Lewis's formula, which is meant to define fiction and not narrative, is fully compatible with the "experiential" conception of narrativity.

11. See von Wright's (1967) logic of action, which, however, consists of only options 1 and 3.

12. On these narrative types, see Dannenberg (2008).

13. Compare the proverb "For the want of a shoe the horse was lost; for the want of a horse the rider was lost; for the want of a rider the battle was lost; for the want of a battle the kingdom was lost; and all for the want of a horseshoe nail."

14. Storyspace hypertext fictions are produced in Storyspace editing software, which allows writers to connect chunks of text (known as "lexia") via hyperlinks. They have been distributed by Eastgate Systems Ltd. on CD-ROM since the late 1980s, and thus many Storyspace works represent some of the earliest forms of hypertext fiction, with some published before the web became publicly accessible.

References

Adams, Robert M. 1979. "Theories of Actuality." In *The Possible and the Actual: Readings in the Metaphysics of Modality*, edited by Michael J. Loux, 190–209. Ithaca NY: Cornell University Press.

———. 1981. "Actualism and Thisness: Synthese." *Demonstrative and Indexical Reference, Part I* 49 (1): 3–41.

Alber, Jan. 2011. "The Diachronic Development of Unnaturalness: A New View on Genre." In *Unnatural Narratives, Unnatural Narratology*, edited by Jan Alber and Rüdiger Heinze, 41–67. Berlin: de Gruyter.

———. 2016. *Unnatural Narrative: Impossible Worlds in Fiction and Drama.* Lincoln: University of Nebraska Press.

Allén, Sture, ed. 1988. *Possible Worlds in Humanities, Arts and Sciences: Proceedings of Nobel Symposium 65.* Berlin: de Gruyter.

Aristotle. 1998. *Poetics.* Edited by Malcolmm Heath. London: Penguin.

Ashline, William L. 1995. "The Problem of Impossible Fictions." *Style* 29 (2): 215–34.

Barthes, Roland. 1981. "The Discourse of History." Translated by Stephen Bann. In *Comparative Criticism: A Yearbook*, 7–20. Cambridge: Cambridge University Press.

Bell, Alice. 2010. *The Possible Worlds of Hypertext Fiction*. New York: Palgrave Macmillan.

———. 2014. "Media-Specific Metalepsis in *10:01*." In *Analyzing Digital Fiction*, edited by Alice Bell, Astrid Ensslin, and Hans Kristian Rustad, 21–38. Routledge Studies in Rhetoric and Stylistics. New York: Routledge.

———. 2016. "'I Felt Like I'd Stepped Out of a Different Reality': Possible Worlds Theory, Metalepsis and Digital Fiction." In *World Building: Discourse in the Mind*, edited by Joanna Gavins and Ernestine Lahey, 15–32. London: Bloomsbury.

Bell, Alice, and Jan Alber. 2012. "Ontological Metalepsis and Unnatural Narratology." *Journal of Narrative Theory* 42 (2): 166–92.

Bordwell, David. 2002. "Film Futures." *SubStance* 31 (1): 88–104.

Bremond, Claude. 1972. *Logique du récit*. Paris: Seuil.

Bricker, Phillip. 2008. "Concrete Possible Worlds." In *Contemporary Debates in Metaphysics*, edited by Theodore Sider, John Hawthorne, and Dean W. Zimmerman, 111–34. Malden MA: Blackwell.

Buckland, Warren. 2004. "Between Science Fact and Science Fiction: Spielberg's Digital Dinosaurs, Possible Worlds, and the New Aesthetic Realism." In *Liquid Metal: The Science Fiction Film Reader*, edited by Sean Redmond, 24–34. New York: Columbia University Press.

Cohn, Dorrit. 1999. *The Distinction of Fiction*. Baltimore MD: Johns Hopkins University Press.

Currie, Gregory. 1990. *The Nature of Fiction*. Cambridge: Cambridge University Press.

Dannenberg, Hilary. 2008. *Coincidence and Counterfactuality: Plotting Time and Space in Narrative Fiction*. Lincoln: University of Nebraska Press.

Divers, John. 2002. *Possible Worlds*. London: Routledge.

Dohrn, Daniel. 2009. "Counterfactual Narrative Explanation." In "The Poetics, Aesthetics, and Philosophy of Narrative." Special issue, *Journal of Aesthetics and Art Criticism* 67 (1): 37–47.

Doležel, Lubomír. 1976a. "Extensional and Intensional Narrative Worlds." *Poetics* 8:193–212.

———. 1976b. "Narrative Modalities." *Journal of Literary Semantics* 5:5–14.

———. 1988. "Mimesis and Possible Worlds." *Poetics Today* 9:475–96.

———. 1998. *Heterocosmica: Fiction and Possible Worlds*. Baltimore MD: Johns Hopkins University Press.

———. 2010. *Possible Worlds of Fiction and History*. Baltimore MD: Johns Hopkins University Press.

Eco, Umberto. 1984. *The Role of the Reader: Explorations in the Semiotics of Texts*. Bloomington: Indiana University Press.

Fludernik, Monika. 1996. *Towards a "Natural" Narratology*. London: Routledge.

Fořt, Bohumil. 2016. *An Introduction to Fictional Worlds Theory*. Frankfurt am Main: Peter Lang.

Herman, David. 2009. *Basic Elements of Narrative*. Chichester: Wiley-Blackwell.

Hintikka, Jaakko. 1988. "Exploring Possible Worlds." In *Possible Worlds in Humanities, Arts and Sciences: Proceedings of Nobel Symposium 65*, edited by Sture Allén, 52–73. Berlin: de Gruyter.

Hutcheon, Linda. 1988. *A Poetics of Postmodernism: History Theory Fiction*. London: Routledge.

Jameson, Fredric. 1975. *The Prison-House of Language*. Princeton NJ: Princeton University Press.

Jenkins, Henry. 2006. *Convergence Culture: Where Old and New Media Collide*. New York: New York University Press.

Juul, Jesper. 2014. "On Absent Carrot Sticks: The Level of Abstraction in Video Games." In *Storyworlds across Media: Toward a Media-Conscious Narratology*, edited by Marie-Laure Ryan and Jan-Noël Thon, 173–92. Lincoln: University of Nebraska Press.

Kripke, Saul. 1963. "Semantical Considerations on Modal Logic." *Acta Philosophica Fennica* 16:83–94.

———. 1972. "Naming and Necessity." In *Semantics of Natural Language*, edited by Donald Davidson and Gilbert Harman, 253–355. Dordrecht: Reidel.

Lavocat, Françoise. 2010. "Avant-propos." In *La théorie littéraire des mondes possibles*, edited by Françoise Lavocat, 5–11. Paris: CNSR Editions.

Lewis, David K. 1973. *Counterfactuals*. Cambridge: Cambridge University Press.

———. 1978. "Truth in Fiction." *American Philosophical Quarterly* 15:37–46.

———. 1979. "Possible Worlds." In *The Possible and the Actual: Readings in the Metaphysics of Modality*, edited by Michael J. Loux, 182–89. Ithaca NY: Cornell University Press.

———. 1986. *On the Plurality of Worlds*. Oxford: Blackwell.

———. 1983. "Postscript to 'Truth in Fiction.'" In *Philosophical Papers*, 1:276–79. Oxford: Oxford University Press.

Loux, Michael J. 1979. Introduction to *The Possible and the Actual: Readings in the Metaphysics of Modality*, edited by Michael J. Loux, 15–64. Ithaca NY: Cornell University Press.

Maître, Doreen. 1983. *Literature and Possible Worlds*. Middlesex: Middlesex Polytechnic Press.

Martin, Thomas L. 2004. *Poiesis and Possible Worlds: A Study in Modality and Literary Theory*. Toronto: University of Toronto Press.

McHale, Brian. 1987. *Postmodernist Fiction*. London: Routledge.

———. 1992. *Constructing Postmodernism*. London: Routledge.

Nolan, Daniel P. 2002. *Topics in the Philosophy of Possible Worlds*. New York: Routledge.

Pavel, Thomas. 1975. "Possible Worlds in Literary Semantics." *Journal of Aesthetics and Art Criticism* 34:165–76.

———. 1986. *Fictional Worlds*. Cambridge MA: Harvard University Press.

———. 2010. "Univers de fiction: Un parcours personnel." In *La théorie littéraire des mondes possibles*, edited by Françoise Lavocat, 307–13. Paris: CNSR Editions.

Plantinga, Alvin. "Actualism and Possible Worlds." In *The Possible and the Actual: Readings in the Metaphysics of Modality*, edited by Michael J. Loux, 253–73. Ithaca NY: Cornell University Press.

Punday, Daniel. 1997. "Meaning in Postmodern Worlds: The Case of *The French Lieutenant's Woman*." *Semiotica* 115 (3/4): 313–43.

———. 2014. "Seeing into the Worlds of Digital Fiction." In *Analyzing Digital Fiction*, edited by Alice Bell, Astrid Ensslin, and Hans Kristian Rustad, 57–72. Routledge Studies in Rhetoric and Stylistics. New York: Routledge.

Rescher, Nicholas. 1988. "The Ontology of the Possible." In *The Possible and the Actual: Readings in the Metaphysics of Modality*, edited by Michael J. Loux, 166–81. Ithaca NY: Cornell University Press.

Ronen, Ruth. 1994. *Possible Worlds in Literary Theory*. Cambridge: Cambridge University Press.

Ryan, Marie-Laure. 1985. "The Modal Structure of Narrative Universes." *Poetics Today* 6 (4): 717–56.

———. 1991. *Possible Worlds, Artificial Intelligence and Narrative Theory*. Bloomington: Indiana University Press.

———. 1992. "Possible Worlds in Recent Literary Theory." *Style* 26 (4): 528–52.

———. 2001. *Narrative as Virtual Reality: Immersion and Interactivity in Literature and Electronic Media*. Baltimore MD: Johns Hopkins University Press.

———. 2006a. *Avatars of Story*. Minneapolis: University of Minnesota Press.

———. 2006b. "From Parallel Universes to Possible Worlds: Ontological Pluralism in Physics, Narratology and Narrative." *Poetics Today* 24 (7): 633–74.

———. 2015. *Narrative as Virtual Reality 2: Revisiting Immersion and Interactivity in Literature and Electronic Media*. Baltimore MD: Johns Hopkins University Press.

Saint-Gelais, Richard. 2011. *Fictions transfuges: La transfictionnalité et ses enjeux*. Paris: Seuil.

Saler, Michael. 2012. *As If: Modern Enchantment and the Prehistory of Virtual Reality*. Oxford: Oxford University Press.

Saussure, Ferdinand de. 1966. *Course in General Linguistics*. Translated by Wade Baskin. New York: McGraw Hill.

Searle, John. 1975. "The Logical Status of Fictional Discourse." *New Literary History* 6:319–32.

Semino, Elena. 1997. *Language and World Creation in Poems and Other Texts*. London: Longman.

Swift, Elizabeth. 2016. "What Do Audiences Do? Negotiating the Possible Worlds of Participatory Theatre." *Journal of Contemporary Drama in English* 4 (1): 134–49.

Tegmark, Max. 2003. "Parallel Universes." *Scientific American*, May, 40–51.

Todorov, Tzvetan. 1969. *Grammaire du Décaméron*. The Hague: Mouton.

——. (1970) 1975. *The Fantastic: A Structural Approach to a Literary Genre*. Translated by Richard Howard. Ithaca NY: Cornell University Press.

Traill, Nancy. 1991. "Fictional Worlds of the Fantastic." *Style* 25 (2): 196–210.

——. 1996. *Possible Worlds of the Fantastic: The Rise of the Paranormal in Fiction*. Toronto: University of Toronto Press.

Uhl, Nele. 2013. "On the Concept of Diegese, Possible Worlds, and the Aesthetics of Illness." In *(Dis)Orienting Media and Narrative Mazes*, edited by Julia Eckel, Bernd Leiendecker, Daniela Olek, and Christine Piepiorka, 205–20. Bielefeld: Transcript Verlag.

Vaina, Lucia. 1977. "Les mondes possible du texte." *Versus* 17:3–13.

Van Looy, Jan. 2005. "Virtual Recentering: Computer Games and Possible Worlds Theory." *Image and Narrative* 12, http://www.imageandnarrative.be/inarchive/tulseluper/vanlooy.htm.

Voegelin, Salome. 2014. *Sonic Possible Worlds: Hearing the Continuum of Sound*. London: Bloomsbury.

von Wright, Georg Hendrik. 1967. "The Logic of Action: A Sketch." In *The Logic of Decision and Action*, edited by Nicholas Rescher, 121–36. Pittsburgh: University of Pittsburgh Press.

Walton, Kendall. 1990. *Mimesis as Make-Believe: On the Foundations of the Representational Art*. Cambridge MA: Harvard University Press.

Wolf, Mark J. P. 2012. *Building Imaginary Worlds: The Theory and History of Subcreation*. London: Routledge.

PART 1 | *Theoretical Perspectives of Possible Worlds*

1 Porfyry's Tree for the Concept of Fictional Worlds

LUBOMÍR DOLEŽEL

In 1975 an article by Thomas G. Pavel titled "Possible Worlds in Literary Semantics" appeared in the *Journal of Aesthetics and Art Criticism*. This study substantially enriched literary theory by linking it to the modal logic of possible worlds. Pavel, then professor of linguistics at the University of Ottawa, was trying to develop a new approach to the theory of fiction. He read an article on modal logic by the logician Saul Kripke that he found inspiring, and fictional theory based on possible worlds was born. Pavel continued his research in fictional theory, and in 1986 Harvard University Press published his book *Fictional Worlds*, which became a classic in this growing field.

I approach the problem of fictionality from the same position as Thomas Pavel—as a theorist of literature originally trained as a linguist. The theory I present here is formulated primarily with regard to literary and, more specifically, narrative fiction. That does not mean that I restrict fictionality to literature. I believe that other genres of literature, lyric poetry, and drama, as well as theater, fiction film, fictional genres in television, ballet, painting, and sculpting, each by its own semiotic means creates or constructs fictional worlds. Necessarily, the problem of fictionality is not a monopoly of literary scholars; instead, developing and evaluating conceptions of fictionality are interdisciplinary tasks.

At present, the two most active centers of this inquiry are narratology— itself an interdisciplinary field—and analytic philosophy. My efforts over the years have been aimed at synthesizing the main theoretical ideas and suggestions that emerged in these two fields.

Every theory rests on some tacit assumptions. I find it necessary to make explicit one of them because it determines the fundamental position that

I take in my work. It is the choice of the research tradition, in the sense of Larry Laudan (1977), in which we place ourselves as researchers. Let me just mention without argumentation that even those scholars who deny the relevance or even the existence of tradition proceed in the framework of the tradition denying tradition. I believe that the only research tradition in which the concepts of possible and fictional worlds can be developed is the tradition of a rigorous and explicit theory and concept formation. There is no possibility to discuss fictional world in a fuzzy, impressionistic language.

In the twentieth century our disciplines developed this tradition in Prague and in Parisian structuralism and semiotics. American new criticism should be considered a special branch of this tradition. Since this tradition was rejected by poststructuralism, we can see the theory of possible/fictional worlds as a sign of the emergence of post-poststructuralism.

In this chapter, placing myself in the tradition of rigorous and explicit theory and concept formation, I use the method of the tree to delineate the concept of fictional worlds. The "data structure" known as the tree has a venerable history (see Eco 2014), originating with the third-century philosopher Porfyry, and it has recently achieved a new prominence by being widely used in contemporary sciences, especially in biology, linguistics, and computer science. In the tree structure, the logical history of the concept of fictional worlds will be seen as a hierarchically arranged succession of binary nodes; at each of these nodes we will choose one of two alternative directions (see fig. 1.1).

I believe that the journey is worth undertaking for two reasons. First, it represents the logical structure of the concept dynamically: as we look backward we will discover more and more general frameworks in which the concept of fictional worlds is placed. Second, we can develop alternative conceptions of fictionality for comparative purposes.

Node 1: Semantics or Pragmatics

There is a frightful confusion today about the relationship between semantics and pragmatics. It is caused, in my opinion, by the neopragmatists' claim that pragmatics is the supreme, even exclusive dimension in the study of signs. Semantics is downgraded, sometimes even erased. The transfer of responsibility for concept and theory formation to the users of signs (i.e., the readers of literature, the viewers of visual signs, etc.) has had fatal consequences—an uncontrollable relativization.

PHILOSOPHY OF LANGUAGE

PRAGMATICS — SEMANTICS

CONSTRUCTIVISM — REALISM

ONE WORLD — POSSIBLE WORLD

POSSIBILISM — ACTUALISM

TOTAL P-WORLD — SMALL P-WORLD

POSSIBLE WORLDS THEORY
OF LITERARY FICTION

PERFORMATIVES

TEXT THEORY

CONSTANTIVES

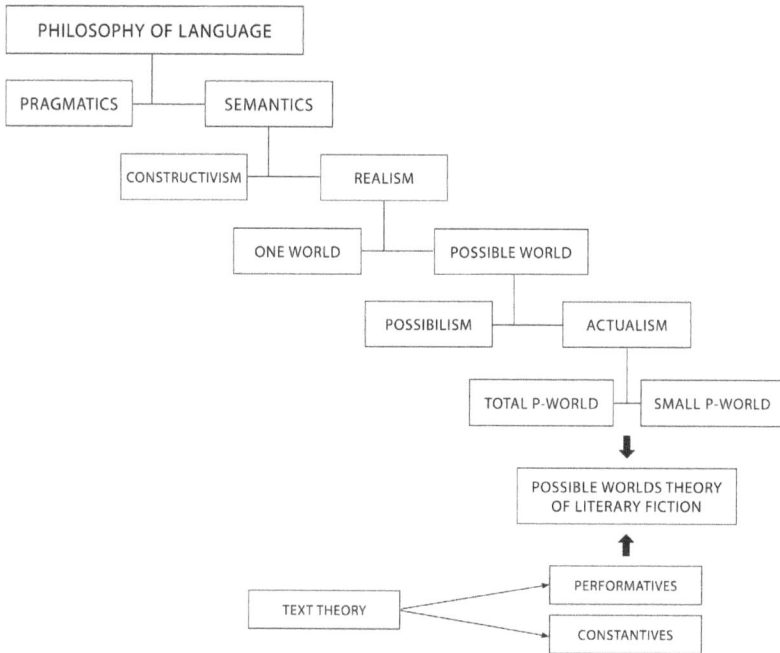

Fig. 1.1. Tree diagram to delineate the concept of a fictional world.

In the study of literature, specifically of literary reception, one neo-pragmatic conception has gained prominence: the German *Rezeptionsäs-thetik* (e.g., Iser 1978; Jauss 1982). The representatives of this school assigned text interpretation to anonymous readers. They denied identity to the literary text. In the Anglo-American version of neopragmatism, fictionality is most frequently taken as a speech-act convention. "The essence of fiction," writes Nicholas Wolterstorff, "is to be located in the nature of the speech acts performed when telling or writing a narration" (1988, 248). The paradigmatic version of fictional pragmatics, proposed by John Searle, treats fictional speech acts as pretended assertions: "The author of a work of fiction pretends to perform a series of illocutionary acts, normally of the assertive type, without any intent to deceive" (1979, 65).

The assumption about the pretended character of the fictional speech act is empirically unverifiable. For me, it is at this point irrelevant, because it offers explanation for the speech act of fiction making, not for its result, the fictional world. I will deal with the pragmatic aspect of the fictional speech act when I get to the reverse phase of the tree evolution.

The weaknesses of the pragmatic interpretations lead us to choose at this junction the direction toward semantic conceptions of fictionality. However, due to the contemporary confusion in the concepts of semantics and pragmatics, I decided to return to the original distinction made by one of the founders of the semiotic theory, the American Charles Morris. He distinguished three "subordinate branches" of semiotics: syntactics, semantics, and pragmatics. Syntactics studies the formal relations between signs, semantics concerns "the relations of signs to their designata," and pragmatics focuses on "the relation of signs to their interpreters" (Morris 1938, 8, 21). At the same time, however, he emphasized that "the various dimensions are only aspects of a unitary process" (30). It is within Morris's framework that I claim that "fictional world" is a semantic notion. Its ground is not in the character of the fictional speech act but in the specificity of its domain of reference. It is precisely on this axis that the concept of the fictional world emerges: fictions have a reference that is not the actual but a possible world. Following Philip Bradley and Norman Swartz (1979), we can strengthen this argument by pointing to the logic of possible worlds: their truth conditions (i.e., semantic conditions) are stated as "true in/of a possible world."

Node 2: Realism versus Constructivism

In order to build a semantics of fiction, we have to choose its ontological base, a certain general conception of reality. Our choice at this intersection could be traditional, the metaphysical distinction of realism and idealism. However, the "linguistic turn" of the twentieth century and the field of semiotics allow us to restate the basic ontological question as the opposition of realism and constructivism.

The Czech analytic philosopher Petr Koťátko (2006) presents the realist position under the designation "naive realism." His designation hints at the traditional metaphysical notion that any metaphysical system is philosophically naive because none can be supported by a consistent and generally acceptable logical argument. The undecidability of metaphysics has always been felt; recently, it has been explicitly articulated by a practitioner of this ancient philosophical discipline. In connection with David Lewis's "modal realism," Phillip Bricker states: "The debate goes on; as with other metaphysical debates, a decisive outcome is not to be expected. . . . There seems to be a fundamental rift—unbridgeable by argument—between ontologically conservative philosophers who have what Bertrand Russell called 'a robust sense of reality,' and ontologically liberal philosophers who respond, echoing Hamlet: 'There is more on heaven and earth than is dreamt of in your philosophy'" (2008, 131).

To avoid this undecidability, Koťátko placed the basic ontological problem in the general semantics of signs (semiotics). He formulated the basic choice as questions: "Do we express ourselves in language about the world and about objects existing independently of our utterances and of our language, or is what we express ipso facto formed (structured, organized) by language? Do we express ourselves about a linguistic construct?" (2006, 25). And he answers the questions by affirming the realist position: language is "one of the means of our interaction with our environment and with each other"; "the ability of language to serve for speaking about entities independent of our utterances and of our language is anchored in the very constitution of language and in the role that it plays in our way of life" (27).

The position of constructivism, that is, the view that reality is a social construct, was succinctly and unambiguously expressed by Nelson Goodman: "We can have words without a world, but no worlds without words or other symbols" (1978, 6). Goodman did not answer, did not even ask, where we could find "words without a world." It seems that in general constructivists have difficulty answering Ian Hacking's (1999) question: "Social construction of what?"

Consequences of radical constructivism can be best observed in the postmodern philosophy of history, where this view has achieved wide popularity. It was announced by Roland Barthes (following Nietzsche): "From the moment language intervenes (and when would it not intervene?), the fact can only be defined in a tautological fashion. . . . The fact can only have a linguistic existence (as a term of a discourse), and yet everything proceeds as if this existence were nothing but a pure and simple 'copy' of another existence situated in the extrastructural domain, in the 'real'" ([1967] 1981, 16–17). Armed with this presupposition, Barthes was ready to answer his original question: "Does this narration [the narration of past events] differ, in some specific trait, in some indubitably pertinent feature, from imaginary narration, as we find it in the epic, the novel, the drama?" His answer is negative (65, 73).

Hayden White provided further ammunition to the view that there is no fundamental distinction between historiographic and fictional narrative. He claims that explanation in history consists in matching "a specific plot structure with the set of historical events that he [the historian] wishes to endow with a meaning of a particular kind. This is essentially a literary, that is to say *fiction-making*, operation" (White 1978, 85, emphasis added). British historian Alun Munslow dragged this position to a radical extreme: "The past is not discovered or found. It is created and represented by the historian as a text" (1997, 118). Here, I feel, constructivism reveals its counterintuitive character.[1]

A recently formulated dichotomy, in my opinion, contributes substantially to our choice at this node: Jaakko Hintikka's "ultimate presupposition of twentieth-century philosophy." It harks back to Leibniz's project of a universal regimented language (*characteristica [lingua] universalis* and *calculus ratiocinator*), but Hintikka's immediate inspiration was a brief paper on Gottlob Frege's logic by Jean van Heijenoort (1967). Van Heijenoort distinguished between logic as "calculus" and logic as "language." Hintikka (1988, 1997) transferred this distinction into the philosophy of language, speaking about two conceptions of language: language as calculus and language as universal medium. In his later contribution, Hintikka noted that the term "calculus" has "multiple connotations" and therefore can be misleading; instead, he suggested speaking "of the *model-theoretical tradition* in logic and philosophy of language" (1997, xi).

Hintikka's suggestion was significantly enriched by Martin Kusch, another Finnish analytic philosopher. He undertook a thorough analysis of the philosophy of language of prominent phenomenologists of the twentieth century and came to this conclusion: Husserl accepts the concept of language as calculus, while Heidegger's and Gadamer's conceptions treat it as a universal medium (Kusch 1989, 130–34, 225–28, 257).

Hintikka differentiates the two positions fundamentally in their answer to a critical question: Can we or can we not "escape our language"? He explains that if you treat language as calculus, "you so to speak stop your language and step off. In less metaphoric terms, you can discuss the semantics of your language and even vary systematically its interpretation." This implies, in my opinion, that you can "get through" language and gain a view of the world as existing independently of its verbal representations. In contrast, when we see language as the universal medium "we cannot in the last analysis escape our language and as it were look at it and its logic from the outside" (Hintikka 1988, 53–54). From this distinction Hintikka draws a very important conclusion: "One of the most important consequences of the view of language as the universal medium is the uniqueness of our language and of its interpretation. All that language is good for on this view is to enable us to talk about this world. We cannot (unless a great deal of further explanation is given) use language to discuss other possible worlds. . . . Thus the very possibility of possible-worlds semantics depends on some version of the assumption of language as calculus" (54). Hintikka's formulation, together with the previous critique of constructivist semantics, leads us to take at this node the direction toward the realist position in the philosophy of language.

Node 3: One World or Plurality of Worlds

At this binary choice we have to decide whether a satisfactory conception of fiction will be placed in the frame of one-world semantics or in the frame of a semantics based on the plurality of worlds. The one-world frame is the base of a popular tradition established by Bertrand Russell: "There is only one world, the 'real world.' . . . It is the very essence of fiction that only the thoughts, feelings etc. in Shakespeare and his readers are real, and that there is not, additional to them, an objective Hamlet" (1919, 169). According to Russell, fictional entities (such as Odysseus) are nonexistent entities and as such have no properties; fictional terms (the name Odysseus) lack reference (are "empty"); and fictional sentences are false. This view spells disaster for fictional entities, especially for fictional characters. By denying them properties, Russell's conception is the exact opposite of what the creators of fictions do, namely, assign specific properties to their fictional persons.

The second one-world conception of fictionality is the doctrine of mimesis, which ties fictions to the actual world, explaining them as its imitations or representations. This conception has been dominant in the Western cultural tradition since its emergence in antiquity (Socrates, Plato, Aristotle). It achieved wide popularity, especially in its Aristotelian guise, which transforms fictional individuals into actual universals (types). And despite its rejection by modernist poets and artists, it has survived until today in various guises.[2] The semantics of fictional worlds requires a conception of fiction broad enough to accommodate not only "realist" fictions but also various types of nonstandard and experimental fictions of the past, the present, and the future. Modern fiction making, a supreme and autonomous exercise of creative imagination, has cut ties to the actual world.

In contrast to one-world theories of fictionality, the "Leibnizian conception," based on the idea of the plurality of worlds, enables us to formulate the concept of fictional worlds as possible worlds. It is well known that the modernized notion of possible worlds was originally suggested as the model for modal semantics formulated by Saul Kripke (1963).[3] But soon it proved to be very useful in a wide range of theoretical disciplines. Let me quote the opinions of two philosophers who agree on this point, although they hold very different views on what possible worlds are. According to Joseph Melia, "The philosophical benefits that possible worlds offer are rich indeed" (2008, 135), but he did not go beyond this generality. Bricker is more specific: "Philosophers agree for the most part that possible worlds talk is extremely useful for explicating concepts and formulating theories." He points to a number of philosophical fields in which this "talk" has proved its usefulness: "analytic metaphysics, philosophy of language, philosophy of science, epistemology, and ethics" (Bricker 2008, 111). Unfortunately, he did not take notice of the key document of the interdisciplinary reach of the idea of possible worlds, namely, the proceedings of Nobel Symposium 65 (Allén 1988). In this volume the concept was tested in a number of disciplines, ranging from philosophy, history of science, and linguistics through literary and art theory to quantum mechanics and cosmology.

Node 4: Actualism or Possibilism

In its original version as formal semantics of modality, the concept of possible worlds was ontologically neutral. This neutrality was formulated at that time by a Russian logician: possible worlds semantics should be taken "simply as mathematical models of the corresponding logical calculi, without any philosophical interpretation" (Slinin 1967). But outside formal semantics the model could not preserve its ontological innocence. As recognized by Robert Adams (1989), a fundamental split exists within the doctrine of possible worlds, namely, the opposition between actualism and possibilism. For possibilism, the actual world "does not have a different status" within the set of possible worlds, while for actualism, the actual world is "a standpoint outside the system of possible worlds from which judgments of actuality which are not world-relative may be made" (Adams 1989, 202).

I do not claim that a semantics of fiction on the basis of possibilism could not be developed. But I have two reasons for choosing actualism at this node. First, actualism is consistent with the realist position in the philosophy of language, which I have chosen at the second node. Second, if there is a need to defend the borderline between fiction and reality, it is actualism that offers us support. And in our time the strengthening of this borderline is necessary because certain trends in postmodern thought (such as the constructivist conception of historiography mentioned above) weakened it or even tried to erase it.

Node 5: Total or Small Worlds

Now we are faced with the final binary choice, which some philosophers consider a barrier preventing them from treating fictions as possible worlds. It is well known that the possible worlds of Kripke's model are "total" and "maximally comprehensive" states of affairs, or, as Takashi Yagisawa put it, "maximal cohesive mereological sums of possibilia" (1968, 180). In other words, the possible worlds of modal logic are infinite and complete sets of abstract entities. John Perry calls this conception "the strong version of possible-worlds theory" (1988, 125) and names David Lewis and Robert Stalnaker as philosophers who adhere to it. The infinite size, number, and variety of possible worlds can be handled by logical formalisms but is beyond the reach of tools and models of empirical research. For all empirical researchers, this caveat has been expressed by Barbara H. Partee: "A maximal set is not appropriate for empirical research, such as, for example, linguistics" (1988, 118). Are we to leave possible worlds in their original purely formal manifestation and refuse them as a theoretical base of empirical inquiries?

In answering this question, we are again offered a helping hand from Hintikka. He considers the claim that possible worlds have to be infinite a "hangover" from the conception of language as the universal medium. But in the conception of language as calculus, where "we really are free to re-interpret our language," we can also choose freely the universe of discourse language refers to. This universe hence does not have to be an entire world in the commonplace sense of the word, that is, a possible world history; it can be a "'small world,' that is, a relatively short course of local events in some nook or corner of the actual world" (Hintikka 1988, 55). The concept of small worlds was taken up by Umberto Eco, who extended its application to fictional worlds. Eco also emphasized that outside formal semantics we need "furnished" possible worlds made up of "individuals endowed with properties" (Eco 1989, 343). Small and concrete possible worlds are a legitimate base of theorizing in empirical disciplines. Correspondingly, we conceive of fictional worlds as small structured worlds consisting of a finite number of possible particulars: persons, events, actions, places, and so on.

A semantics of literary fiction based on this conception of possible worlds as small worlds was launched as early as the 1970s. In the late 1980s and especially in the 1990s a number of synthesizing works laid a firm foundation for a comprehensive possible worlds semantics of literary fictions.[4] Soon other literary scholars expanded the project.[5]

The discovery of possible worlds semantics would seem to end our journey in search of a semantics of literary fictions. However, we have not yet answered a very important question: How are these worlds created?

According to Leibniz's amendment of the story of creation, the divine mind had the ability to survey and evaluate an infinite number of possible worlds and was able to select the best of them for the act of creation. Contemporary thinking about possible worlds does not locate possible worlds in some transcendental depository where they await *discovery*. As Kripke put it, "Possible worlds are *stipulated*, not discovered by powerful telescopes" (1980, 44), and M. J. Cresswell specifies: "Possible worlds are things we can talk about or imagine, suppose, believe in or wish for" (1988, 4). How then are possible worlds of literary fictions "stipulated"? They are constructed by the creative activity of writing. By writing a text, the author creates a fictional world that had not been available prior to this act. There is no other medium of construction (and reconstruction) of fictional worlds of literature than the literary text. In order to serve this function, the fictional text has to possess a special world-creating power. How do we explain this power? In order to answer this question, we have to reverse the direction of our journey and take *text theory* as the second base for our conception of fiction. And we will have to choose again between two options (see fig. 1.1).

My explanation of the world-creating power of fictional texts will be given in two steps. The first step is the claim that fictional texts lack truth value. In this thesis, I follow Frege ([1892] 1960, 62), who recognized that fictional texts (sentences; he calls them *Dichtung*) are neither true nor false. Indeed, it makes no sense to ask whether Gustave Flaubert was telling the truth or not when he made Emma Bovary die by poisoning herself. There was no world, no life, no death of Emma prior to Flaubert's writing; therefore, there was no basis for the truth valuation of his sentences.

The second, no less important step in the development of our conception of fictional poiesis is the recognition of a specific illocutionary force of fictional texts. To explain this force, I turn to the theory of speech acts, specifically to J. L. Austin's concept of performative speech acts. He suggested this concept in his well-known book, *How to Do Things with Words* (1962), and elaborated it in a paper, first published in French the same year and later translated into English (Austin 1971). The paper is important because in it the concept of the performative is specified by being contrasted to the constative. The distinction harks back to Aristotle, who removed certain classes of texts (such as invocations, prayers, etc.) from the authority of logic and relegated them to the domain of rhetoric (*De interpretatione* 17a). According to Austin, a performative speech act "has its own special job, it is used to perform an action" (1971, 13). A performative speech act gains this power not by truth conditions but by felicity conditions. A necessary (although not the only) felicity condition is the speaker's authority to perform a certain action by words (e.g., the judge's authority to sentence somebody to prison).

I explained the specific world-creating power of the fictional text by the theory of authentication: a possible world is converted into a fictional world when it is authenticated by a felicitous (i.e., authoritative) fictional text (1998, chap. 6). It is as authenticated possibles that unicorns and fairies, Odysseus and Raskolnikov, Brobdingnag and Chevengur exist and that readers can gain access to them, fear them, or feel pity for them, as well as talk and argue about them at any time—as they do with respect to actual entities.

The story of authentication in narrative texts is, however, more complicated. Because authentication can be achieved by different narrative text modes—third-person narration (also known as Er-form), first-person narration (also known as Ich-form), subjective narration, and so on—as well as explicitly or implicitly, we are forced to speak about various degrees or ranks of fictional existence. Some fictional facts exist absolutely, others with a subjective tinge, some as definite, others as virtual, and so on. Does it mean that our semantics of fiction has to accept a broad (Meinongian) conception of existence? The Hungarian fictional worlds theorist Zoltan Kanyó thought so, and Marie-Laure Ryan (2001) presupposes so in speaking about "virtual worlds." I am not imposing this ontology, but I maintain that not only possible worlds semantics of fiction but also various developments in today's science and technology force us to struggle anew with the very concept of existence. What we learned in deriving the concept of fiction can thus provide us with arguments in the perennial but again topical philosophical conflict: the conflict over what exists and what does not exist. Fictional worlds seem to challenge our standard binary thinking about existence.

Notes

1. For a detailed critique of the constructivist philosophy of history, see Doležel (2010).
2. See especially Erich Auerbach ([1946] 1957). Some contemporary scholars who defend the doctrine of mimesis have made the term fuzzy.
3. For recent developments in the philosophy of possible worlds, see the anthology *Possible Worlds: Logic, Semantics and Ontology*, edited by Guido Imaguire and Dale Jaquette.
4. See Pavel (1986); Ryan (1991); Eco (1994); Ronen (1994); and Doležel (1998).
5. See Semino (1997); Červenka (2003); Fořt (2005). The attention of my readers should not escape the popularity of possible worlds semantics of fiction in contemporary Czech theory of fiction and narratology. It is a result of the expansion of the domain of structural thematics initiated by the Czech literary structuralists Jan Mukařovský and Felix Vodička (see Bremond et al. 1995).

References

Adams, Robert M. 1989. "Theories of Actuality." In *The Possible and the Actual: Readings in the Metaphysics of Modality*, edited by Michael J. Loux, 190–209. Ithaca NY: Cornell University.

Allén, Sture, ed. 1988. *Possible Worlds in Humanities, Arts and Sciences: Proceedings of Nobel Symposium 65.* Berlin: de Gruyter.

Auerbach, Erich. (1946) 1957. *Mimesis: The Representation of Reality in Western Literature.* Garden City: Doubleday.

Austin, John Langshaw. 1962. *How to Do Things with Words*. Cambridge MA: Harvard University Press.

———. 1971. "Performative-Constative." In *The Philosophy of Language*, edited by J. R. Searle, 13–22. Oxford: Oxford University Press.

Barthes, Roland. (1967) 1981. "The Discourse of History." In *Comparative Criticism: A Yearbook*, vol. 3, translated by S. Bann. Cambridge: Cambridge University Press.

Bradley, Philip, and Norman Swartz. 1979. *Possible Worlds: An Introduction to Logic and Its Philosophy*. Indianapolis: Hackett.

Bremond, Claude, et al., eds. 1995. *Thematics*. Albany: State University of New York Press.

Bricker, Phillip. 2008. "Concrete Possible Worlds." In *Contemporary Debates in Metaphysics*, edited by Theodor Sider et al., 111–34. London: Blackwell.

Červenka, Miroslav. 2003. *Fikční světy lyriky* [Fictional worlds of lyric poetry]. Prague: Paseka.

Cohn, Dorrit. 1998. *The Distinction of Fiction*. Baltimore MD: Johns Hopkins University Press.

Cresswell, M. J. 1988. *Semantical Essays: Possible Worlds and Their Rivals*. Dordrecht: Kluwer.

Crittenden, Charles. 1991. *Unreality: The Metaphysics of Fictional Objects*. Ithaca NY: Cornell University Press.

Doležel, Lubomír. 1998. *Heterocosmica: Fiction and Possible Worlds*. Baltimore MD: Johns Hopkins University Press.

———. 2010. *Possible Worlds of Fiction and History: The Postmodern Stage*. Baltimore MD: Johns Hopkins University Press.

Eco, Umberto. 1988. "Report on Session 3: Literature and Arts." In *Possible Worlds in Humanities, Arts and Sciences: Proceedings of Nobel Symposium 65*, edited by Sture Allén, 343–55. Berlin: de Gruyter.

———. 1989. "Small Worlds." *Versus* 52/53:53–70.

———. 1994. *Six Walks in the Fictional Woods*. Cambridge MA: Harvard University Press.

———. 2014. *From the Tree to the Labyrinth: Historical Studies on the Sign and Interpretation*. Cambridge MA: Harvard University Press.

Fořt, Bohumil. 2005. *Uvod do sémantiky fikcnich světů* [An introduction to the semantics of fictional worlds]. Brno: Host.

———. 2016. *An Introduction to Fictional Worlds Theory*. New York: Lang.

Frege, Gottlob. (1892) 1960. "On Sense and Reference." In *Philosophical Writings of Gottlob Frege*, edited by G. P. Geach and M. Black, 56–78. Oxford: Blackwell.

Goodman, Nelson. 1978. *Ways of Worldmaking*. Indianapolis: Hackett.

Hacking, Ian. 1999. *Social Construction of What?* Cambridge MA: Harvard University Press.

Hintikka, Jaakko. 1988. "Exploring Possible Worlds." In *Possible Worlds in Humanities, Arts and Sciences: Proceedings of Nobel Symposium 65*, edited by Sture Allén, 52–73. Berlin: de Gruyter.

———. 1997. *Lingua Universalis vs. Calculus Ratiocinator: An Ultimate Presupposition of Twentieth-Century Philosophy*. Dordrecht: Kluver.

Imaguire, Guido, and Dale Jaquette, eds. 2010. *Possible Worlds: Logic, Semantics and Ontology*. Munich: Philosophia.

Iser, Wolfgang. 1978. *The Act of Reading: A Theory of Aesthetic Response*. Baltimore MD: Johns Hopkins University Press.

Jauss, Hans Robert. 1982. *Toward an Aesthetic of Reception*. Translated by Timothy Bahti. Minneapolis: University of Minnesota Press.

Kanyó, Zoltan. 1980. "Semantik für heimatlose Gegenstände: Die Bedeutung von Meinongs Gegenstandtheorie für die Theorie der Fiktionalität." Edited by Z. Kanyó. *Studia Poetica* 3:3–114.

Koťátko, Petr. 2006. *Interpretace a subjektivita* [Interpretation and subjectivity]. Prague: Filosofia.

Kripke, Saul A. 1963. "Semantical Considerations on Modal Logic." *Acta Philosophica Fennica* 10:83–94.

———. 1980. *Naming and Necessity*. Cambridge MA: Harvard University Press.

Kusch, Martin. 1989. *Language as Calculus vs. Language as Universal Medium: A Study in Husserl, Heidegger and Gadamer*. Dordrecht: Kluver.

Laudan, Larry. 1977. *Progress and Its Problems*. Berkeley: University of California Press.

Melia, Joseph. 2008. "Ersatz Possible Worlds." In *Contemporary Debates in Metaphysics*, edited by Theodor Sider et al., 135–51. London: Blackwell.

Morris, Charles W. 1938. *Foundations of the Theory of Signs*. In *International Encyclopedia of United Science*, vol. 1, no. 2. Chicago: University of Chicago Press.

Munslow, Alun. 1997. *Deconstructing History*. London: Routledge.

Partee, Barbara H. 1988. "Possible Worlds in Model-Theoretic Semantics: A Linguistic Perspective." In *Possible Worlds in Humanities, Arts and Sciences: Proceedings of Nobel Symposium 65*, edited by Sture Allén, 93–123. Berlin: de Gruyter.

Pavel, Thomas. 1975. "Possible Worlds in Literary Semantics." *Journal of Aesthetics and Art Criticism* 34:165–76.

———. 1986. *Fictional Worlds*. Cambridge MA: Harvard University Press.

Pavel, Thomas, Claude Bremond, and Joshua Landy, eds. 1994. *Thematics: New Approaches*. New York: SUNY Press.

Perry, John. 1988. "Possible Worlds and Subject Matter: Discussion of Barbara H. Partee's Paper 'Possible Worlds in Model-Theoretic Semantics: A Linguistic Perspective.'" In *Possible Worlds in Humanities, Arts and Sciences: Proceedings of Nobel Symposium 65*, edited by Sture Allén, 124–37. Berlin: de Gruyter.

Ronen, Ruth. 1994. *Possible Worlds in Literary Theory*. Cambridge: Cambridge University Press.

Russell, Bertrand. 1919. *Introduction to Mathematical Philosophy*. London: Allen & Unwin; New York: Macmillan.

Ryan, Marie-Laure. 1991. *Possible Worlds, Artificial Intelligence and Narrative Theory*. Bloomington: Indiana University Press.

———. 2001. *Narrative as Virtual Reality: Immersion and Interactivity in Literature and in Electronic Media*. Baltimore MD: Johns Hopkins University Press.

Searle, John R. 1979. *Expression and Meaning: Studies in the Theory of Speech Acts*. Cambridge: Cambridge University Press.

Semino, Elena. 1997. *Language and World Creation in Poems and Other Texts*. New York: Longman.

Slinin, J. A. 1967. "Teorija modal'nostej v sovremennoj logike" [Theory of modalities in contemporary logic]. In *Logičeskaja semantika i modal'naja logika* [Logical semantics and modal logic], edited by P. V. Tavanec, 119–47. Moscow: Nauka.

van Heijenoort, Jean. 1967. "Logic as Language and Logic as Calculus." *Synthèse* 17:324–30.

White, Hayden. 1978. *Tropics of Discourse: Essays in Cultural Criticism*. Baltimore MD: Johns Hopkins University Press.

Wolterstorff, Nicholas. 1988. "Discussion of Lubomír Doležel's Paper 'Possible Worlds and Literary Fictions.'" In *Possible Worlds in Humanities, Arts and Sciences: Proceedings of Nobel Symposium 65*, edited by Sture Allén, 243–49. Berlin: de Gruyter.

Yagisawa, Takashi. 1968. "Beyond Possible Worlds." *Philosophical Studies* 53:175–204.

2 From Possible Worlds to Storyworlds

On the Worldness of Narrative Representation

MARIE-LAURE RYAN

The metaphor of world to designate what is presented to the imagination by a narrative text has been informally used in literary theory and narratology for a very long time. No less time-honored is the association of narrative fiction with the domain of the possible: in the *Poetics*, Aristotle contrasts the task of the historian, which is to describe what is, to the task of the poet, which is to describe "what could be according to possibility and probability" (*Poetics* 9.2). When philosophers and logicians developed possible worlds (PW) theory, they established a connection between worldness and possibility that held great promise for scholars interested in the narrative experience, despite the differences in perspective and goals between philosophers and narratologists: the former conceive possible worlds as tools to solve problems in modal logic, while the latter view them as constructs of the imagination, as objects of aesthetic contemplation, and as conditions of narrative immersion. In this chapter I examine the relations between the worlds of PW theory and the notion of storyworld, which has recently gained traction as the designation of that which narrative texts, whatever their medium, display to the mind of the reader, spectator, or even player. First, I attempt to define the general properties of storyworlds. Then I explore the variety of storyworlds, comparing them on the basis of three variables: distance from the actual world, size, and ontological completeness. I conclude with the discussion of two texts that suggests different answers to the question of completeness.

Basic Properties of Storyworlds

Insofar as it can apply to both fictional and factual stories, the notion of storyworld is broader than the more traditional term *fictional world*. In the case of nonfiction, the storyworld as image of a world must be distinguished from the world being represented, since this world exists independently of any text; but in the case of fiction this distinction becomes void because the text creates its own world. Yet storyworlds have to fulfill more stringent conditions than fictional worlds because these conditions have to ensure narrativity. One can imagine a purely descriptive fictional world lacking a temporal dimension, but this world would not be a storyworld. The relation between storyworlds and fictional worlds is thus one of overlap: some storyworlds are not fictional, some fictional worlds are not storyworlds, but most imaginary worlds are both.

Building on the OED's definition of worlds as "all that exists," I regard storyworlds as totalities that encompass space, time, and individuated existents that undergo transformations as the result of events. Worlds can be thought of in two ways: as containers for entities that possess a physical mode of existence (events can be considered such entities because they affect solid objects and are anchored in time and space) and as networks of relations between these entities. By insisting on existents, events, and change, this conception of worlds links them to the basic conditions of narrativity, and it concurs with David Herman's definition of storyworlds as "global mental representations enabling interpreters to frame inferences about situations, characters, and occurrences either explicitly mentioned or implied by a narrative text or discourse" (2009, 106).

As totalities that encompass both time and space, storyworlds solve a problem that has dogged narratology and text typology ever since Gérard Genette distinguished narration and description and regarded the latter as a "pause" in narration (1976, 6): the role of description in narrative texts. Text typologists (Chatman 1978; Virtanen 1992; Herman 2009) consider narration and description to be distinct text types: one is concerned with events that take place in time, the other with the properties of entities that exist in space. But while texts that represent the descriptive type on the macrolevel are rather rare (they are illustrated by academic papers in ethnography or human geography), description is widely found in the narrative text type. Text typologists (e.g., Virtanen 1992) contour this problem by claiming that text types can exist on both the macro- and the microlevels, but even if a text is considered narrative on the macrolevel, the descriptions of the microlevel constitute islands of nonnarrativity that need to be filtered out to get at the narrative meaning of the text. This is rather counterintuitive, since without descriptions readers could not form a mental image of characters and settings. Description constitutes, therefore, an integral dimension of narrativity. If narrative is conceived as the creation of a storyworld that extends in both space and time, rather than simply as the recounting of a sequence of events, then descriptions can be fully integrated into narrative meaning because they contribute as much to the image of this world as the report of events.

The concept of storyworld that I am proposing differs from other, more informal, and traditional uses of the term *world* in literary theory in several important ways. When critics speak of "the world of Proust" or "the world of Kafka," they mean the totality of meanings associated with a given author. These large worlds can contain contradictions, since authors may defend different ideas during their career. Storyworlds, by contrast, relate to specific texts or groups of texts, and their links to individual authors are loose: authors may create several different storyworlds, as will be the case when science fiction writers produce different series of novels, while a storyworld can be developed by different authors, as will be the case in the phenomenon that Richard Saint-Gelais (2005, 2011) describes as "transfictionality."

An important difference between storyworlds and the global vision of particular authors lies in the essentially concrete nature of storyworlds. While "the world of Proust" contains all the opinions and ideas that can be derived from *À la recherche du temps perdu* (as well as from Proust's other texts), these aspects of meaning are not necessarily part of the storyworld of the novel because they can be messages indirectly conveyed by the author, who is not a member of the storyworld. It could be argued that even the voiced opinions of impersonal third-person narrators do not belong to storyworlds since these narrators are extradiegetic, which means located outside the storyworld.[1] For an abstract idea to form a constitutive element of a storyworld it must correspond to the content of a mental event or of an act of communication actually performed by a member of this world. Storyworlds are not made of general statements such as "love hurts" but of particular events such as "Juliet thought that love hurts."

Yet another common conception of worlds from which storyworlds must be distinguished is their association with spatial objects such as islands and planets. Narratives that represent travel between different worlds in the planetary or insular sense, such as *Gulliver's Travels* and *Star Wars*, still present only one storyworld. Yet if one regards the beliefs, wishes, obligations, and dreams of characters as constituting private worlds (Ryan 1991), then storyworlds are not just worlds but entire universes, since they contain not only an actual world of narrative facts but a multitude of possible worlds created by the mental activity of characters.

In contrast to "textualist" literary doctrines that postulate an absolute dependency of worlds on texts (so that if one changes one word of the text, one also changes the world), the concept of storyworlds that I am proposing entertains loose relations with texts and narratives. Three cases are possible (Ryan 2015). (1) A narrative text may present several ontologically distinct worlds, for instance, when it describes multiple conflicting outcomes for the same situation, as in the novel *The French Lieutenant's Woman* and the film *The Butterfly Effect*. (2) A text may project a unified world that includes many different stories, as in the film *Babel* and the novel *Cloud Atlas*, which consist of several stories taking place in different places (*Babel*) or different times (*Cloud Atlas*) but connected by common objects. (3) Several texts may contribute to the building of the same world, as in the already mentioned phenomenon of transfictionality, to which I return later.

Distance

The notion of distance presupposes a point of reference. Through its opposition of one actual or real world to a multitude of nonactual possible worlds, pw theory suggests using the actual world (i.e., the world we inhabit and that determines our life experience) as the standard of comparison.[2] The distance between our world and storyworlds can be measured by so-called ontological rules that specify what can be found and what cannot in a storyworld or in a type of storyworld. For instance, an ontological rule governing fairy tales states that the laws of nature that govern the actual world can be broken by magic and that fairy tales' biological inventory can include species that cannot be found in reality, such as fairies, witches, and talking animals. Overall distance between worlds will depend on how many of the rules that describe one world are broken by the other. If we draw an analogy between ontological rules and what pw theory calls "accessibility relations," the distance of a storyworld from the actual world is a function of the number of accessibility relations connecting the two worlds.[3]

The most general way to assess ontological distance relies on a story's possibility of realization. A storyworld can entertain three basic types of relation to the actual world: it can be verified in it (this will happen in the case of accidentally true fiction, as well as in truthful factual narratives); it can be possible in it (realistic Victorian novels, fictionalized history, some science fiction); or it can be clearly impossible (fairy tales, the fantastic).[4] The facts narrated in *Madame Bovary*, for instance, could have happened in the real world, because the storyworld of the novel only differs from the real world in that it adds a few individuals to its inventory while respecting its geography, history, and natural laws.

Fantastic stories may not be actualizable in the real world (though this is to some extent a matter of opinion: ghost stories could be credible for people who believe in the occult), but they remain imaginable and logically consistent. PW theory would regard their worlds as possible. We must therefore distinguish the pragmatically impossible (e.g., people being transformed into animals) from the logically impossible, which breaks the laws of noncontradiction (not p AND ~p) and of Excluded Middle (either p OR ~p). A distinction should further be made between logical impossibilities born out of interesting plot situations and "pure" logical impossibilities presented for their own sake. In the first category are the paradoxes inherent to time travel (cf. the grandfather paradox), ontological metalepses (fictionally fictional characters interacting with fictionally real ones), causes preceding their effects, or the replacement of the past by different events (Ryan 2009).[5] While such narratives open logical holes in the fabric of storyworlds, their inconsistencies are limited to certain areas, and they do not contaminate the entire storyworld, despite the claim of logicians that when a single contradiction enters a system of propositions, anything can be inferred, and no world can be constructed. Readers process these texts according to what I call a "Swiss cheese strategy": they close their eyes on the holes and process the rest of the text according to normal inference processes. This kind of contradiction thus remains compatible with world building and immersion. The second category, contradiction for its own sake, is exemplified by the folklore form of nonsense poetry, as well as by some postmodern texts, especially those of the French New Novel, a school whose explicit goal was to "free" the novel from the conventions of nineteenth-century narrative. As Lubomír Doležel writes about Alain Robbe-Grillet's *La maison de rendez-vous*, this novel "constructs contradictions of different orders: (1) one and the same event is introduced in several conflicting versions; (2) a place (Hong Kong) is and is not the setting of the novel; (3) the same events are ordered in reversed temporal sequence (A precedes B and B precedes A); and (4) one and the same world entity recurs in several modes of existence—as a literary fictional fact, as a theater performance, as a sculpture, as a painting" (1998, 164). Such a systematic use of contradiction can have only one purpose, that of subverting the notion of storyworld, preventing immersion, and forcing—as Doležel concludes—a metafictional or metanarrative reading.

In a system that ranks texts according to the distance of their worlds from the actual world, texts that use contradiction for its own sake could be said to represent the most remote possible worlds, but this would mean that there are impossible possible worlds, an obvious oxymoron. For some scholars familiar with PW theory, the possibility of contradiction is reason enough to distinguish its possible worlds, which must respect the laws of logic, from fictional worlds, which do not. These scholars have no qualms about talking of impossible fictional worlds. Thus Doležel: "The writing of impossible worlds . . . cancels the entire world-making project. However, literature turns the ruin of its own enterprise into a new achievement: in designing impossible worlds, it poses a challenge to the imagination no less intriguing than squaring the circle" (1998, 165). Or Ruth Ronen: "With postmodernism, impossibilities, in the logical sense, have become a central poetic device, which shows that contradictions in themselves do not collapse the coherence of a fictional world" (1994, 55).[6] The idea of impossible fictional worlds is particularly popular with the school known as unnatural narratology. In his book *Unnatural Narrative: Impossible Worlds in Fiction and Drama*, Jan Alber writes (citing Ronen 1994, 57): "Like Ronen . . . I refuse to view logical impossibilities in fictional worlds as violations of possible-worlds semantics. Rather I see them as 'domains for exercising creative powers' that we readers are invited to make sense of" (2016, 32). Alber's claim that impossible fictional worlds still respect possible worlds semantics implies that this semantics embraces the oxymoron of impossible possible worlds, which I find highly doubtful. It is, however, unclear what PW theory does with representations that lie beyond the horizon of logically possible worlds. Are these worlds or nonworlds?

Even if we regard these representations as nonworlds, this does not exclude meaning and interpretation, because texts can convey ideas by simply exercising the purely literary or linguistic possibility of freely combining contradictory or incompatible terms. Yet while it is easy to write "square circle" or "colorless green ideas sleep furiously" (Chomsky's famous example of a syntactically well-formed but semantically deviant sentence), it is quite another problem to build a plot and its supporting storyworld around such entities. Can one still speak of world when a text asks the imagination to perform acrobatics that stretch it to the breaking point? I simply cannot picture in my mind a situation where both p and –p obtain at the same time, no more than I can imagine a square circle or a flat sphere.[7] Without denying their potential for meaningfulness, I regard texts that use contradictions for their own sake as refusing to construct a world. For a text to have a storyworld, it should be possible to build a mental representation compatible with the whole text (or, alternatively, a mental representation that builds a continuous solid area around the logical holes); but when a text openly asserts p and –p, all the imagination can do is contemplate a subworld where p, and then a subworld where –p, without reaching a synthesis. Thus when I try to form a mental picture of the nonsense rhyme "a young old man, sitting on a wooden stone, was reading a newspaper folded in his pocket in the light of a street lamp that had been turned off," I imagine various permutations of the conflicting elements, for instance, a world where "an old man sitting on a stone was reading his newspaper" and another where "a young man sitting on a pile of wood had a newspaper folded in his pocket," but I cannot conflate these versions into one world.[8]

Size

The size of a storyworld is a function of the amount of information it gives about the world it purports to describe. A thousand-page narrative, a series of novels, or a transmedial franchise has a large storyworld, unless it is highly repetitive; a three-hundred-page stand-alone novel has a medium storyworld; and a short story, a joke, or a text of microfiction has a small storyworld. Here I would like to take a look at the problems raised by the two extremes: minimalist storyworlds and very large storyworlds created by multiple texts.

The genre of microfiction, which is currently gaining popularity, raises the question of the minimal conditions for a text to create a storyworld. Even if we assume that the worlds of PW theory are maximal worlds that assign a positive truth value to one of each pair of contradictory propositions, these worlds can be very small in terms of what exists in them. If we give a negative truth value to all the propositions that assert the existence of something, except for the proposition "there is a rock," we will generate an ontologically complete possible world that consists of a rock and nothing else. (What if even this proposition is false? Can there be empty possible worlds?) Now consider the minimalist story proposed by E. M. Forster as an example of plot: "The king died, then the queen died of grief" ([1927] 1953, 82). If there is a possible world that contains only a rock, there should also be a possible world with just a king, a queen, and the two events that make up Forster's example. But while this would be a possible world in a logical sense, it would not be a *story*world in a phenomenological or experiential sense because it lacks the ability to stimulate the imagination. We read Forster's narratoid as a collection of propositions to which we assign a positive truth value, but we do not attempt to construct a world in which these propositions hold true. In other words, we do not relate emotionally to the grief of the queen; we do not picture her death in our mind; and we do not try any interpretation, such as asking if the king loved her as much as she loved him, because there is nothing beyond the text. This purely propositional mode of understanding is typical of the way we process plot summaries, as opposed to the texts that implement these plots. (And indeed, one could write a fascinating novel based on Forster's sketch.) We read plot summaries to find out what a certain narrative is about and whether we may like it, but we do not become immersed in them, nor do we derive aesthetic pleasure from our reading.

While I would deny worldness in any sense but a strictly logical one to Forster's example (or to the examples of minimal narrative proposed by Gerald Prince [1982], such as "John was rich, then he gambled, then he was poor"), I do not attribute this lack of worldness to the brevity of the text but, rather, to its failure to perform what Mary Louise Pratt (1977) calls a display of its content, that is to say, an invitation to the reader to engage with the reported events. It is certainly much more difficult for a short text than for a long one to create an immersive storyworld, since the reader is quickly expelled from it as the text comes to an end, but it is not impossible. Compare the Forster example to this famous example of flash fiction, attributed to Hemingway by a popular legend: "For sale. Baby shoes. Never worn."[9] I am much more tempted to construct a world out of this minimalist narrative than out of the Forster example because it gives far greater room to my imagination. With the Forster text I do nothing more than process the information because there is no need to make any inferences, but with "baby shoes" I have to fill in gaps and construct past events to explain a puzzling situation. My filling of gaps leads me to imagine the plight of a young mother who lovingly prepared everything her baby would need but tragically lost the infant. This mother is so poor that she needs to sell the items that have become useless, or maybe the sight of the shoes is so painful for her that she has to get rid of them. Whether a text displays a storyworld or only asserts propositions is admittedly a subjective decision, since readers differ in their willingness to engage with certain types of content, but the decision rests on a dependable guideline: when a text creates a storyworld, *we imagine that there is more to this world than what the text represents.*

While the small semantic domains of microfiction raise the problem of the phenomenological difference between projecting a storyworld and simply asserting propositions, the large, expandable domains of transfictionality and transmedia storytelling raise the problem of the identity of storyworlds. Transfictionality is defined by Richard Saint-Gelais (2005) as the sharing of elements, mostly characters, but also imaginary locations, events, and entire fictional worlds, by two or more works of fiction. Transmedia storytelling, the much-talked-about phenomenon responsible for the creation of large commercial franchises such as *Star Wars*, *Harry Potter*, and *The Lord of the Rings*, is a combination of transfictionality and adaptation: like adaptation, it spreads narrative content across multiple media; though unlike adaptation, it usually involves more than two; and like transfictionality, it builds storyworlds through multiple texts. Henry Jenkins defines it in this way, though most of the big commercial franchises fail his definition because they exploit the success of a popular narrative originally conceived as monomedial through sequels, prequels, and adaptations, rather than deliberately distributing narrative content across many media: "Transmedia storytelling represents a process where integral elements of a fiction get *dispersed systematically across multiple delivery channels* for the purpose of creating *a unified and coordinated entertainment experience*. Ideally each medium makes its own *unique contribution* to the unfolding of the story" (2007, n.p., emphasis original).

Whether it uses one or several media, transfictionality relies on a number of basic operations: (1) extension, which adds new stories to the fictional world while respecting the facts established in the original; (2) modification, which changes the plot of the original narrative, for instance, by giving it a different ending; and (3) transposition, which transports a plot into a different temporal or spatial setting, as, for instance, when the musical *West Side Story* sets the plot of *Romeo and Juliet* in the New York City of the 1950s.[10] To this basic catalog of transfictional operations one could conceivably add two more: (4) mash-up, or crossover, an operation that allows characters imported from different narratives to coexist within the same storyworld, as when the heroes of different nineteenth-century novels meet each other in the novels of Jasper Fforde or in the comic book series *The League of Extraordinary Gentlemen*. On the level of storyworld configuration, the mash-up operation allows generic storyworlds to be contaminated by foreign elements, as when the gentle aristocratic world of Jane Austen is invaded by creatures from the horror genre in the novel *Pride and Prejudice and Zombies* by Seth Grahame-Smith. We could also add (5) embedding, an operation by which a storyworld exists in another storyworld as fiction rather than as part of reality. Thus, the characters in the TV series *Futurama* can watch *The Simpsons* on TV, and vice-versa.

Insofar as it maintains ontological boundaries, embedding can be considered a special case of expansion. A new show appears on the TV screen of the Simpson family, and they may talk about it, but the show does not acquire reality status, and it does not threaten the autonomy of the Simpson storyworld. Mash-up and crossovers, by contrast, create brand-new storyworlds through a process of hybridization: half of the world of *Pride and Prejudice and Zombies* comes from Jane Austen, the other half from the horror genre. If the mash-up is constructed as the migration of characters into a different storyworld where they must fight zombies, it becomes a case of transposition, especially since the plot remains roughly the same: Mr. Darcy and Elizabeth marry after a complicated courtship. This leaves us with only three basic transfictional operations: expansion, modification, and transposition.

While all three operations are found in postmodern fiction, as Doležel demonstrates (1998, 199–226), only the first, expansion, is acceptable for the fans of the transmedia franchises of popular culture because it is the only one that respects the integrity of the storyworld. With expansion, the names of characters refer to the same individuals, the facts established by the other texts are respected, and the storyworld established on the basis of the whole system is free of contradictions. The operation of modification, by contrast, creates contradictory versions that challenge the logical consistency of the storyworld; it is widely practiced in fan fiction, but fan fiction is not canonical. Modification can only be regarded as a legitimate way to build storyworlds if we adopt a broad imaginative conception of world rather than a narrow logical one. To fight contradiction, producers of large franchises create compilations of facts known as Bibles that authors of tie-ins are asked to respect, and to maintain control over the growth of storyworlds, they may declare some texts canonical and others noncanonical. When the Disney Company rebooted the *Star Wars* franchise, it excluded from the canon many tie-ins that the Lucas Company had accepted as world defining, thereby changing their ontological status from descriptions of the actual world of the system to descriptions of merely possible counterfactual worlds.[11] As for transposition, it creates an entirely different storyworld, thereby conflicting with the main reason for the popularity of transmedia franchises: the loyalty of audiences to a given world and to its characters and their desire for more information about them.

When two texts are linked by relations of expansion, characters bearing the same name can be considered the same individual, since they present the same core of properties. In the case of modification, however, the same name can refer to characters with different personal histories. If one accepts Saul Kripke's 1972 theory of proper names as rigid designators, which tells us that names refer to the same individual regardless of changes in their properties, these homonymous characters will be considered counterparts of each other in different possible worlds. The counterpart relation allows readers to submit these characters to what I have called "the principle of minimal departure" (Ryan 1991): construct them as close as possible to the characters of the original text, except for the changes imposed by the new text.[12] Transposition presents a more complicated case because the corresponding characters may or may not have the same name. Maria in *West Side Story* is not literally Juliet, even though she suffers similar obstacles to the fulfillment of her love. In this case, the two characters are linked to each other by analogical rather than counterpart relations. But what if the characters in the transposed story have the same names as in the original? In Curtis Sittenfeld's *Eligible*, a transposition of *Pride and Prejudice* to contemporary Cincinnati, we find characters named Jane, Elizabeth, Mary, Kitty, and Lydia Bennet, as well as a Fitzwilliam Darcy and a Chip Bingley. True to contemporary culture, the sisters are busy with texting, yoga, painting their nails, Paleo diet, and exercising, and the three youngest live at home, unable to achieve financial independence. Darcy is a rich doctor, and Bingley is the star of a reality TV show, *Eligible*, on which he must choose a bride from a pool of bachelorettes. Are these characters mere homonyms, or are they counterparts of the same individuals in different worlds? If the counterpart solution is chosen (and I do choose it), an interpretation suggested to the reader by strong similarities in both plot and personalities, the text will be processed as "what would the Bennet sisters do in contemporary culture?" (cf. the popular guideline "what would Jesus do?"); if it is not chosen, the sisters of *Eligible* would be merely typical millennials.[13]

When two or more texts are written by the same author, and when the setting and all the character names remain the same, the answer to the question of whether or not the texts refer to the same world is usually positive. But this answer is not automatic. The question of world and character identity has been recently raised by the 2015 publication of *To Set a Watchman* by Harper Lee, the author of the celebrated novel *To Kill a Mockingbird* (1960). The earlier novel describes the efforts of a white Alabama lawyer, Atticus Finch, to defend an African American man named Tom Robinson wrongly accused of assaulting a white woman. The whole story is narrated from the perspective of Atticus's young daughter, Scout. Written before *Mockingbird* and initially rejected by publishers, *Watchman* is set some fifteen years after *Mockingbird*. The novel describes the visit of an adult Scout to her family in Alabama and her disagreement with the racial politics of her father, a lawyer also named Atticus Finch who has joined an association that defends segregation. The setting, Maycomb, Alabama, is identical, and so are the names of most characters. Many readers were disappointed to find out that the heroic Atticus of *Mockingbird* has turned into a racist in his old age. But given the fact that no mention is made of the Robinson trial in *Watchman* and that Lee completely reconceived the early manuscript when she wrote *Mockingbird*, can one automatically assume that the *Mockingbird* Atticus is the same person as the *Watchman* Atticus and that there is a continuous ideological evolution connecting the two? The textualist school would say that Harper Lee created a brand new storyworld when she rewrote *Watchman* and turned it into *Mockingbird*, so that the two Atticuses are really different persons; but the disappointment of readers demonstrates the strength of the tendency to imagine a large world encompassing both texts.

Completeness

The question of ontological completeness has been one of the most controversial issues in the application of PW theory to storyworlds. For a world to be complete it must possess the property of maximality and excluded middle, which stipulates that for every contradictory pair of propositions, one must be true and another false in that world. Completeness is a property of the actual world and of the worlds of PW, since they represent alternative ways the real world might have been: it would be too farfetched to imagine that a complete world could have been incomplete. But as Doležel observes, "It would take a text of infinite length to construct a complete fictional world. Finite texts, the only texts that humans are capable of producing, are bound to create incomplete worlds. For this reason, incompleteness is a universal extensional property of the fictional-world structuring" (1998, 169). This reasoning is supported by the famous controversy regarding the number of children of Lady Macbeth, first raised by Lionel Charles Knight in 1933, about which philosopher Nicholas Wolterstorff writes, "We will never know how many children had Lady Macbeth. That is not because to know this would require knowledge beyond the capacity of human beings. It is because there is nothing of the sort to know" (1980, 133). The thesis of the incompleteness of fictional storyworlds presupposes a perspective external to these worlds and a sustained awareness of the textual origin of fictional creatures (what I call "textualism") that inhibits make-believe and makes it difficult to explain immersion.

In addition to its incompatibility with immersion (who would care for fictional characters if they are not perceived as ontologically like us?), the idea of fictional incompleteness encounters difficulties when complete real-world entities, such as Paris and Napoleon, enter fictional storyworlds and interact with native characters. Three solutions to this problem are possible: (1) The inventory of the storyworld is split between complete and incomplete entities—a solution that conflicts with the sense of unity and homogeneity conveyed by realistic storyworlds. (2) Real-world entities become incomplete when they enter fictional worlds because they are ontologically recreated by the text. Ruth Ronen claims, for example, that the Paris of Stendhal's *Le rouge et le noir* loses its geography because none of the places of the real Paris are mentioned in the novel (1994, 128 ff.). This reduces the two Parises to mere homonyms and makes the proposition "Julien Sorel moved to a city on the Seine" either false or indeterminate in the world of the novel, a rather counterintuitive implication (3). Both native and imported entities are experienced by readers as complete, provided the text presents a sufficient degree of mimeticism to construct a storyworld.

The third interpretation is the one that I would like to defend, as I did in my 1991 work. In contrast to possibility 2, possibility 3 adopts the world-internal viewpoint of the readers who relocate themselves imaginatively into a storyworld rather than the external perspective typical of philosophers who look at fiction from the perspective of the real world and oppose a fictional mode of existence that encompasses *all* fictional entities to a real mode. Unless narrative texts practice the illusion-destroying self-reflectivity that we have come to expect from postmodernism, they present their characters as real people within the storyworld and not as textual constructs. While readers *know* that the storyworld would not exist without the text (or texts), they pretend that it has an autonomous existence and that the text represents it rather than creates it. This means that readers construct storyworlds and their characters as sharing the ontological status of the real world and of its inhabitants unless otherwise specified.[14] If we imagined Emma Bovary and Lady Macbeth as presenting ontological gaps, they would differ from actual human beings in ways not mandated by the text. While we don't know how many children Lady Macbeth had, and we will never know, we still regard her as somebody who had a determinate number of children. It's just that the text does not specify this number. We consequently treat it as missing information, rather than as ontological gap. Similarly, we don't know and we may never know how many children were born to the historical character of Cleopatra, but this does not make Cleopatra ontologically incomplete. Wolterstorff would probably object that in the case of Cleopatra this information may surface someday, while it will not in the case of Lady Macbeth, but this argument takes an external perspective on the world of Macbeth rather than adopting the attitude of make-believe that defines our experience of fiction (Currie 1990; Walton 1990).

Yet while most narratives present their storyworlds as complete, some fictions do indeed create worlds with ontological gaps. In contrast to the textualist position that regards all fictional storyworlds as incomplete, the difference between them being a matter of what Doležel calls their "saturation" (1998, 169–84), I want to argue for a qualitative difference between complete and incomplete storyworlds (if the latter can still be called storyworlds). I will take as example two dramatic texts, the seventeenth-century French tragedy *Phèdre* by Jean Racine, and Samuel Beckett's twentieth-century play *En attendant Godot / Waiting for Godot*. As a performance-centered type of narrative, which means as a spectacle, the theater depends heavily on what is shown onstage, but because its storyworld can include elements that exist beyond the stage, it provides a particularly good test of the difference between ontologically full and gappy worlds and characters. As Philip Auslander (2015) has argued, the theater oscillates between two poles: the mimetic pole of narrative and fictional representation and the antimimetic pole of pure performance. The spectacles of the mimetic pole present a classic ontology whose space and time extend beyond what is shown onstage, while the spectacles representing the pole of pure performance (such as nonnarrative modern dance) limit space and time to the "here" and "now" occupied by the bodies of the performers.

The plot of *Phèdre* can be summarized as follows: Phèdre is the wife of Thésée (Theseus), king of Trézène. She has fallen in love with Hippolyte, Thésée's son from an earlier marriage. At the beginning of the play Thésée has been absent for six months. When the news of his death arrives, Phèdre confesses her passion to a horrified Hippolyte, who is in love with Aricie, a young woman he cannot marry because she comes from an enemy house. But the news of Thésée's death is soon overturned, and he returns to Trézène. With the consent of Phèdre, Oenone, her nurse, tells Thésée that Hippolyte has tried to force himself on Phèdre. Furious, Thésée asks the god Neptune to take revenge on Hippolyte and banishes him from the kingdom. Soon after, Théramène, Hippolyte's advisor, arrives with the news that Hippolyte has been killed by a sea monster. Full of remorse, Phèdre confesses her lie to Thésée and dies onstage after having taken poison.

Phèdre clearly represents the mimetic/narrative pole. Its world, as well as the world of all strongly mimetic forms of drama, can be divided into three circles: circle 1, the space-time of the action shown onstage; circle 2, the space-time of the action taking place offstage, such as narrated events; and circle 3, the space-time of the geographic and historical context in which the action takes place.[15] In *Phèdre* the location of circle 1 is not a specific place, as a private room would be, but rather an abstract space, a pure thoroughfare where characters come and go freely without specific motivation. How else could one explain that in the same location Phèdre confesses her love to Hippolyte, Hippolyte confesses his love to Aricie, Oenone suggests to Phèdre to accuse Hippolyte of sexual advances, Thésée curses Hippolyte, and Phèdre comes to die? This abstract space is commonly conceived as "the antechamber of the palace," but the stage directions only say "the action is in Trézène."

The second circle, located beyond the stage, literally in the wings, is the realm of the diegetic mode of narration, as opposed to the mimetic mode of the stage action. As the seventeenth-century poet and critic Nicolas Boileau-Despréaux wrote, "Ce qu'on ne doit point voir qu'un récit nous l'expose" (let a narrative tell what cannot be shown) (*L'art poétique*, canto 3). The rules of classical French tragedy do not allow showing violent events onstage, but the death of Hippolyte away from the palace can be narrated in its most grisly details by Théramène. The events of this second circle fully respect the rules, which called for unity of place and time, since they take place between the beginning and the end of the stage action, and they are located in places sufficiently close to be reached within the prescribed time frame.

The third circle consists of the geography of Greece and of all the stories of Greek mythology. When a narrative mentions a real-world location, the principle of minimal departure (see note 10) tells us that its storyworld encompasses all of real-world geography. For instance, when Théramène mentions "the two seas separated by Corinth," the spectator is entitled to assume that the storyworld of *Phèdre* encompasses not only Trézène on the Peloponnese but also Athens, Sparta, and all the islands of the Aegean Sea. This explains why the Larousse edition offers a map of ancient Greece as a "reading tool." Racine's text also includes numerous references to ancient Greek mythology. These narratives are not presented as fictions but as a historical past whose influence plays a crucial role in the plot. For instance, Hippolyte cannot inherit the throne of Thésée because he is the son of an Amazon, that is, of a stranger, and he cannot marry Aricie because her brothers once plotted to dethrone Thésée.

By filling the three circles of its actual world with existents, *Phèdre* verifies the principle stated above: when a text creates a (full) storyworld, we imagine that there is more to this world than the text represents (or shows onstage, in the case of drama). This principle does not hold for *Godot*, as we can see from its handling of the three circles. The first one contains everything that exists beyond doubt in the world of *Godot*. Scenic space is less abstract than in *Phèdre*; the stage directions describe it as "A country road. A tree. Evening" (1952/54, 7). There is also a rock, on which Estragon is sitting. While in *Phèdre* the dramatic action is entirely dependent on the dialogue, in *Godot* gestures are so prominent and so elaborately described by the stage directions that they turn the play into a pantomime. The dialogue, on the other hand, plays a marginal role in the dramatic progression because most of the time it means much more through its incoherence than through its actual content: one could imagine a teacher of creative writing asking students to rewrite the dialogue of *Godot*, aiming for the same absurdist effect, but it would be unthinkable to replace the dense, intricately wrought verses of Racine with the creations of amateurs.

As we have already seen, circle 2 consists of all the events relevant to the plot that take place outside the stage. In *Godot* this circle is as good as empty. In the first act Vladimir and Estragon are waiting for Godot; in the second act they are still waiting, and one can imagine that they will wait forever, because Godot will never come. There is a semblance of external event when a young boy enters the stage with a message from Mr. Godot for Vladimir and Estragon, a message that informs them that Mr. Godot will not come that evening. This event is repeated in both acts (165, 345). It presupposes an act of communication between the boy and Godot in circle 2, an event that presupposes in turn the existence of Godot in this circle. But Godot's existence becomes doubtful when, in act 2, the boy declares that he didn't bring a message on the previous day, a day that spectators would normally associate with act 1. Was it another boy, is the boy lying, or does the world of Godot transgress the principle of noncontradiction? Whatever the answer, one cannot conclude that Godot exists in circle 2, because instead of giving a *de re* interpretation of the boy's claim that he has a message from Godot, according to which there is an individual named Godot who gave a message to the boy, one can settle for a *de dicto* interpretation, according to which there is a boy who claims he has a message from somebody named Godot, but this claim could be false while the whole proposition remains true.

Another indication of the emptiness of circle 2 is the fact that a character named Pozzo can see in act 1 but is blind in act 2. Such a change of state would normally be caused by an event temporally located between act 1 and act 2, but the text does not allude to such an event. Nothing happens between act 1 and act 2, and the change is purely arbitrary. Though spectators normally expect that act 2 follows act 1 unless otherwise suggested, there is no reason to assume that time passes between the two acts.

Circle 3 in *Godot* is barely fuller than circle 2. While the world of *Phèdre* participates in a rich mythological tradition, a tradition that characters regard as history, the world of *Godot* is locked in an almost complete ontological isolation. A few real-world place-names are mentioned, for instance, the departments of Vaucluse, Seine, and Seine-et-Oise in the French version, but these toponyms are chosen for their sonorities and not for their geographical connotations: in the English version, also written by Beckett, Seine and Seine-et-Oise become Fordham and Clapham. I have mentioned above that when a fictional text mentions a real-world toponym, all of real-world geography becomes implicitly part of its world; but this principle does not operate in *Godot*: in this text, names are pure signifiers without referent.

Toward the end of the play (262 ff.), it turns out that space is limited to the space of the stage. Vladimir and Estragon feel threatened, and they try to escape, but they are unable to do so, because there is no elsewhere. Not only is the storyworld reduced to the area of the stage, it is itself a flat area comparable to the worldview traditionally (but wrongly) associated with medieval belief. When Pozzo and Lucky leave the stage a loud noise is heard: they fell from the edge of the world. The absence of space beyond the stage also explains the last lines: "Well, shall we go?" says Vladimir. "Let's go," answers Estragon (357); then the curtain falls. When there is nowhere to go, movement becomes impossible.

Not only is there no space that allows movement, there is no time that allows change.[16] Vladimir and Estragon have always waited for Godot and will always do so. They already know each other at the beginning of the play, but the circumstances of their meeting do not exist, because they do not have personal biographies. They seem from time to time to have distinct personalities, but most of the time they are interchangeable, so that Vladimir's lines could be given to Estragon and vice-versa without significant consequences. They do have a belief world (Godot exists, and they must wait for Godot), but beyond this belief one cannot say anything about them. They are not human beings but allegories. The principle of minimal departure, which tells us to imagine characters on the model of ontologically complete real-world people, does not apply to them.[17]

Phèdre clearly occupies what Auslander calls the mimetic/narrative pole, but *Godot* is more difficult to categorize: Should one place Beckett's play halfway between the two poles, on the ground that it projects an embryo of storyworld, a world that maintains some substance despite its ontological gaps and that remains capable of immersing the spectator in the existential plight of the characters? Or should one locate the play near the pole of pure performance on the ground that its lack of a continuous time and space render narrative development impossible? For Vladimir and Estragon, there is a world that stretches beyond the stage, a world where Godot resides and whose time will perhaps stop when Godot arrives, but for the spectator who doubts the existence of Godot, there is nothing more than the spectacle on the stage and the dialogue of the characters, nothing more than the here and the now. The play thus rests on a conflict between the "objective" ontology of the world in which Vladimir and Estragon live, an ontology far remote from our life experience, and their private conception of this ontology, which retains the properties of a classic ontology. This conflict goes a long way toward explaining the poignant character of the play.

Can one still speak of storyworld in the case of *Godot*, or does the play illustrate the case of a fictional world that fails to develop into a storyworld? (Try summarizing the plot!) If we regard mimesis as essential to narrativity (*pace* the school of unnatural narrative, whose members claim that there are nonmimetic narratives [Alber et al. 2010]), and if we regard the type of mimesis that defines narrative as the representation of a world whose members have *roughly* the same reasons for acting as we have in the real world, then *Godot* fails this criterion. The gestures and talk of Vladimir and Estragon are so random, so absurd, that they cannot be said to implement "the implicit inferential logic of action guiding our real-world experience," as Jean-Marie Schaeffer and Ioana Vultur (2004, 310) describe Paul Ricoeur's conception of mimesis. Vladimir and Estragon perform a verbal and corporeal ballet closer to the gestures of the performers in an abstract dance spectacle than to the kind of strategic moves and occasionally irrational but always goal-oriented actions that we find in *Phèdre*. The closer a text to Auslander's pole of antimimetic pure performance, the less of a storyworld it displays to the imagination.

Conclusion

The introduction of the concept of world, or storyworld, in narratology can be considered a paradigm shift with respect to the school of thought that I call textualism, a school represented by New Criticism, poststructuralism, and deconstruction. Textualism is a theory of high culture and literary narrative. It privileges the signifier over the signified (cf. Barthes's description of the ideal literary text as "galaxies of signifiers" [1974, 5]); it considers literary texts to be primarily about language, not about the kinds of issues that preoccupy human beings; it believes in the infinity, ineffability, and fundamental ambiguity of literary meaning; and it insists on a radical ontological distinction between the flesh-and-blood inhabitants of the real world and the language-made creatures of fiction, so that fictional characters are collections of semantic features rather than imaginary human beings. The storyworld approach, by contrast, applies to all narrative media and embraces both high and popular culture. Regarding texts as "blueprints for worldmaking" (Herman 2009, 195) it rests on the idea that storyworlds, though created by texts, are imagined as existing independently of the medium and as containing more than the text can describe. This idea has important theoretical consequences:

The notion of storyworld provides the surrounding environment required for immersion. Whatever name one gives to the experience of being totally absorbed in a story, of being present on the scene of the events, of feeling empathy for the characters, of eagerly awaiting to find out how the story ends, this experience cannot take place without the sense that the text projects a world that encompasses both characters and events.[18]

The notion of storyworld justifies the practice of transfictionality. If worlds are imagined as existing independently of texts, they escape the control of the original author, and they become expandable. The characters acquire a life of their own, and they can be placed in other circumstances than those described in the original text. And since PW theory tells us that "things could have been different from what they are," it becomes feasible to create alternatives to established fictional worlds.

In language-based narrative, the notion of storyworld encourages a mode of reading based on imagining, visualizing, and mentally simulating the action, rather than on extracting the propositional content of sentences. In contrast to a strict focus on propositional content, these modes of experiencing narrative set no limits on what can be mentally contemplated.

Without a notion of storyworld, it would be difficult to justify fan behavior, such as drawing maps, compiling encyclopedias, constructing genealogies, writing fan fiction, and even dressing up as characters in a cosplay event. These behaviors demonstrate the strength of the need of audiences not only to immerse themselves in storyworlds but to share them with others and to participate in their creation.

The notion of storyworld does not reduce all fictions to a uniform model, because "worldness" can be realized to different degrees. The narrativity of a text is a function of its worldness, and its worldness is a function of its ability to build a mental representation that satisfies the three conditions discussed in this chapter: being logically consistent, large enough to stimulate the imagination, and experienced as complete.

Notes

1. This does not mean that the narrator's opinions do not influence the reader's construction of the storyworld; they certainly do, but they do it in the same way the soundtrack of a film, which is clearly extradiegetic, affects the spectator's experience.

2. The distance of a nonactual possible world from the actual world can be measured, at least theoretically, in terms of the number of propositions whose value differs in each case, though this method does not distinguish important propositions (Napoleon was emperor of France) from rather trivial ones (Napoleon had brown eyes) and therefore cannot account for the fact that a world in which Napoleon is not emperor but does have brown eyes will generally be judged farther from the actual world than a world in which Napoleon has blue eyes but does become emperor, an event that has significant consequences for history.

3. See Ryan (1991, chap. 2) for a systematic exploration of accessibility relations.

4. To these three ontological categories, Doreen Maître (following Todorov's personal definition of the fantastic) adds a fourth: storyworlds in which there is a hesitation, often unresolvable, between could-be-actual and could-never-be-actual events, as, for instance, when an event could be

caused by either supernatural forces or strange manifestations of the laws of nature. (Henry James's *The Turn of the Screw* is widely regarded as an illustration of this category: the text does not assert the existence of supernatural beings, but strange events happen that can be regarded as either the hallucination of a governess or the work of ghosts.) However, Maître's fourth category differs from the other three in that it is not ontological but epistemological. Her taxonomy rests, therefore, on mixed criteria.

5. The grandfather paradox concerns a time traveler who goes back into the past and kills his grandfather; consequently, he is not born and does not travel into the past; therefore, his grandfather is not killed, and the time traveler is born (etc. etc. in an infinite loop).

6. I assume that Ronen means coherence in a thematic or an aesthetic, not a logical, sense.

7. As for the circle famously squared by Sherlock Holmes, a favorite example of philosophers, it is not an impossible object but a procedure that has been geometrically proven to be impossible. According to Wikipedia, "It is the challenge of constructing a square with the same area as a given circle by using only a finite number of steps with compass and straightedge." I don't feel that a story in which Sherlock squares the circle would construct an impossible world: it would, rather, be a world that challenges Euclidean geometry or a world where Sherlock proves mathematicians to be wrong. Of course, the event could be taken as a metaphor of Sherlock's incredible problem-solving ability, which would erase impossibility.

8. Users will differ in what they do with contradictions: some will be deeply bothered by them, some will just ignore them, some will accept the existence of impossible objects without trying to imagine them because the text tells them to do so; and Jan Alber has even suggested a mystical "Zen mode of reading" (2016, 54) by which contradictions will be seen as forming a harmonious whole.

9. According to Wikipedia, "The May 16, 1910 edition of the *Spokane Press* had an article titled 'Tragedy of Baby's Death is Revealed in Sale of Clothes.' At that time, Hemingway would only have been aged ten, and years away from beginning his writing career" (https://en.wikipedia.org/wiki/For_sale:_baby_shoes,_never_worn).

10. Doležel may have been the first to distinguish these three operations in his treatment of postmodern rewrites in *Heterocosmica*, but he uses "displacement" for what I refer to as modification (1998, 206–7). While popular in postmodernism, the phenomenon of transfictionality is much older. It goes back at least to the sequel to *Don Quixote* written by Alonso Fernández de Avellaneda during Cervantes's lifetime (expansion), to the 1681 alternative

version of Shakespeare's *King Lear* by Nahum Tate (modification), and to the multiple transpositions of the *Robinson Crusoe* saga in the eighteenth and nineteenth centuries (e.g., *Swiss Family Robinson*).

11. See https://en.wikipedia.org/wiki/Star_Wars_canon.

12. The principle normally works between the real world and fictional story-worlds, telling us to fill in gaps in the latter on the basis of our life experience unless otherwise specified by the text, but in the case of transfictionality it constructs a fictional storyworld as the closest possible to a preexisting fictional world.

13. One character that I interpret as homonym rather than as a counterpart is the famous feminist Kathy de Bourgh, whose name is reminiscent of Lady Catherine de Bourgh in *Pride and Prejudice*. I expected Kathy de Bourgh to be an obnoxious character who would try to derail the romance between Liz and Darcy, as does Lady Catherine in Austen's novel, but on the contrary, she turns to be warm, wise, and supportive.

14. What about characters who regard themselves as fictional? This is a paradox that breaks ontological boundaries, since by acknowledging their fictionality these characters look at themselves from the perspective of the world of the author, where they do not exist, not from the perspective of the world they inhabit.

15. This division into three circles can also be used for diegetic narratives such as novels, but the distinction between circle 1 and circle 2 is not as clear-cut as in drama, since in drama one circle is enacted and the other narrated, while in diegetic narrative both are narrated. However, circle 2 could be associated with the stories told by characters about the storyworld, as opposed to the main narrator's representation. In *The Odyssey*, circle 2 would be Odysseus's first-person narration of his adventures to the king of Scheria (books 9–12) and circle 1 the third-person narration of all the other books.

16. The loss of sight of Pozzo could be regarded as change, but it cannot be attributed to a temporally situated event.

17. In this reading of *Godot* I stress the incompleteness of its world, especially of its space and time, but the play also contains a good deal of contradiction, for instance, Pozzo being both blind and able to see; the young boy having and not having given a message to Vladimir and Estragon in act 1.

18. Though I disagree with his position, Richard Walsh (forthcoming) is very consistent in rejecting the notions of both world and immersion. His argument is as follows: "World" is a spatial concept, while "narrative" is a temporal concept. A narrative text is a blend of descriptive passages, which mobilize our "spatial cognition" but during which time stands still, and of properly narrative passages, which mobilize our "narrative cognition." Ac-

cording to Walsh, the notion of world carries an implication of totality and completeness that would force readers into superfluous attempts to fill in the blanks in the text. He cites as an example of a frivolous attempt to construct a world the map included in the English-language edition of Alain Robbe-Grillet's *La jalousie*. Rejecting what I have called the principle of minimal departure as requiring the construction of meaningless details, Walsh proposes instead a "relevance" theory of reading that limits mental activity to those imaginings that allow readers to make sense of fictional texts despite their lack of real-world truth. Since there is no such thing as a storyworld, there is no phenomenon such as immersion: Walsh regards immersion as a property of media, not of narratives. The minimalist, rather puritanical mode of reading prescribed by the criterion of relevance prevents indeed any kind of immersive experience, for immersion requires far richer acts of imagination than a strict adherence to the propositional content of the text, to which "relevance" seems to be limited. My arguments against Walsh are as follows: (1) The notion of storyworld does not require an exhaustive filling in of its space: there is a difference between assuming that there is a continuous spatial fabric between the locations mentioned in a narrative text and having to visualize every point in this fabric. (2) It is possible to imagine too little to make sense of a narrative text, but readers cannot be guilty of imagining too much as long as they respect textual information. Mapping *La jalousie* is a way to engage with the text. (3) Narrative cannot be reduced to the temporal, no more than worlds can be reduced to the spatial. Walsh claims that a term such as *spatiotemporal* is just a conceptual juxtaposition, not a synthesis, but any attempt to imagine character movements demonstrates the opposite.

References

Alber, Jan. 2016. *Unnatural Narrative: Impossible Worlds in Fiction and Drama*. Lincoln: University of Nebraska Press.

Alber, Jan, Stefan Iversen, Henrik Skow Nielsen, and Brian Richardson. 2010. "Unnatural Narrative, Unnatural Narratology: Beyond Mimetic Models." *Narrative* 18 (2): 113–36.

Aristotle. 1945. *Poetics*. Translated and introduction by Malcolm Heath. New York: Penguin Books.

Auslander, Philip. 2015. "Théâtre et performance: L'Évasion de la représentation." In *Corps en scènes*, edited by Catherine Courtet, Mireille Besson, Françoise Lavocat, and Alain Viala. Paris: CNRS Edition.

Barthes, Roland. 1974. *S/Z*. Translated by Richard Miller. New York: Farrar, Straus and Giroux.

Beckett, Samuel. 1952/54. *En attendant / Waiting for Godot*. Bilingual edition translated from the French by the author. New York: Grove Press.

Chatman, Seymour. 1978. *Story and Discourse*. Ithaca NY: Cornell University Press.

Currie, Gregory. 1990. *The Nature of Fiction*. Cambridge: Cambridge University Press.

Doležel, Lubomír. 1998. *Heterocosmica: Fiction and Possible Worlds*. Baltimore MD: Johns Hopkins University Press.

Forster, E. M. (1927) 1953. *Aspects of the Novel*. London: E. Arnold.

Genette, Gérard. 1976. "The Boundaries of Narrative." *New Literary History* 8:1–13.

Herman, David. 2009. *Basic Elements of Narrative*. Malden MA: Wiley-Blackwell.

Jenkins, Henry. 2007. "Transmedia Storytelling 101." *Confessions of an Aca-Fan*, March 22. http://henryjenkins.org/2007/03/transmedia_storytelling_101.html.

Knight, Lionel Charles. (1933) 1964. "How Many Children Had Lady Macbeth? An Essay in the Theory and Practice of Shakespeare Criticism." In *Explorations*, 15–54. New York: New York University Press.

Kripke, Saul. 1972. "Naming and Necessity." In *Semantics of Natural Language*, edited by D. Davidson and G. Harman, 253–355. Dordrecht: Reidel.

Maître, Doreen. 1983. *Literature and Possible Worlds*. London: Middlesex Polytechnic Press.

Nabokov, Vladimir. 1980. *Lectures on Literature*. Edited by Fredson Bowers. New York: Harcourt Brace Jovanovich.

Pratt, Mary Louise. 1977. *Toward a Speech Act Theory of Literary Discourse*. Bloomington: Indiana University Press.

Prince, Gerald. 1982. *Narratology*. The Hague: Mouton.

Racine, Jean. 1998. *Phèdre*. Petits classiques Larousse, presented, edited, and annotated by Laurence Giavarini and Eve-Marie Rollinat-Levasseur. Paris: Editions Larousse-Bordas.

Ronen, Ruth. 1994. *Possible Worlds in Literary Theory*. Cambridge: Cambridge University Press.

Ryan, Marie-Laure. 1991. *Possible Worlds, Artificial Intelligence and Narrative Theory*. Bloomington: Indiana University Press.

———. 2009. "Temporal Paradoxes in Narrative." *Style* 43 (2): 142–64.

———. 2011. "Narratology and Cognitive Science: A Problematic Relation." *Style* 44 (4): 469–95.

———. 2015. "Texts, Worlds, Stories: Narrative Worlds as Cognitive and Ontological Concept." In *Narrative Theory, Literature, and New Media: Narrative Minds and Virtual Worlds*, edited by Mari Hatavera, Matti Hyvärinen, Maria Mäkelä, and Frans Mäyrä, 13–28. London: Routledge.

Ryan, Marie-Laure, and Jan-Noël Thon, eds. 2014. *Storyworlds across Media*. Lincoln: University of Nebraska Press.

Saint-Gelais, Richard. 2005. "Transfictionality." In *The Routledge Encyclopedia of Narrative Theory*, edited by David Herman, Manfred Jahn, and Marie-Laure Ryan, 612–13. London: Routledge.

———. 2011. *Fictions transfuges: La transfictionnalité et ses enjeux*. Paris: Seuil.

Schaeffer, Jean-Marie, and Ioana Vultur. 2004. "Mimesis." In *The Routledge Encyclopedia of Narrative Theory*, edited by David Herman, Manfred Jahn, and Marie-Laure Ryan, 309–10. London: Routledge.

Todorov, Tzvetan. (1970) 1975. *The Fantastic: A Structural Approach to a Literary Genre*. Translated by Richard Howard. Ithaca NY: Cornell University Press.

Virtanen, Tuija. 1992. "Issues of Text Typology: Narrative—a 'Basic' Type of Text?" *TEXT* 12:293–310.

Walsh, Richard. 2017. "Beyond Fictional Worlds: Narrative and Spatial Cognition." In *Emerging Vectors of Narratology*, edited by John Pier and Philippe Roussin, 461–78. Berlin: Walter de Gruyter.

Walton, Kendall. 1990. *Mimesis as Make-Believe: On the Foundations of the Representational Arts*. Cambridge MA: Harvard University Press.

Wolterstorff, Nicholas. 1980. *Worlds of Works of Art*. Oxford: Clarendon Press.

3 Interface Ontologies

On the Possible, Virtual, and Hypothetical in Fiction

MARINA GRISHAKOVA

In *The Logic of Life: A History of Heredity* and *The Possible and the Actual*, François Jacob gives a brief overview of cultural constructions of monstrosity. Whereas in sixteenth-century zoology books monsters were pictured as part of the actual world, many Enlightenment thinkers tended to see monstrosity as a possible but accidental violation of the natural order. Further, the study of embryology and physiology in the late eighteenth to early nineteenth century demystified monstrosity, considering it as a developmental peculiarity, as another order rather than a random disorder in the natural world. Contemporary science fiction books, where monsters appear to be products of a recombination of various organisms living on Earth (Jacob 1982, 124), maintain the naturalizing view on monstrosity. Jacob concludes that these monsters "show how culture handles the possible and marks its limits. Whether in a social group or in an individual, human life always involves a continuous dialogue between the possible and the actual" (354). Not only arts or politics but also scientific investigation "begins by inventing a possible world, or a small piece of a possible world," "a preconception of what is possible," "a certain representation of the unknown" (362–63).

Jacob's examples illustrate that probing the borders between the actual and possible is a central function of culture. Narrative as an important cultural tool manifests a similar bridging dynamics. The forward-looking, epistemic function of narrative, that of a delayed recognition of meaningful events in the dynamics between known and unknown, was discussed in detail by Arthur Danto. According to Danto (1985), the passage of time plays a crucial role in historical descriptions: assessment of what is possible and identification of what counts as event are only available in retrospection, thereby leaving the past open for further interpretations. Narration is propelled by future, virtual, not-yet-existent possibilities and accustoms us to thinking in terms of an open-ended future.

The possible worlds approach presents persuasive counterclaims to the view on narrativity as a reductive mold, as pictured by Gary Saul Morson, among others: "Narratives . . . tend to create a single line of development out of the multiplicity. Alternatives once visible disappear from view, and an anachronistic sense of the past surreptitiously infects our understanding" (1994, 6). The possible worlds approach reveals that, instead of reducing the multiplicity, fictional narratives bring to life numberless embedded alternative worlds. In the subsequent discussion, I focus on two specific narrative manifestations of the possible—virtual narratives and virtual voices—and their role in narrative dynamics. Drawing on Charles Bally's (1965) actualization theory, I consider the relations of the actual-virtual as an "interface ontology," using the concept as a modeling metaphor for the text-reader interaction, indicating that the *surface* (discursive, stylistic, narrative) interpretive choices are guided by the deep-level frames or macrounits of meaning and, in their turn, *actualize* those frames, thereby providing felicity conditions for narrative processing.

The Possible and the Virtual

Umberto Eco was one of the first to systematically apply possible worlds theory to fictional narratives. His approach integrates elements of modal logic, philosophical theories of reference and fictionality, and narrative theory. The subsequent approaches retained a certain eclecticism of Eco's conception, which was itself a consequence of the hybrid nature of fictional worlds as both textual and imaginary constructs. Possible worlds in fiction have been considered by Eco and other scholars as (PW1) sets of propositions that may be assessed as true or false; (PW2) textual and imaginary constructs—world matrices, each with its own assortment of objects and existents, their properties and relations; (PW3) hypotheses and inferences on events within the story or alternative scenarios readers are stimulated to create. Ultimately, Eco ([1979] 2005, 132) suggests, "possible worlds" as series of inferences and alternative scenarios inscribed in culturally constructed systems, such as railway networks, chess games, and novels, refer to structural rather than ontological-metaphysical possibilities. In fiction, their emergence is contingent on the structures of narrative dynamics, such as suspense, turning points (narrative "disjunctions"), gaps, and cruxes.[1] In contrast with two static types of possible worlds (PW 1 and 2), the third one (PW 3) emerges in narrative dynamics. It could be productively related to Alfred North Whitehead's (1978) conception of *prehension*—the act of grasping a constitutive presence (concrescence) of earlier experiences in actual experience.[2]

First, PW 3 could be defined in terms of alternate narrative paths, potential ways of plotting, and forecasts. Eco's metaphor of narrative text as "*a machine for producing possible worlds*" has been widely cited (1984, 246, emphasis original). Making forecasts and inferences from textual cues, readers can imagine possible worlds where Romeo and Julia are happily reunited, the lonely sentimental monster created by Frankenstein is embraced by humanity, and Prince Myshkin rescues Nastasya Filippovna. Importantly, possible worlds stem from *both* a reader's inferences or expectations and a narrator's strategies. These two aspects are inextricably entwined: narrative texts invite close cooperation between narrator and reader and manipulate reader's attitudes and expectations.

Alternate versions of the story, inferences, and hypotheses on its further development may be based on the reader's background knowledge and the availability of various cultural templates or interpretive frames, for instance, generic conventions (that of crime fiction, fantasy, romance, or realistic novel) or specific textual features. The reader familiar with constitutive generic conventions takes them in her stride: specific generic rules, rather than the rules of verisimilitude, determine the reader's expectations and lead her to take the possible world for granted, even if it includes incoherences and doesn't obey the reality principle.[3] If generic texts provide rules and instructions for the reader, many experimental narratives offer only "construction kits" (Ryan 2015, 378) to let the reader make her or his own story.

Second, possible worlds emerging in narration (PW3) may be contingent on *characters'* expectations, hypotheses, intentions, wishes, or fantasies manifested in virtual embedded narratives: "story-like constructs contained in the private worlds of characters," as Marie-Laure Ryan (1991, 156) puts it. Ryan shows how these possible worlds generated in characters' minds contribute to narrative dynamics by entering conflicting relations either with the "textual actual world" or with other private worlds and thereby causing changes and turns in the development of fictional events. Ryan's (1991, 158) model radically revises the concept of story by including virtual dimensions in narrative dynamics and showing that even imaginary events and unactualized possibilities (including failures, unsuccessful actions, broken promises, mistaken interpretations) contribute to the emergent story. Not unlike Tolstoy's "history," which is, presumably, a differential of many infinitesimal disparate, conflicting, or similar, as well as personal or collective, strivings and actions, an emergent story appears to be guided and modified by many virtual forces. It emerges from narrative agents' interaction and resulting communicative "deviation," every agent's intentions being modified, suppressed, or enhanced by those of other agents. The story stems from the difference between the possible (an agent's intentions and goals) and the actual (the agent's intentions and goals modified by other agents), but it also constantly generates this difference anew at various levels (see also Grishakova 2012d).

Ryan's model of the dynamics of the actual and virtual is plot oriented: it works well for interestingly dramatic, intrigue-based fictions. However, it seems less suitable to describe fictions whose narrativity is weak and whose central interest lies in "inner adventure": the narrator's or character's mindscapes, thoughts, and feelings (e.g., stream-of-consciousness or confession novels); narrations by elusive or metamorphic narrators; or polyvocal (multiteller, multivoiced, or "multipersoned") narratives displaying a polyphony of blended or separate voices.[4] In sum, Ryan's model is less suitable for fictional narratives that, rather than featuring collisions or convergences of various "doxastic worlds" (worlds of opinion, belief, or knowledge in Eco's terminology) and respective types of plotting, keep the very *doxa* at bay by taking a critical and negotiating perspective on the doxastic forms of truth and knowledge (Grishakova 2018).

Ryan's dynamics of a reader's navigation (recentering) between possible (private, character) worlds and textual actual world implies the existence of distinct worlds—a "hard-fact" actual world, as well as worlds of character knowledge, wishes, intentions, obligations, and fantasies. Conversely, modernist and postmodernist fiction develop increasingly opaque and hybrid discursive spaces, blurring the ontological distinctions—starting with Flaubert, with his elusive narrators and a combination of a narrator's over- and underdistancing regarding a character's world (Hayman 1987, 3, 19–42), up to polyvocal novels with a multiplicity of narrators or narrator-like figures and embedded, layering types of narration. Early modernist authors easily combine two or more perspectives in a single sentence. For example, the beginning of Anton Chekhov's short story "Rothschild's Fiddle" inconspicuously merges the narrator's and character's perspective: "It was a small town, worse than a village, and almost the only people living in it were old men, *who died so rarely that it was actually quite annoying*" (cited by Paducheva 2011, 19, emphasis added). The italicized part of the sentence includes the perspective of the character Yakov, a coffin maker, tinged with narrator's irony, which could be assessed only retrospectively, after the character has been introduced.[5] In *Problems of Dostoevsky's Poetics*, Mikhail Bakhtin (1999, 199) defines various forms of interaction of narrator's and characters' discourses and their explicit or implicit dialogization via objectification, stylization, parodic or polemical relation, covert dialogue, or "sideward glance" based on the actual or virtual copresence of two or more voices. In experimental polyvocal fiction, the subjectivity "zones"—analogues to Bakhtin's (1981, 316) "character zones," inflected with subjectivity markers and individual "accents"—extend far beyond their nominal and pronominal pivots to distanced realms: the classical realist narrator yields the discursive space to multiple voices.[6]

To account for these types of narrative poetics, I (Grishakova 2011) coined the concept of *virtual voice* as a counterpart of Ryan's virtual narrative—a hypothetical discourse that might be, but allegedly is not, pronounced by the purported speaker, being instead attributable to other narrative agent. Virtual voice ascribed to a hypothetical speaker is *actualized* by another narrative agent (narrator or character). Similarly to Ryan's virtual narrative, virtual voice is not fully contingent on linguistic manifestations (it may be "spelled out in great detail, suggested by a few words, or left entirely implicit" [1991, 168]), retaining the ontological status of a mental act. It is most often implicit or inferred by the reader from textual cues. However, "virtual narrative" as a subcategory of the *disnarrated* belongs to the level of plot dynamics: "virtual narratives" are unrealized or unrealizable plot versions that, ultimately, contribute to the development of the plot, even if negatively. In a broad sense, the disnarrated may be defined as counterfactual (what could or might have happened but didn't), and as such it is part of the plotting. Conversely, virtual voice is not an unrealized or discarded possibility of plot development or an alternative scenario but an actualized discursive effect, a means of perspectivization whose value is interpretive.

At the same time, virtual voice should be distinguished from the overlapping linguistic-stylistic categories of hypothetical or imagined speech and thought.[7] Virtual voice is a structural-ontological category: rather than being a local stylistic effect, it contributes to the dynamics of narrative world-making as a subjectively constructed version of the actual world. Within the category of virtual voice, I distinguished six subcategories.

1. *Mediated* or *embedded voice*: A voice embedded in a narrator's or character's actualized discourse. Insofar as the fictional narrator's or character's direct discourse is taken as "actual" and as having a constitutive force by virtue of a basic fictional convention, any *embedded* (*mediated*) thought and speech representation (psychonarration, free indirect discourse, quoted monologue) may qualify as "virtual voice"—a narrator's or character's verbalization of another's potential or internal speech, which has allegedly not been verbalized by its purported speaker and remains "on the threshold of verbalization" (Cohn 1978, 103).[8] As an example of skillful exploitation of embedded or mediated voices I used the novel *The Accidental* (2005) by Scottish author Ali Smith, with the ambiguous role of Amber, alias Alhambra, as a character and a narrator. The novel includes three parts, "The Beginning," "Middle," and "The End," each part comprising sections of third-person narration with extensive embedded fragments of free indirect discourse by four members of the Smart family. Free indirect discourse in these sections ultimately transforms into quoted monologue that, in its turn, may encompass other voices. For instance, Eve Smart's section takes the form of a self-interview, her monologue splitting into the third-person interviewer's and the first-person interviewee's voices. These sophisticated strategies make critics wonder whether the novel is a narration by a single narrator or by five narratorial voices. The novel is imbued by Amber/Alhambra's presence: Amber's sudden intrusion in the Smarts' family life, her provocative moves and attempts at turning family members' monologues into a polylogue (i.e., making them communicate with one another), is parallel to Alhambra's narrative intrusions, her first-person sections embedding other narrations, at the opening and the end and in-between three parts of the novel. This embedding leads the reader to identify Alhambra with the authorial narrator. As a result, the characters' sections, with free indirect discourse serving as a vehicle for quoted monologue, reveal their mediated nature. Additionally, the authorial-narratorial presence, epitomized by Amber/

Alhambra's crucial role in the novel, manifests itself in an alternatingly ironic or empathic engagement with characters' voices.

2. *Hypothetical voice*: Usually combined with hypothetical focalization (Herman 1994) and presented in subjunctive mood, for instance, the description of Mr. Golyadkin's desperate run in the stormy night before meeting his double in Dostoevsky's *The Double*:

> If some disinterested outside observer had now glanced, just like that, from the outside, at Mr Golyadkin's miserable gait, even he would at once have been pierced by all the terrible horror of his misfortunes and would without fail have said that Mr Golyadkin looked now as if he himself wanted to hide somewhere from himself, as if he himself wanted to escape somewhere from himself. Yes, it really was so! We shall say more: Mr Golyadkin now not only wished to escape from himself, but even completely to annihilate himself, not to be, to turn to dust. (Dostoevsky 2004, 41)

A precursor and progenitor of modernist multiperspectival poetics, Dostoevsky observes his characters from many perspectives and surrounds them with many incomplete or distorted reflections. The disinterested outside observer's discourse is not much different from the nervous, repetitive speech of the authorial narrator, which, in its turn, echoes a character's compulsive nervousness and incertitude. What is typical of Dostoevsky's poetics is the presentation of a subjectively colored discourse as a seemingly objective report and the fusion of third-person narration with various subjective perspectives as a means to reach a higher (intuitive) degree of objectivity.[9]

3. *Generalized* or *impersonal voice* (*one* or *we* narration): In the conversational discourse the sustained *we* refers to some kind of group unified by common goals or part of a social structure. In fiction the sustained *we* tends to be unstable, provisional, and often *fictive* as a result of a narrator's wishful thinking or generalization, particularly when applied to mental activity or experience: "we" can grow or shrink to accommodate very different sized groups (Richardson 2006, 14). Moreover, "inner states and mental episodes are usually understood to be separate, private, and, barring telepathy and mind reading, inaccessible to others. They cannot form constituents of a higher-order group mental action of a different kind, nor can they be interpersonally coordinated or influence each other as such.

(This can be done only once they are verbalized in the public domain, by which time they become verbal acts by definition.) A group mental action can at most consist of the coaction of many" (Margolin 2000, 605).

"We" can split into individual voices, merge in ever new entities, or translate into third-person "they," as in Monique Wittig's writing (analyzed by Margolin [2000] and Richardson [2006]) or in Joseph Conrad's *The Nigger of the "Narcissus"* (Richardson 2006, 39–43). Gabriel García Márquez's *The Autumn of the Patriarch* (1975) combines *we* narration with omniscient third-person narration. *We* refers to the presumable witnesses of a patriarch's life and is expected to render a reliable report. However, instead of being a voice of authority, *we* narration turns out to be a speculation by the uninformed collective voice, encompassing a plethora of intermediary unreliable narrators (Labanyi 2007, 152).

4. *Fictive* or *projected voices*: For example, voices of narrators and characters allegedly invented by the narrator, as in Samuel Beckett's *The Unnamable* (see Richardson 2006, 76), or voices of dead, inanimate, or other nonhuman narrators in nongeneric contexts where the nonhuman narrators are not a standard generic convention and where their ontological status remains ambivalent. The narrator of the first section ("Past") of Ali Smith's *Hotel World* (2002) is the ghost of a dead girl, a hotel chambermaid, who has fallen to her death in a hotel food elevator. As if teetering on the brink of life and death, the narrator once and again associates herself with the dead girl, using the first-person plural form when referring to their previous coexistence: "We were a girl, we died young; the opposite of the old, we died it. We had a name and nineteen summers; it says as much on the stone. Hers/mine. She/I." Ultimately, the narrator dissociates herself from the dead body, referred to in third-person form: "Actually it is very nice, where they buried her" (Smith 2002, 9).

5. *Metaleptic voice*: Crossing narrative levels, for instance, the authorial narrator's speech addressed to the character in Nabokov's *Transparent Things*: "Here's the person I want. Hullo, person! Doesn't hear me. . . . Hullo, person! What's the matter, don't pull me. I'm not bothering him. Oh, all right. Hullo, person . . . (last time, in a very small voice)" (1989b, 1).

6. *Alternative voices*: Belonging to the same subject but retaining their separate quality or even ascribed to separate fictive agents, for example, a subject's social or psychological roles and projections, voices of schizophrenic characters (the anonymous narrator's two voices in Sasha

Sokolov's *A School for Fools* [1976]), or characters with split personality disorder (Norman Bates in Robert Bloch's 1959 novel *Psycho* and Hitchcock's 1960 film adaptation).

As a result of the polyphonic layering, fictional discourse becomes imbued with voices—manifestations or traces of subjective speech, thought, and perception that are not always attributable to characters or narrators. Virtual voices are means of perspectivization and interpretation: they problematize the authorial-narratorial authority; introduce multiple alternative perspectives on the events; instill a sense of otherness and dialogue; question the validity of essentialist conceptions of representation, knowledge, and identity, for example, in metafictional works (Vladimir Nabokov, Julio Cortázar, Italo Calvino), queer and feminist works (Margaret Atwood, Ali Smith, Jeanette Winterson), or postcolonial fiction (Salman Rushdie, Toni Morrison). However, the "virtual voice" remains a weak category unless incorporated in the process of narrative worldmaking. In the next section, I discuss the dynamics of virtualization and actualization constitutive of this process.

The Virtual and the Actual

Ryan's model, capitalizing on David Lewis's modal realism, renders the dynamics of actualization and virtualization via the reader's "transportation" or "imaginative recentering": arguably, readers navigate their way through the text by recentering, which propels them into alternative systems of actuality/possibility, the world where readers relocate, becoming the actual world. This model has an intuitive appeal as an analogue of real-life cognitive orientation, navigation, and displacement, activated in play, exploratory activities, and the work of imagination. The inferential capacity to distinguish between one's own and another's conceptual perspective has been considered an important part of human cognitive "equipment" in education theory and developmental psychology: "The ability to 'displace' in time and space, including seeing things from another's perspective, is thought to be a key factor in linguistic and cognitive development—indeed, arguably, 'displacement' is one of the defining characteristics of human intelligence" (Emmott 1997, ix).

However, specific textual features may foster or impede "transportation," or block or facilitate access to fictional worlds. To account for textual mechanisms that facilitate transportation, Ryan's possible worlds model has been complemented with other cognitively oriented models, such as deictic shift theory (Galbraith 1995). For example, in his study of viewpoint in drama, Dan McIntyre (2006) combines Ryan's and Mary Galbraith's frameworks with Catherine Emmott's (1997) theory of contextual frames. Contextual frames are mental representations of settings, characters, and their actions within these settings based on the information retrieved from the text and stored by readers in the process of reading. Emmott's model suggests that priming (bringing a contextual frame to a reader's attention) and binding (integrating frames into a coherent narrative) are two basic mechanisms of narrative processing and comprehension.

Storage of contextual frames or deictic shifting are, again, plot- and character-oriented strategies that do not fully account for the perspective-oriented (voice, subjectivity) types of narrations. The perspective is not always character bound—it enters third-person narration as projected perceptions, expressive features, implicit value judgments, and preferences or is filtered through the multiple alternative perspectives in polyvocal narration. Third-person (seemingly "impersonal") narration is far from neutral: it is imbued with implicit value judgments, verbal and perceptual encodings of subjectivity, for example, subjectively colored expressivity features (see Fludernik 1993, 226–74; Uspensky 1973). Although the majority of Monika Fludernik's (1993, 223) examples refer to a character as the source of expressivity, the expressivity features in fiction neither qualify consistently as markers of quoted or reported speech nor always enable a character attribution. They may be also attributable to virtual experiencers or perceivers (Fludernik 1993, 253) or serve as actualizers of extra- and intertextual frames (such is, for example, the function of Latin in Umberto Eco's novels, or French as an alternative, stylistically, and pragmatically distinct mode of the Russian nobility's conversation in Tolstoy's *War and Peace*).[10]

Indeed, as Ruth Ronen (1994, 195) observes, information about fictional worlds is always perspectively determined. Nelson Goodman's radical constructivist model describing a multitude of subjectively constructed actual worlds without a privileged Actual World could be considered as a close match to multiperspectival narration (Bell 2010, 57), or one could accept a moderate version of constructivism implying the existence of the Actual World beyond its constructed versions, at least potentially (Ryan 1998, 148; Bell 2010, 59). However, the ontological issues seem to be not of primary relevance in multiperspectival poetics whose main concerns are epistemological—exploration of mindscapes, "epistemic spaces" (Chalmers 2011), or draft scenarios (PW3) as subjective versions of the actual world—rather than building full-fledged world matrices.

Charles Bally's (1965, 77–83) linguistic theory defines actualization as a contextualization and localization of linguistic entities (words or word combinations), determining their spatial and temporal aspects regarding the speaking subject, or, in other words, their placing in a definite perspective. In fiction, the real-world existents, such as speaker, are replaced with the imaginary narrative agents, and the real-world coordinates are replaced with the imaginary deictic set-ups. Fictional settings are perspective bound, their representation depending on how they are viewed, perceived, experienced, or conceptualized by various narrative agents. Extending Bally's concept of actualization to narrative poetics, I would define actualization as *priming of a perspective-bound discursive space*, bringing it to a reader's attention through the use of various actualizers. It is an alteration of discursive spaces that guides a reader's navigation through the text.[11] The actualized or primed discursive space belongs to a baseline or access level of narrative, or, to use Barbara Dancygier's (2012, 63) cognitively oriented terminology, the "on-stage" as distinct from the "off-stage" space. The baseline actualized narrative level is a level of minimal narrative mediation. Whereas in the story- and character-oriented possible worlds approaches, third-person (diegetic) narration is usually deemed the default access level, the discursively oriented model accounts for the changeable relations between the actual and the virtual in fictional communication.[12] The mimetic types of discourse, such as direct discourse and quoted monologue, have the status of an actual event in the fictional world, whereas free indirect discourse and psychonarration retain the status of a subjective rendering or "virtual quotation," the narrator coming "more and more to intervene, mediating between the character's discourse and the reader" (McHale [1978] 2004, 197). The slipping perspective and hybridization of discourses (i.e., interaction and interchangeability of the reported utterance and reporting context) account for the "heightened subjectivity" (208) of mixed types of speech and thought representation. The less mediated the discourse, the more probable its actualization: it is the discourse that a reader encounters at the entry level of narrative act and takes in stride while processing long stretches of narrative. The sustained first-person narration or quoted monologue, even if attributable to an unreliable narrator as the only source of information (e.g., Humbert Humbert in Nabokov's *Lolita* or Mr. Stevens in Ishiguro's *The Remains of the Day*) may serve as the actualized context for interpolated virtual discourses, whereas the authoritative pattern remains virtualized and not easily available. As Tamar Yakobi justly observes,

> As concerns the immediacy of encounter with the narrated object, readers always find themselves in an inferior position vis-à-vis every speaker or subject within the fictional world. This holds true in comparison, not only with omniscient or authoritative reporters (e.g., the sleuth in the detective story) but with constrained and dubious sources of information as well (the Watson or the suspect in the detective story). After all, the reporter ("mediator") confronts the object directly or at least exists within the same world. His is, therefore, an eye-witness (or at least inside) account, and we readers depend on it for information—sometimes, as in a "first person" novel like *Moby Dick* or *Doctor Faustus*, exclusively so. Not only do we readers lack access to the object; we cannot count on an alternative representation, either. (2015, 505)

In the above-cited article on "normative pattern" and unreliability in fiction, Yakobi demonstrates that even if the authoritative reporter's "normative pattern" (i.e., an authorial set of values and preferences) is available in such types of first-person narration, certain work of detection and interpretation is required to uncover it. Moreover, the normative pattern is neither postulated in advance nor fixed or conventional (Yakobi 2015, 507): the covert authorial system of values and preferences may be subject to change in the process of narration. Respectively, the relations of the embedded and embedding, actual and virtual voices also appear to be unstable, ambivalent, or reversible.

For instance, Nabokov's Humbert Humbert is an elusive, metamorphic, and, at the same time, self-conscious narrator, anticipating and fencing off various potential diagnoses and verdicts (juridical, psychiatric, psychoanalytical, moral) that his confession may provoke, by providing scholarly references and literary allusions and parodying the potential reader's desire for turning Humbert's confession into a "case study."[13] Nabokov uses a similar strategy in his postface, "On a Book Entitled *Lolita*": while anticipating critical reactions to and psychoanalytical interpretations of his book, he refers to "a newspaper story about an ape in the Jardin des Plantes" (Nabokov 2000, 311) as a presumable source of inspiration both for writing the novel's prototext (the short story "The Enchanter") and for resuming (in 1949) the work on what eventually turned out to be the novel. According to Elizabeth Phillips's (1960) astute guess, the indirect reference to Edgar Allan Poe's "Murders in the Rue Morgue" (via the ape's story in the Jardin des Plantes) is actually a double allusion: it brings to the reader's attention a Freudian analysis of Poe's life as it is illuminated through his fiction, Marie Bonaparte's 1933 book *The Life and Works of Edgar Allan Poe: A Psychoanalytic Interpretation* (translated into English in 1949). In Poe's fiction, Mme Bonaparte argues, the ape appears to be a father figure, the epitome of both a primeval beast and a hunter pursuing the beast. Both Quilty and Humbert, the most obvious doubles in the novel, are often alluded to as beasts and hunters.

Nomi Tamir-Ghez (1979) described the strategies of the narrator's, implied reader's, and narrative situation's doubling in Humbert's discourse: the shift of personal forms and the resulting split of the speaker, the alternation of the two genres of narration (diary and memoir) and two speech situations (court speech and written confession) with different pragmatics. These strategies, which permanently channel a reader's expectations beyond the actual narrative situation and prompt him or her to seek explanations beyond the actual frame, allow Humbert to escape the reader's conclusive verdict. Humbert's narration projects various generic (romance, fairy tale, western, confession, detective, pulp fiction) and intertextual frames: his story allows for various (Romantic, aesthetic-decadent, parodic, psychiatric, and other) encodings. Distinctions between the author's and narrator's perspective are not clear-cut. Is it Humbert who surreptitiously introduces a fictive "initial girl-child," an imaginary Annabel Leigh, in his story, or is it the author who encodes the story of Humbert's first love as an imaginary story by evoking Poe's "Annabel Lee"? Does the author's actual voice embed the character-narrator's imaginary voice, or is it the character-narrator's voice that forges the author's image through multiple anagrams, citations, and allusions? Humbert's strategy of merging autobiographical and fictional detail is, likewise, a Nabokovian strategy (see Grishakova 2012a, 2012c). As with other Nabokov novels, *Lolita* involves some provocative and playful metaleptic transgressions. This playful reversal of the author-character's relations and respective discursive spaces made a certain critic state that "Nabokov *should*, perhaps, at least on one level, have a more exacting moral in tow" (Clegg 2000, 102).

Not only the positioning at the entry level but also a degree of manifestation or foregrounding serve as criteria distinguishing the virtualized and the actualized layers of narrative. Fictional narratives use the actualizing force of entry-level narration to manipulate the reader's expectations and to produce surprising effects of recentering when the whole deictic set-up is reoriented, along with what counts as actual or virtual parts of the fictional world. Margaret Atwood's *The Blind Assassin* (2000) is another example of a sophisticated narrative puzzle involving a reversal of the actual and virtual parts of narration. The main diegetic level of the female protagonist's (Iris Chase) first-person memoir embeds a third-person virtual narrative (fiction within fiction): Iris's sister Laura Chase's novel *Blind Assassin*, with two characters referred to through the pronouns "she" and "he" only. Due to thematic matches between the embedding and embedded story, the latter is perceived as a virtual counterpart of the former, as something underreported and underrepresented in the main narrative: Laura's fictionalized voice narrates her own story, the story of her love affair with the young leftist activist Alex Thomas. However, the embedded fictional story remains incomplete, gappy, and fragmentary, and its status remains indeterminate, which is taken for granted by the reader, given the marginality of Laura's voice and position, that of a rebel, nonconformist, and, ultimately, victim in the actual narrative depicting the world of the successful and prosperous, where Iris, married to a rich businessman with political ambitions, belongs.

Only the last sections of Iris's embedding memoir cast doubt on the coreferential decoding of the embedded narrative's "he" and "she" as Alex and Laura of the main narrative. The coreference is, finally, revised and reversed: Iris turns out to be the embedded novel's author and Alex Thomas's lover, and Laura's sacrificial loveless affair with Iris's husband as a means of saving Alex Thomas is disclosed. Similarly, the relationship between the "actual world" of the story and what appeared to be its virtual fictionalized counterpart is reversed: the embedded fictional story is actualized as the core narrative, rather surprisingly presenting a suppressed or hypothetical story as Iris's actual life story, including her and Alex Thomas's extramarital child, whereas the other, seemingly central narrative line—

the story of Iris's marriage and her high social position in elite society—appears to be its virtual counterpart.

Many narratives feature a gap or a discrepancy between their actual and virtual counterparts while avoiding closure and retaining ambiguity as to what counts as "actual" and what counts as "virtual." Henry James's *The Turn of the Screw* is a famous example of such a postclosure type of poetics. In Don DeLillo's *Point Omega* (2010), the first-person narration by the filmmaker Finley, who visits the Iraq War expert Elster in his forlorn house in the Arizona desert to discuss a documentary film project and meets his daughter, Jessie, is juxtaposed to the art installation episodes. The latter include a cinematic ekphrasis—a detailed description of a film performance, alluding to the art installation *24 Hour Psycho* by Douglas Gordon (1993). Gordon's *24 Hour Psycho* was an appropriation of Hitchcock's movie muted and slowed down, lasting twenty-four hours. The art installation episode features an anonymous male character, a viewer in a gallery, immersed in the film show. The episode is narrated in the third person and permeated with the anonymous character's virtual speech and thought. Initially presented as a virtual counterpart of the "hard-fact story," the film performance, centered on Hitchcock's notorious murder scene in the shower, is eventually actualized as the only available interpretive frame from which the reader is expected to collect clues on what happened to Jessie after her mysterious disappearance, leaving no trace. The filmic episode opens and ends the novel, forming the embedding frame of Finley's story—two chapters titled "Anonymity" and "Anonymity 2." The links between the embedding (gallery) and the embedded (desert) episodes eventually accumulate: not only the anonymous male character seems to be a projection of Finley's film-obsessed mind, but also other anonymous characters in the gallery remind readers of the characters in Finley's story. Whereas the "hard-fact" perspective proves to be inconsistent and breaks apart insofar as Jessie disappears and Finley's film project fails, the "virtual" perspective of film viewing absorbs the reality and gains the status of the actual. However, the links between the counterparts remain obscure: instead of mutual decoding, the counterparts seem to converge on an ideal point (point Omega, where "consciousness accumulates" and "begins to reflect upon itself" [DeLillo 2010, 72]), evoking an unsettling sense of a reality contingent on human perception, attention, and consciousness that is akin to filmic reality—as pointed out by the early film psychologist Hugo Münsterberg, film shows the physical reality "clothed in the forms of our consciousness" ([1916] 1970, 24).

Conclusions

In *Useful Fictions: Evolution, Anxiety, and the Origins of Literature* (2010), Michael Austin discusses fiction's ability to respond to anxiety as its adaptive value. He refers to the use of Bakhtin's theory of voice in the treatment of obsessive-compulsive disorders, when obsessions, often difficult to distinguish from rational beliefs, are considered as unresolved dialogues between multiple virtual narratives. The lesson one could learn from these examples is the natural polyvocality of human existence composed of numerous, potentially contradictory stories. "Living in reality is a matter of degree": normal cognitive functioning requires us to "exist in a gradient of awareness where the plausibility of different possibilities is associated with distinct senses of reality" (Austin 2010, 33).

Virtual parts of narration—incomplete, gappy, or not easily accessible—should be distinguished from the full-fledged possible worlds or world matrices. The status of the "virtual" is a matter of degree: it is always indexed by what is taken as the baseline "actual," and, together with the actual, it constitutes narrative dynamics. Rather than being separate full-fledged world matrices, these are extensions, splits, and layerings within a baseline narrative ontology; they may prove to be embryonic alternative ontologies, however. Some of them remain open and contribute to narrative dynamics as underpinnings of or alternatives to the actualized structures or structures competing for actualization, while others are closed or ruled out in the course of narration. The narrative dynamics is guided by the epistemic functions (elimination of possibilities, negotiation of what counts as knowledge). Possible worlds and virtual scenarios as discursive interfaces are cognitive-epistemic rather than solely linguistic objects: they cut across linguistic surfaces and create bridges between the surface and in-depth semantic-interpretive frames. They would, therefore, require modal-conceptual rather than solely linguistic mapping on the scale between what is deemed inevitable or highly probable; predictable or anticipated; possible, feasible, or likely; hypothetical or imaginable; to improbable and impossible. As situated between "tacit" and "explicit" knowledge and belief, between mental and tangible, the virtual could be also assessed as contingent on the degree of its manifestation: virtual as anticipated; potential, latent; hypothetical, based on reasoning or mental prognosis; conceivable, imaginable, thinkable; invented or imaginary.

Notes

Research for this chapter was supported by the Estonian Research Council (PUT 192 and 1481) and by the European Union Regional Development Fund (Center of Excellence in Estonian Studies).

1. Crux: "a critical point, often a gap, in a fictional narrative where there is an insufficiency of cues, or where cues are sufficiently ambiguous, to create a major disagreement in the intentional interpretation of the narrative" (Abbott 2008, 231).
2. "Whitehead conceived of specific physical occasions as defined by the incessant assimilation of adjacent occasions into a new descendant occasion, via a process he termed *prehension* (roughly, 'grasping'). In this process, each physical occasion assimilates features of adjacent occasions, and changes accordingly" (Deacon 2012, 77).
3. For instance, the episode of Humbert's last rendezvous with married and pregnant Lolita in Nabokov's novel alludes to the romantic plot of the adulterous beloved (Carmen) as the interpretive frame, yet its implied tragic ending is ironically discarded. The effect of the scene is contingent on the "minus-device" (Lotman 1977, 51) or a "non-utilization" of the expected generic elements e: the generic frame is activated and then revoked. Interestingly, Humbert splits into the first-person narrator and third-person character in this scene:

   > *Carmencita, lui demandais-je* . . . "One last word," I said in my horrible careful English, "are you quite, quite sure that—well, not tomorrow, of course, and not after tomorrow, but—well, some day, any day, you will not come to live with me? . . ."
   >
   > "No," she said smiling, "no."
   >
   > "It would have made all the difference," said Humbert Humbert.
   >
   > Then I pulled out my automatic—I mean, this is the kind of fool thing a reader might suppose I did. It never even occurred to me to do it. (Nabokov 2000, 280)

   The very conventions of fictional communication erect an ontological barrier between fictional reality and the reader (Yakobi 2015, 503) both in fictional works that cast a seemingly transparent illusion of mimetic reality and in those that project hybrid, heterogeneous worlds where "various components are distributed among different frameworks of reality" (505; see also Lavocat 2016, 402–12).

4. Brian Richardson distinguishes between four categories of multipersoned works: "works that systematically oscillate between different narrative positions, those that collapse apparently different types of narration into a single voice, works whose narration remains fundamentally ambiguous, and texts that employ narrational stances that would be impossible in nonfictional discourse" (2006, 243).

5. For other examples of such shifting, see Fludernik (1993, 114–24).

6. Similar types of overlapping or merging perspective-bound sequences may be found in nonverbal or mixed media. Film narration may cue subjective (individual, internally stimulated) experience as objective (shared, externally stimulated) or vice versa while using such strategies as ambiguous, multiple, or false attribution of subjective shots; dissociation of soundtrack and image; dissociation of distal/proximal stimuli (e.g., zoom-in and close-up representing heightened attention rather than physical movement); "mental process narration" (thoughts, dreams, memories) cued as an actual-world action sequence; "impossible shots" where the viewer identifies with the camera, such as the view from inside the brain in David Fincher's *Fight Club* (1999) or from inside John Malkovich's consciousness in Spike Jonze's *Being John Malkovich* (1999) (see Grishakova 2012b).

7. The category seems to be rather vast and vague: examples of hypothetical thought and speech include what appears to be *actual* thought and speech about alleged or anticipated events and, similarly, intentions, plans, and prognoses that do not qualify as hypothetical speech acts (boldface emphasis in the original): "She told me that from that day on I was allowed **to call her Doris**, rather than Miss Speed" (Sally Beck, *Queen of the Street: The Amazing Life of Julie Goodyear* [1999, 101], cited in Semino, Short, and Wynne 1999, 329) and "A boy aged twenty-one—we'll call him Colin—wrote to tell us that he and his girlfriend were getting engaged at Christmas-time and he thought it would be a lovely surprise **if he could propose to her on the show**" (Cilla Black, *Step Inside* [1985, 96], cited in Semino and Short 2004, 161).

8. For instance, the passages of interior monologue in Joyce's *Ulysses* that capture "the working of the consciousness at a level below that of complete verbalization" (Leech and Short 2007, 202).

9. Karen Jacobs argues that "the modernist observance of the embodied and partial nature of vision takes the form of multiperspectivalism, with its implicit acknowledgement of the limits of isolated points of view" (2001, 9).

10. Eco stresses that the "real world" is, similarly to the fictional world, a cultural construct that is available to us solely through a multitude of different descriptions.

11. I found Barbara Dancygier's cognitive-linguistic approach (in her *Language of Stories*) particularly helpful in my reflections on the actualization-virtualization dynamics. Dancygier (2012, 36) uses the concept of narrative space that is structured by viewpoint phenomena in her description of narrative dynamics. To avoid the "container metaphor" (narrative space as a container for discourse) and the implications of the narrowly understood correspondence theory of representation, somewhat characteristic of literary and linguistic cognitivism (a viewpoint as a synonym for human-like entities such as narrator and character), and to highlight the importance of low-level (discursive) choices contributing to narrative construction, I use "discursive spaces" instead. The actualizers include various means of deictic (perceptual, spatial, temporal, relational, textual, compositional; see Stockwell 2002, 45–46) as well as para- and intertextual priming.

12. See also Helmut Bonheim ([1982] 1992) on the virtual narrative mode as a "transformative mode" that any other narrative mode, except for comment, may take. There are four standard narrative modes in Bonheim's classification: speech, report, description, and comment. Respectively, he discusses imagined speech, imaginary (conceivable rather than actual) report, and imaginary description as kinds of the virtual mode (34–36).

13. See Alfred Appel's comments to *Lolita* (Nabokov 2000, 333).

References

Abbott, Porter H. 2008. *The Cambridge Introduction to Narrative*. Cambridge: Cambridge University Press.

Austin, Michael. 2010. *Useful Fictions: Evolution, Anxiety, and the Origins of Literature*. Lincoln: University of Nebraska Press.

Bakhtin, Mikhail. 1981. *The Dialogic Imagination*. Edited by Michael Holquist. Austin: University of Texas Press.

———. 1999. *Problems of Dostoevsky's Poetics*. Edited and translated by Caryl Emerson. Minneapolis: University of Minnesota Press.

Bally, Charles. 1965. *Linguistique générale et linguistique française*. Berne: Éditions Francke.

Bell, Alice. 2010. *The Possible Worlds of Hypertext Fiction*. Houndmills, Basingstoke: Palgrave Macmillan.

Bonheim, Helmut. (1982) 1992. *The Narrative Modes: Techniques of the Short Story*. Woodbridge, England: D. S. Brewer.

Chalmers, David J. 2011. "The Nature of Epistemic Space." In *Epistemic Modality*, edited by Andy Egan and Brian Weatherson, 60–107. Oxford: Oxford University Press.

Clegg, Christian, ed. 2000. *V. Nabokov, "Lolita": A Reader's Guide to Essential Criticism*. Cambridge: Icon Books.

Cohn, Dorrit. 1978. *Transparent Minds: Narrative Modes for Presenting Consciousness in Fiction*. Princeton NJ: Princeton University Press.

Dancygier, Barbara. 2012. *The Language of Stories: A Cognitive Approach*. Cambridge: Cambridge University Press.

Danto, Arthur. 1985. *Narration and Knowledge*. New York: Columbia University Press.

Deacon, Terrence W. 2012. *Incomplete Nature: How Mind Emerged from Matter*. New York: W. W. Norton.

DeLillo, Don. 2010. *Point Omega*. London: Picador.

Dostoevsky, Fyodor. 2004. *The Double*. London: Hesperus.

Eco, Umberto. (1979) 2005. *Lector in Fabula*. Translated into Estonian by Ülar Ploom, edited by Daniele Monticelli. Tartu: Tartu Ülikooli Kirjastus.

———. 1984. *The Role of the Reader: Explorations in the Semiotics of Texts*. Bloomington: Indiana University Press.

Emmott, Catherine. 1997. *Narrative Comprehension: A Discourse Perspective*. Oxford: Clarendon Press.

Fludernik, Monika. 1993. *The Fictions of Language and the Languages of Fiction*. London: Routledge.

Galbraith, Mary. 1995. "Deictic Shift Theory and the Poetics of Involvement in Narrative." In *Deixis in Narrative: A Cognitive Science Perspective*, edited by Judith F. Duchan, Gail A. Bruder, and Lynn E. Hewitt, 19–59. Hillsdale NJ: Lawrence Erlbaum.

Grishakova, Marina. 2011. "On the Typology of Virtual Narrative Voices." In *Strange Voices in Narrative Fiction*, edited by Per Krogh Hansen et al., 175–90. Berlin: De Gruyter.

———. 2012a. *The Models of Space, Time and Vision in V. Nabokov's Fiction: Narrative Strategies and Cultural Frames*. 2nd rev. ed. Originally published in 2006. The Hague: Open Access Publications in European Networks. http://www.oapen.org/search?identifier=421498.

———. 2012b. "On Cognitive and Semiotic Functions of Shifters." *Chinese Semiotic Studies* 8 (2): 227–38.

———. 2012c. "Stranger Than Fiction, or Jerome David Salinger, Author of 'Lolita': Real, Implied and Fictive Authorship." In *Narrative, Interrupted: The Plotless, the Trivial and the Disturbing in Literature*, edited by Markku Lehtimäki, Laura Karttunen, and Maria Mäkelä, 238–53. Berlin: De Gruyter.

———. 2012d. "The Voices of Madness: Performativity and Narrative Identity." In *Disputable Core Concepts in Narratology*, edited by Göran Rossholm and Christer Johansson, 131–46. Bern: Peter Lang.

———. 2018. "Multi-teller and Multi-voiced Stories: The Poetics and Politics of Pronouns." In *Pronouns in Literature: Positions and Perspectives*, edited by Alison Gibbons and Andrea Macrae, 193–216. Houndmills, Basingstoke: Palgrave Macmillan.

Hayman, David. 1987. *Re-forming the Narrative: Toward a Mechanics of Modernist Fiction*. Ithaca NY: Cornell University Press.

Herman, David. 1994. "Hypothetical Focalization." *Narrative* 2:230–53.

Jacob, François. 1982. *The Logic of Life: A History of Heredity; The Possible and the Actual*. London: Penguin Books.

Jacobs, Karen. 2001. *The Eye's Mind: Literary Modernism and Visual Culture*. Ithaca NY: Cornell University Press.

Labanyi, Jo. 2007. "Language and Power in *The Autumn of Patriarch*." In *Gabriel García Márquez*, edited by Harold Bloom, 145–58. Updated ed. New York: Chelsea House.

Lavocat, Françoise. 2016. *Fait et fiction: Pour une frontiére*. Paris: Seuil.

Leech, Geoffrey, and Mick Short. 2007. *Style in Fiction: A Linguistic Introduction to English Fictional Prose*. 2nd ed. London: Pearson Education Ltd.

Lotman, Jurij. 1977. *The Structure of the Artistic Text*. Translated by G. Lenhoff and R. Vroon. Ann Arbor: University of Michigan Press.

Margolin, Uri. 2000. "Telling in the Plural: From Grammar to Ideology." *Poetics Today* 21 (3): 591–618.

McHale, Brian. (1978) 2004. "Free Indirect Discourse: A Survey of Recent Accounts." In *Narrative Theory: Critical Concepts in Literary and Cultural Studies*, vol. 1, edited by M. Bal, 187–296. London: Routledge.

McIntyre, Dan. 2006. *Point of View in Plays: A Cognitive Stylistic Approach to Viewpoint in Drama and Other Text-Types*. Amsterdam: John Benjamins.

Morson, Gary Saul. 1994. *Narrative and Freedom: The Shadows of Time*. New Haven CT: Yale University Press.

Münsterberg, Hugo. (1916) 1970. *The Film: A Psychological Study*. New York: Dover Publications.

Nabokov, Vladimir. 1989a. *Speak, Memory: An Autobiography Revisited*. New York: Vintage.

———. 1989b. *Transparent Things*. New York: Vintage International.

———. 2000. *The Annotated Lolita*. Edited by Alfred Appel Jr. London: Penguin Books.

Paducheva, Elena. 2011. *The Linguistics of Narrative: The Case of Russian*. Moscow: Lambert Academic Publishing.

Phillips, Elizabeth. 1960. "The Hocus-Pocus of Lolita." *Literature and Psychology* 10 (2): 97–101.

Richardson, Brian. 2002. "Beyond Story and Discourse: Narrative Time in Postmodern and Non-mimetic Fiction." In *Narrative Dynamics: Essays on Time, Plot, Closure and Frames*, 47–63. Columbus: Ohio University Press.

———. 2006. *Unnatural Voices: Extreme Narration in Modern and Contemporary Fiction*. Columbus: Ohio State University Press.

Ronen, Ruth. 1994. *Possible Worlds in Literary Theory*. Cambridge: Cambridge University Press.

Ryan, Marie-Laure. 1991. *Possible Worlds, Artificial Intelligence, and Narrative Theory*. Bloomington: Indiana University Press.

———. 1998. "The Text as World versus the Text as Game: Possible Worlds Semantics and Postmodern Theory." *Journal of Literary Semantics* 27 (3): 137–63.

———. 2015. "Impossible Worlds." In *The Routledge Companion to Experimental Literature*, edited by Joe Bray, Alison Gibbons and Brian McHale, 368–79. London: Routledge.

Semino, Elena, and Mick Short. 2004. *Corpus Stylistics: Speech, Writing and Thought Presentation in a Corpus of English Writing*. London: Routledge.

Semino, Elena, Mick Short, and Martin Wynne. 1999. "Hypothetical Words and Thoughts in British Narratives." *Narrative* 1:307–34.

Smith, Ali. 2002. *Hotel World*. London: Penguin Books.

Stockwell, Peter. 2002. *Cognitive Poetics: An Introduction*. London: Routledge.

Tamir-Ghez, Nomi. 1979. "The Art of Persuasion in Nabokov's *Lolita*." *Poetics Today* 1 (1/2): 65–83.

Uspensky, Boris. 1973. *A Poetics of Composition: The Structure of the Artistic Text and Typology of a Compositional Form*. Berkeley: University of California Press.

Whitehead, Alfred North. 1978. *Process and Reality*. Gifford Lectures delivered at the University of Edinburgh during the session 1927–28. New York: Free Press.

Yakobi, Tamar. 2015. "Narrative and Normative Pattern: On Interpreting Fiction, with Special Regard to (Un)Reliability." *Poetics Today* 36 (4): 499–528.

PART 2 | *Possible Worlds and Cognition*

4 Ungrounding Fictional Worlds

*An Enactivist Perspective on the
"Worldlikeness" of Fiction*

MARCO CARACCIOLO

The history of the term "possible worlds" and its offshoots in narrative theory has been told multiple times—not least, in this book's introduction. Even beyond the scholars who have drawn directly on possible worlds semantics (Eco 1979; Pavel 1986; Ryan 1991; Doležel 1998), the language of worlds has entered the vocabulary of narrative theory in a looser, metaphorical meaning. An influential example is David Herman's notion of "storyworlds," which he defines as psychological "models built up on the basis of cues contained in narrative discourse" (2002, 20). While Herman acknowledges and discusses earlier work on narrative and possible worlds semantics, the exact sense in which mental models count as "worlds" remains unclear in his treatment. Yet Herman's broad use of the notion of world captures an intuition widely shared by contemporary readers, namely, that there is a certain world-like quality to narratives. This is especially true for the fictional narratives I will focus on in this chapter: fictional texts ask us to imagine consistent or recognizable domains that can be compared to worlds. In the following pages I attempt to specify this quality of fiction—which I call "worldlikeness"—by drawing on recent work in the mind sciences, particularly approaches that go under the heading of "enactivism." In essence, I argue that some of the implications of the world metaphor are unhelpful to think about audiences' engagement with narrative. Yet the metaphor can still be salvaged—provided that we conceptualize "worldlikeness" in the right way. This is what enactivism will enable me to do.

Trouble with Worlds

To understand why the world metaphor is potentially problematic, I suggest turning to Richard Walsh's provocative—if controversial—critique of the concept. That critique has been articulated in *The Rhetoric of Fictionality* (2007) and—more fully—in a recent essay (Walsh 2017). Walsh's approach to fiction builds on Dan Sperber and Deirdre Wilson's (1995) relevance theory: in broad strokes, he argues that engaging with fiction is an inferential, context-bound activity whereby readers work out the relevance of a text based on "the implication of various cognitive interests or values that are not contingent upon accepting the propositional truth of the utterance itself" (2007, 30). Since Walsh sees audiences' engagement with fiction as a dynamic process, his view would seem largely compatible with Herman's equation between storyworlds and mental models generated during comprehension. However, Walsh takes issue with the idea that texts construct domains separate from the real world and that readers have to "complete" these domains in any meaningful way. For him, the extraction of relevance—which is both a hermeneutic and an emotional process—precedes and trumps readers' commitment to the quasi-ontological separateness of fiction. Thus, the idea of worlds carries an ontological baggage that is undesirable in theorizing about fiction, because readers' meaning making is always projected against a background of real-world interests and expectations.

A further difficulty, which Walsh explores in his later essay, is that there is a fundamental tension between narrative sense making and the associations of stability and persistence in space that come with the world metaphor. Narrative has to do with the "semiotic articulation of linear temporal sequence" (2017, 473), whereas the world metaphor takes us in the different—and, for Walsh, fundamentally separate—direction of *spatial* cognition. Indeed, he argues that "this complementarity [between narrative and spatial meaning making, or stories and worlds] is irreducible in cognitive terms; like the word 'spatiotemporal' itself, the whole is a product of conceptual juxtaposition, not a synthesis" (474). Walsh's conclusion about the mutual irreducibility of space and time is problematic in a number of ways: think only of how our understanding of time relies on spatial patterns ("the meeting has been pushed *back* two weeks"; see Boroditsky 2000). In fact, experiencing time without spatial motion can be extremely difficult. But Walsh is right to say that the world metaphor for fiction often emphasizes the relative stability of space over the temporal dynamics of narrative. In a paradoxical reading of Alain Robbe-Grillet's novel *La jalousie*, Walsh offers a reductio ad absurdum of the view that reading fictional narrative works via "an inference to the global, or to a spatio-temporal whole" (2017, 476): readers' mental modeling of story-worlds is driven by other interests than the need for a complete, stable, gap-free representation of space.

I'm quoting at length from Walsh's discussion of the world metaphor not because I subscribe to his argument and conceptual framework (both of which call for a more in-depth, and critical, examination than I can offer here) but because Walsh's ideas can help me expose two assumptions that are typically bound up with the idea of world. I call these assumptions "ontological segregation" and "representational stability." The former idea clashes with the way in which readers bring to bear real-world interests and values on the fictional texts they read; the latter is contradicted by how, in texts that call for narrative sense making, temporal progression takes precedence over readers' spatial mapping activity—as Marie-Laure Ryan puts it succinctly, "People read for the plot and not for the map" (2003, 138). Thus, in my approach to the world metaphor I aim to shift the emphasis from these assumptions to a feature of worlds that has not received sufficient attention in narrative theory: I call it "logic of unfolding." The logic of unfolding is the way in which a fictional narrative opens itself to its readers, creating a distinctive rhythm based on patterned interactions between the audience and various aspects of a text. I claim that such distinctive logic accounts for the worldlikeness of narrative, but it can be uncoupled from assumptions of ontological segregation or representational stability: it is based on a fully hermeneutic process and therefore takes into consideration a text's relevance to its readers; it is temporally extended, and while it may reflect spatial features of a text, it does not entail that readers have to form a complete and stable model of the storyworld. Yet that process is structurally analogous to how we come to know the real world—hence the value of the world metaphor. I stress that this is a *structural* analogy; it has nothing to do with the contents of narrative representation, which may depart significantly from everyday experience (as scholars in the field of unnatural narratology have pointed out; see Alber et al. 2010).

My approach to narrative's worldlikeness is inspired by enactivist thinking in the contemporary mind sciences, as we'll see, but clear parallels can be found with Martin Heidegger's (1996) philosophy of "Being-in-the-World" (see, e.g., Dreyfus 1991) and with two antecedents of enactivism that will be discussed in the next section: Jakob von Uexküll's notion of Umwelt and James J. Gibson's ecological psychology. In my view, when readers and scholars talk about the world of a text in the broad sense, they are implicitly (and unintentionally) taking on board the relational notion of world proposed by these thinkers more than ideas of ontological segregation and representational stability. From an enactivist perspective, the worldlikeness of narrative arises from its capacity to evoke the patterns of interaction that accompany our engagement with a world that is fundamentally "groundless," in that it first emerges in a process of embodied exploration (and only later on may be conceptualized as an autonomous domain preexisting the subject). I note, in passing, that this use of the word "groundless" and of the verb "ungrounding" in my title does not imply incompatibility with Lawrence Barsalou's notion of "grounded cognition," by which he means that cognitive activities are deeply shaped by "modal simulations, bodily states, and situated action" (2008, 617). On the contrary, we'll see that a focus on bodily states and actions can help us unground fictional worlds in the ontological sense of "grounding."

I acknowledge that revising the notion of world in this way takes us far from modal logic (where possible worlds theory originated) and from Walsh's view of narrativity as the "semiotic articulation" of time. But I do think there are dividends to be reaped from this operation, if only because it unsettles the rigid distinctions of narratology (e.g., between temporality and narrative space) and opens up perspectives on the dynamic nature of audiences' engagement with narrative. In this sense, the account offered in this chapter does not contradict existing theorizations of possible and fictional worlds in narratology but rather aims to complement them by insisting on the processual and dynamic nature of "worldling the story," to borrow Herman's (2013, 2) terminology. Broadly speaking, possible worlds theorists have sidelined the dynamically unfolding nature of storyworlds, tending to see them as textual constructs rather than mental ones. To the extent that scholars have conceptualized worlds in psychological terms, they have done so in a way that emphasizes these worlds' cognitive stability, not their experiential fluidity. Ryan discusses this limitation of current approaches to storyworlds: the "'worldness' of fictional worlds needs to be explored from a phenomenological rather than a purely logical point of view. The thesis of the radical incompleteness of fictional worlds is undoubtedly correct from a logical perspective, but we also need to describe fictional worlds as a lived imaginative experience" (2013, sec. 4.1). All the available empirical evidence suggests that narrative understanding is driven by emotion and therefore experience (see, e.g., Tan 1996; Miall 2011; Hogan 2011), not by "cold" reasoning and inference making. The values implicated in narrative sense making are affective and experiential through and through, as I have argued in *The Experientiality of Narrative* (2014a). Factoring in these experiential dynamics allows us to capture storyworlds in their phenomenological becoming, as called for by Ryan. Thus, after laying out the central ideas of enactivist philosophy in the next two sections, I will explore its ramifications for fictional worlds. I will also exemplify this account by discussing Jonathan Lethem's *Girl in Landscape*, a science fiction–inspired novel originally published in 1998.

A Stroll through Worlds without Ground

A brief genealogy of enactivism will allow me to bring into focus its contribution to the mind sciences. I begin by singling out two historical moments in which protoenactivist themes emerged in twentieth-century psychology, with specific emphasis on the idea of world. In *A Stroll through the Worlds of Animals and Men* (1957), originally published in 1934, Estonian-born biologist Jakob von Uexküll introduced the term "Umwelt" (literally, "surrounding world") to describe how reality presents itself to various animals as a function of their size and perceptual possibilities. Uexküll's notion has gained popularity in narrative theory, particularly in work by Marina Grishakova (2006, 2009) and Herman (2011). But the exact implications of this notion for the world metaphor of engaging with fiction are still underexplored. Uexküll effectively collapses the illusion of an external and relatively stable world into a myriad Umwelten or worlds as subjectively perceived by animals (human and nonhuman). The world of the tick is different from the world of the snail, and both are distinct from the worlds of humans. These worlds do overlap to some extent, of course, as evidenced by the many cases in which humans coordinate their actions with those of nonhuman animals. An external reality—Uexküll calls it "the environment"—does exist, but we can access it through feedback loops of perception and action that are specific to the kind of animal that we are. The key idea is that, for Uexküll, the notion of world—in the sense of Umwelt—begins to lose its ontological grounding: our world is constructed through patterns of interaction that display a certain kind of regularity, reflecting biological and anatomical structures but also (in the case of humans) cultural propensities.

Uexküll's account of the Umwelt anticipates the movement of "ecological psychology" associated with James J. Gibson's work in the 1970s. For Gibson, the environment contains invariant structures that afford certain possibilities of interaction to animals; Gibson (1986, 18–19) calls these structures "affordances." Further, Gibson (127) argues that affordances have a certain "meaning" or "value" that can be directly perceived: when an animal is trying to avoid a predator, for example, the perception of a nearby tree, the possible action of climbing it, and the "refuge" value of the tree are closely bound up. Note that these values are much more basic than semiotic, conceptual meanings: for Gibson, something has meaning when it has a use, when it bears (positively or negatively) on the survival and well-being of a particular animal.

Uexküll's and Gibson's insights into "the complementarity of the animal and the environment" (Gibson 1986, 127) are further extended and developed in the enactivist account of experience put forward by Francisco Varela, Evan Thompson, and Eleanor Rosch in their landmark *The Embodied Mind*. Seeking to bring together phenomenology and the mind sciences, Varela, Thompson, and Rosch challenge three assumptions that, they claim, have held sway in cognitive science: "(1) the world is pregiven; (2) our cognition is of this world—even if only to a partial extent; and (3) the way in which we cognize this pregiven world is to represent its features and then act on the basis of these representations" (1991, 135). Varela, Thompson, and Rosch summarize these assumptions through the metaphor of an experiencing subject that is "parachuted" into a pregiven world. By distinct contrast, *The Embodied Mind* argues that subject and world emerge concurrently: the world is, in the authors' language, enacted or "brought forth." With this idea, Varela, Thompson, and Rosch are taking Uexküll's Umwelt and Gibson's affordances one radical step further. They are not just arguing that the world is shaped by the ways in which we can interact with it. They are suggesting that these interactions—when projected against a certain evolutionary and (in humans) cultural history—are constitutive of an animal's identity and experience: as they put it, "Organism and environment enfold into each other and unfold from one another in the fundamental circularity that is life itself" (217).

From this perspective, animals live in "worlds without ground" (i.e., a stable ontological substrate), and cognition can be seen as an act of "laying down a path in walking" (Varela, Thompson, and Rosch 1991, 237). Two aspects of this process are worth highlighting. First, enacting a world is a patterned activity, and the patterns Varela, Thompson, and Rosch focus on are sensorimotor in nature; they are physical movements, or the potentiality to move one's body in certain ways. Second, the act of bringing forth a world is hermeneutic insofar as it involves selecting "a domain of significance out of the background of [an organism's] random milieu" (156)—an idea that can be traced back to Gibson's emphasis on the meaning or value of environmental affordances.

All this goes a long way toward evacuating the assumptions of ontological segregation and representational stability that we associate with the idea of world. Surely, humans are able to conceive worlds in this abstract sense, as collections of objects that preexist an experiencing subject. But this conception comes relatively late, phylogenetically and ontogenetically. Could it be that the enactivist notion of world as a "domain of significance" that arises with the subject through embodied engagements can shed light on our understanding of fictional narratives? Clearly, Varela, Thompson, and Rosch are concerned with basic experiences—patterns of interaction that humans share with other living beings. How does this model "scale up" to something as complex as the cultural experience of fiction? Answering this question requires delving deeper into enactivist philosophy, particularly into the account of social cognition offered by Ezequiel Di Paolo, Marieke Rohde, and Hanne De Jaegher.

Coconstructing Worlds in Social Interaction

For Gibson, and later for Varela, Thompson, and Rosch, values are already "given" in our experience: they are the fabric of our groundless worlds. Thus, Di Paolo, Rohde, and De Jaegher's point of departure is that a value "is simply an aspect of all sense-making, as sense-making is, at its roots, the evaluation of the consequences of interaction for the conservation of an identity" (2010, 45). For basic organisms, like bacteria, the only value is the fulfillment of nutritional needs. But as the complexity of an organism increases, so does the degree of mediacy of its values. Di Paolo, Rohde, and De Jaegher regard play as the activity (or set of activities) in which more complex animals, including humans, experiment with the mediacy of their values: "Play becomes a way of substitution for real satisfaction and a way of dealing with an insurmountable mediacy. Soon the value-generating properties of play become evident and the activity is done for its own sake" (77). Despite being a fully embodied activity, play puts at stake values that are *not* given in the here and now. In cultural transactions, play thus helps us forge a connection between our embodied engagement with reality and values that are either abstract or nonactual. In other words, play develops our "capacity to 'unstick' meanings from a given situation and 'stick' novel ones onto it (to put it graphically), or, generally, [our] capacity to influence meaning generation" (76).

The upshot is that, even when values become more mediated and abstract than in the bacterium's self-preservation, they emerge in a patterned fashion. In fact, Di Paolo, Rohde, and De Jaegher focus on patterns or dynamics of coordination between participants. The centrality of play in their approach to social cognition resonates with theories, such as Brian Boyd's (2009), that see narrative and play as intrinsically linked in evolutionary terms. In storytelling, as well as other cultural activities, the value manipulation gives rise to a certain dynamic that is the equivalent—in the conceptual domain—of play's patterns of embodied interaction. The key concept is "interaction rhythm," which "refers to the diverse aspects of the temporality of the interaction—a necessary, though not sufficient, aspect of establishing, maintaining, and closing social interactions. Timing coordination in interaction is done at many different levels of movement, including utterances, posture maintenance, and so on" (Di Paolo, Rohde, and De Jaegher 2010, 69). Could narrative meaning making be seen in this light, as an interactive and participatory process? This is what narrative theorist Yanna Popova has suggested in a book that builds on Di Paolo, Rohde, and De Jaegher's enactivist work. Since audiences tend to engage with fictional narratives in the absence of their authors or creators, we cannot posit a *direct* interaction with them. Instead, Popova argues that readers coordinate their interpretation of narrative with a narrator in the broad sense (i.e., a narrating instance, whether it is a character or a constructed image of the author). In Popova's words: "The interaction between narrator and reader is best captured as a kind of rhythmic coordination between tension and release in the narrative pace itself, as the contrast between scene and summary, between the oscillation of short punctual events and temporally unconstrained moments of evaluative pausing" (2015, 83). Importantly, a number of experiential values are implicated in this rhythmic progression and negotiated through them.

Consider, for example, the case of suspense—one of the three "universals" of narrative, according to Meir Sternberg (2001). In a typical scenario, suspense presupposes an investment of value in an identity (the character's) and in a situation that potentially endangers his or her identity. However, this value is attached to a scenario that we know to be nonactual and often fictional. Put otherwise, the values involved in narrative may be similar to real-life situations, but they are leveraged with a higher degree of mediacy, which often implies different behavioral consequences. Just like play in Di Paolo, Rohde, and De Jaegher's account, narrative allows us to "unstick" values from our everyday interactions, negotiating them through the safe distance afforded by semiotic cues and nonactual situations (see also Caracciolo 2014a, 78–79). Moreover, narrative implicates real-world values while asking us to devolve part of our control over those values to cues that have been prestructured by a storyteller. The text displays a value (e.g., the character's survival) while delaying the fulfillment of that value in a concrete narrative outcome: this gives rise to a temporally unfolding pattern of interaction or rhythm, which (in the case of suspense) we tend to characterize as a "buildup" of affect and its eventual release.

Note, however, that in moving from basic experiences (in Varela, Thompson, and Rosch's account) to social and cultural experiences (as conceptualized by Di Paolo, Rohde, and De Jaegher), we've lost track of the notion of world. Surely, it is much easier to grasp how an organism may enact a world when we consider an individual organism confronting a spatially bounded environment. Human worlds are enacted in a highly complex act of coordination with countless other humans, living and dead, who make up our social milieu or have had a lasting influence on our culture. Perhaps it is this sophisticated machinery that fuels our illusion of living in a grounded world, a preexisting reality into which we are "parachuted" at birth. But in fact worlds first arise through patterns of negotiation with the physical and social environments to which we are exposed in the course of our lives. Not only do narratives, including fictional narratives, participate in this dynamic, but they owe their worldlikeness to the ways in which they are able to recreate and—potentially—reconfigure the patterning of our interactions with reality. This patterning is discussed in the next section as a narrative's logic of unfolding.

Rhythm and Archbuilders: A Closer Look at the Logic of Unfolding

Intuitively, we all know that narrative has a certain rhythm. We call an action movie "fast-paced," or we complain about the extremely slow pace of—for instance—Marcel Proust's *Recherche*. Narrative theorists have devoted some attention to questions of pace and speed (Hume 2005; Baetens and Hume 2006), but some of the most interesting implications of narrative's rhythmicity have yet to be addressed. I have started thinking about these issues in an article (Caracciolo 2014b); with the aid of Popova's account of narrative comprehension I would like to go further in exploring how a certain rhythm emerging from narrative may result in a sense of worldlikeness. Rhythm is, in essence, temporal patterning; we can think of it as the "form" of experienced time. But this form is never an exclusively formal (in the sense of abstract and disembodied) phenomenon, because rhythm has deep roots in our bodies. First, time is shaped by motion through the patterns of embodied interaction with the world highlighted by enactivist philosophers. Walking at a leisurely pace gives time a very different shape from a mad rush to catch a train. In the domain of cultural expression, the link between rhythm in music and the experience of motion has been widely studied (see, e.g., Jones 1981). Second, the rhythm of time is always affective: like a magnet, rhythm attracts whatever emotional values happen to co-occur with it, reflecting both the external context and an organism's psychological states and predispositions.

As a practice that deals with the segmentation of experienced time (see Fludernik 2005), narrative has a built-in rhythmicity that involves both the representation of bodily movements and the negotiation of affective values. In face-to-face, conversational narrative and in narrative media such as theater, the bodily element is provided by the speaker's gestures and posture, which contribute—along with semiotic cues—to the audience's meaning making. In prose narrative, these movements are a matter of semiotic representation rather than direct perception: nevertheless, our imagination of characters moving in narrative space is still to a large extent based on patterns arising from our embodied interaction with the world (Caracciolo 2013a; Troscianko 2014). Affective values derive from the situations being represented by narrative. Consider again the case of suspense: if the protagonist is facing a life-or-death predicament, the experienced slowness of the narrative will be inevitably colored by a sense of anxious apprehension. But the same slowness may take on a completely different affective value in a different narrative context (e.g., a love scene).

The suspense example might give the impression that narrative rhythm emerges only in specific episodes. While it is undeniable that rhythm is likely to become experientially more salient in conjunction with specific situations and storytelling strategies, it is a global feature of narrative. A sense of rhythmic temporality is at the heart of the worldlikeness of a story because it mirrors the affectively laden patterns of our interaction with reality: narrative is enacted in ways that are structurally analogous to how we "bring forth" a world in engaging with an environment.

To specify these ideas, I will discuss Jonathan Lethem's novel *Girl in Landscape*. I choose this text partly because its science fiction–themed narrative would seem to foreground the notion of world in the "grounded," ontological sense: the novel's adolescent protagonist, Pella, and her family leave Earth to settle on a distant planet where a handful of humans coexist with an enigmatic (but peaceable) alien race, the Archbuilders. We may be tempted to see this planet as a "world" that preexists the human settlers, but in fact I argue that the novel's storyworld presents the same dynamic unfolding as that of *any* other fictional text. My reading of this novel thus aims to show how readers' engagement with fiction functions more generally, if we take seriously the enactivist insights outlined over the previous pages. The narrative is rich in descriptive details, painting a vivid picture of a desolate landscape strewn with abandoned buildings (most of the Archbuilders, we are told, have left the planet; only a handful of them remain, ghostly presences in this twilight of the Archbuilder civilization). Yet this space is not a stable backdrop to our imagination of the storyworld. Rather, the description of the planet is drawn into the rhythm of the plot and tinges affectively its progression. Ultimately, the mysterious planet of the Archbuilders allows Lethem to capture Pella's alienation as she comes face-to-face with the complex and often harsh realities of adulthood. The title suggests precisely this close link between the planet's nonhuman landscape and Pella's Bildungsroman. But the macrostructural narrative pattern that accompanies Pella from childhood to adulthood emerges from a series of small-scale patterns—those of characters' embodied actions. Consider, for instance, the beginning of the novel:

> Mother and daughter worked together, dressing the two young boys, tucking them into their outfits. The boys slithered under their hands, delighted, impatient, eyes darting sideways. They nearly groaned with momentary pleasure. The four were going to the beach, so their bodies had to be sealed against the sun. The boys had never been there. The girl had, just once. She could barely remember.
>
> The girl's name was Pella Marsh.
>
> The family was moving to a distant place, an impossible place. Distance itself haunted them, the distance they had yet to go. It had infected them, invaded the space of their family. So the trip to the beach was a blind, a small expedition to cover talk of the larger one. (Lethem 2011, 1)

The first few sentences are richly patterned: the verbs implying action or motion ("worked," "dressing," "tucking," "slithered," "darting") are like a sequence of brushstrokes—embodied gestures that quickly and effectively sketch out a fictional reality. Readers respond to these cues through a psychological mechanism known as "motor resonance" (Zwaan and Taylor 2006): they internally and unconsciously enact the characters' movements by combining traces of their past interactions with reality. In this way, readers' engagement with these lines mirrors the embodied nature of animals' engagement with their Umwelten—and an inchoate sense of worldlikeness can emerge. The boys' groaning "with momentary pleasure" introduces an affective element to these embodied transactions, reminding us that a perceptual pattern is never purely perceptual: it is always invested with expectations and goals that are emotionally laden.

After the third sentence, the narrative seemingly shifts gears: it zooms out of these small-scale embodied happenings and reveals the larger project behind these actions (the characters' trip to the beach). The scale of the narrative becomes even larger as their excursion is mapped onto the family's planned relocation to the planet of the Archbuilders—an action that is extended in time and points to a faraway space. By remarking that "the trip to the beach was a blind, a small expedition to cover talk of the larger one," the narrator is implicitly drawing a parallel that helps readers connect three levels of the narrative: the embodied preparations described in the first paragraph, the trip to the beach that will be narrated in this first chapter, and the overall plot arc (Pella's life on the planet of the Archbuilders). This bridging of temporal scales serves to establish a sense of patterned progression that involves not just external actions (actual or planned) but also the characters' emotional responses to them: the planet feels impossibly far off, its distance "haunts" the family, and so on.

In the following two chapters, Pella's mother falls ill and dies unexpectedly, but the family decides to leave for the distant planet nevertheless. This trauma compounds Pella's estrangement from the new, unfamiliar reality that surrounds her. Not only is this Archbuilder planet compared to a world in which one may wake up after a "seizure" (2011, 78), but it has a direct and profound impact on Pella's psychology: as Pella soon realizes, whenever she falls asleep she somehow takes on the body (and consciousness) of one of the small, rodent-like animals that inhabit the planet. These nearly invisible creatures are known as "household deer," and the exploration of their Umwelt again brings to the fore spatial, embodied patterns: "The deer [Pella during one of her "dreams"] ran to deny its mistake now, to forget the person in the chamber [Pella's human self]. Running to forget wasn't as pure as running for no reason at all, but it was still a consolation to zip along implacably, . . . making silent ribbons across the surface of the world" (160). These embodied "ribbons" do not just denote a way of being that is alternative to Pella's ordinary human perception and perhaps more suitable to this alien location; they fall into the larger trajectory of Pella's psychological development—and therefore of the Bildungsroman plot—by affording Pella insight into aspects of reality that would remain hidden from her as a human child. For instance, becoming a household deer allows Pella to discover the machinations of Efram Nugent, an authoritarian, malicious man to whom Pella nevertheless feels sexually attracted. Efram is accusing the Archbuilders of child abuse in order to deepen the rift between the human colonists and the harmless aliens. As Pella gradually realizes, Efram's agenda is to exterminate the Archbuilders and their culture. To complete her Bildungsroman, Pella has to embrace the alienness of the planet: she becomes household deer and uses their perceptual perspective to disclose the violence at the heart of the human.

As we read the novel, we follow this narrative arc by coordinating with the storyteller's narrative strategies in a process of participatory sense making, as argued by Popova. Our understanding of this macrostructural pattern builds on the small-scale, embodied patterns traced by the characters' interactions on (and with) the planet of the Archbuilders. Further, the planet's deserted landscape contributes to the affective qualities of this progression insofar as the emotional values of the spatial descriptions are infused into readers' engagement with the Bildungsroman plot: the "[fallen] bridges, incomplete towers, [and] demolished pillars" (2011, 48) left behind by the Archbuilders, along with the desolate, dusty hills, set the emotional tone for the character's initiation into adulthood. The planet represents a core of alienness that Pella has to interiorize—by blending with it and becoming a "girl in landscape"—in order to fully grasp the depths of human psychology. Narrative space thus participates in the plot and in the meanings plot brings into play, as I discuss more at length elsewhere (Caracciolo 2013b).

This temporally extended, affective dynamic, which for most readers will be spread out over a number of reading sessions, is the narrative's logic of unfolding: the patterned way in which it constructs an imaginary reality—a fictional world—by capitalizing on both the characters' embodied actions and the spatial locations in which those actions take place. In fictional, literary narratives like Lethem's, this affective dynamic can be so carefully orchestrated that it coalesces in a certain mood or atmosphere—an intangible but distinctive quality that is also part of the plot's worldlikeness. In this sense, I argue that the fictional world is *enacted* by readers—with the important proviso that it is a groundless world that doesn't meet the two criteria (implicit in Walsh's critique of world talk) of representational stability and ontological segregation. In the rhythmic flow of the narrative, we may be aware that the events we are imagining are not *actual*, but any sense of clear-cut ontological separation from the real world is absent: the perceptual patterns and affective dynamics from which fictional worlds are woven are fundamentally the same as those inherent in our transactions with reality. Our apprehension of the narrated space is oriented toward the characters' actions and the situations in which they are embedded: there is no need for—or indeed time to construct—a stable spatial model of this world, because readers' attention is driven by the narrative progression. Space is relevant only insofar as it enriches the affective logic of the narrative. If there is mimesis, it is not in any ontologically grounded sense—as an "accessibility relation" across semiautonomous worlds—but only because there is a fundamental continuity between our imagination of this novel and the patterned nature of our embodied, social cognition. This background of continuity explains a striking feature of fictional worlds, which Ryan (1991) discusses under the heading of the "principle of minimal departure"—namely, the idea that readers will assume fictional worlds to work similarly to the real world unless they are explicitly told otherwise. Readers make this default assumption because fictional worlds are fluid, unstable constructs that build on and mirror the affective and embodied structure of our interactions with reality.

Conclusion

One of the core claims of enactivist philosophy is that basic experience does not need mental representations, that is, the construction of an internal model of the world. The world is simply "out there," available to our perception via bodily engagements. As Alva Noë puts it, "Just as you don't need to download, say, the entire *New York Times* to be able to read it on your desktop, so you don't need to construct a representation of all the detail of the scene in front of you to have a sense of its detailed presence" (2004, 50). In the case of the semiotically mediated realities evoked by narratives, some form of mental representation is clearly unavoidable: there is extensive psycholinguistic evidence that readers do construct mental models of the scenarios represented by narrative—Teun van Dijk and Walter Kintsch (1983) call them "situation models." However, we shouldn't rush to the conclusion that these mental models are a psychological basis for the notion of fictional worlds, because, as I have argued in this chapter, the idea of worlds can have unwanted implications. Situation models are volatile, ad hoc constructs that readers update as they process a narrative: they don't present the stability in time and space that is generally associated with worlds. A fortiori, situation models have little in common with the surgical precision of the possible worlds of modal logic.

Theorists of possible worlds in narratology may have avoided these difficulties to a large extent, but they have taken on board the world metaphor without fully coming to terms with the experiential fluidity of the storyworlds of fiction. If these storyworld-based approaches have merit, and I'm convinced they do, it is because there is indeed a certain world-likeness to our engagement with narratives, especially with the carefully constructed narratives of fiction. However, to correctly understand this worldlikeness we need to rethink it from a processual, phenomenologi-cal perspective, drawing inspiration from the enactivist view that world and experience coemerge in a groundless pattern of interaction. Fictional worlds are similarly groundless: they arise from a series of rhythmic trans-actions that involve the reader, the text, and the storyteller behind it. The nature of these transactions is both embodied (since they mirror the char-acters' own embodied engagement with a nonactual reality) and affective (since they reflect the emotional values implicated in narrative situations). Moreover, these patterns exist at many levels of analysis: their rhythmic convergence helps close the divide between the reader's moment-by-moment engagement with narrative situations and their involvement in plot as a narrative macrostructure.

The account of fictional worlds I've offered in this chapter is admit-tedly speculative: I have considered the conceptual difficulties involved in a certain understanding of world, and I have sketched an alternative picture from a different theoretical position. However, I take these ideas to be fundamentally consistent with empirical work on the affective and embodied nature of narrative comprehension: psycholinguist Rolf Zwaan, for instance, writes that we understand stories via "the integration and sequencing of traces from actual experience cued by the linguistic input" (2004, 38). The sensorimotor patterns I've alluded to are among these "traces" derived from experience, and they are reenacted or simulated whenever we engage with semiotic representations. More work, empiri-cal and conceptual, remains to be done, particularly with regard to global narrative patterns: Is the idea of "rhythm" a helpful way of understand-ing readers' engagement with plots? When does this implicit rhythm give rise to an experienced sense of fastness or slowness?

There is an assumption, whenever we talk about narrative, that it is what happens that fuels our involvement. Rethinking fictional worlds as I have tried to do in this chapter begins shifting the emphasis from the "what" of representation to the "how" of dynamic enactment. This con-ceptual shift is a step toward a more comprehensive account of narrative engagements—one in which our absorption in stories is not just a func-tion of the intrinsic interest generated by the states of affairs being repre-sented; it is induced and consolidated by the experienced *patterns* traced by the story. In this sense, narrative is perhaps not so fundamentally dif-ferent from music. This would explain why we can be gripped by a suspenseful story even if we already know how it ends—in the famous case of "anomalous suspense" (Gerrig 1993). Adopting an enactivist perspective on narrative, even if it is for the time being only a speculative endeavor, can lay bare the prerepresentational, affective patterns that underlie—and perhaps, in some respects, drive—our engagement with narrative representations.

References

Alber, Jan, Stefan Iversen, Henrik Skov Nielsen, and Brian Richardson. 2010. "Unnatural Narratives, Unnatural Narratology: Beyond Mimetic Models." *Narrative* 18 (2): 113–36.

Baetens, Jan, and Kathryn Hume. 2006. "Speed, Rhythm, Movement: A Dialogue on K. Hume's Article 'Narrative Speed.'" *Narrative* 14 (3): 349–55.

Barsalou, Lawrence W. 2008. "Grounded Cognition." *Annual Review of Psychology* 59 (1): 617–45.

Boroditsky, Lera. 2000. "Metaphoric Structuring: Understanding Time through Spatial Metaphors." *Cognition* 75 (1): 1–28.

Boyd, Brian. 2009. *On the Origin of Stories: Evolution, Cognition, and Fiction.* Cambridge MA: Harvard University Press.

Caracciolo, Marco. 2013a. "Blind Reading: Toward an Enactivist Theory of the Reader's Imagination." In *Stories and Minds: Cognitive Approaches to Literary Narrative*, edited by Lars Bernaerts, Dirk De Geest, Luc Herman, and Bart Vervaeck, 81–106. Lincoln: University of Nebraska Press.

———. 2013b. "Narrative Space and Readers' Responses to Stories: A Phenomenological Account." *Style* 47 (4): 425–44.

———. 2014a. *The Experientiality of Narrative: An Enactivist Approach.* Berlin: de Gruyter.

———. 2014b. "Tell-Tale Rhythms: Embodiment and Narrative Discourse." *Storyworlds* 6 (2): 49–73.

Di Paolo, Ezequiel A., Marieke Rohde, and Hanne De Jaegher. 2010. "Horizons for the Enactive Mind: Values, Social Interaction, and Play." In *Enaction: Toward a New Paradigm for Cognitive Science*, edited by John Stewart, Olivier Gapenne, and Ezequiel A. Di Paolo, 33–87. Cambridge MA: MIT Press.

Doležel, Lubomír. 1998. *Heterocosmica: Fiction and Possible Worlds.* Baltimore MD: Johns Hopkins University Press.

Dreyfus, Hubert L. 1991. *Being-in-the-World: A Commentary on Heidegger's "Being and Time," Division I.* Cambridge MA: MIT Press.

Eco, Umberto. 1979. *The Role of the Reader: Explorations in the Semiotics of Texts.* Bloomington: Indiana University Press.

Fludernik, Monika. 2005. "Time in Narrative." In *Routledge Encyclopedia of Narrative Theory*, edited by David Herman, Manfred Jahn, and Marie-Laure Ryan. London: Routledge.

Gerrig, Richard J. 1993. *Experiencing Narrative Worlds: On the Psychological Activities of Reading*. New Haven: Yale University Press.

Gibson, James J. 1986. *The Ecological Approach to Visual Perception*. New York: Psychology Press.

Grishakova, Marina. 2006. *The Models of Space, Time and Vision in V. Nabokov's Fiction: Narrative Strategies and Cultural Frames*. Tartu: Tartu University Press.

——. 2009. "Beyond the Frame: Cognitive Science, Common Sense and Fiction." *Narrative* 17 (2): 188–99.

Heidegger, Martin. 1996. *Being and Time*. Translated by Joan Stambaugh. Albany: State University of New York Press.

Herman, David. 2002. *Story Logic: Problems and Possibilities of Narrative*. Lincoln: University of Nebraska Press.

——. 2011. "Storyworld/Umwelt: Nonhuman Experiences in Graphic Narratives." *SubStance* 40 (1): 156–81.

——. 2013. *Storytelling and the Sciences of Mind*. Cambridge MA: MIT Press.

Hogan, Patrick Colm. 2011. *Affective Narratology: The Emotional Structure of Stories*. Lincoln: University of Nebraska Press.

Hume, Kathryn. 2005. "Narrative Speed in Contemporary Fiction." *Narrative* 13 (2): 105–24.

Jones, Mari Riess. 1981. "Music as a Stimulus for Psychological Motion: Part 1. Some Determinants of Expectancies." *Psychomusicology: Music, Mind and Brain* 1 (2): 34–51.

Lethem, Jonathan. 2011. *Girl in Landscape: A Novel*. New York: Knopf.

Miall, David S. 2011. "Emotions and the Structuring of Narrative Responses." *Poetics Today* 32 (2): 323–48.

Noë, Alva. 2004. *Action in Perception*. Cambridge MA: MIT Press.

Pavel, Thomas. 1986. *Fictional Worlds*. Cambridge MA: Harvard University Press.

Popova, Yanna. 2015. *Stories, Meaning, and Experience*. New York: Routledge.

Ryan, Marie-Laure. 1991. *Possible Worlds, Artificial Intelligence and Narrative Theory*. Bloomington: Indiana University Press.

——. 2003. "Cognitive Maps and the Construction of Narrative Space." In *Narrative Theory and the Cognitive Sciences*, edited by David Herman, 214–42. Stanford CA: CSLI Publications.

——. 2013. "Possible Worlds." In *The Living Handbook of Narratology*, edited by Hühn Peter. Hamburg: Hamburg University Press. http://www.lhn.uni-hamburg.de/article/possible-worlds.

Sperber, Dan, and Deirdre Wilson. 1995. *Relevance: Communication and Cognition*. Malden MA: Wiley-Blackwell.

Sternberg, Meir. 2001. "How Narrativity Makes a Difference." *Narrative* 9 (2): 115–22.

Tan, Ed S. 1996. *Emotion and the Structure of Narrative Film: Film as an Emotion Machine*. Mahwah NJ: Lawrence Erlbaum.

Troscianko, Emily. 2014. *Kafka's Cognitive Realism*. New York: Routledge.

Uexküll, Jakob von. 1957. "A Stroll through the Worlds of Animals and Men: A Picture Book of Invisible Worlds." In *Instinctive Behavior: The Development of a Modern Concept*, edited by Claire H. Schiller, 5–80. New York: International Press.

van Dijk, Teun A., and Walter Kintsch. 1983. *Strategies of Discourse Comprehension*. New York: Academic Press.

Varela, Francisco J., Evan Thompson, and Eleanor Rosch. 1991. *The Embodied Mind: Cognitive Science and Human Experience*. Cambridge MA: MIT Press.

Walsh, Richard. 2007. *The Rhetoric of Fictionality: Narrative Theory and the Idea of Fiction*. Columbus: Ohio State University Press.

———. 2017. "Beyond Fictional Worlds: Narrative and Spatial Cognition." In *Emerging Vectors of Narratology*, edited by Per Krogh Hansen, John Pier, Philippe Roussin, and Wolf Schmid, 461–78. Berlin: Walter de Gruyter.

Zwaan, Rolf A. 2004. "The Immersed Experiencer: Towards an Embodied Theory of Language Comprehension." In *The Psychology of Learning and Motivation*, edited by Brian H. Ross, 44:35–63. San Diego: Elsevier Academic Press.

Zwaan, Rolf A., and Lawrence J. Taylor. 2006. "Seeing, Acting, Understanding: Motor Resonance in Language Comprehension." *Journal of Experimental Psychology* 135 (1): 1–11.

5 Postmodern Play with Worlds
The Case of At Swim-Two-Birds

W. MICHELLE WANG

Patricia Waugh observes that "all art is 'play' in its creation of other symbolic worlds" (1984, 34). In this essay, I argue that the readerly play involved in delineating textual possible worlds is a defining feature of "postmodernist fiction" (McHale 1987, 10), where worlds tend to be multiple, complex, or even kaleidoscopic in nature. Postmodern fiction typically instantiates an aesthetics of play in which ontological questions about the sorts of worlds characters inhabit and the ways in which readers orient to these worlds constitute a central readerly concern.

In association with Mikhail Bakhtin's concept of the "carnivalesque," Roger Caillois's category of "*ilinx*" productively captures the nature of play in postmodern fiction, particularly in the way it foregrounds the affective disorientation that readers sometimes experience in their encounters with chaotic postmodern textual worlds. Referring to games "based on the pursuit of vertigo and which consist of an attempt to momentarily destroy the stability of perception and inflict a kind of voluptuous panic upon an otherwise lucid mind" (Caillois [1958] 1961, 23), Marie-Laure Ryan observes that "*ilinx* expresses the aesthetics, sensibility, and conception of language of the postmodern age" (2001, 186). While the "jarring fragmentation and incoherencies" of postmodern play worlds have their own "stimulating aesthetic (and cognitive) effect," Richard Shusterman notes that the "human need to perceive and experience satisfying unities in the disordered flux of experience" also "motivates our interest in [literary] art" (2000, 75–77). Since *ilinx* is characterized by the pleasurable, *momentary* destruction of stable perceptions, it is simultaneously implied that coherence-restoring cognitive processes complement the disorienting effects of play.

I suggest that the cognitive disorientation readers tend to experience in their encounters with postmodern textual worlds spurs what Friedrich Schiller terms the "formal instinct" ("Letter XII," in [1794] 1902) into action, as readers attempt to comprehend the text and restore stability of perception by imposing some form of (artificial and/or temporary) "global coherence" (Ryan 2001, 223). While classical aesthetics dominantly locates such harmonizing tendencies in the artifact's formal design—as a product of the artist's efforts—postmodern literature modifies our understanding of contemporary aesthetics by displacing the latent energies of coherence, order, and harmony from the artifact/artist to the reader/perceiver/participant/player. This shared onus of formal coherence promotes the "active and playful participation of the reader" (195–96), whereby order and coherence are no longer readily perceptible characteristics of the artifact but are (partially) relocated to readers' consciousness. Using Flann O'Brien's *At Swim-Two-Birds* as a case study, I suggest that the possible worlds approach functions as a particularly useful apparatus for capturing readers' cognitive attempts at managing the complexities of postmodern fiction's disorienting, playful textual worlds.

Mediating Accessibility Relations: Finessing the Possible Worlds Model

Ryan's account of possible worlds theory designates *reality* as a universe that is "the sum of the imaginable," with the "actual world" (AW) at the center of its system and satellite worlds that are products of "mental activity, such as dreaming, imagining, foretelling, promising, or storytelling" (2005b, 446–48). Theorists like David Lewis and Nicholas Rescher have further debated and finessed the concept, but for my purpose, the AW refers to the world inhabited by flesh-and-blood authors and readers, including the late Brian O'Nolan (better known by his pseudonym, Flann O'Brien) and readers of *At Swim-Two-Birds*. Ryan explains that though there is only one AW, fictional texts establish their own pretended actual world, with "its own horizons of possibilities," which she calls the "textual actual world" (TAW) (447). The process of "fictional recentering" occurs when we read fiction and shift our attention from the AW to the TAW, becoming "in make-believe temporary members of the recentered system" (Ryan 1991, 24–26).

Ryan suggests that readers minimize such distance "between the textual universe and our own system of reality" by a default reliance on "the principle of minimal departure" (1991, 51), which states that "when readers construct fictional worlds, they fill in the gaps in the text by assuming the similarity of the fictional world to their own experiential reality. This model can only be overruled by the text itself" (2005b, 447).[1] Scholars who dispute aspects of the minimal departure principle include Lubomír Doležel, who argues that the principle's assumption of "ontologically complete" fictional worlds is problematic because "incompleteness [is] the distinctive feature of fictional existence. He argues that by filling the gaps, readers would reduce the ontological diversity found in fictional worlds to a uniform structure" (Ryan 2005b, 447; see also Ryan's chapter in this volume addressing this debate).

The other objection comes from Thomas Pavel, who suggests that when "confronted with radical oddities," readers are likely instead to anticipate "'maximal departure' from the real world" (1986, 93; cf. Alber 2009, 82; Ryan 1991, 57). The main difference between minimal and maximal departure relates to the cognitive premise from which readers proceed: if minimal departure relies on a default assumption of the fictional world's similarity to our own experiential reality, I propose that maximal departure proceeds from readerly expectations that such real-world frames are repurposed, reconfigured, and retooled as mere building blocks of the fictional universe; the distinction lies in readers' attitudes toward the functions of these frames of reference. Under the principle of maximal departure, the fantastic, strange, and nonsensical (to borrow from J. R. R. Tolkien) are not anomalous but default modes of the fictional world. It is crucial to note that the principle of maximal departure does not completely cancel the effects of minimal departure, since we overwhelmingly use such real-world frames in our everyday processing of the world— including fiction. Instead, it is useful to consider the principles of minimal and maximal departure as being two ends on the same spectrum of fictional credulity, whereby readers adopt a point of departure based on their attentiveness to textual cues in the work of fiction.

To address Doležel's contention that incompleteness is distinctive of fictional worlds and attests to their ontological diversity and Pavel's suggestion that readers anticipate maximal departure when confronted with radical oddities, I propose that three factors mediate accessibility relations, which help readers determine the shape and nature of (postmodern) textual worlds. I use the possible worlds model to explain the functional purpose of some of postmodern fiction's difficulties in terms of their effects on the reading experience and to explore possible strategies that readers intuit or undertake in coping with the challenges posed by such texts.

Ryan proposes that nine orders of "accessibility relations from AW [are] involved in the construction of TAW"—qualities that readers use to determine the relevance of assuming that principles operating in the AW will continue to operate in the TAW. The criteria of comparison, in "decreasing order of stringency," include (1) "identity of properties," (2) "identity of inventory," (3) "compatibility of inventory," (4) "chronological compatibility," (5) "physical compatibility," (6) "taxonomic compatibility," (7) "logical compatibility," (8) "analytical compatibility," and (9) "linguistic compatibility" (1991, 32–33). Two domains of such accessibility relations govern our mental blueprints of the fictional universe: "transuniverse relations" articulate relationships between the AW and TAW, "function[ing] as the airline through which participants in the fictional game reach the world at the center of the textual universe," while "intrauniverse relations" articulate relationships linking the TAW to its own textual alternate possible worlds (32). The notion of play thus implicitly characterizes Ryan's model in terms of readers' projections and coconstructions of textual possible worlds.

In my revision to Ryan's model, I propose that three types of textual cues mediate our beliefs/knowledge about the distance/proximity of the AW from the TAW and, correspondingly, of the TAW from its TAPWs:

1. At which point or how far into the narrative do departures take place?
2. How frequently do we encounter departures?
3. What is the qualitative nature of these departures?

I use the word *departures* in reference to accessibility relations: for instance, a departure or deviation from "logical compatibility" is evident in *At Swim-Two-Birds*, where sexual relations and procreation are possible between an author and his character (Orlick Trellis is begotten after Dermot Trellis assaults his own fictional creation, Sheila Lamont). The qualitative nature of departures relates both to how explicitly such departures are signaled in the text and to the perceived degree of estrangement: the lower its position on Ryan's list of accessibility relations, the more readers are likely to regard such deviations as radical.

The position, frequency, and nature of the textual universe's departures from the AW determine whether readers are likely to adopt the principle of minimal or maximal departure. In general, readers likely assume *minimal* departure the *later* a deviation occurs, the *fewer* the number of departures, the more *implicit* authors are about them (such that readers likely fail to observe their occurrence), and/or the *less radical* the nature of these departures. Conversely, readers likely assume *maximal* departure the *sooner* they notice deviations from the AW, the more *frequently* they observe them, the more *explicitly* authors signal them, and/or the more *radical* the nature of these departures. Furthermore, indeterminacy or "undecidable relations"—such as "when epistemic access to these facts is denied" (Ryan 1991, 39)—is also likely to facilitate the principle of maximal departure. I suggest that readers remain engaged in discerning accessibility relations even in textual worlds that cue maximal departure, since it is a pertinent cognitive act that gives us traction for gaining a "foothold" in these fictional worlds, however slippery and tentative.

I begin my analysis with a review of critical approaches to *At Swim-Two-Birds*, which highlights the difficulties critics and readers have encountered in cognitively processing the play with possible worlds in O'Brien's novel. By elucidating the novel's transuniverse and intrauniverse relations, I explain how my three factors mediating accessibility relations bear on the principle of minimal or maximal departure in each world. In so doing, I hope to more clearly explicate the imaginative range of the novel's tangled textual worlds and to explain the functional purposes of some of its interpretive difficulties. I suggest that navigating the novel's labyrinthine fictional universe is part of the challenge O'Brien invites his readers to participate in through the aesthetics of play that characterizes the novel's overarching textual design.

Textual Universe of *At Swim-Two-Birds*

Brian McHale theorizes that unlike modernist fiction, which is preoccupied with epistemological issues, "the dominant of postmodernist fiction is *ontological*" (1987, 10). Therefore, questions such as "What is a world? What kinds of worlds are there, how are they constituted, and how do they differ?" and "How is a projected world structured?" are concerns brought to the fore in postmodern fiction (10). The frequently problematic structures of worlds are a central readerly concern in postmodern texts such as Italo Calvino's *The Castle of Crossed Destinies* (1973), Alasdair Gray's *Lanark* (1981), Paul Auster's *The New York Trilogy* (1985–86), and especially O'Brien's *At Swim-Two-Birds*, where discerning the very shape of its textual universe becomes a key readerly game-task, particularly given the ambiguity or uncertainty surrounding attempts to map out these worlds.

Consider the amount of critical effort that has been expended in attempts to offer a comprehensible structure of O'Brien's novel. Thomas Shea observes, "From the beginning, we assume that [the characters] Finn, Furriskey, and The Pooka exist adjacent to one another. . . . Not until the fifth autobiographical reminiscence do we find that Finn has been 'demoted' a level, serving as a character of Dermot Trellis who is himself a character of the undergraduate. Once we think we have it settled, however, our quandary begins anew" (1992, 58). David Herman describes the novel as a "baroquely hypodiegetic narrative" with characters like Orlick Trellis, whose "diegetically unstable status" allows him to "metaleptically migrate to a frame positioned somewhere between O'Brien's narrator and Dermot Trellis" (1997, 136–39). Shea notes that "critics often struggle to impose thematic shape onto *At Swim*" (1992, 74) and the very tentativeness of the language these critics use (e.g., "struggle," "somewhere between," and "quandary") evinces the difficulties they have had navigating the text's ontological challenges.

Anne Clissmann (1975, 84–85), Rüdiger Imhof (1985, 168), and William Gass (1998, ix) are generally in agreement that O'Brien's book (B1) comprises the homodiegetic student-narrator's book (B2), which in turn contains Dermot Trellis's book (B3), which in turn frames Dermot's son, Orlick Trellis's book (B4). Gass points out that the four books "are not hermetically sealed from one another," but like "salvage from the sea, flotsam from this or that wrecked narrative washes up on foreign shores" (1998, ix). Though this four-book model is widely used, Kimberly Bohman-Kalaja points out that it has "one fundamental drawback" (2007, 51): readers tend to accept Dermot "Trellis as a narrator because they are told to, but his book on sin occupies virtually no textual space," since he "never succeeds in creating any manuscript at all" (76). Bohman-Kalaja rightly observes that we never read a word of Dermot's manuscript; in fact, most of B3's events occur when Dermot is drugged and asleep and hence could

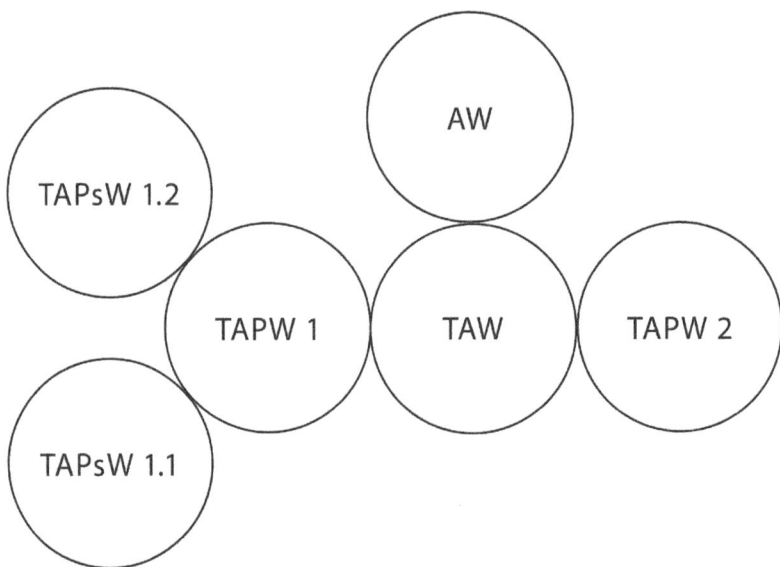

Fig. 5.1. Possible worlds model of *At Swim-Two-Birds*.

have no possible knowledge of them. Furthermore, even within this four-book structure, Imhof points out that it is "possible to establish yet another level," depending on what readers do with "the tale about Finn MacCool, who in turn tells the romance about Mad King Sweeny": while some critics regard it as part of B3, others "regard the Finn part as a 'book' in its own right" (1985, 168). Reliance on this four-book structure thus presents significant interpretive challenges.

My adaptation of the possible worlds approach makes it possible to untangle some of these navigational nightmares, since I rely on textual cues about storylines and characters to answer McHale's questions "What kinds of worlds are there, how are they constituted, and how do they differ?" (1987, 10). In so doing, I employ a critical approach that offers an apparatus for aiding readerly comprehension of the fabula. Possible worlds theory thus serves as a useful model for approaching postmodern fiction's kaleidoscopic textual worlds, giving us a sense of how readers might possibly handle *At Swim-Two-Birds'* ontological challenges.

With reference to figure 5.1 and table 5.1, AW refers to the *actual world* inhabited by flesh-and-blood authors and readers. TAW refers to the *textual*

Table 5.1. Possible worlds of *At Swim-Two-Birds*

TEXTUAL WORLDS	INHABITANTS
Textual actual world (TAW)	Student-narrator
	Brinsley
	Byrne
	Cryan
	Kerrigan
	Kelly
	Verney Wright
	Student-narrator's uncle
	Mr. Connors
	Mr. Fogarty
	Mr. Corcoran
	Mr. Hickey
	William Falconer
Textual alternate possible world 1 (TAPW 1): characters in the student-narrator's manuscript	Dermot Trellis
	Orlick Trellis
	Sheila Lamont
	Antony Lamont
	John Furriskey
	Peggy
	William Tracy
	Paul Shanahan (cowboy)
	Slug Willard
	Peter (Shorty) Andrews
	Red Indians
	Henderson
	Red Kiersay
	Unnamed Belgian author
	Timothy Danaos
	Dona Ferentes
	Good Fairy
	Pooka (Fergus MacPhellimey)
	Finn MacCool
	Dermot
	Granya
	Sweeny
	Jem Casey
	Detective-Officer Snodgrass
	Superintendent Clohessy
	Mr. Lamphall
	Teresa
Textual alternate possible subworld 1 (TAPSW 1.1): characters in Finn MacCool's imaginings (Correspondingly, also characters in the student-narrator's manuscript)	Conán
	Diarmuid Donn
	Caolcrodha Mac Morna
	Liagan Luaimneach O Luachair
	Dheaghaidh
	Gearr mac Aonchearda

TEXTUAL WORLDS	INHABITANTS
Textual alternate possible subworld 2 (TAPSW 1.2): characters in Orlick's manuscript (Correspondingly, also characters in the student-narrator's manuscript)	Dermot Trellis (accused)
	Paul Shanahan (philosopher)
	Justice Sweeny
	Justice Lamont
	Justice Casey
	Justice Andrews
	Justice Lamphall
	Justice Furriskey
	Supt. Clohessy
	Mr. Sweeny
	F. MacCool
	S. Willard
	R. Kiersay
	M. Tracy
	Pooka
	Good Fairy
	Moling
	Unnamed cleric
	Short-horn cow
Textual alternate possible world 2 (TAPW 2): characters in William Falconer's "The Ship-wreck"	Master
	Albert
	Rodmond
	Arion
	Palemon
	Anna

actual world inhabited by the student-narrator and his family and friends. TAPW 1 refers to the dominant *textual alternate possible world* inhabited by Dermot Trellis and his fellow authors, as well as their created and hired characters. Embedded within TAPW 1 are at least two *textual alternate possible subworlds*, TAPSW 1.1 (characterized by Finn MacCool's imaginings) and TAPSW 1.2 (characterized by the events that occur in Orlick Trellis's manuscript). TAPW 2 refers to a minor *textual alternate possible world* as characterized by the events of William Falconer's epic poem "The Ship-wreck." By explicating the configuration of textual worlds in *At Swim-Two-Birds* with reference to the position, frequency, and nature of their departures from the AW, I focus on moments that cue fictional recentering to show how a possible worlds approach allows us to account for some of the novel's difficulties in terms of their effects on the reading experience.

Critics who use the four-book structure tend to agree on the relative diegetic stability of the novel's TAW, inhabited by the homodiegetic student-narrator and his family and friends. Part of the reason for this agreement is that fictional recentering from its alternate possible worlds back to the TAW is signposted by an italicized heading—such as *"Biographical reminiscence, part . . ."* or *"Extract from my typescript"* (O'Brien [1939] 2007, 8–9)—which signal that the narration is about to change gears as the student-narrator moves from describing events taking place around him to explicating parts of his book manuscript. However, headings are used not only to cue fictional recentering but also to gloss information that the student-narrator provides about objects in the TAW, such as the *"Quality of rasher in use in household"* or the student-narrator's *"Description of my uncle"* (6). In other words, not every use of a heading signals a contextual shift, which is part of the disorienting confusion readers are likely to experience and with increasing intensity when *At Swim-Two-Birds* becomes populated by more and more characters and subworlds. Though readers appear to be able to rely on these headings for shifts in contexts, like other O'Brien devices (such as the chapter title on the very first page), the headings turn out to be one of O'Brien's illusionistic tricks: playful red herrings that contribute to the novel's comic appeal.[2]

In general, however, the headings signal transitions from the novel's satellite worlds back to the TAW—a world characterized by few departures from the AW, none of which is radical, such that readers, without any great leaps of imagination, can readily adopt the belief that the homodiegetic student-narrator plausibly lived in Dublin, Ireland, of the AW at some point. Readers are thus cued to approach the TAW using the principle of minimal departure. It is when we leave the TAW that worlds start to become muddied.

TAPW 1 is characterized by frequent and radical departures from the AW and TAW. Readers learn that Dermot Trellis—a product of the TAW student-narrator's story and hence of TAPW 1—buys "a ream of ruled foolscap and is starting on his story. He is compelling all his characters to live with him in the Red Swan Hotel so that he can keep an eye on them. . . . Trellis has absolute control over his minions but this control is abandoned when he falls asleep. Consequently he must make sure that they are all in bed before he locks up and goes to bed himself" (O'Brien [1939] 2007, 31). Readers are thus directed to approach TAPW 1 using the principle of maximal departure, since we are explicitly cued early on to make a radical break with the AW. Furthermore, the comic purpose of such radical departures—of a dictatorial author sharing the same physical space as his characters—prompts readers to take a playful attitude toward TAPW 1.

Such logical incompatibilities (in relation to the AW and TAW) are ad hoc features of TAPW 1 that are continually foregrounded: Dermot, for instance, sexually assaults his fictional creation, who later gives birth to a son, Orlick Trellis (O'Brien [1939] 2007, 58, 142–43). Furthermore, like the character John Furriskey, Orlick is born into TAPW 1 as a fully grown man rather than a baby through the process of "aestho-autogamy" (36–37, 142–43). To compound the challenges readers face in cognitively processing TAPW 1, its inhabitants are not fully fleshed out early in the narrative discourse: consider the Good Fairy, who enters only midway through the novel, significantly modifying our existing mental model of TAPW 1, which has thus far largely been confined to the Red Swan Hotel and its inhabitants. Part of the reader's game-task is to figure out who belongs (and how) to which world—an issue I take up more fully in the following section on intrauniverse relations.

The effect of creating a TAW that is very similar to our sense of AW reality to buffer the AW and TAPW 1 is that it prevents us from simplistically reading (or, worse still, dismissing) *At Swim-Two-Birds* as pure fantasy. By juxtaposing these worlds that operate on different principles within the same textual universe, O'Brien foregrounds issues of metafictionality by preserving the strange and wonderful texture of TAPW 1 (operating on maximal departure) alongside overt confrontations about the nature of fiction writing thus raised in the TAW (operating on minimal departure). Waugh notes that postmodern metafictional novels function "through the problematization rather than the destruction of the concept of 'reality'" (1984, 40–41). The mimetic TAW thus serves as *At Swim-Two-Birds*' tenuous anchor to the AW, creating an alternative to (rather than replacement/substitution/destruction of) reality. In so doing, ontological readerly game-tasks are foregrounded as we are forced to continually engage with our own AW sense of reality even as we are kept busy in the shuffle of fictional recentering between the novel's satellite worlds. O'Brien further problematizes the very idea of a fictional "center" by displacing its centrality altogether; most of the novel's action, so to speak, occurs not in the TAW but in TAPW 1 and TAPSW 1.2, such that we are likely to feel more invested in the outcomes of characters populating these satellite worlds (as compared to characters in the mimetic TAW, with whom we are more marginally engaged).

Intrauniverse Relations: Delineating TAPW 1 from Its Subworlds

One of the key interpretive difficulties that characterizes O'Brien's novel is determining if and when fictional recentering is supposed to be taking place—a challenge compounded by the stylistic continuities that characterize different textual worlds (e.g., italicized headings that gloss the TAW and signpost TAPW 1) and stylistic incongruities that characterize the same textual world (e.g., Finn MacCool's grandiloquence is jarringly juxtaposed with Shanahan's colloquialism in TAPW 1).[3] The difficulties entailed in delineating TAPW 1 from its subworlds are aggravated by O'Brien's playful use of naming functions, as he employs both "homonymy" (Ryan 2001, 232) and "transworld identity" (Bell and Alber 2012, 171) to perpetuate further readerly confusion.[4] The possible worlds approach thus becomes an especially useful "cheat sheet" for navigating O'Brien's disorienting, tangled play worlds. By grasping the novel's complex "internal configuration" through its "intrauniverse relations" (Ryan 1991, 32), readers gain a clearer sense of the brilliant construction underlying its textual universe instead of simply dismissing *At Swim-Two-Birds* as a chaotic mishmash.

The expansive TAPW 1 is at least partly modeled on AW Ireland: readers are told that the Red Swan Hotel is located in "Lower Leeson Street," and Shanahan reminisces about "Dublin in the old days" (O'Brien [1939] 2007, 22, 49). TAPW 1's inhabitants include author figures (Dermot Trellis, William Tracy, Henderson, the poet Jem Casey, and an unnamed "Belgian author" [99]), created characters (Trellis creates Furriskey, Peggy, Sheila Lamont, and the Pooka; Tracy creates Shanahan, Slug, Shorty, and the Red Indians—some of whom Trellis borrows), "hired" characters (Antony Lamont of unknown origin and Finn MacCool from Celtic mythology [57–58]), at least one begotten character (Orlick Trellis), familiar figures from Celtic folk and fairy lore (the Good Fairy and Sweeny), and Teresa of the Red Swan Hotel.

This eclectic configuration of characters that constitute TAPW 1 comically stages O'Brien's "irritation" with Ireland's intellectual environment of his time (Taaffe 2008, 27–28). Published in 1939, *At Swim-Two-Birds* was composed during a period of volatile cultural and political change as an increasingly independent Ireland moved from the formation of the Irish Free State to the establishment of its own constitution in 1937. Carol Taaffe notes that though O'Brien was "disdainful of modernism's elitism, he was also nevertheless ambivalent in his attitude to the populism extolled by Gaelic Revivalists and other cultural nationalists" (3). This "impatience with all forms of literary pomposity" (31) is playfully invoked in *At Swim-Two-Birds* when Finn MacCool's recitations of Celtic lays and ballads are constantly interrupted by Shanahan's complaints ("bloody blather" being one of his choice responses) that the old Irish lays fail to account for "the man in the street" like himself (O'Brien [1939] 2007, 9–16, 69–77, 82).

O'Brien's response was finally to playfully parody all of these attitudes, mercilessly poking fun at them both in his novels and in "Cruiskeen Lawn," his newspaper column in the *Irish Times*. His playful irreverence is emphasized by the decision to situate this diverse "rag-bag" of characters and "incongruous styles" (Taaffe 2008, 40) in TAPW 1—a world that operates on the principle of maximal departure and is characterized by frequent and radical departures from the AW he was responding to. O'Brien's decision to situate these characters and their corresponding voices—a parody of the inherent conflict that characterized Ireland's intellectual environment at the time—in a textual world twice removed from AW reality implies how far removed such polemical attitudes were to the fruitful development of a rich, independent Irish culture.

Though I situate Finn MacCool in TAPW 1, what we are to make of the character (particularly given his bardic tendencies) remains critically disputed. Even within the conventional four-book structure many O'Brien critics favor, there are debates as to whether the tale about Finn MacCool is "part of the Trellis book" or "a 'book' in its own right" (Imhof 1985, 168). Compounding the confusion is the fact that the Finn mythology exists in the AW—and by the principle of minimal departure, we take it to exist in the TAW as well—leading readers to wonder if Finn's narrative possibly warrants a new TAPW of its own, like the narrated events from William Falconer's poem "The Shipwreck."[5]

Readers are explicitly told from the beginning that "Finn MacCool was a legendary hero of old Ireland" who was subsequently "hired by Trellis on account of [his] venerable appearance and experience, to act as [Peggy's] father" (O'Brien [1939] 2007, 5, 57). Finn, however, turns out to be an abusive cad of an adoptive father, since Peggy's "virtue has already been assailed" by him a quarter way into the novel (57). Some critics are inclined to delineate two different Finns in *At Swim-Two-Birds*, one being the cad-like adoptive father and the other being the legendary Irish giant who recites Celtic lays and ballads. However, using my revision of the possible worlds model based on mediated accessibility relations, I suggest that we are dealing with the same Finn in both cases (excepting the judge/jury member "F. MacCool" [193], who indeed belongs to a different textual world—a point to which I shall return).

Readers are likely to consider Finn as part of TAPW 1 based on several textual cues. First, like other characters in TAPW 1, Finn recognizes his own existence as a character and remarks on his own fictionality: "Small wonder, said Finn, that Finn is without honour in the breast of a sea-blue book, Finn that is twisted and trampled and tortured for the weaving of a story-teller's book-web. Who but a book-poet would dishonour the God-big Finn for the sake of a gap-worded story?" (O'Brien [1939] 2007, 15). Not only do we learn early on that authors and their created characters coinhabit TAPW 1, but we are explicitly and repeatedly reminded that this is a world in which characters are aware of their own roles as characters: Shanahan, for instance, recalls being soundly chastised by his creator, Tracy, when he responds to a false summons from someone impersonating Tracy (49–50).

The Pooka's account of "one of the old Irish sagas" (O'Brien [1939] 2007, 138) ultimately allows readers to pin Finn to TAPW 1. As the Pooka and others await the birth of Dermot Trellis's son at the Red Swan Hotel, the Pooka relates having "played a small part" in "the old story about Dermot and Granya" a "long time ago" (138–42). The old story to which the Pooka refers—"The Pursuit of Diarmuid and Gráinne" (original Celtic forms of the Anglicized names Dermot and Granya)—is a well-known tale from the Fenian cycle of Celtic mythology, a series of narratives centered on Finn MacCool, wherein Granya rejects her betrothal to the aged Finn and elopes with one of his warriors, who is named Dermot.[6] Since the Pooka met Dermot and Granya while they were on the run, readers are thus cued to treat the Finn narrative as events that happened at an earlier time in TAPW 1, such that AW myth is transposed into TAPW 1 history.[7] When the mythological in the AW is made historical in TAPW 1, readers are correspondingly prompted to consider the potentially "mythic" dimensions of historical accounts rendered in our own AW—not in order to negate the existence/reality of events that did occur in the AW past, to paraphrase Waugh, but to foreground the difficulties of comprehensively rendering accurate accounts of those events, that is, what we call "history." To simply treat the Finn narrative as a separate TAPW would be to miss such nuances.

At *Swim-Two-Birds* does, however, feature at least two subworlds that are satellites of TAPW 1. Though the mythologies that Finn narrates (first his own and later Sweeny's) belong to the "historical fabric" of TAPW 1, so to speak, I suggest that the companions who prompt Finn to relate his story at the beginning of *At Swim-Two-Birds* belong to the subworld TAPSW 1.1, which I identify as part of Finn's imaginings. Finn's recitation begins and then stalls repeatedly, even as Conán, Diarmuid Donn, Caol-crodha Mac Morna, Liagan Luaimneach O Luachair Dheaghaidh, and Gearr mac Aonchearda urge him on in turn (O'Brien [1939] 2007, 9–16).[8] Like Finn, all five characters are adapted from the Fenian cycle of Celtic mythology, but several textual cues suggest that Finn's interactions with these characters exist only in his own mind. Adrian Oţoiu, for instance, notes that Finn "seems to have . . . lost his eye-sight, or to be sitting in complete darkness," as he addresses his "invisible" companions (2012, 295–96). Furthermore, Conán, who initially instigates Finn to tell these stories, is later revealed as "hidden Conán" (O'Brien [1939] 2007, 12, 60).

We encounter Conán once more when Finn, Furriskey, Lamont, and Shanahan are gathered in a room after Dermot has fallen asleep: "Relate, said hidden Conán, the tale of the Feasting of Dún na nGedh. Finn *in his mind* was nestling with his people" (O'Brien [1939] 2007, 60, emphasis added). Even though Conán's remarks are interspersed with Furriskey's, Lamont's, and Shanahan's comments, Conán remains ontologically distinct from TAPW 1 and likely exists only in Finn's mind, since the other three characters do not react or respond to Conán's remarks. I thus suggest that the interactions between Finn and Conán (and likely their other "invisible" contemporaries mentioned earlier) exist only in Finn's mind, TAPSW 1.1, though the stories he tells are part of his memories and belong to the historical fabric of TAPW 1. The shift between worlds here is relatively covert and infrequently encountered, since it happens only twice, making it easy for the reader to misread these moments as belonging to TAPW 1. O'Brien's textual worlds thus constantly threaten to collapse or blend into each other if our attention lapses even momentarily. We have to constantly shift gears as we traverse between worlds in order to make sense of the chaotic, game-like structures that characterize *At Swim-Two-Birds'* textual universe. Using possible worlds theory to delineate such ontological shifts suggests how readers gain a tentative interpretive foothold in O'Brien's complex, disorienting layering of worlds.

Orlick Trellis, Shanahan, Lamont, and Furriskey are members of TAPW 1 who fantasize about wreaking vengeance on Dermot Trellis, with Orlick recording these imaginings in his manuscript, the events of which constitute TAPSW 1.2. Inhabitants of TAPSW 1.2 include Shanahan the philosopher, Justice Lamont, Justice Furriskey, other jurors/judges/witnesses (including Sweeny, F. MacCool, M. Tracy, J. Casey, R. Kiersay, a talking cow), the Pooka, a Sweeny-like Dermot Trellis, and other characters adapted from the Sweeny/*Suibhne* legend (including Moling and an unnamed cleric likely to be Ronan).[9] Dermot is recast as the protagonist of Orlick's rescrambled *Suibhne* tale in TAPSW 1.2, but continual interruptions from characters in TAPW 1 cause the events of TAPSW 1.2 to be restarted several times (O'Brien [1939] 2007, 163, 168, 170)—yet another game-like quality of O'Brien's postmodern textual universe. The impish spirit inherent to *At Swim-Two-Birds* is evident in the explicit, deliberate overlap in the taxonomy of character names between TAPW 1 and TAPSW 1.2, which heightens the affective disorientation we experience in our attempts to make sense of O'Brien's tangled textual worlds.

Toward the end of *At Swim-Two-Birds*, while TAPSW 1.2 Dermot is on trial for his life and about to be put to death, Teresa finds "to her surprise" in TAPW 1 that Dermot's room is empty—an unusual occurrence, since we learn early on that he rarely leaves his bed and spends his days mostly in a drugged coma (O'Brien [1939] 2007, 214). It is only when, by "a curious coincidence," she accidentally burns "the pages which made and sustained the existence of Furriskey and his true friends" in TAPW 1 that "just at that moment, Teresa heard a knock at the hall-door," and it turns out to be Dermot (215). The "curious coincidence" of TAPW 1 Dermot's reappearance immediately after Teresa burns the pages containing TAPSW 1.2 strongly suggests that intrauniverse relations between the two worlds have been deliberately muddied, as O'Brien coyly implies the confluence of Dermots from TAPW 1 and TAPSW 1.2.[10] Dermot's identity comes into question, since "taxonomic compatibility" (Ryan 1991, 33) between the two worlds becomes an "undecidable relation": is this an instance of "transworld identity" (Bell and Alber 2012, 171) or of "homonymy"? (Ryan 2001, 232). Leaving this accessibility relation indeterminate leaves room for our playful imaginations to fill these gaps as we will, reinforcing the fluid shapes of worlds operating according to the principle of maximal departure.

Conclusion: An Aesthetics of Play

Postmodern texts like *At Swim-Two-Birds* frequently foreground fiction's "text-as-game" mode, whereby much of the readerly pleasure we encounter in these texts is driven by their engagement of our cognitive capacities in their play with "informational chaos" (Ryan 2001, 240). A large part of the fun involved is the difficult yet pleasurable process of navigating these texts' complex worlds, which are not simply given but gradually uncovered during the reading process.

Play, which I argue is the dominant aesthetic mode of postmodern fiction, has been identified by "neuroscientists, developmental biologists, psychologists, social scientists, and researchers" to be a "profound biological process" that correlates to cognitive processing (Brown and Vaughan 2010, 5, 33–35). Drawing on the neuroscientific work of Nobel laureate Gerald Edelman, Stuart Brown and Christopher Vaughan note that human "perceptual experiences are coded within the brain in scattered 'maps,'" the vitality of which "depends on the active and incessant orchestration of countless details. It seems likely that this orchestration happens most fully through play" and our engagements in "storytelling, art," and other sorts of play activities (35–36; see also Brian Boyd's chapter, "Art as Cognitive Play," in *On the Origin of Stories* [2010, 80–98]). By attending to textual cues such as the position, frequency, and nature of the novel's deviations from the AW, my analysis works to explicate one way by which readers orchestrate the myriad details involved in our cognitive processing of ontologically complex postmodern fictional worlds.

One possible objection that may be raised against my use of possible worlds theory to interpret texts like *At Swim-Two-Birds* is that the approach—in its "clean" delineation of worlds—violates postmodern fiction's fundamental spirit of entropic play. I do not deny that postmodern novelists intend for these worlds to appear extremely chaotic, but I attempt to critically elucidate the text in a way that best approximates the reading experience by using textual cues that mediate accessibility relations to account for how readers deal with the textual mayhem. I suggest that many postmodern fictional worlds are designed to *simulate* pandemonium, forcing the formal instinct to kick into play as readers attempt to dispel the feeling of vertigo and restore stability of perception in order to apprehend the novel's larger concerns (in the case of *At Swim-Two-*

Birds, with metafictionality and parodying sociocultural politics). Furthermore, as I pointed out in my analysis, there are certain characteristics of O'Brien's textual universe that remain indeterminate or undecidable; thus, my use of the possible worlds approach is not incompatible with postmodern fiction's purposeful chaos and ambiguity but functions as a useful heuristic tool to explicate some of the implicit cognitive tasks we likely engage in when we encounter such anarchic texts.

The revised possible worlds model works as an interpretive apparatus that allows readers to establish provisional formal order based on textual cues. Through our participation in their puzzle- or game-like structures, postmodern texts partly shift the onus of co-orchestrating narrative form onto readers. In this way, postmodern literature redefines aesthetic experience by bilocating the form-impulse: both as part of the author's textual design and of readers' participation in the task of cognitively coconstructing the textual universe.

Notes

1. Experiential reality not only refers to readers' firsthand knowledge and experience of the AW but also includes various forms of textual knowledge (fictional or otherwise) that we use as frames of reference in the AW (Ryan 1991, 54). Thus, depending on each individual's experience, knowledge, and "literary competence" (Culler 1980, 101), readers' sense of what departs from experiential reality will vary.

2. Critics including Andrew Shipe (1997, 291) and Monique Gallagher (2005, 2) observe that no other chapters appear in the rest of the novel.

3. Cathal G. Ó Háinle (1987) notes that the use of "various kinds of linguistic register and stylistic detail is utterly haphazard" (42), while Herman (1997, 144) observes that O'Brien's use of "register-switching" and "register-mixing" makes it difficult to rely solely on stylistic delineations to order narrative structure in *At Swim-Two-Birds*.

4. Ryan explains *homonymy* as "a proper name borne by two different characters" (2001, 232), while the term *transworld identity* has been used by numerous critics to describe a character's "identity across possible worlds" (Mackie and Jago 2013; cf. Ryan 1991, 52).

5. We are cued to consider narrated events from Falconer's poem as a satellite world of the TAW (rather than of TAPW 1) because we are explicitly told that this is a poem that the student-narrator peruses in "a volume [he took] from the mantelpiece" (O'Brien [1939] 2007, 207, 209–10).

6. The play on nomenclature arguably creates an "undecidable relation" (Ryan 1991, 39), since readers are unable to determine for certain if this Dermot refers only to the mythological Diarmuid or if the two Dermots (Gráinne's Diarmuid and Dermot Trellis) have been playfully cobbled together.

7. Crucially, the figure of Finn MacCool has repeatedly weaved back and forth between the pages of AW Celtic myth and history: "Originally a mythological figure . . . confined in the learned lore of the eighth, ninth and tenth centuries," Finn was then believed to be a historical figure by eleventh-century chroniclers, only to be displaced yet again "to the realm of mythology" by later historians (Ó Hainle 1987, 15; Oṭoiu 2012, 302). O'Brien reverses this displacement in *At Swim-Two-Birds* by transposing myth into (fictional) history once more, insistently exposing their porous frontiers.

8. Ó Háinle identifies this scene as being modeled on two Fenian tales, where Conán is drawn from *Feis Tighe Chonáin* (or "The Feast in Conán's House"), while the remaining four characters are drawn from *Tóraigheacht an Ghiolla Dheacair* (alternately known as "The Pursuit of the Hard Gilly / Difficult Servant" or "The Adventures of the Troublesome Fellow") (Ó Háinle 1997, 25, 32; Oṭoiu 2012, 304; MacKillop 2004).

9. *Buile Suibhne* recounts the legend of Mad King Sweeny, whose violent temper and confrontations with the cleric Ronan lead the latter to put a curse on him (O'Keeffe 1913). The bulk of the *Suibhne* narrative deals with the consequences of this curse, with Sweeny eventually finding absolution with the help of the cleric Moling shortly before his death.

10. The physical abuse sustained by Dermot in TAPSW 1.2—extracts from Orlick's manuscript note that many of Dermot's bones were broken (O'Brien [1939] 2007, 194)—does not seem to translate to any (lasting?) physical damage on Dermot in TAPW 1 once the pages sustaining the existence of Furriskey and company are burnt. TAPW 1 Dermot does, however, seem to carry physical traces of TAPSW 1.2 Dermot's time in the woods, going by the "dead leaves attached to the soles of his poor feet" and his being attired in a "night-shirt," since TAPSW 1.2 Dermot was unceremoniously yanked out of bed and sent on his travails when Orlick's narrative began (182, 215, 163).

References

Alber, Jan. 2009. "Impossible Storyworlds—and What to Do with Them." *Storyworlds: A Journal of Narrative Studies* 1:79–96.

Aldama, Frederick Luis. 2015. "The Science of Storytelling: Perspectives from Cognitive Science, Neuroscience, and the Humanities." *Projections* 9 (1): 80–95.

Aldama, Frederick Luis, and Patrick Colm Hogan. 2014. *Conversations on Cognitive Cultural Studies: Literature, Language, and Aesthetics*. Columbus: Ohio State University Press.

Asbee, Sue. 1991. *Flann O'Brien*. Boston: Twayne Publishers.

Bateson, Gregory. 2006. "A Theory of Play and Fantasy." In *The Game Design Reader: A Rules of Play Anthology*, edited by Katie Salen and Eric Zimmerman, 314–28. Cambridge MA: MIT Press.

Bell, Alice, and Jan Alber. 2012. "Ontological Metalepsis and Unnatural Narratology." *Journal of Narrative Theory* 42 (2): 166–92.

Bohman-Kalaja, Kimberly. 2007. *Reading Games: An Aesthetics of Play in Flann O'Brien, Samuel Beckett, and Georges Perec*. Champaign IL: Dalkey Archive Press.

Booker, M. Keith. 1995. *Flann O'Brien, Bakhtin and Menippean Satire*. Syracuse NY: Syracuse University Press.

Boyd, Brian. 2010. *On the Origin of Stories: Evolution, Cognition, and Fiction*. Cambridge MA: Belknap Press.

Brooker, Joseph. 2005. *Flann O'Brien*. Devon: Northcote House Publishers.

———. 2010. "Irish Mimes: Flann O'Brien." In *A Companion to Irish Literature*, vol. 2, edited by Julia M. Wright, 176–92. Malden MA: Wiley-Blackwell.

Brown, Stuart, and Christopher Vaughan. 2010. *Play: How It Shapes the Brain, Opens the Imagination, and Invigorates the Soul*. New York: Avery.

Burgess, Anthony. 1985. "Probably a Masterpiece." In *Alive Alive O': Flann O'Brien's "At Swim-Two-Birds,"* edited by Rüdiger Imhof, 70–72. Dublin: Wolfhound Press.

Cahn, Steven M., and Aaron Meskin, eds. 2008. *Aesthetics: A Comprehensive Anthology*. Malden MA: Blackwell Publishing.

Caillois, Roger. (1958) 1961. *Man, Play, and Games*. Translated by Meyer Barash. New York: Free Press.

Calinescu, Matei. 1987. *Five Faces of Modernity: Modernism, Avant-Garde, Decadence, Kitsch, Modernism*. Durham NC: Duke University Press.

Clissmann, Anne. 1975. *Flann O'Brien: A Critical Introduction to His Writings (The Story-Teller's Book-Web)*. Dublin: Gill and Macmillan.

Comer, Todd A. 2008. "A Mortal Agency: Flann O'Brien's *At Swim-Two-Birds*." *Journal of Modern Literature* 31 (2): 104–14.

Culler, Jonathan. 1980. "Literary Competence." In *Reader-Response Criticism: From Formalism to Post-Structuralism*, edited by Jane Tompkins, 110–17. Baltimore MD: Johns Hopkins University Press.

Currie, Gregory. 2004. *Arts & Minds*. Oxford: Oxford University Press.

Detweiler, Robert. 1976. "Games and Play in Modern American Fiction." *Contemporary Literature* 17 (1): 44–62.

Dewsnap, Terence. 1993. "Flann O'Brien and the Politics of Buffoonery." *Canadian Journal of Irish Studies* 19 (1): 22–36.

Dole, Nathan Haskell. 1902. Foreword. In *Aesthetical and Philosophical Essays*, vol. 7, by Friedrich Schiller. Boston: F. A. Niccolls.

Doležel, Lubomír. 2010. *Possible Worlds of Fiction and History: The Postmodern Stage*. Baltimore MD: Johns Hopkins University Press.

Dufrenne, Mikel. 1973. *The Phenomenology of Aesthetic Experience*. Translated by Edward S. Casey, Albert A. Anderson, Willis Domingo, and Leon Jacobson. Evanston IL: Northwestern University Press.

Eco, Umberto. 1979. *The Role of the Reader: Explorations in the Semiotics of Texts*. Bloomington: Indiana University Press.

Egenfeldt-Nielsen, Simon, Jonas Heide Smith, and Susana Pajares Tosca. 2008. *Understanding Video Games: The Essential Introduction*. New York: Routledge.

Flor, Carlos Villar. 2011. "Flann O'Brien: A Postmodernist Who Happens to Be a Thomist." *Review of Contemporary Fiction* 31 (3): 62–77.

Gallagher, Monique. 2005. "Frontier Instability in Flann O'Brien's *At Swim-Two-Birds*." In *"At Swim-Two-Birds" by Flann O'Brien: A Casebook*, edited by Thomas C. Foster. Normal: Dalkey Archive Press. http://www.dalkeyarchive.com/product/at-swim-two-birds-by-flann-obrien/.

Gass, William H. 1998. Introduction. In *At Swim-Two-Birds*, by Flann O'Brien, v–xviii. Normal: Dalkey Archive Press.

Habermas, Jürgen. 2002. "Modernity—an Incomplete Project." In *The Anti-aesthetic: Essays on Postmodern Culture*, edited by Hal Foster, 1–13. New York: New Press.

Herman, David. 1997. "Toward a Formal Description of Narrative Metalepsis." *Journal of Literary Semantics* 26 (2): 132–52.

Herman, David, Manfred Jahn, and Marie-Laure Ryan, eds. 2005. *Routledge Encyclopedia of Narrative Theory*. London: Routledge.

Hopper, Keith. 2011. *Flann O'Brien: A Portrait of the Artist as a Young Postmodernist*. 2nd ed. Cork: Cork University Press.

Huizinga, John. (1950) 1955. *Homo Ludens: A Study of the Play-Element in Culture*. Boston: Beacon Press.

Humicke, Robin, Marc LeBlanc, and Robert Zubek. 2004. "MDA: A Formal Approach to Game Design and Game Research." Northwestern University. http://www.cs.northwestern.edu/~hunicke/pubs/MDA.pdf.

Hutcheon, Linda. 1988. *A Poetics of Postmodernism: History, Theory, Fiction*. New York: Routledge.

Imhof, Rüdiger, ed. 1985. *Alive Alive O': Flann O'Brien's "At Swim-Two-Birds."* Dublin: Wolfhound Press.

Iser, Wolfgang. 1980. "The Reading Process: A Phenomenological Approach."
In *Reader-Response Criticism: From Formalism to Post-structuralism*, edited
by Jane Tompkins, 50–69. Baltimore MD: Johns Hopkins University Press.

Jameson, Fredric. 1984. "Postmodernism: Or, the Cultural Logic of Late
Capitalism." *New Left Review* 146:53–92.

———. (1995) 2009. "Transformations of the Image in Postmodernity."
In *Beauty*, edited by Dave Beech, 107. London: White Chapel Gallery;
Cambridge MA: MIT Press.

Jenkins, Henry. 2006. "Game Design as Narrative Architecture." In *The Game
Design Reader: A Rules of Play Anthology*, edited by Katie Salen and Eric
Zimmerman, 670–89. Cambridge MA: MIT Press.

Kant, Immanuel. (1790) 1971. "From 'Critique of Judgment.'" In *Critical Theory
Since Plato*, translated by J. H. Bernard, edited by Hazard Adams, 377–99.
New York: Harcourt Brace Jovanovich.

———. (1790) 1978. *The Critique of Judgement*. Translated by J. C. Meredith.
Project Gutenberg.

———. (1790, 1978) 2008. "Critique of Judgement." In *Aesthetics: A
Comprehensive Anthology*, edited by Steven Cahn and Aaron Meskin.
Malden MA: Blackwell Publishing.

Knight, Stephen. 1985. "Forms of Gloom." In *Alive Alive O': Flann O'Brien's "At
Swim-Two-Birds,"* edited by Rüdiger Imhof, 86–101. Dublin: Wolfhound Press.

LeBlanc, Marc. 2006. "Tools for Creating Dramatic Game Dynamics." In *The
Game Design Reader: A Rules of Play Anthology*, edited by Katie Salen and
Eric Zimmerman, 438–59. Cambridge MA: MIT Press.

Lyotard, Jean-François. 1984. *The Postmodern Condition: A Report on
Knowledge*. Translated by Geoff Bennington and Brian Massumi.
Minneapolis: University of Minnesota Press.

Mack, Michael. 2011. *How Literature Changes the Way We Think*. London:
Continuum.

Mackie, Penelope, and Mark Jago. 2013. "Transworld Identity." In *Stanford
Encyclopedia of Philosophy*. http://plato.stanford.edu/archives/fall2013
/entries/identity-transworld/.

MacKillop, James. 2004. *A Dictionary of Celtic Mythology*. Oxford: Oxford
University Press.

Mays, J. C. C. 1985. "Literalist of the Imagination." In *Alive Alive O': Flann
O'Brien's "At Swim-Two-Birds,"* edited by Rüdiger Imhof, 81–86. Dublin:
Wolfhound Press.

McHale, Brian. 1987. *Postmodernist Fiction*. London: Methuen.

Mellamphy, Ninian. 1985. "Aestho-autogamy and the Anarchy of Imagination:
Flann O'Brien's Theory of Fiction in *At Swim-Two-Birds*." In *Alive Alive

O': *Flann O'Brien's "At Swim-Two-Birds,"* edited by Rüdiger Imhof, 140–60. Dublin: Wolfhound Press.

Mercier, Vivian. (1962) 1969. *The Irish Comic Tradition.* London: Oxford University Press.

Meyer, Jürgen. 2011. "Flann O'Brien's Anti-esotericism: *The Third Policeman* and *The Dalkey Archive*." *European Journal of English Studies* 15 (3): 267–78.

Murphy, Neil. 2005. "Flann O'Brien." *Review of Contemporary Fiction* 25 (3): 7–41.

Murphy, Neil, and Keith Hopper, eds. 2011. "Editors' Introduction: A(nother) Bash in the Tunnel." *Review of Contemporary Fiction* 31 (3): 9–20.

Nolan, Val. 2011. "Flann, Fantasy, and Science Fiction: O'Brien's Surprising Synthesis." *Review of Contemporary Fiction* 31 (3): 178–90.

O'Brien, Flann. (1939) 2007. *At Swim-Two-Birds.* In *Flann O'Brien: The Complete Novels.* New York: Everyman's Library.

Ó Háinle, Cathal G. 1987. "Fionn and Suibhne in *At Swim-Two-Birds*." *Hermathena* 142:13–49.

O'Keeffe, J. G., ed. 1913. *Buile Suibhne (The Frenzy of Suibhne).* 1629–1722. London: Irish Texts Society. https://archive.org/details /builesuibhnethefl2okee.

Oțoiu, Adrian. 2012. "Hibernian Choices: The Politics of Naming in Flann O'Brien's *At Swim-Two-Birds*." In *Name and Naming: Synchronic and Diachronic Perspectives*, edited by Oliviu Felecan, 295–309. Newcastle upon Tyne: Cambridge Scholars Publishing.

Pavel, Thomas G. 1986. *Fictional Worlds.* Cambridge MA: Harvard University Press.

Pier, John. 2005. "Metalepsis." In *Routledge Encyclopedia of Narrative Theory*, edited by David Herman, Manfred Jahn, and Marie-Laure Ryan, 303–5. London: Routledge.

Rescher, Nicholas. 1973. "Possible Individuals, Trans-world Identity, and Quantified Modal Logic." *Nous* 7:330–50.

Robin, Thierry. 2009. "Flann O'Brien and the Concept of Ideology." In *Political Ideology in Ireland: From the Enlightenment to the Present*, edited by Olivier Coquelin, Patrick Galliou, and Thierry Robin, 162–79. Newcastle upon Tyne: Cambridge Scholars Publishing.

———. 2011. "Representation as a Hollow Form, or the Paradoxical Magic of Idiocy and Skepticism in Flann O'Brien's Works." *Review of Contemporary Fiction* 31 (3): 33–48.

Ryan, Marie-Laure. 1991. *Possible Worlds, Artificial Intelligence, and Narrative Theory.* Bloomington: Indiana University Press.

———. 2001. *Narrative as Virtual Reality: Immersion and Interactivity in Literature and Electronic Media.* Baltimore MD: Johns Hopkins University Press.

———. 2005a. "Narrative, Games, and Play." In *Routledge Encyclopedia of Narrative Theory*, edited by David Herman, Manfred Jahn, and Marie-Laure Ryan, 354–56. London: Routledge.

———. 2005b. "Possible-Worlds Theory." In *Routledge Encyclopedia of Narrative Theory*, edited by David Herman, Manfred Jahn, and Marie-Laure Ryan, 446–50. London: Routledge.

Salen, Katie, and Eric Zimmerman, eds. 2006. *The Game Design Reader: A Rules of Play Anthology*. Cambridge MA: MIT Press.

Schiller, Friedrich. (1794) 1902. *Aesthetical and Philosophical Essays*, vol. 7. Edited by Nathan Haskell Dole. Boston: F. A. Niccolls.

Shea, Thomas F. 1992. *Flann O'Brien's Exorbitant Novels*. Cranbury: Associated University Presses.

Shipe, Andrew. 1997. "Flann O'Brien (1911–1966)." In *Modern Irish Writers: A Bio-critical Sourcebook*, edited by Alexander G. Gonzalez, 289–95. Westport CT: Greenwood Press.

Shusterman, Richard. 2000. *Pragmatist Aesthetics: Living Beauty, Rethinking Art*. 2nd ed. Lanham MD: Rowman & Littlefield.

Smethurst, Paul. 2000. *The Postmodern Chronotope: Reading Space and Time in Contemporary Fiction*. Amsterdam: Rodopi.

Stevenson, Randall. 2000. "Greenwich Meanings: Clocks and Things in Modernist and Postmodernist Fiction." *Yearbook of English Studies* 30:124–36.

Stewart, Susan. 1978. *Nonsense: Aspects of Intertextuality in Folklore and Literature*. Baltimore MD: Johns Hopkins University Press.

Sutton-Smith, Brian. 2006. "Play and Ambiguity." In *The Game Design Reader: A Rules of Play Anthology*, edited by Katie Salen and Eric Zimmerman, 296–313. Cambridge MA: MIT Press.

Taaffe, Carol. 2008. *Ireland through the Looking-Glass: Flann O'Brien, Myles na gCopaleen and Irish Cultural Debate*. Cork: Cork University Press.

Vygotsky, L. S. 1978. *Mind in Society: The Development of Higher Psychological Processes*. Edited by Michael Cole, Vera John-Steiner, Sylvia Scribner, and Ellen Souberman. Cambridge MA: Harvard University Press.

Walton, Kendall. (1970) 2008. "Categories of Art." In *Aesthetics: A Comprehensive Anthology*, edited by Steven M. Cahn and Aaron Meskin, 521–37. Malden MA: Blackwell Publishing.

———. (1978) 2008. "Fearing Fictions." In *Aesthetics: A Comprehensive Anthology*, edited by Steven M. Cahn and Aaron Meskin, 637–50. Malden MA: Blackwell Publishing.

Waters, Maureen. 1984. *The Comic Irishman*. Albany: State University of New York Press.

Waugh, Patricia. 1984. *Metafiction: The Theory and Practice of Self-Conscious Fiction*. London: Methuen.

Welch, Robert Anthony. 2014. *The Cold of May Day Monday: An Approach to Irish Literary History*. Oxford: Oxford University Press.

Zeki, Semir. 2009. *Splendors and Miseries of the Brain: Love, Creativity, and the Quest for Human Happiness*. Malden MA: Wiley-Blackwell.

6 Logical Contradictions, Possible Worlds Theory, and the Embodied Mind

JAN ALBER

The basis of possible worlds theory is "the set-theoretical idea that reality—the sum of the imaginable—is a universe composed of a plurality of distinct elements. This universe is hierarchically structured by the opposition of one well-designated element, to all the other members of the set" (Ryan 2005, 446). Possible worlds theorists such as Lubomír Doležel, Umberto Eco, Thomas Pavel, Ruth Ronen, and Marie-Laure Ryan place the actual world (AW), the world in which we are all located, at the center of their model, while what they call "alternate possible worlds" (APWs) (such as our dreams, visions, utopias, hallucinations, and fictional narratives) revolve around the center (the AW) to which they are all connected and form alternatives. Furthermore, the relations between APWs and the AW may involve different types of accessibility. An APW can entertain closer or more distant relations to the AW, but in general, a world only counts as being an APW if it is accessible from the AW, the world at the center of the system.

In 1699 Gottfried Wilhelm Leibniz imposed a restriction on possible worlds by arguing that "possible things are those which do not imply a contradiction" (1969, 513). This statement clearly influenced the ways in which theorists and critics have since thought about APWs in general and fictional worlds in particular. Marie-Laure Ryan writes that the most common view in possible worlds theory associates possibility with logical laws: "Every world that respects the principles of non-contradiction and the excluded middle is a PW" (2005, 446). From this vantage point, worlds that include or imply contradictions are unthinkable or empty. Indeed, the standard view in logic is that if a single contradiction enters a system of propositions, anything can be inferred, and it becomes impossible to construct a world out of these propositions (Goldstein 2005, 92).

However, Marie-Laure Ryan has shown that this view is too strict in the case of fiction because readers of literary narratives do not treat logical inconsistencies as an excuse for giving up the attempt to make inferences: "If contradictions are limited to certain areas—to what [she calls] the holes in a Swiss cheese—then it remains possible to make stable inferences for the other areas and to construct a world" (2006, 671n28). She also writes that "texts such as nonsense rhymes, surrealistic poems, the theater of the absurd, or postmodernist fiction may liberate their universe from the principle of noncontradiction" (Ryan 1991, 32; see also Ryan 2009).

Similarly, Ruth Ronen elaborates on the notion of logical impossibility as follows: "Although logically inconsistent states of affairs are not restricted to specific literary periods or genres, with postmodernism, impossibilities, in the logical sense, have become a central poetic device, which shows that contradictions in themselves do not collapse the coherence of a fictional world" (1994, 55; see also Ashline 1995; Littlewood and Stockwell 1996; and Stefanescu 2008). The philosopher Graham Priest likewise argues that "there are, in some undeniable sense, logically impossible situations or worlds. . . . In particular, a [logically] impossible world/situation is (partially) characterized by information that contains a logical falsehood but that is closed under an appropriate inference relation" (1997, 580; see also Priest 1998). His short story "Sylvan's Box" (Priest 1997), for example, confronts its readers with a box that is empty and full at the same time. The narrator describes this box as follows: "At first, I thought it must be a trick of the light, but more careful inspection certified that it was no illusion. The box was absolutely empty, but also had something in it. . . . *The experience was one of occupied emptiness. . . . The box was really empty and occupied at the same time. The sense of touch confirmed this*" (Priest 1997, 575–76, emphasis added).

Lubomír Doležel is also willing to entertain the idea of logically impossible worlds. However, he argues that the writing of impossible worlds in the strict logical sense "is, semantically, a step backward in fiction making; it voids the transformation of nonexistent possibles into fictional entities and thus cancels the entire world-making project. However, literature turns the ruin of its own enterprise into a new achievement: in designing impossible worlds, it poses a challenge to the imagination no less intriguing than squaring the circle" (1998, 165).[1] My own position parallels that of Ryan, Ronen, and Priest and therefore goes beyond the thesis that Umberto Eco presents in *The Limits of Interpretation*: Eco merely points out that logically impossible worlds can be "mentioned" because "language can name nonexistent and inconceivable entities." But he argues that we can draw nothing but "the pleasure of our logical and perceptual defeat" from them (1990, 76–77).

In J. K. Rowling's *Harry Potter and the Prisoner of Azkaban*, for instance, Hermione Granger receives a time-turner that allows her to attend several classes at the same time. According to Professor Dumbledore, the time-turner enables the same person "to be in two places at once" (Rowling 1999, 528). In the case of this fictional world, Hermione can be at different locations at the same time. Hence, *p* and non-*p* are simultaneously true. This APW violates the principle of noncontradiction, but I do not see how or why this logical impossibility should lead to the reader's perceptual defeat. I argue that readers can accept such a scenario under certain conditions. In this specific case, they can attribute the logical inconsistency to the possibility of magic in the represented world.

In contrast to Eco, who simply gives up the interpretive process, I will show in this chapter that readers can indeed make sense of worlds that contain logical contradictions. For me, all propositions representing events or states of affairs are ultimately the result of somebody's subjective experience or imagination. In other words, all narrative representations—regardless of whether they involve logical impossibilities or not—somehow reflect human motivation, which is part of their very texture (see also Fludernik 1996; Ludwig 1999, 194). Like Ruth Ronen, therefore, I refuse to view logical impossibilities as incompatible with the notion of fictional world and with sense-making operations; rather, I see them as a "domain for exercising . . . creative powers" (Ronen 1994, 57) that we as readers are invited to make sense of.

Jan-Noël Thon distinguishes between two types of logical impossibility. On the one hand, he discusses the representation of logically incompatible situations (such as the various scenarios or plotlines listed in Robert Coover's "The Babysitter" [1969]). On the other hand, he mentions local situations that contain logical contradictions (such as Hermione's magical ability to be at two locations at the same time). Thon comments on this distinction as follows: "As far as the narrative representation of local situations is concerned, I tend to agree with Lubomír Doležel (and others) that situations represented as contradictory are not imaginable, or at least not imaginable in the ways that situations represented as noncontradictory are" (2016, 59).

In this chapter, I will deal with both kinds of logical impossibility. As I will show, it is not only the case that humans can come to terms with lists of logically incompatible scenarios; we can also process local (fictional) situations in which, say, a character is here and not here at the same time (or one in which the narrator or a character is alive and dead simultaneously).

More specifically, I argue that it is because logical contradictions elicit emotional responses—they may make us feel uneasy, confused, afraid, fearful, joyful, or pleased—that we build interpretations on the basis of the "experiential feel" (Caracciolo 2014, 55) they evoke in us.[2] Despite the existence of logical impossibilities in the storyworld, we can enact what happens in the narrative. In the case of *Harry Potter and the Prisoner of Azkaban*, for instance, we enact Hermione's attending two different classes at the same time (including her feelings of delight regarding this possibility). It is joyful to experience how this likeable overachiever outsmarts the school system at Hogwarts. As Caracciolo explains, "The main thrust of enactivism is that experience, far from being the computational process whereby we construct an internal model of the environment, is an embodied, evaluative exploration of the world" (2014, 97). Caracciolo also writes that "while the imaginative contents and experiential qualities of reading fiction may deviate from real-world engagements, the underlying structure of interaction is the same: readers respond to narrative on the basis of their experiential backgrounds" (5).

My readings of logically impossible phenomena are based on the notions of enactivism and the embodied mind, that is, the idea that mental processes can be found on a continuum with brain-related bioevolutionary phenomena and cultural practices such as storytelling (Varela, Rosch, and Thompson 1991). Karin Kukkonen and Marco Caracciolo distinguish between first- and second-generation theories in the cognitive sciences as follows: "'Second generation' refers to a specific strand in contemporary cognitive science, one foregrounding the embodiment of mental processes and their extension into the world through material artifacts and cultural practices. 'First generation' theories in the cognitive sciences conceive of the mind as based on abstract, propositional representations. Like a computer, the first-generation mind would process information as largely independent from specific brains, bodies, and sensory modalities" (2014, 261).

Like Kukkonen and Caracciolo, I foreground the fundamental embodiment of mental processes. My basic argument here is that our emotional reactions to logical contradictions serve as a first orientation or "protointerpretation": it is because of our bodily reactions that we deal with logical impossibilities in the first place.

Let me discuss some examples of APWs that contain logical contradictions by first highlighting the emotional effect that they have on me before moving on to more detailed interpretations. I define an emotional response as one specific type of bodily reaction to narratives. More specifically, I follow Patrick Colm Hogan, who discusses emotions in terms of four components. For him, emotions involve (1) eliciting conditions that then evoke (2) a feeling or phenomenological tone. This feeling in turn leads to (3) an expressive outcome (i.e., physiological manifestations of the emotion), and this outcome then determines (4) our attentional focus (2003, 169–70). My examples concern different narrative parameters. In what follows, I will look at logical contradictions in relation to narrators, narrative endings, and temporalities.[3] Furthermore, my examples are ordered in such a way that the degree of incoherence increases as I move from one example to the next: the texts of my corpus become more and more extreme.

Logical Contradictions in Fictional Worlds

Dead Narrators

As Franz Karl Stanzel has shown, there are authors who present the gradual dissolution of a dying first-person narrator's consciousness up to the threshold of life. He calls this type of narration "dying in the first person" and argues that "the difficulties arising from the presentation of the death of a narratorial 'I' have not deterred authors from selecting the first-person form for the fictional presentation of this extreme situation" ([1979] 1984, 229–32, 229). As I will show, various authors even go one step further and confront us with narrators who have already died but are for some reason still capable of narrating. Such narrators violate the principle of noncontradiction because they are alive (i.e., not dead) and dead (i.e., not alive) at the same time.

Alice Sebold's novel *The Lovely Bones*, for instance, opens as follows: "My name was Salmon, like the fish; first name, Susie. I was fourteen when

I was murdered on December 6, 1973" (2002, 5).[4] Later on, we learn that the narrator, who was raped and murdered by her neighbor, Mr. Harvey, has entered heaven and speaks from there (16). In the words of Lisa Zunshine, we are here presented with "a violation of our intuitive ontological expectations, which forces us to reconsider all familiar social scenarios concerning death" (2008, 72). *The Lovely Bones* transcends our real-world parameters, and we are invited to work on our reading frames to come to terms with the novel's storytelling situation. I argue that we are urged to activate our knowledge about people who are alive (and able to tell stories) and our awareness of the fact that the dead cannot speak. In a second step, we combine these schemata to picture a scenario in which somebody who is dead nevertheless speaks to us.

When we are confronted with dead narrators, we can generate new frames by blending preexisting schemata. Mark Turner explains the process of blending by pointing out that "cognitively modern human beings have a remarkable, species-defining ability to pluck forbidden mental fruit—that is, to activate two conflicting mental structures . . . [such as *corpse* and *living person*] and to blend them creatively into a new mental structure . . . [such as *speaking corpse*]" (2003, 117). As an example, Turner mentions the character of Bertran de Born in Dante's *Inferno*. This character is "a talking and reasoning human being who carries his detached but articulate head in his hand like a lantern." Turner argues that "this is an impossible blending, in which a talking human being has an unnaturally divided body" (1996, 62, 61).

From my vantage point, the described blending process goes hand in hand with our emotional reactions to such figures. While Bertran de Born (like the ghosts in Gothic novels) presumably elicits feelings of fear, the phenomenological tone in the case of *The Lovely Bones* is of a different nature. The following passage gives readers an idea of what it is like to experience heaven in the novel. As recipients, we can enact the experiences of Susie Salmon: "When I first entered heaven I thought that everyone saw what I saw. That in everyone's heaven there were soccer goalposts in the distance and lumbering women throwing shot put and javelin. That all the buildings were like suburban northeast high schools built in the 1960s" (Sebold 2002, 16). Later on, the first-person narrator tells us that each dead person inhabits his or her own private version of heaven: "After a few days in heaven, I realized that the javelin-throwers and the shot-putters and the boys who played basketball on the cracked blacktop were all in their own version of heaven. Theirs just fit with mine—didn't duplicate it precisely, but had a lot of the same things going on inside" (17).

In the words of Caracciolo, readers enact the narrator's consciousness just as they enact the represented narrative space (in this case, the space of heaven) by "simulating a hypothetical bodily-perceptual experience on the basis of both their experiential background and the textual cues" (2014, 104).[5] In my case, the elicited phenomenological tone is one of calmness and contentedness.

These feelings serve us a first clue regarding an interpretation of this dead narrator scenario. *The Lovely Bones* invites us to picture a situation in which a dead girl continues to interact with the world she had to leave. Perhaps one can explain this scenario in terms of our difficulties to envision death as the definite end of our existence or in terms of the wishes of the bereaved that the dead somehow continue to exist. Indeed, Greta Olson argues that the position of the narrator highlights "the novel's major theme: How does a lovable family, each member of which is both frail and human, all too human in her or his frailty, move on after one of its members has been brutally ripped out of its midst?" (2005, 138). For instance, at one point, Susie's father builds "a balsa wood stand to replace" her, and he starts talking to her: "Susie, my baby, my little sailor girl, . . . you always liked these smaller ones [ships in bottles]" (Sebold 2002, 46). In this context, Mark Turner points out that "a child who died in the past is still mentally with us. The child never leaves, is always there to cast her shadow on the day, even though our days have changed radically since her death. In the blend, we can imagine her living and appropriately aged" (2002, 16).

On the other hand, one might also argue that in this storyworld, the dead Susie continues to interact with the actual world because heaven actually exists and allows her to right a wrong. In other words, readers are urged to posit a transcendental realm in which the dead narrator can still act, and her dealings make sure that poetic justice is achieved after all. The dead Susie is objectively involved in Mr. Harvey's punishment through death at the end of the novel, and it is highly unlikely that he will enter heaven as well. Both of my readings are in fact based on my first emotional reaction: the wish of the bereaved that the dead may somehow continue to exist and the idea of poetic justice closely correlate with feelings of calmness and contentedness.

Multiple Endings

B. S. Johnson's "Broad Thoughts from a Home" is a fictional narrative that contains logical contradictions of a different kind. This short story confronts its readers with a list of mutually exclusive endings. It "ends" as follows:

> *Magnanimous gesture*: the reader is offered a choice of endings to the piece. *Group One: The Religious.* (a) The quickest conversion since St. Paul precipitates Samuel into the joint bosoms of Miss Deane and Mother Church. (b) A more thorough conversion throws Samuel to the Jesuits. (c) A personally delivered thunderbolt reduces Samuel to a small but constituent quantity of impure chemicals. *Group Two: The Mundane.* (a) Samuel rapes Miss Deane in a state of unwonted elation. (b) Miss Deane rapes Samuel in a state of unwonted absentminded-ness. (c) Robert rapes both of them in a state of unwonted aplomb (whatever that may mean). *Group Three: The Impossible.* The next post contains an urgent recall to England for (a) Samuel (b) Robert (c) both; on account of (i) death (ii) birth (iii) love (iv) work. *Group Four: The Variable.* The reader is invited to write his own ending in the space provided below. If this space is insufficient, the fly-leaf may be found a suitable place for any continuation. Thank you. (1973, 110)[6]

The enactment of these endings involves a certain experiential feel: I find this proliferation of endings rather amusing. I think it is funny that Johnson refuses to provide a clear ending or definite closure and instead presents us with a list of endings (but I can see that others might find this disorienting, worrisome, or annoying).

Let me take the elicited phenomenological tone as the starting point of my interpretation. The ontological pluralism of this passage may in fact serve different purposes. To begin with, these endings ridicule our rea-derly expectations concerning a stable and reliable ending that provides closure. Many narratives (such as Shakespearean plays, Victorian novels, and Hollywood films) have a definitive ending (such as a wedding or the death of the protagonist). "Broad Thoughts from a Home," by contrast, tries to take us out of the realm of the familiar and the well-known. This narrative invites us to actively reflect upon our expectations regarding stability and security through its anticlosural or open-ended character.

In addition, we are invited to laugh at ourselves and our (perhaps ridiculous) yearning for closure.

Alternatively, one can explain the various endings of Johnson's short story by assuming that "the contradictory passages in the text are offered to the readers as material for creating their own stories" (Ryan 2006, 671). From this perspective, the narrative serves as a construction kit or collage that invites free play with its elements. "Broad Thoughts from a Home" invites us to choose the ending that we prefer for whatever reason.[7] This interpretation closely correlates with Roland Barthes's ideas about "the birth of the reader," which, according to him, must be "at the cost of the death of the Author" ([1968] 2001, 1470). Barthes argues that "to give a text an Author is to impose a limit on that text, to furnish it with a final signified, to close the writing. . . . When the Author has been found, the text is 'explained'—victory to the critic" (1469). In stories such as "Broad Thoughts from a Home," however, the author cannot be found. Johnson is absent and does not guide his readers at all. Hence, they are urged to make up their own minds, choose their own endings, and construct their own stories. As in my first example, the initially elicited phenomenological tone (i.e., the impression that Johnson's list of logically incompatible endings is amusing or funny) feeds into the playfulness with which my two readings correlate.

Time Travel into the Past

My final and most difficult example concerns time travel into the past. As we all know, time travel is not possible in the real world but common in genres such as fantasy and science fiction. In such texts, the characters are in the possession of either a magical device or a time machine that enables them to visit the worlds of the past (or sometimes the future). It is perhaps also worth noting that journeys into the past are markedly different from journeys into the future: "In spite of its psychological plausibility, time travel into the past seems to be a logical impossibility, because any alteration of history is implicitly paradoxical" (Stableford 2006, 532).[8] The logical impossibility of time travel into the past is usually illustrated on the basis of the so-called grandfather paradox, which poses the following questions: "What happens if an assassin goes back in time and murders his grandfather before his (the assassin's) own father is conceived?

If his father is never born, neither is the assassin, and so how can he go back to murder his grandfather?" (Nahin [1997] 2011, 114, see also 7).[9]

The basic argument is that if we travel into the past and change the past by killing our grandfather, we also change the present because we no longer exist. This new present would make it logically impossible for us to travel into the past in the first place. The impossibility of time travel into the past is also asserted by the nuclear physicist Enrico Fermi, who argues that "the absence of present evidence of time travellers from the future is proof enough of the impossibility of time travel into the past" (Stableford 2006, 534). In an interview, Fermi said, "If we are not alone [in the universe], where are they?" (Stableford 2006, 178–79).

However, once we accept the possibility of time travel in an APW, we can easily picture situations in which history is changed (through interventions by the time traveler) so that certain events in the past are determined by instances of time travel in the present. Science fiction narratives typically form causal loops because despite the time traveler's interventions, it is still the case that time in the storyworld moves forward so that the past "automatically" leads to the present and the present to the future. Brian Stableford argues that "such causal loops . . . have an intrinsic aesthetic fascination, . . . especially when they are ingeniously convoluted" (2006, 354).

Robert A. Heinlein's short story "All You Zombies" confronts its readers with an excessive number of perverted causal sequences through which an intersexual time traveler creates himself and in addition becomes both his father and his mother.[10] "All You Zombies" is told by a time traveler who works as a bartender at Pop's Place in New York City. In 1970 he meets an unnamed man who calls himself "unmarried mother" (Heinlein [1959] 1980, 205) because he writes stories in confession magazines for women. This man tells the first-person narrator (i.e., the bartender) that he used to be a little girl who was left at an orphanage in Cleveland in 1945. In 1963 she was impregnated by an older man who then left her: "He . . . kissed me good night and never came back" (208). After having given birth to her daughter "Jane" (211) in 1964, which involved "a Caesarian" (209), the doctors discovered that the mother was in fact intersexual and that complications during the birth procedure forced them to turn her into "a man" (209). The unnamed man also tells the bartender that the baby was "stolen from the hospital nursery" (210). We are here invited to enact the experiences of the "unmarried mother." Heinlein's short story urges us to address the question of what it is like to have such experiences. I feel pity for the unnamed man who seems to be an innocent victim: s/he was an orphan; s/he was abused by an older man; the baby was taken away; and s/he was forced to undergo a sex change.

In the second part of "All You Zombies" this sad bar story turns into a convoluted science fiction/time travel narrative. To begin with, the bartender informs the unnamed man that he knows the whereabouts of the father of the baby: it is in fact the unnamed man himself. In the bar's storeroom, the bartender reveals himself to be a temporal agent, and with the help of his time machine, a "USFF Coordinates Transformer Field Kit, series 1992, mod. II" (Heinlein [1959] 1980, 212), the two characters travel back in time to the city of Cleveland, Ohio, in 1963, and we learn what actually happened in the unnamed man's life:

1. On April 3, 1963, the unnamed man meets his former female/intersexual self (before s/he underwent a sex change), and they become a couple (212–13).
2. The time agent travels to March 10, 1964, in Cleveland and steals the baby ("Jane") to whom the intersexual person (the former self) has given birth in the meantime (213).
3. The temporal agent takes the baby back to September 20, 1945, in Cleveland and leaves her at an orphanage (where she will eventually develop into the intersexual woman the unnamed man has sex with in 1963) (213).
4. The time agent travels to April 24, 1963, in Cleveland to pick up the unnamed man after he has impregnated his former female/intersexual self (213–14).
5. On August 12, 1985, the temporal agent leaves this person (who is now a man due to the sex change) at the *Sub Rockies Base* (214, emphasis original), the time patrol he works for, where the man will then gradually become the temporal agent we read about.
6. The time agent returns to November 7, 1970, in New York City to give his share of the bar to the day manager (215).
7. The temporal agent travels to January 12, 1993, to sleep at the Sub Rockies Base (215).

"All You Zombies" contains various reversed causalities in which an earlier event is caused by an instance of time travel at a later point in time. Furthermore, we gradually learn that all the figures in the story (including the baby) are "instances from the same character trace" (Ryder 2003, 217). Since the unnamed man impregnates his former female/intersexual self, he is both the father and the mother of Jane. Furthermore, the baby, who gets taken to the year 1945 by the time traveler, develops into the female/intersexual version of the unnamed man of 1963, who in turn develops into the unnamed man, who talks to the bartender in New York in 1970. Finally, at the Sub Rockies Base, the unnamed man of 1985 develops into the time traveler, who has ultimately caused all the events (starting in 1945) by traveling into the past from his present, that is, 1993.[11] The most important reversed causality has to do with the fact that the narrator travels back in time to create himself, which can aptly be described as a "strange act of self-creation *ex nihilo*" (Gomel 2010, 53).

Elana Gomel argues that this "splintering of the temporal continuity of the self" parallels the postmodernist idea of the "death" of the traditional humanist subject (2010, 53). Indeed, at first glance, the excessive time traveling that leads to the coexistence of character duplicates seems to be yet another postmodernist celebration of the multiplicity of conflicting positions that the subject can assume in the multifaceted world in which we live. Stuart Sim, for instance, defines the postmodern understanding of the self as follows:

> Postmodernism has rejected the concept of the individual, or "subject," that has prevailed in Western thought for the last few centuries. For the latter tradition, the subject has been a privileged being right at the heart of cultural process. Humanism has taught us to regard the individual subject as a unified self, with a central "core" of identity unique to each individual, motivated primarily by the power of reason. . . . [For] . . . postmodernists, the subject is a fragmented being that has no essential core of identity, and is to be regarded as a process in a continual state of dissolution rather than a fixed identity or self that endures unchanged over time. (Sim 2011, 299)

But let me also take my emotional response to this story into consideration. When I experience the various instances of time travel described in Heinlein's narrative, I do not inspect a preexisting picture-like image.

Instead, I engage in an embodied exploration of and thus enact what is experienced in the storyworld. Indeed, "What really matters," according to Caracciolo, is "the experiential nature of our imaginings" (2014, 100).

It is notably not only the case that the "unmarried mother" is extremely sad; the temporal agent and first-person narrator, the ultimate source of the character duplicates, is decidedly unhappy as well. At the end, he realizes that he only deals with versions of him- or herself and thus longs for real Otherness. More specifically, the temporal agent seeks to reach beyond the boundaries of the text by addressing the implied reader: "I *know* where *I* came from—but *where did all you zombies come from*?" (Heinlein [1959] 1980, 215, emphasis original). Furthermore, he says, "*You* aren't really there at all. There isn't anybody but me . . . here alone in the dark. I miss you dreadfully" (215, emphasis original).

Given this desperate (and perhaps even heartbreaking) yearning for real Otherness, one might read this short story as a critique of the solipsism with which the self-referentiality of postmodernism correlates (see also Currie [1998] 2011, 171). In the preface to "All You Zombies," we are told that "solipsism" is "the theory that nothing really exists outside the self." In addition, it "can be a terrifying concept in the hands of a skilled writer like Robert A. Heinlein" (Heinlein [1959] 1980, 205). Indeed, in Heinlein's narrative, the first-person narrator has "engineered a world where he/she . . . is its own first and final cause" (Slusser and Heath 2002, 14) but has become tired of engaging in the construction of convoluted event sequences that involve only duplicate versions of him/herself. Instead, s/he yearns for a real dialogue or confrontation with somebody else, a true encounter of Otherness. In the words of Elana Gomel, "All the significant others in his/her life are him/herself"; "s/he has never had a relationship with an Other" (2010, 57).

Conclusions

From my perspective, logical contradictions in APWs neither cancel the entire world-making project nor imply our perceptual defeat. On the contrary, logical impossibilities can lead to highly stimulating textual phenomena such as the ones discussed in this article. In fictional narratives, characters can be at two different locations at the same time (*Harry Potter and the Prisoner of Azkaban*); a box may be simultaneously empty and full ("Sylvan's Box"); narrators can be alive and dead (*The Lovely*

Bones); narratives may present us with multiple mutually exclusive endings ("Broad Thoughts from a Home"); and the logical impossibility of time travel into the past (including its disconcerting consequences) can be negotiated ("All You Zombies").

As I have shown, we can come to terms with such phenomena by attributing them to, say, the realm of magic; our wishes and desires (including the wish that the dead may continue to exist in a transcendental realm); the mocking of our readerly expectations regarding closure; the idea of narrative as a construction kit that invites free play with its elements; or a critique of solipsism. Regardless of the specific interpretive path we choose to follow, logical impossibilities do not paralyze our interpretive faculties. I believe that this is so because all narratives—even those that contain logical contradictions—activate what Caracciolo calls "our experiential backgrounds." He argues that "engaging with narrative has an experiential feel not only because it activates traces of our past interactions with the world, but also because it reproduces the network structure of *any* kind of experience" (2014, 55, emphasis original).

In other words, our evaluative enactments on the basis of our sensorimotor skills (which are derived from our bodily experience of the world) lead to practical engagements concerning the question of "what it is like" to have a certain experience. In general, APWs that contain logical impossibilities are accessible from the perspective of the AW because they trigger our experiential backgrounds and elicit a certain emotional response. The only limit case I can think of is constituted by logical contradictions that are created for their own sake, as in nonsense poetry, some of Alain Robbe-Grillet's novels, or some of the films by David Lynch. These cases may elicit a certain phenomenological tone, but it is very difficult—if not impossible—to develop our emotional reactions into proper interpretations. In all other cases, the resulting experiential feel serves as an instinctive "protointerpretation" on which we can build our more sophisticated readings. I think it is because the discussed logical impossibilities touch our bodies that we try to interpret them and the APWs in which they occur.

Notes

1. On the other hand, Doležel has recently written (more positively) that postmodernist narratives "do not resolve contradictions but let all flowers,

however incompatible, however disharmonious, bloom in one and the same garden bed" (2010, 5).

2. Marco Caracciolo argues that the term "experiential feel" closely correlates with the reader's ability to get a sense of what it is like to have a certain experience; it denotes "a distinct phenomenal character . . . that cannot easily be reduced to the linguistic meaning of the text" (2014, 101). Similarly, Hans-Ulrich Gumbrecht states that "any form of human communication, through its material elements, will 'touch' the bodies of the persons who are communicating," and this is what he calls "presence effects" (2004, 17).

3. According to James Phelan and Wayne C. Booth, "The narrator is the agent or, in less anthropomorphic terms, the agency or 'instance' that tells or transmits everything—the existents, states, and events—in a narrative to a narratee" (2005, 388). Narratives are often argued to consist of beginnings, middles, and endings. Endings, in turn, may or may not provide closure, which refers to "the satisfaction of expectations and the answering of questions raised over the course of any narrative" (Abbott 2005, 65–66). Temporalities are in a sense more basic than stories or plots: story (or plot) entails time (or temporal progression), but temporal progression does not necessarily entail plot (or story).

4. Dead narrators proliferate in twentieth- and twenty-first-century fiction: the narrators of Samuel Beckett's "The Calmative" (1954), Flann O'Brien's *The Third Policeman* (1967), Vladimir Nabokov's "Terra Incognita" (1968), Nabokov's *Transparent Things* (1972), Robertson Davies's *Murther and Walking Spirits* (1991), Percival Everett's *American Desert* (2004), and one of the narrators of Orhan Pamuk's *My Name Is Red* (2001) are also dead; the narrator of "Past," the first section of Ali Smith's *Hotel World* (2001), is the ghost of a chambermaid who had fallen into a food elevator, while *Destiny and Desire* (2011) by Carlos Fuentes is narrated by the severed head of Josué Nadal, a young attorney; the narrator of Markus Zusak's *The Book Thief* (2005) is the allegorical figure of Death itself; and in Maggie Gee's *Dying, in Other Words* (1981) and *The Burning Book* (1983), the world ends so that nobody is left to report it—nevertheless, we are presented with reports in both cases.

5. Perhaps one could define Caracciolo's approach as an embodied or enactivist version of Ryan's principle of minimal departure. Ryan's principle predicts that "we project upon [fictional] worlds everything we know about reality, and . . . make only the adjustments dictated by the text" (1991, 51). Ryan argues that readers only alter their realist expectations if a narrative text explicitly tells them to do so. While Ryan's principle involves the idea of real-world knowledge, Caracciolo argues that we engage in an embodied exploration as we enact the narrative on the basis of our prior experiences.

6. Further examples of forking-path narratives are Ts'ui Pen's novel in Jorge Luis Borges's "The Garden of Forking Paths" (1941), Vladimir Nabokov's *Pale Fire* (1961), Ayn Rand's *Night of January 16th* (1963), Alain Robbe-Grillet's *La maison de rendez-vous* (1965), John Barth's "Lost in the Funhouse" in *Lost in the Funhouse* (1968), John Fowles's *The French Lieutenant's Woman* (1969), Robert Coover's "The Babysitter" (1969), Caryl Churchill's *Heart's Desire* (1997), Michael Frayn's *Copenhagen* (1998), the film *Run Lola Run* (*Lola rennt*, 1998) by Tom Tykwer, and Rudolph Wurlitzer's *The Drop Edge of Yonder* (2008). In this context, one can also mention Choose-Your-Own-Adventure Stories, certain computer games, some types of hypertext fiction, and alternate reality games. Christoph Bode discusses all these texts as what he calls "future narratives" (FNs). While many narratives negotiate the future at the level of the content, FNs in the sense of Bode stage the future through their form; they contain "nodal situations" that allow for more than one continuation. These "nodes" are the *conditio sine qua non* of FNs: they use their structure to present the future as open and undecided. FNs thus enable "the reader/player to enter situations that fork into different branches and to actually *experience* that 'what happens next' may well depend upon us" (Bode and Dietrich 2013, 1). In contrast to Bode, I am less interested in the element of choice; I here focus on the logical incompatibility or mutual exclusiveness of the represented scenarios.

7. Similarly, John Ashberry sees Gertrude Stein's "impossible work" as an "all-purpose model which each reader can adapt to fit his own set of particulars" (1957, 251).

8. On the other hand, the physicists Stephen Hawking and Leonard Mlodinow claim that once we have the technological means to do so, "it is possible to travel to the *future*" (2005, 105, emphasis added; see also Nahin [1997] 2011, 29–48).

9. According to Gregory Benford, the so-called many-worlds cosmology is a way of overcoming the grandfather paradox: if one assumes that coexisting universes exist, then one can argue that "the grandson reappeared in a second universe, having traveled back in time, where he shot his grandfather and lived out his life, passing through the years which were forever altered by his act. No one in either universe thought the world was paradoxical" (1993, 186, 189).

10. Another causal loop can be found in Lord Dunsany's play *The Jest of Hahalaba* (1928), where a man receives a copy of tomorrow's newspaper (through magic) and reads his own obituary, which then causes him to die (see Nahin [1997] 2011, 122). In this case, we are presented with a causal loop because the future determines the present (and vice versa). Further examples of

causal loops occur in Robert A. Heinlein's "By His Bootstraps" (1941) and Charles L. Harness's "Time Trap" (1948). See also Brian Richardson's outstanding analysis of reversed causalities in Shakespeare's *Macbeth*. As he demonstrates, the play frequently "inverts the order of cause and effect," and this "submerged 'drama of temporality'" mirrors "the central concerns of the play" (1989, 283–84). Further science fiction novels that contain an excessive number of reversed causalities and display a playful attitude toward identity are Stanislaw Lem's *The Star Diaries* (1971) and David Gerrold's *The Man Who Folded Himself* (1973), both of which I would place on the overlap between science fiction and postmodernism. In *The Star Diaries* Ijon Tichy splits into an uncontrollable number of avatars that continuously argue with each other, while in *The Man Who Folded Himself* Daniel Eakins, the first-person narrator, generates so many character duplicates that he keeps "running into versions of [him]self" (Gerrold 1973, 83) at all times. The narrator describes this populous community of duplicates as follows: "I am not one person. I am many people all stemming from the same root" (86).

11. At the end, the narrator notes that "a Caesarian leaves a big scar but I'm so hairy now that I don't notice it unless I look for it" (Heinlein [1959] 1980, 215).

References

Abbott, H. Porter. 2005. "Closure." In *Routledge Encyclopedia of Narrative Theory*, edited by David Herman, Manfred Jahn, and Marie-Laure Ryan, 65–66. London: Routledge.

Ashberry, John. 1957. "The Impossible." *Poetry* 90:250–54.

Ashline, William S. 1995. "The Problem of Impossible Fictions." *Style* 29 (2): 234–51.

Barthes, Roland. (1968) 2001. "The Death of the Author." In *The Norton Anthology of Theory and Criticism*, edited by Vincent B. Leitch, 1466–70. New York: Norton.

Benford, Gregory. 1993. "Time and *Timescape*." *Science Fiction Studies* 20 (2): 184–90.

Bode, Christoph, and Rainer Dietrich. 2013. *Future Narratives: Theory, Poetics, and Media-Historical Moment*. Narrating Futures. Berlin: De Gruyter.

Caracciolo, Marco. 2014. *The Experientiality of Narrative: An Enactivist Approach*. Berlin: De Gruyter.

Currie, Mark. (1998) 2011. *Postmodern Narrative Theory*. New York: St. Martin's Press.

Doležel, Lubomír. 1998. *Heterocosmica: Fiction and Possible Worlds*. Baltimore MD: Johns Hopkins University Press.

———. 2010. *Possible Worlds of Fiction and History: The Postmodern Stage.* Baltimore MD: Johns Hopkins University Press.

Eco, Umberto. 1990. *The Limits of Interpretation.* Bloomington: Indiana University Press.

Fludernik, Monika. 1996. *Towards a "Natural" Narratology.* London: Routledge.

Gerrold, David. 1973. *The Man Who Folded Himself.* New York: Random House.

Goldstein, Rebecca. 2005. *Incompleteness: The Proof and Paradox of Kurt Gödel.* New York: Norton.

Gomel, Elana. 2010. *Postmodern Science Fiction and Temporal Imagination.* London: Continuum.

Gumbrecht, Hans-Ulrich. 2004. *Production of Presence: What Meaning Cannot Convey.* Stanford CA: Stanford University Press.

Hawking, Stephen, and Leonard Mlodinow. 2005. *A Briefer History of Time.* New York: Bantam Books.

Heinlein, Robert A. (1959) 1980. "All You Zombies." In *The Arbor House Treasury of Modern Science Fiction*, edited by Robert Silverberg and Martin H. Greenberg, 205–15. New York: Arbor House.

Hogan, Patrick Colm. 2003. *Cognitive Science, Literature, and the Arts.* New York: Routledge.

Johnson, B. S. 1973. "Broad Thoughts from a Home." In *Aren't You Rather Young to Be Writing Your Memoirs?*, 91–110. London: Hutchinson.

Kukkonen, Karin, and Marco Caracciolo. 2014. "Introduction: What Is the 'Second Generation'?" *Style* 48 (3): 261–74.

Leibniz, Gottfried Wilhelm. 1969. *Philosophical Papers and Letters*, vol. 2. Edited and translated by Leroy E. Loemker. Dordrecht: Reidel. Originally published in 1699.

Littlewood, Derek, and Peter Stockwell, eds. 1996. *Impossibility Fiction: Alternativity, Extrapolation, Speculation.* Amsterdam: Rodopi.

Ludwig, Sämi. 1999. "Grotesque Landscapes: African American Fiction, Voodoo Animism, and Cognitive Models." In *Mapping African America: History, Narrative Formation, and the Production of Knowledge*, edited by Maria Diedrich, Carl Pedersen, and Justine Tally, 189–202. Hamburg: Lit.

Nahin, Paul J. (1997) 2011. *Time Travel: A Writer's Guide to the Real Science of Plausible Time Travel.* Baltimore MD: Johns Hopkins University Press.

Olson, Greta. 2005. "Introducing Alice Sebold's *The Lovely Bones*." In *Twenty-First Century Fiction: Readings, Essays, Conversations*, edited by Christoph Ribbat, 137–47. Heidelberg: Winter.

Phelan, James, and Wayne C. Booth. 2005. "Narrator." In *Routledge Encyclopedia of Narrative Theory*, edited by David Herman, Manfred Jahn, and Marie-Laure Ryan, 388–92. London: Routledge.

Priest, Graham 1997. "Sylvan's Box: A Short Story and Ten Morals." *Notre Dame Journal of Formal Logic* 38 (4): 573–82.

———. 1998. "What Is So Bad about Contradictions?" *Journal of Philosophy* 95 (8): 410–26.

Richardson, Brian. 1989. "'Hours Dreadful and Things Strange': Inversions of Chronology and Causality in *Macbeth*." *Philological Quarterly* 68 (3): 283–94.

Ronen, Ruth. 1994. *Possible Worlds in Literary Theory*. Cambridge: Cambridge University Press.

Rowling, J. K. 1999. *Harry Potter and the Prisoner of Azkaban*. London: Bloomsbury.

Ryan, Marie-Laure. 1991. *Possible Worlds, Artificial Intelligence, and Narrative Theory*. Bloomington: Indiana University Press.

———. 2005. "Possible-Worlds Theory." In *Routledge Encyclopedia of Narrative Theory*, edited by David Herman, Manfred Jahn, and Marie-Laure Ryan, 446–50. London: Routledge.

———. 2006. "From Parallel Universes to Possible Worlds: Ontological Pluralism in Physics, Narratology, and Narrative." *Poetics Today* 27 (4): 633–74.

———. 2009. "Temporal Paradoxes in Narrative." *Style* 43 (2): 142–64.

Ryder, Mary Ellen. 2003. "I Met Myself Coming and Going: Co(?)-Referential Noun Phrases and Point of View in Time Travel Stories." *Language and Literature* 12 (3): 213–32.

Sebold, Alice. 2002. *The Lovely Bones*. Boston: Little, Brown and Company.

Sim, Stuart. 2011. "Critical Terms: A–Z." In *The Routledge Companion to Postmodernism*, edited by Stuart Sim, 227–304. 3rd ed. London: Routledge.

Slusser, George E., and Robert Heath. 2002. "Arrows and Riddles of Time: Scientific Models of Time Travel." In *Worlds Enough and Time: Explorations of Time in Science Fiction and Fantasy*, edited by Gary Westfahl, George Slusser, and David Leiby, 11–24. Westport CT: Greenwood Press.

Stableford, Brian M. 2006. *Science Fact and Science Fiction: An Encyclopedia*. New York: Routledge.

Stanzel, Franz Karl. (1979) 1984. *A Theory of Narrative*. Translated by Charlotte Goedsche, with a preface by Paul Hernadi. Cambridge: Cambridge University Press.

Stefanescu, Maria. 2008. "World Construction and Meaning Production in the 'Impossible Worlds' of Literature." *Journal of Literary Semantics* 37:23–31.

Thon, Jan-Noël. 2016. *Transmedial Narratology and Contemporary Media Culture*. Lincoln: University of Nebraska Press.

Turner, Mark. 1996. *The Literary Mind*. New York: Oxford University Press.

———. 2002. "The Cognitive Study of Art, Language, and Literature." *Poetics Today* 23 (1): 9–20.

———. 2003. "Double-Scope Stories." In *Narrative Theory and the Cognitive Sciences*, edited by David Herman, 117–42. Stanford CA: CSLI.

Varela, Francisco J., Eleanor Rosch, and Evan Thompson. 1991. *The Embodied Mind: Cognitive Science and Human Experience*. Cambridge MA: MIT Press.

Zunshine, Lisa. 2008. *Strange Concepts and the Stories They Make Possible*. Baltimore MD: Johns Hopkins University Press.

PART 3 | *Possible Worlds and*
Literary Genres

7   Escape into Alternative Worlds and Time(s) in Jack London's *The Star Rover*

CHRISTOPH BARTSCH

"Time" is not only a basic condition of our world and real-life experience but also a constitutive element of the fictional realities evoked by narratives. There are two arguments for this assertion. First, a world can in general be understood as a "constellation of spatiotemporally linked elements" (Ronen 1994, 199). These two parameters, space and time, are the fundamental constituents of what we call "world," whether this be real or fictional. Thus, when we metaphorically call—as narrative theorists commonly do—the virtual domain referred to by a work of fiction a "world," one of the conceptual implications of this notion is that this domain is somehow temporally organized.[1] Second, it is a fundamental assumption in narratology that a fictional plot is a narration of a succession of fictive events (Rimmon-Kenan 2002, 2), and an event necessarily involves an element of change (Schmid 2010, 2). So the *narrativity* of a text depends on its projection of temporal units that function as components of a story. Reciprocally, the reader of a narrative always bears implicitly in mind not only a space *where* but also a time *when* the narrated events take place.

While holding a central position in narrative discourse, time is still a "blind spot" in possible worlds theory, despite its unquestionable significance for narrative world creation.[2] This chapter attempts to fill that gap by focusing on the importance of fictional (and partly *unnatural*) time structures for the evocation of narrative worlds.

On Fictive Time(s)

Fictive sentences describe alternative states of affairs inasmuch as they refer not to real but to imaginary conditions. Similarly, possible worlds stipulated by propositions in the discourse of modal logic and analytical philosophy are also semantic projections of nonactual, that is, counter-factual, situations. In this respect the fictive worlds of literature can analogously be described in the taxonomy of possible worlds (Doležel 1998, 31).[3] But while possible worlds in propositional discourse remain abstract concepts of (total) ways the world might have been (Kripke 1980, 18), the possible worlds of fictional discourse can be regarded as virtual but in a way autonomous: often based on extensively detailed descriptions of their texture, they ostensibly attain a self-sufficient substantiality in the act of reading. As Doležel puts it, "Fictional texts are performative: they call possible worlds into fictional existence" (2010, 42). This property establishes a criterion for distinguishing fictive worlds not only from possible worlds in modal logic but also from possible historiographical images of past conditions and events in our own "real" world. In fact, the statements of historiographical texts are "constative," constructing possible worlds as verifiable (or falsifiable) models of an "actual" past (42). That is to say, the worlds of fictional storytelling should not, even if they coincide in part with reality, be regarded as portrayals of events that might under other circumstances have "really happened." On the contrary, they constitute an "independent parallel ontology" (Ronen 1994, 198). Their "history" is only analogous to our real world in that their courses of events mainly correspond. So this is a matter not just of diverging time lines within one world but of autonomous worlds—"excellent counterparts"—whose history may at times resemble our own but then departs from it to follow its own course (Lewis 2001, 70). Taking up David Lewis's and Marie-Laure Ryan's (1991, 18) indexical concept of actuality, a fictional narrative establishes a *textual actual world* (TAW) in which readers immerse themselves by an act of deictic recentering, recognizing it imaginatively as the ontological heart of an autonomous modal system.

The fundamental semantic premise of possible worlds theory, that fictional narrations evoke autonomous worlds, entails the independence and alterity of narrated time. That is, regarding fictional worlds as ontologically independent systems allows for conceptions of time that differ from our experience of real-world time. Since fictive events do not refer immediately to the real world, their temporal dimension is emancipated from that of "reality," so temporal qualities such as linearity, progression, and so on must be thought of there as contingent (Weixler and Werner 2015, 6). Given that each TAW established in a fictional text possesses what

I call its own *textual actual time* (TAT), the conditions that describe our real-life experience of time could, then, be fundamentally different in the domain of fiction, most notably in the worlds evoked by unnatural narratives. Unnatural phenomena like backward causality and temporal circularity are common scenarios in fantasy, science fiction, and time travel stories (Heinze 2013).

Textual actual time, as I use the phrase, is not exactly the same as the structuralist concept of *storytime*, for the latter solely relates to the duration of the plot (i.e., the time of what is narrated); in this formal respect it mainly functions as a referential parameter for ascertaining *discourse time*. But TAT could be understood as the "higher-level" time that pervades the narrated universe in its entirety: the *diegetic world* as such. Just as Gerárd Genette emphasizes that "the diégèse is . . . not the story but the universe in which the story takes place" (1988, 17), the diegetic time—which I call here TAT—is not the time of the story (storytime) but of the fictive reality in which the course of narrated actions is embedded. TAT, then, points beyond the surface of the story line to the specific fabric of the respective narrated world in its historical and ontological dimension.

However, in spite of their ontological independence, fictive worlds of literature are "parasites of reality"—as Umberto Eco (1989, 63) labeled them—in view of the fact that their mental construction in the act of reading is determined by the reader's knowledge of conditions governing "his" own real world. They are established against the background of reality, that is, the historicocultural "reality" of the viewer (Lewis 1978, 44). Readers imagine fictive worlds to be as like as possible to the actual world they live in, and deviations are only made if they are prompted by the text. More precisely, readers compensate for the inevitable incompleteness of a fictive world (Doležel 1998, 22) by assuming an analogy with the real world—unless a departure from these conventions is indicated either explicitly or retrospectively (e.g., by the later incursion of unnatural events) in the text itself or by the (paratextually marked) conventions of the genre. Ryan calls this basic rule the "principle of minimal departure" (1991, 48).

The assumed agreement of the laws pertaining in fictive worlds with those of the reader's actual world has a profound impact on fictive time, since the reader will assume that fictional time is similar to actual time unless the authorial text stipulates something different. Following the principle of minimal departure, a narrative world will be seen to obey laws of historical and natural sequentiality, whether calendrical, chronological, or chronometrical, analogous to those of our own world. Ronen (1994, 200) observes that this is, in fact, one of the most stable of all constructive mechanisms in the evocation of fictive universes.[4]

On Time and Narrativity

Influenced by perdurantists like Lewis, my further reflections on time as *the* constitutive element of worlds (whether real or fictive) will advance the idea that every possible world consists of numerous *temporal parts* (Lewis 2001, 76). This notion is based on the mereological sense proposed by Lewis, according to whom a world is a maximum sum of entities—for which he uses the student-dorm metaphor of "worldmates" (69)—related to each other in a spatiotemporal framework. In that relation they constitute their unique world: if they are not spatiotemporally related, they necessarily belong to different worlds, between which there can be no causal interdependence (70). Each world in this perdurantist view has spatial as well as "temporal parts" and its own space-time (or analogous) dimension (76); and each temporal part exists at its own specific moment (202; Benovsky 2006, 19). Conversely, every entity within a world consists of many temporal parts: a caterpillar and a butterfly, for example, are distinct temporal parts of one and the same insect (Schwarz 2009, 36). Differences between two temporal parts of one and the same entity are observable and describable as "changes."

These basic considerations are of specific importance for narrative worlds and times because they build a bridge between the notion of possible worlds in general and specific narratological premises of plot. A narratological focus on the parameter of time reveals a difficulty of principle in the application of possible worlds theory arising from the transfer of a static concept from analytical philosophy to the description of narrated worlds, which are, as such, essentially changing and dynamic—for, as previously observed, modal logic regards possible worlds as possible states of the real world (Kripke 1980, 18).

Arthur C. Danto prominently described the basic relation between narration and event as one of explanation, placing individual events or instances in a temporal and causal context: "We require, of stories, that they have a beginning, a middle, and an end. An explanation then consists in filling in the middle between the temporal end-points of a change" (2007, 233). Accordingly, a minimal narration will posit two states (constituting the end points of change) linked temporally and causally by an intermediate explanatory element. And the end point of one event may be the beginning of another, a link in a larger chain that can itself be thought of as an "event."

Temporality is thus the prior condition for *eventfulness*, which is again essential for the *narrativity* of what is told. Therefore, a "narrative" world (in the narrow sense of the word) cannot be based simply on spatial parts (that would just describe a "frozen" environment), it must definitely feature temporal parts that allow the realization of change. In other words, the possible world of a narrative is not just the projection of textual states of affairs as such: it represents a *succession* of textual states (Eco 1979, 235).[5] The start and end points of an event can, then, be understood as temporal parts of a world whose qualitative differences are describable in terms of change. And a narrative text is a set of propositions enacting the fictive states of affairs that constitute the temporal parts of its world.

Conversely, the conventional premise that the worlds evoked by narratives are temporally structured is used as a reading strategy for ordering and making sense of the many states described by a particular text. In the perspective of modal logic, every logically possible proposition requires a possible world in which it is true. Worlds of narrative fiction, however, are constituted not by a single proposition but by a whole set of sentences (or narrative propositions) that the reader has to cohere into a consistent, noncontradictory whole (Csúri 1991, 6). The reader will accomplish that by integrating the textual states into a meaningful succession of events, that is, by ordering them performatively into a continuous structure of temporal parts. Of course, in Danto's notion of narrative explanation, the temporal parts of a narrated world follow each other not just sequentially but causally; but the event to be explained need not be explicitly expressed: it can be left as a gap to be filled by the reader's own cognitive-inferential processes (Martínez 2011, 4).

On External Time and Personal Time

It is a logical consequence arising from the notion of temporal parts that each worldmate, that is, each constituent of the world in question, also consists of temporal parts. Every individual, in fact, can be seen as the sum of its temporal parts, linked through causal dependence of one sort or another into a single lifeline—which in the case of humans is their personal identity (Lewis 2001, 81). Temporal parts of an individual set up a thread connecting the end points of a human life (birth and death) like beads on a string and can be regarded as an individual's personal time line. Following a terminological distinction proposed by Lewis (1986, 69), I call this chain of temporal parts *personal time* in order to distinguish it from the overall continuum of *external time*. Personal time is not personal in the sense of a subjective perception of time.[6] It should be thought of instead as time measured by a wrist watch worn continuously by the person in question. It will normally correspond with external time (i.e., the world's enduring time), just as a personal biography normally corresponds with its own historical time.

This can be different in the worlds of fiction: time travel stories, for example, are unnatural narratives evoking fictive worlds in which this correspondence is overridden. For Lewis, time travel is based on a discrepancy between the external time span separating the moments of departure and arrival, on the one hand, and the personal time covered by the journey, on the other (1986, 67–72). When a time traveler like the main character in Jack London's *The Star Rover* moves into the past, his arrival (moment t_2) immediately follows his departure (moment t_1) in his personal time, but, measured in the continuum of external time, t_2 may be a long way before t_1.

The ambiguity between these two manifestations of time is of special interest with regard not only to time travel stories in particular but to narrative communication in general: stories are often mediated through the voice of a first-person narrator who inhabits the fictive world related there (a "homodiegetic" narrator in Genette's terminology [1980, 248]); furthermore, the narrated world is frequently told from the viewpoint of a focalized figure. As a consequence, the reader of such a narrative has (more or less) direct access to a character's personal time, whereas the external "empirical" time of the narrated world must be abstracted from contextual information. To illustrate this, one might think of an autobiography describing the events and issues of one's personal lifetime vividly and in detail, while external time manifests itself only via chrononyms interspersed throughout the text (the opposite would be a pure chronicle, namely, an enumeration of occurrences situated solely in the domain of external time).

So the integration of temporal parts into a continuous world (i.e., the reader's primary strategy for making sense of fictional narratives) is often made difficult by narrative techniques, for, in contrast with the possible worlds of modal logic, the fictive worlds of storytelling are only accessible through the perspective of a text-internal mediator—a narrator or focalized figure. And their modal heterogeneity may also hinder their integration by recipients, for the fictional "truth" of a narrative proposition is linked to the reliability of its speaker or focalizer. To get a consistent idea of the course of the narrated world, readers of narrative fictions have not only to reconstruct the correct order of textual states but also to consider very carefully whether the textual states stipulated by the narration are "really" temporal parts of the fictive world in question (i.e., components of its external time line) or parts of a personal course of time experienced by a narrating or focalized figure. While an authorial narrator generally conveys a reliable picture of the TAW and its temporality (TAT), the version of the world transmitted by a first-person or internally focalizing narrator may diverge from this.[7]

Following Ryan's (1991, 113–19) idea of modal universes projected by narratives, readers then immerse themselves not into the textual actual world but into the virtual private domain of the figure in question and must reconstruct the reality of the fictive world in the process of reading. Inconsistencies may be resolved by the division of a narrated world into a number of per se coherent subworlds (e.g., private domains) that may have their own temporal structures.

As Ronen puts it, "Temporal relations can serve as a primary criterion for drawing the dividing line between worlds" (1994, 199), so fictive events that cease to fulfill the basic condition of the world's temporal homogeneity have to be attributed to separate (sub)worlds. Different states of affairs in fiction may in this sense be temporal parts of different subworlds.[8] Hence, readers have to decide which of the fictional states of affairs described by the text are temporal parts of the TAW (i.e., parts of the TAT) and which might belong to other temporal (sub)dimensions (e.g., the experienced time of a character's dream).

According to Ryan (1991, 119), plot dynamics requires an initial state of conflict between at least two worlds of such a narrative modal system, for example, between a character's private world and the TAW. What Ryan calls "move" (i.e., change) occurs through the action of a character aiming to achieve an optimum balance between these domains. The fictive time dimension of a narrative cannot, therefore, be reduced to the manifest events of the TAW: it must be seen as a parameter framing numerous, possibly conflicting temporal subsystems. Hence, in order to grasp the complexity of temporal structures pervading the modal universe of the narrative in question, a narratological analysis should consider not only how TAT links discrete events into a storyline but also how the characters' personal times are interrelated with this.

Against the background of these theoretical considerations I will now turn to a tale whose world reveals an extremely complex configuration of time: Jack London's fantasy prison-novel *The Star Rover* (1915). As will be shown in the following sections, the tale is an interesting example of how a narrative can evoke more than one world time, for the protagonist's personal time differs from the text world's external time in a highly unconventional manner.

Narrated Time(s) in Jack London's *The Star Rover*

The Narrated World

The application of possible worlds theory to the various conceptions of time that inform narrated worlds is for the most part confined to fantasy, science fiction, and time travel texts, for which time is often an explicit theme.[9] And time in these instances generally diverges from what we know as "reality." In fact, narratology seems especially interested in time when it is "unnatural" because such deviances bring into focus basic mechanisms of temporal configuration that are usually taken for granted. In London's late novel *The Star Rover*, time is also a constitutive element of the action, but its ontological penetration of the narrated world sets the novel apart from other, more typical time travel texts. Narrated time cannot here be univocally defined, for the novel posits several time dimensions that mutually interact and even amalgamate and that differ in both duration and direction.

London's novel contains the memoirs, published by a fictive editor, of Darrell Standing, one-time professor of agronomy, now an inmate of the federal prison in Folsom, California, condemned to death by hanging. The first-person narrator devotes the remaining hours of his life to chronicling his past eight years in jail with the aim of making the "cotton-wool citizen" (London 1915, 52) aware of the inhuman conditions prevailing in the prisons of the time (Haslam 2008). Standing had been sentenced to life imprisonment for murdering a university colleague. Incarcerated in the notorious San Quentin state prison, he is denounced by a fellow inmate who wants to ingratiate himself with the prison director as an informer. Standing is accused of having smuggled several kilograms of dynamite into the prison for use in a planned breakout and of concealing the explosives in the prison grounds. Constantly tormented by the warders on account of his intellectual superiority, he is now put in solitary confinement in an underground cell and, in order to extract information about the hiding place of the nonexistent dynamite, subjected to increasing periods of torture in the "jacket"—a rough canvas straitjacket enveloping the entire body and tied like a corset at the back. Forced into immobility for hours or even days at a time, Standing suffers stenocardiac pain to the point of losing consciousness. During his hours of "recuperation" out of the straitjacket he manages to communicate—by tapping on the cell wall—with his neighbor, Ed Morrell, who teaches him a secret technique he calls "the little death" (London 1915, 252). This enables Standing to free his mind temporarily from his racked body and to escape mentally from present place and time to reinhabit the bodies indwelt by his immortal soul in former lives. Among many astral journeys only summarily or anecdotally mentioned, Standing describes at some length his earlier life as the Dutch sailor Adam Strang, whose brilliant career at the court of a sixteenth-century Korean king ended abruptly with a palace intrigue, compelling him to live henceforth as a beggar and vagrant; or as the eight-year-old Jesse Fancher, whose family was murdered in a Mormon ambush in Mountain Meadows while leading a trek to the American West; or, again, as Ragnar Lodbrog, Roman ambassador, who witnessed the sentencing of Christ in ancient Palestine; as the French Count Guillaume de Sainte-Maure, beset by curial intrigues in medieval Paris; or as the shipwrecked English sailor Daniel Foss, stranded for eight years on a rock-bound island in the ocean. When he finally makes a bid to escape and strikes a warder in the face, Standing's life sentence is changed to death, and in the narrative present he is awaiting execution.

The narrator begins his report with the following words: "I am Darrell Standing. They are going to take me out and hang me pretty soon. In the meantime I say my say, and write in these pages of the other times and places" (London 1915, 8). Strikingly, the past the narrator will write about is plural: while narrative present (the moment of writing) and expected future (after writing) are spatiotemporally clearly defined (waiting in a prison cell and execution outside the cell, respectively), the past extends not only to the years of the narrator's imprisonment but to other, quite separate continua. The temporal dimension of an autobiography usually runs from the birth of the narrator to the time of writing, but Standing announces his intention of writing as an eye-witness of times long before his birth. Moreover, he speaks repeatedly of these memories as being of "other worlds," comparing them with a child's intuitive knowledge of things that could not have entered its experience: "These child glimpses are of other-worldness, of other-lifeness, of things that you had never seen in this particular world of your particular life. Then whence? Other lives? Other worlds?" (1).

The Time(s) of the Narrated World

"I write these lines to-day in the Year of Our Lord 1913, and to-day, in the Year of Our Lord 1913, men are lying in the jacket in the dungeons of San Quentin" (London 1915, 59). The present of fictional discourse (and with it the TAW of the novel) maintains wide accessibility relations here to the *actual world* (AW) of the reader, minor deviations being typical of the "realistic" or historical novel (Ryan 1991, 35). Thus the basic spatiotemporal features of the narrated world are analogous to those of the real world: toponyms (San Francisco, San Quentin, and Folsom) and chrononyms (the year 1913) belong to both worlds, for the principle of minimal departure allows no other interpretation. Differences occur only in those entities of the TAW that do not analogously belong to the environment of the AW: the "Folsom Prison 1913" of *The Star Rover*, for all its similarity, diverges from AW reality in one respect: its inmate Darrell Standing. Standing's worldmate Ed Morrell, on the other hand—the man from whom he learns the technique of astral projection—is a counterpart of the real prisoner Edward H. Morrell (1886–1946), and London's detailed descriptions of conditions in San Quentin and of the straitjacket torture derive largely from reports related by Morrell after his release in 1909; these also covered his mental and emotional experiences in jail (Lacassin 1983). There are, then, many correspondences between AW and TAW that also give the fictive events of the tale a "real" relevance. Thus when Standing reviews his work at the end of the novel with the words "I read hastily back through the many lives of many times and many places. I have never known cruelty more terrible, nor so terrible, as the cruelty of our prison system of today" (London 1915, 326), the deictic "our" and "today" refer not only to the present of the TAW but also to that of the reader and to the real abuses of the American prison system at that time.

The principle of minimal departure leads the reader to assume a correspondence between the time of our real world and the diegetic time of the TAW, that is, the textual actual time (TAT), for the linear structure of the respective temporal parts is analogous. Furthermore, this assumed similarity of time lines provides underlying information about the history of the narrated world: the existence of Shakespeare and Napoleon can be taken for granted there, even if neither of them is explicitly mentioned, so the reader has no problem accepting figures like Pilate and Jesus, or the historically documented Fancher family with whom Standing interacts on his astral voyages. The only difference is that the narrative existence of Shakespeare remains virtual, but that of Jesus and the Fancher clan is actual. Thus the many past times and events that Standing relates in the course of the novel fit seamlessly into an implicit history evoked by the reader as latently underlying the TAT.

However, while the time line of the TAW matches that of our actual world, the narrator's (auto)biography does not. The periods he lives through are irreconcilable with our knowledge of a human lifetime, for the auto-diegetically narrated time comprises not only Standing's eight years of imprisonment (1905–13) but also all those passages and periods that lie—sometimes centuries—earlier. This is an inconsistency typical, or indeed constitutive, of the unnatural time travel genre to which *The Star Rover* is sometimes assigned (Rivers 1997, 24). As explained above, time travel can be characterized as a divergence between external time and personal time (using Lewis's terminology). Normally both time lines coincide, but in the case of time travel the course of external time differs from the traveler's personal time. In *The Star Rover* the situation is even more complex because the time travel experiences of the first-person narrator are unconventional, inasmuch as only his spirit regularly returns to past times, while his body stays in the present.

As stated above, Lewis's idea of external time could be identified with the "empirical" time of the fictional world (TAT), whereas personal time is bound to an individual of that world and contains the temporal parts whose sum constitutes that person's identity. Due to its first-person narrator structure, the reader of *The Star Rover* has immediate access only to the personal time of Darrell Standing. His autobiographical memoirs (narrated time) follow the course of this dimension, whereas external time can in the absence of an authorial voice only be indirectly reconstructed by the reader. Hence the continuum of the narration remains linear, despite the time travel episodes: the flow of personal time never falters, irrespective of the temporal part of the TAW in which Standing happens to find himself. During his metempsychoses his body is strapped into the straitjacket in external time (TAT) and suffers the increasing debilitation proper to that dimension; but his spirit moves in a personal time that is independent of TAT. Standing's time travel implies an ambiguity between correlative and divergent temporal relations: when he is mentally in his "real" body, in the narrated present of the prison, his personal time is that of TAT, but when he is "out of his body" this correspondence is broken, and an external past is experienced as the personal present.

Consistently with this perspective, Standing proposes an idea of human personality that closely approximates—albeit on a macrological level—Lewis's understanding of the ego as the sum of its temporal parts: "Since human personality is a growth, a sum of all previous existences added together, what possibility was there . . . to break down my spirit in the inquisition of solitary? I am life that survived, a structure builded up through the ages of the past—and such a past! What were ten days and nights in the jacket to me?—to me, who had once been Daniel Foss, and for eight years learned patience in that school of rocks in the far South Ocean?" (London 1915, 282).

The passage emphasizes the complexity of *The Star Rover*'s temporal asymmetries. Personal time and external time not only diverge, they also differ in duration: Daniel Foss's eight years on his rocky outcrop and Adam Strang's forty years as a tramp on the streets of Korea far exceed the time Standing spends in the straitjacket. Even the inception of a metempsychotic state is accompanied by an extended perception of time: "The extension of time was equally remarkable. Only at long intervals did my heart beat. Again a whim came to me, and I counted the seconds, slow and sure, between my heart-beats. At first, as I clearly noted, over a hundred seconds intervened between beats. But as I continued to count the intervals extended so that I was made weary of counting" (London 1915, 79).

The intervals of Standing's mental time not only are displaced on the axis of TAT but also evidently belong to a different temporal continuum. But before addressing this disparity in detail, Standing's time experience(s) must be subjected to closer ontological scrutiny.

The (Un)reliability of Narrated Time(s)

Standing's experiences are evidently alien to the narrated world (TAW) as well, for he explicitly cautions at the outset of the novel: "I am neither fool nor lunatic. I want you to know that, in order that you will believe the things I shall tell you" (London 1915, 3). Nevertheless, there are further grounds for doubting his reliability as a narrator: not that he seeks consciously to deceive the reader, but the rigors of solitary confinement and the mind-bending torture of the "jacket" might have permanently so twisted his perceptions that one could justifiably interpret them as hallucinations—the more so in view of statements like the following: "Much of this time I was physically numb and mentally delirious. Also, by an effort of will, I managed to sleep away long hours" (60).

This seems to be the line actually taken by a critical figure within the TAW, Standing's fellow inmate Jake Oppenheimer, who dismisses his report of extracorporeal experiences as a "fairy story" (London 1915, 67) and "pipe-dream" (209): "I ain't saying you lied. I just say you get to dreaming and figuring in the jacket without knowing you're doing it" (293). Oppenheimer rationalizes Standing's apparently detailed knowledge of historical persons and events as unconscious traces of conversations, historical reading, museum visits, and so on captured in the peripheral memory that in Standing's delirious state are thrown up in distorted configurations to the surface: "You don't remember that you ever heard of it. . . . But you must have just the same. Though you have forgotten about it, the information is in your brain all right, stored away for reference, only you've forgot where it is stored. You've got to get woozy in order to remember" (294). It does not seem far-fetched to read Standing's experiences in this way as escapist fantasies projected to block, at least internally, the impact of his imprisonment.

Oppenheimer's skepticism finds further justification in Standing's frequent comments on his emotional condition. These already begin with the complaint: "In solitary one grows sick of oneself in his thoughts, and the only way to escape oneself is to sleep" (London 1915, 32); or "there was nothing to do, and my thoughts ran abominably on in vain speculations" (35). When he is not asleep, Standing sinks into consciously evoked imaginations, playing chess with himself, for instance, and becoming in his own words an "expert at this visualized game of memory" (33). These introverted activities force him to "split my personality into two personalities" (33), anticipating the plurality of selves that the prisoner believes himself to undergo in the straitjacket. In this sense his astral journeyings can be interpreted as a fragmentation of the self, a diffusion of the individual personality induced by the prison regime.[10] This is, if anything, confirmed by his comments on the vivid nature of the dreams into which he increasingly sinks during his periods in the "jacket"—even before he has learned from Morrell the ability to separate his mind from his body by an act of will: "During the first period of the jacket-inquisition I managed to sleep a great deal. My dreams were remarkable. Of course they were vivid and real, as most dreams are. What made them remarkable was their coherence and continuity" (63).

Whether Standing really embarks on astral journeys or whether these are not rather the product of a distraught imagination remains entirely undecided. Tzvetan Todorov (1975, 26) sees ontological ambiguity of this sort as constitutive of the fantastic, and Ryan (1991, 37) specifies Todorov's seminal insight in terms of the compatibility between the real and narrated worlds: either the TAW is subject to the same natural laws as the AW, in which case many statements of the narrator are unreliable (i.e., metempsychoses are also impossible in the TAW, and Standing is hallucinating), or the TAW and AW are governed by different laws, in which case a reliable narrator is communicating what the reader understands to be a hybrid "unreliable world" (Jedličková 2008, 297) where astral projections are possible and really experienced by Standing. Caught in the ambiguity, the reader does not know which statements of the autodiegetic narrator are "fictionally true" (i.e., can be coherently integrated into the TAW) and which are "fictionally false." Applied to the time dimension, the question is whether Standing's reincarnations actually transpose him to the TAT (of which they are, therefore, temporal parts) or whether his real experience is purely in the imagination, and the reincarnations are temporal parts of a projected, counterfactual world internal to the fiction. The ambiguity is heightened when research undertaken by the (fictive) editor of Standing's memoirs is explicitly cited in support of their veracity:

"Since the execution of Professor Darrell Standing . . . we have written to Mr. Hosea Salsburty, Curator of the Philadelphia Museum, and, in reply, have received confirmation of the existence of the oar and the pamphlet" (London 1915, 285). Standing, it is asserted, could not have known of the actual existence of this oar, on which his "alter ego," the shipwrecked sailor Daniel Foss, had scratched a message; for although it had been inventoried by the museum as early as 1821, the oar "is not on exhibition in the public rooms" (284).

The Experience of Narrated Time(s)

If one reads Standing's astral journeys as hallucinations whose temporal structure deviates from that of TAT, they can, following Ryan (1991, 119), be classified as *fantasy worlds*. While other private domains might establish specific subjective versions of a TAW based on the knowledge, ignorance, beliefs, desires, intentions, sense of duty, and so on of a figure with respect to its actual world, a fantasy world internal to a narration establishes an independent textual actual subworld modally related (i.e., on a second level) to other such possible subworlds (e.g., book in book, tale in tale, dream, hallucination, fantasy of a fictional character, etc.). Such internal mental transpositions enable a dreamer to believe while dreaming in the world of the dream, and for both dreamer and reader the fantasy world in such a case temporarily replaces the TAW. Such a world creates its own spatiotemporality independent of the TAW/TAT of its master text.

The ambiguity observed above can, therefore, be described as follows: Standing's personal time serves as a continuously available hinge between two external time levels, namely, the external time of the TAW and that of his fantasy worlds. He himself can only view this continuity from the ontologically superior perspective of the TAW. He remembers his experiences in the fantasy worlds, but his various avatars know nothing of Darrell Standing—a state of affairs he seeks to explain on the basis of the chronological course of TAT. Thus his spontaneous expression of identity during his first incarnation as Count Guillaume de Sainte-Maure is that "everything was the natural and the expected. I was I, be sure of that. *But I was not Darrell Standing. . . .* Nor was I aware of any Darrell Standing—as I could not well be, considering that Darrell Standing was yet unborn and would not be born for centuries" (London 1915, 83, emphasis original). Far from subverting the dream hypothesis, such an utterance confirms it, for the self of the dream, as a rule, knows nothing of the dreamer, but the awakened dreamer may well remember the self of the dream.

In this respect, Standing's fantasy worlds reveal a striking consistency in their plot dynamics. His reincarnated selves are invariably confronted with tribulations against which they actively pit their own powers of survival. They anticipate possible situations (temporal parts) of their actual world and give their all to turn a hic-et-nunc deficit to their advantage. In contrast to his avatars, Standing himself, however, has neither hopes, plans, nor fears: condemned to vegetate in the straitjacket, he stoically bears the tortures inflicted upon him and awaits his fate with resignation. He sees no possible future, let alone the prospect of turning it to his advantage: "It seemed certain, if I did not do a miracle, . . . that all the years of my life would be spent in the silent dark" (London 1915, 32). As he has no real hope of change, time compresses to a single extended moment, a temporal part divorced from any form of continuity. In this sense, the prison represents an atemporal microcosm, a heterotopical enclave beyond world and time: "The world, so far as we were concerned, practically did not exist. It was more a ghost-world. Oppenheimer, for instance, had never seen an automobile or a motor-cycle. . . . We were buried alive, the living dead" (162).

When Standing describes his solitary confinement as a "living grave" (London 1915, 37), he is not, then, just referring to the oppressive darkness of the subterranean "cells of silence" (29); and when he greets his fellow prisoners sporadically incarcerated in the neighboring cell as "Dantes . . . in our inferno" (163), he means this not just in reference to the tortures they must undergo but also in analogy to postmortal timelessness. For time "in that dark hole of man's inhumanity" (21) is structured only by the repetitive incursions of the power apparatus: "Time was marked by the regular changing of the guards" (32); and the enduring monotony of his state—"out of the sunshine and the light of day" (15)—is enhanced by the absence of any sense stimulus. Consistently, the stasis of external time threatens to petrify the personal time that the condemned man needs for his integrity: "Time was very heavy" (33), "one could only lie and think and think" (32), and "the hours were very long in solitary" (35).

Faced with the experiential emptiness of solitary confinement and above all of the "jacket," Standing takes refuge in worlds of fantasy bursting with temporal parts from whose contingency and continuity he can reweave the thread of personal time. To escape the extended moment of

TAT he (unconsciously) creates his own worlds with their own time.[11] These alternative spatiotemporal dimensions, with their openness to the future and their potentially realizable prospects, allow him to regain experientiality. His surrogate selves face trials and torture analogous to those of his own situation, but they differ in having a possible future in which the dissonance of their real and sought-for worlds may be resolved. It is this functional link between the disparate episodes of the novel, both among themselves and with the framing narrative, that provides the work with its inner coherence—an aspect that has been widely overlooked.[12] Wandering the dusty streets of the Korean peninsula as a beggar for forty years, the Dutchman Adam Strang never loses sight of his goal: to take revenge on those responsible for his fate. And in the hour of his death he is successful. Daniel Foss sustains eight years of hardship on his rocky island in the unfailing hope that a passing ship may rescue him—which also happens. Jesse Fancher, crossing the hostile deserts of the American West with his fellow settlers and fighting off the Mormon attacks, is led by his vision of a fruitful coastland on the horizon. And Count Guillaume de Sainte-Maure is strengthened in his nocturnal duel with the papal henchmen by the knowledge that he may soon hold his beloved Duchess Philippa in his arms.

These are not just escapist worlds in which Standing can compensate the passivity of his real situation through imaginative flights of fancy—after all, neither Jesse Fancher nor Count Guillaume survives his ordeals.[13] It is, rather, their temporal structure making changes possible (i.e., the potential for eventfulness) that provides the key to the novel, for the dynamic flow of time in Standing's astral journeys through alternative worlds not only complements and relieves the temporal standstill of his imprisonment but also gives it a successive structure of its own. His time travel enables him to face the narrative present of the death cell with equanimity, for this is now temporally filled: the moment of execution—a fixed point toward which time moves—is consciously approaching, and time is consequently no longer stretched to the point of dissolution. In the end Standing-the-narrator can even regret its passing: "I should like to tell more of those far days, but *time in the present is short. Soon* I shall pass" (London 1915, 313, emphasis added); or again: "I sit in my cell now, while the flies hum in the drowsy summer afternoon, and I know that my time is short. Soon will they apparel me in the shirt without a collar" (318).

Time in *The Star Rover* is not only an objective constituent of the actual textual world (TAT) but also, and crucially, a dimension of the narrating subject's inner psychological experience and as such the basis of his individual integrity and identity. Both world and self are narrative constructs: life is a tale, but without time there can be no narration.

Conclusion

Possible worlds theory has relatively neglected the fact that fictional narratives create not only alternative worlds but also alternative times. The use of the plural is crucial here because one and the same narrative will often deal with different kinds of times. In *The Star Rover* the unnatural time travel of the main character can be "naturalized" as only mental, so the two different dimensions typical for a time travel narrative—distinguished as external time and personal time—can be applied here to different worlds: one to the textual actual world, the other to the figure's dreamlike private domain. Since time (alongside space) is *the* basic element for narrative world making, narrative theory—and possible worlds theory in particular—should definitely take concepts of temporality into account. While classical narratology has mainly focused on discourse time and thereby only scratched the surface of narrative time structures, possible worlds theory can and must highlight temporal configurations on the level of story and, furthermore, conceive them as essential coordinates for the blueprints of textual worlds. Doing so, it can, as I have argued, draw on the conceptual frameworks provided by analytical philosophy for dissecting and describing the temporal idiosyncrasies that govern the realms of narrative fiction.

Notes

This chapter is a revised version of an article that originally appeared in German in Antonius Weixler and Lukas Werner, eds., *Zeiten erzählen: Ansätze—Aspekte—Analysen* (2015). My thanks are due to the editors for permission to republish the article in English. Furthermore, I am indebted to Joseph Swann for his translation and helpful comments on this essay.

1. Referring to the virtual domain in a work of fiction as a "world" is exemplified by Dorrit Cohn: "A work of fiction itself creates the world to which it refers by referring to it" (1999, 13).

2. "Unnatural narratology" has recently infused new vigor into this debate. Thus Rüdiger Heinze (2013, 34), following the established distinction be-

tween story and discourse, differentiates unnatural time scenarios at the level of histoire (e.g., the backward flowing time in Martin Amis's *Time's Arrow* [1991]) from unnatural configurations of time at the level of narration (e.g., the back-to-front ordering of episodes in Christopher Nolan's film *Memento* [2000]).

3. Of course, even fictive domains are only "possible" so long as they are logically consistent. As Ryan (2009) has shown, there are quite a few narratives describing "impossible" worlds with paradoxical time configurations.

4. The principle of minimal departure also applies, mutatis mutandis, to the relation between narrative time and narrated time, for, so long as there are no explicit or implicit indications to the contrary, readers may assume that the order of the narrated events follows that of the discourse: "Our first impulse with any tale when the order of telling is clear is to take the order of occurrence to be the same as the order of telling; we then make any needed corrections in accord with temporal indications given in the narrative and with our antecedent knowledge both of what happened and of causal processes in general" (Goodman 1984, 110).

5. As Eco explains, the possible world of a fabula "is not a simple state of affairs, since it starts from a given state of affairs s_1 and through lapses of time $t_1 \ldots tn$ undergoes successive changes of state, so as to reach a final state sn, each state shifting into the next one through lapse of time" (1979, 235).

6. See Mark Currie (2007, 75) for an elaboration of the differentiation between psychological time and clock time.

7. As Currie points out, the character's experience of time should, moreover, be considered in order to avoid misunderstandings regarding the discrepancy between story order and text order: "When analepsis functions in the mode of [a character's] memory, it needn't be viewed as an anachrony at all, since the memory itself is an event in the fictional present" (2007, 75).

8. That the imagined worlds of narrated figures also have temporal parts merely extends the technical metaphor.

9. Many such narrations are inspired by Hugh Everett's quantum-theoretical "many-worlds" interpretation, which bears some resemblance to possible worlds theory but, instead of a causal-linear or cyclical concept of time, postulates a system of continuously fragmenting and multiplying time lines, each of which enacts its own "possible world," giving rise to further time lines and further (parallel) worlds. Everett's fractal multiversum should not, however, be equated with Lewis's (1986, 44; 2001, 70, 208) concept of a plurality of worlds. Ryan (2006) explicitly contrasts the two systems. Moreover, narrations whose figures move between different parallel time lines (e.g., Ray Bradbury's "A Sound of Thunder" [1953]) should be

distinguished from those (like Christoph Ransmayr's *Morbus Kitahara* [1995]) that propose an alternative history: "The former use time travel and other sf [science fiction] devices, whereas in the latter the only imaginative change is historical difference itself" (Hills 2009, 437).

10. Thus, for example, Kenneth Rivers (1997, 29) sees Standing as a paranoiac personality: "What happens to Standing is that the sensory deprivation causes a shattering psychosis. His psyche is smashed into dozens of different personalities each going off to lead a separate life somewhere that there is an environment with which it can interact" (30).

11. In his psychoanalytic analysis of the novel, Glen Paul Bush (1987, 68) similarly distinguished between "real time," "prison time," and a "dream time" bound, on the one hand, to Standing's introspective immersion in his own subconscious and, on the other hand, to archetypical—and hence "transhistorical"—elements of a collective subconscious.

12. For the largely negative critical response to London's novel and the attempts to counter it, see Rivers (1997, 23).

13. My reading of the novel departs decisively here from that of Rivers (see 1997, 11).

References

Benovsky, Jiri. 2006. *Persistence through Time and across Possible Worlds.* Frankfurt am Main: Ontos Verlag.

Bush, Glen Paul. 1987. "Rebellion, Time, and Death as Archetypical Structures in Jack London's Novels: 'Martin Eden,' 'The Iron Hell,' 'The Star Rover.'" PhD diss., Saint Louis University.

Cohn, Dorrit. 1999. *The Distinction of Fiction.* Baltimore MD: Johns Hopkins University Press.

Csúri, Károly. 1991. "Mögliche Welten, Kohärenztheorie der Wahrheit und literarische Erklärung." In *Strukturuntersuchung und Interpretation künstlerischer Texte,* edited by Hans-Georg Werner and Eberhard Müske, 3–14. Halle: Martin-Luther-Universität.

Currie, Mark. 2007. *About Time: Narrative, Fiction, and the Philosophy of Time.* Edinburgh: University Press.

Danto, Arthur C. 2007. *Narration and Knowledge* (including the integral text of "Analytical Philosophy of History"). New York: Columbia University Press.

Doležel, Lubomír. 1998. *Heterocosmica: Fiction and Possible Worlds.* Baltimore MD: Johns Hopkins University Press.

———. 2010. *Possible Worlds of Fiction and History: The Postmodern Stage.* Baltimore MD: Johns Hopkins University Press.

Eco, Umberto. 1979. *The Role of the Reader: Explorations in the Semiotics of Texts*. Bloomington: Indiana University Press.

———. 1989. "Small Worlds." *Versus: Quaderni di Studi Semiotici* 52:53–70.

Genette, Gérard. 1980. *Narrative Discourse*. Translated by Jane E. Lewin. Oxford: Blackwell.

———. 1988. *Narrative Discourse Revisited*. Translated by Jane E. Lewin. Ithaca NY: Cornell University Press.

Goodman, Nelson. 1984. "Twisted Tales—or Story, Study, and Symphony." In *Of Mind and Other Matters*, edited by Nelson Goodman, 109–21. Cambridge MA: Harvard University Press.

Haslam, Jason. 2008. "'Morality Is a Social Fund': Jack London's Strait-Jacket Ethics." In *Bausteine zu einer Ethik des Strafens: Philosophische, juristische und literaturwissenschaftliche Perspektiven*, edited by Hans-Helmuth Gander, Monika Fludernik, and Hans-Jörg Albrecht, 233–49. Würzburg: Ergon-Verlag.

Heinze, Rüdiger. 2013. "The Whirligig of Time: Toward a Poetics of Unnatural Temporality." In *A Poetics of Unnatural Narratives*, edited by Jan Alber, Henrik Skov Nielsen, and Brian Richardson, 31–44. Columbus: Ohio State University Press.

Hills, Matt. 2009. "Time, Possible Worlds, and Counterfactuals." In *The Routledge Companion to Science-Fiction*, edited by Mark Bould et al., 433–41. London: Routledge.

Jedličková, Alice. 2008. "An Unreliable Narrator in an Unreliable World: Negotiating between Rhetorical Narratology, Cognitive Studies and Possible Worlds Theory." In *Narrative Unreliability in the Twentieth-Century First-Person Novel*, edited by Elke D'hoker and Gunther Martens, 281–302. Berlin: de Gruyter.

Kripke, Saul A. 1980. *Naming and Necessity*. Cambridge MA: Harvard University Press.

Lacassin, Francis. 1983. "On the Roads of the Night: A Search for the Origins of 'The Star Rover.'" In *Critical Essays on Jack London*, edited by Jacqueline Tavernier-Courbin, 180–94. Boston: G. K. Hall.

Lewis, David K. 1978. "Truth in Fiction." *American Philosophical Quarterly* 15 (1): 37–46.

———. 1986. "The Paradoxes of Time Travel." In *Philosophical Papers II*, edited by David Lewis, 67–80. New York: Oxford University Press.

———. 2001. *On the Plurality of Worlds*. Malden MA: Blackwell.

London, Jack. 1915. *The Star Rover*. New York: Macmillan.

Martínez, Matías. 2011. "Erzählen." In *Handbuch Erzählliteratur: Theorie, Analyse, Geschichte*, edited by Matías Martínez, 1–11. Stuttgart: Metzler.

Rimmon-Kenan, Shlomith. 2002. *Narrative Fiction: Contemporary Poetics*. New York: Routledge.

Rivers, Kenneth. 1997. "Infinite Identities, Endless Environments: Jack London's 'The Star Rover.'" *Lamar Journal of the Humanities* 23 (2): 21–33.

Ronen, Ruth. 1994. *Possible Worlds in Literary Theory*. Cambridge: Cambridge University Press.

Ryan, Marie-Laure. 1991. *Possible Worlds, Artificial Intelligence, and Narrative Theory*. Bloomington: Indiana University Press.

———. 2006. "From Parallel Universes to Possible Worlds: Ontological Pluralism in Physics, Narratology, and Narrative." *Poetics Today* 27 (4): 633–74.

———. 2009. "Temporal Paradoxes in Narrative." *Style* 43:142–64.

Schmid, Wolf. 2010. *Narratology: An Introduction*. Berlin: de Gruyter.

Schwarz, Wolfgang. 2009. *David Lewis: Metaphysik und Analyse*. Paderborn: Mentis.

Todorov, Tzvetan. 1975. *The Fantastic: A Structural Approach to a Literary Genre*. Ithaca NY: Cornell University Press.

Weixler, Antonius, and Lukas Werner. 2015. "Zeit und Erzählen—eine Skizze." In *Zeiten erzählen: Ansätze—Aspekte—Analysen*, edited by Antonius Weixler and Lukas Werner, 1–22. Berlin: de Gruyter.

8 "As Many Worlds as Original Artists"

Possible Worlds Theory and the Literature of Fantasy

THOMAS L. MARTIN

One would think that a new approach to literature like possible worlds theory would have been welcomed in fantasy studies, if not across literary studies in general. Alas, it was not to be. Or has yet to be. Perhaps possible worlds theorists are the most hopeful of all theorists not only for their mindfulness toward alternate states of affairs but for their belief that the inherent possibilism in literature will ultimately win out over all theoretical, scientific, and political attempts to constrain it. For all the promise, fantasy studies have yet to take full advantage of possible worlds theory.

Possible worlds theory is a flexible modeling device for mapping various domains and the properties that attend them. In literary studies, it is a means of modeling the worlds that literary language presupposes. It can be applied to texts, to realms within texts, to epistemic attitudes of characters as representations of worlds within texts, and so on. Besides these discursive and recursive functions, possible worlds theory can also be used to track theories "outside" of texts as critics position their own worldviews next to texts, and in this way it can serve as a kind of metatheory for sorting critical viewpoints. Along these lines, possible worlds theory has been an important corrective not only to textualism but to all forms of reductive criticism.

"In a Hole in the Ground": A Context, a Problem

Literary studies after World War II took the path of Saussure over Peirce, of Joyce over Borges, of Derrida over Eco. Imagination was out, science was in; romance was out, realism was in. The scientific certainty that structuralists Saussure and Lévi-Strauss seemed to promise would eventually explain everything under the banner of "the humanities." Lévi-Strauss proclaimed, for instance, that "in other branches of study . . . the real question is the question of language. If you solve the problem of the nature and origin of language, we can explain the rest: what culture is, and how it made its appearance, what art is and what technological skills, law, philosophy, and religion are" (Lévi-Strauss 1969 in Charbonnier 1973, 154–55). The promise of the new paradigm ignited literary researchers to find those linguistic structures that explained all of human culture and creativity. This scientism, which captivated literary theory for a time, accorded well with the realism of prominent literary writers Joyce, Lawrence, and Fitzgerald.

It turns out that the rising prestige of realism was only one of many such cycles in literary history, particularly since the eighteenth century, when scientific pressures sought to exclude the fantastic from serious modern literature. But as with all such cycles, the prominence of realism was not the last word in science or art. If World War II taught us anything, it was that human beings were capable of unimaginable evil, or at least evil unimaginable to the realist mind. Progress as we knew it before World War I was dead. Science itself started to shift away from the staid mechanism bequeathed to it by Enlightenment naturalists, even as technologists who realized the dream of Enlightenment science in an Industrial Revolution started with the steam engine and progressed to the atom bomb. The physicists who made possible those developments, though formerly accustomed to classical causation, came face to face with a realm of subatomic reality that called for radical new ways of understanding.

The industrialization of society and nature had shown us by then that nature mechanized is not so hospitable to humanity as once thought and well may end up destroying the planet in a single stroke. The dissatisfaction with mechanistic science extended beyond dystopian concerns and reached the theoretical. Too much of nature excluded by earlier scientists continued to exert itself, and figures like Planck, Schrödinger, and others introduced us to tracts of reality far beyond our received experience and those that resemble fantasy lands more than anything we knew before. These social, historical, and scientific pressures were accompanied by new pressures being felt in the world of literary art. In the same way these other forces began to reshape culture, so too a literary revolution was under way.

Naturally, none of those changes occurs without the usual resistance any long-standing dogma has in letting go. How hard it was to break the modernist spell of realism. This kind of exclusionary aesthetic was felt most keenly when in 1998 the editorial board of Modern Library drew up its list of the one hundred best novels of the century. Joyce's *Ulysses* tops the list, but no fantasy works appear, and science fiction gets only the slightest of nods in a couple of dystopian works. Kennedy's *Ironweed* appears, Beerbohm's *Zuleika Dobson* appears, and Durrell's *Alexandria Quartet* appears. But, for example, nowhere on the list is Tolkien's *The Lord of the Rings*.[1]

Up until the time when Tolkien's work appeared in the 1950s, there was an undercurrent of important books of fantasy literature in the nineteenth century from such authors as Lewis Carroll, George MacDonald, and William Morris. Authors L. Frank Baum, Lord Dunsany, James Barrie, and others kept the growing interest alive with their unique contributions in the early decades of the twentieth century. By the time we reach the middle of the twentieth century, the movement hits a critical mass with the work of Tolkien, C. S. Lewis, and their literary circle at Oxford, known as the Inklings, who not only raised this growing body of literature to a new level but mounted a defense of its aesthetic principles for modern readers in a modern context.

Readers were taking this literature as serious art, though critics still put these works in their place. When Tolkien's *The Lord of the Rings* was published, it attracted a number of negative reviews that from our vantage point several decades later seem a curiosity. Now notorious for their outright dismissal of the new literature, the rejections give some sense of the resistance. Critics like Edmund Wilson called Tolkien's work "balderdash" and "juvenile trash." Robert Flood called the first book in the series "pretentious snobbery." And Philip Toynbee wrote that the books were "dull, ill-written, whimsical and childish," celebrating in his 1961 review that the "books have passed into a merciful oblivion."[2] Since then, other negative criticisms have appeared,[3] but among the early reviews that turned the tide was W. H. Auden's (1956) comment whose truth still eludes some critics but whose significance is central to this chapter: "Mr. Tolkien's world may not be the same as our own."

The resistance to the fantastic in modern literature was long and concerted, and these few quotations give only the flavor of it. An older scholar at a recent International Conference for the Fantastic in the Arts reminded me just how much of a slog it was to be a scholar interested in fantasy literature during these decades and how the work was frowned upon by most in the profession.[4] But when the cultural pressures mounted, the literary institutions that had held out for so long gradually acquiesced. From its midpoint onward, the twentieth century saw an almost unimaginable expansion of interest in literature of the fantastic. As Farah Mendlesohn and Edward James say in their 2009 *A Short History of Fantasy*,

> At the time of writing, thirty-nine out of the forty top-grossing movies worldwide are fantasy or science fiction. J. K. Rowling is one of the world's best-selling authors. Terry Pratchett's books go straight into the hardback best-seller lists. *Star Wars* tie-ins dominate the *New York Times* paperback lists. A show about a cheerleader who kills vampires proved the cult TV hit of the 1990s and sparked a revival of TV fantasy. J. R. R. Tolkien's *Lord of the Rings*, which has never been out of print, topped almost every poll of favourite books taken in the UK at the end of the twentieth century. (1)

Fantasy books sell not in the millions but in the tens of millions of copies, and some of the series in the hundreds of millions, with *The Lord of the Rings* most often chosen in readers' polls as their favorite modern novel. Critics eventually opened up themselves to the literature and came to know what readers knew all along, that these new or revived forms were capable of great literary power and that they gave to readers something realist literature lacked. Add to this list the literary experiments of surrealists like Breton, the stories of magical realists like Borges and Márquez, and the reality-bending fiction of postmodern writers like Philip K. Dick and Ernest Cline, and the pressures were overwhelming. The more critics opened themselves to Auden's dictum on other worlds, the more they saw how aesthetic principles might vary across these worlds and shift as much as their respective terrains and moods.

Perhaps from the canons of realism, these new works were simply a violation of all the literary establishment deemed sacred. But from a broader historical perspective, the assumptions evident in the earlier judgments against this literature may seem astonishing to anyone who looks at the development of literary genres and the expanding universe of forms that world literature is. As William Coyle projected in 1986, "In A.D. 2222 when (or if) historians assess the literature of the late twentieth century, the most obvious trend is certain to be the diminished prestige of realism, which dominated the literary imagination for about seventy-five years" (1).

Of course, as Kathryn Hume reminds us, the two terms *fantasy* and *realism* are deeply connected and mutually supporting.[5] But in ages of strong opinion one way or the other, the fantastic and the real are set in opposition. And yet the more the one begrudges the other its very existence—and seeks a literary order absent the other—the more the other flourishes. Pure literary forms are more a matter for those who write dictionaries than those who write novels. While the work of the dictionary writer is an important one, allied with the theorist who identifies constitutive rules, artists are free to transcend those bounds as much as observe them.

"Where Is Fancy Bred": Toward a Definition of Fantasy

As for the writing of dictionaries, one place to begin is to define fantasy in terms of impossibility. This is the tack editors John Clute and John Grant take in their prodigious *Encyclopedia of Fantasy*. While wise in most judgments, including the remainder of their capacious definition of fantasy literature with its component elements and various forms, their direct link of fantasy to the impossible may be inadvisable.[6] They qualify that impossibility is a matter of perception but that the impossibility itself is the purpose: "The perceived impossibility of these stories *was their point*—that they stood as a counter-statement to a dominant worldview" (1997, 338, emphasis original). Setting aside for a moment the large gulf between impossibility and divergence from a dominant worldview, we might raise another question. In the present volume, does it make a difference if fantasy is about possible or impossible worlds?[7]

In the context of Auden's statement that the fantasist's world "may not be the same as our own," he is quick to add: "But it is a world of intelligible law, not mere wish; the reader's sense of the credible is never violated" (1956). This does not sound like an impossible world. Auden's "world of intelligible law" that "never violate[s]" the reader's "sense of the credible" sounds like something else. It sounds not only possible but like something the author makes believable. Auden's description sounds like the parameters of a story about which we might like to hear, from which we might learn something of value.

What would be an impossible world, anyway? One that is logically contradictory? One that is incredible? Would it be a nonsense world like the one produced by Carroll or Edward Lear? Carroll's "Jabberwocky" is readable by Alice only in a mirror, and though it sounds like nonsense, once she inverts the writing, she exclaims, "It seems to fill my head with ideas—only I don't exactly know what they are!" As later readers follow Carroll's lexical hints, ideas do arise, and a story emerges.[8] The same occurs on occasion with Lear's limericks or the verse of Peter Beagle's butterfly in *The Last Unicorn*, to take two other notable examples. In these cases, nonsense words highlight the creative powers of the mind as it engages literary language, teasing it into meaning, or back out of it again. Where readers find nonsense language in such creative contexts, they readily play verbal games like these and happily explore where they might lead. Often verbal games open up to meaning and project stories or worlds beyond their strange verbal configurations.

Fantasy literature may be about impossible worlds in this more precise sense of logical inconsistency, but this is not what Clute and Grant have in mind. The problem with defining fantasy in terms of impossibility is that it too easily settles into what Lubomír Doležel calls the true-false axis, which situates most traditional literary theory. This mimetic poetics maintains a one-world bias that is as hard to eliminate from literary theory as the realist bias is from literary practice. For this view, the world of experience is true, and fantasy literature is false. In its deviation from the true world of experience lies this literature's impossibility. But another way to approach the issue altogether is Shelley's, who speaks for it as well as any other: "It [poetry] makes us the inhabitants of a world to which the familiar world is chaos" ([1840] 1891, 42). From the viewpoint of the poetic creation, Shelley suggests that the world of perception may have neither the inevitability we think it has nor the highest truth. Tolkien certainly thought that higher truths were more available in fairy tales than in the daily newspapers. In authors like these, we consider not only the idea of the relativity of all worlds real and imagined but also the inherent superiority of literature in the midst of that plurality to deliver clarity and insight. Compare possible worlds semiotician Umberto Eco on the matter: "Who do we think we are? We for whom Hamlet is more real than our janitor?" ([1988] 2008, 331).

All this points to the inherent believability of the literary worlds of the fantastic. In Auden's account above, the fantasy of Tolkien is not less than "a world of intelligible law" where "the reader's sense of the credible is never violated." Auden's twin principles of intelligibility and credibility argue that worlds of fantasy are eminently possible, and while these sto-

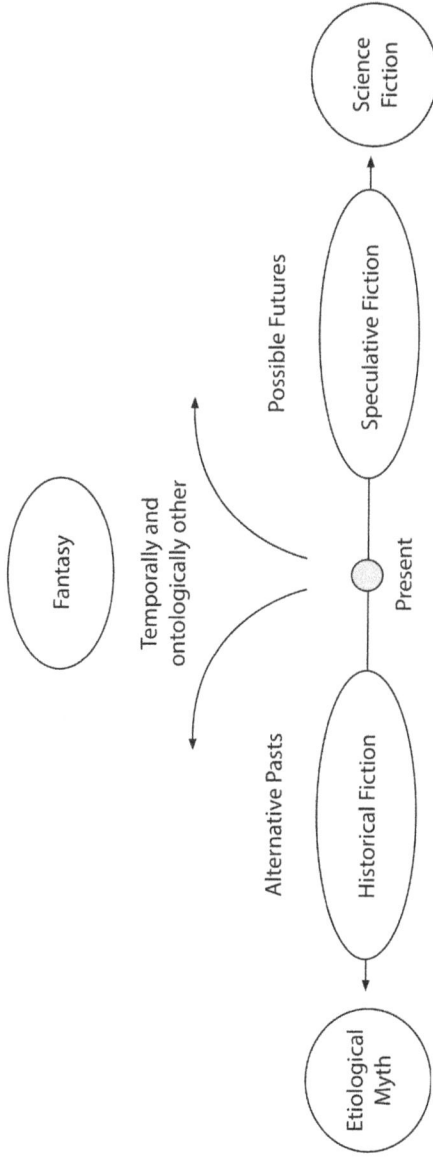

Fig. 8.1. A simple typology of literary worlds based on temporal proximity and remoteness to the reader's assumed reality.

ries make no special appeal to the laws of received science, their internal consistency and the vision and craft by which they are wrought make them compelling on other grounds.

Therefore, instead of referring to real versus impossible worlds, we should speak of actual versus possible worlds. Talk of impossible worlds, or of Eric Rabkin's "direct reversal of ground rules" of reality "turned precisely 180° around" (1976, 14, 28), has been a starting place, but no longer. The approach to fantasy based on a one-world semantics gives way to a possible worlds approach in which a profusion of ontological departures position themselves at various degrees of remoteness and proximity to our received world. Tolkien better distinguishes between the primary world of experience and the secondary world of artistic invention and gets us halfway there. His distinction assumes many artistic worlds and potentially their endless interaction. Proust expresses the idea thus: "Thanks to art, instead of seeing a single world, our own, we see it multiply until we have before us as many worlds as there are original artists" (1948). When we open the semantics of literary kinds in this manner, and not just fantasy, we have available a modeling device that can reckon an extensive typology of literary worlds (fig. 8.1).[9]

Readers do not read these stories in disbelief. They do not typically think, "Well, there is no way this could happen. What I'm reading here is unbelievable." Somehow they understand that what they read is true within the framework of the story. They make assignments about what is true and false there—what is honest and what unreliable, what is reality and what is dream. Those judgments are analogous to judgments they make in the real world. Not every possible world compels readerly belief like this, only those Auden says "do not violate credibility." Fantasy writers go to great lengths to make what otherwise might be incredible into the stuff of readerly belief and wonder.

Always in such discussions someone mentions Coleridge's "suspension of disbelief." Tolkien disagrees that we "suspend our disbelief" when we read fantasy literature, and he again gives some useful guidance. He argues that

> what really happens is that the story-maker proves a successful 'sub-creator.' He makes a Secondary World which your mind can enter. Inside it, what he relates is 'true': it accords with the laws of that

world. You therefore believe it, while you are, as it were, inside. The moment disbelief arises, the spell is broken; the magic, or rather art, has failed. You are then out in the Primary World again. (1947, 60)

Tolkien calls this credence we give to literary fantasy "secondary belief." He insists that readers in these cases do not just suspend disbelief, which perhaps may apply more to the relative inadequacy of linguistic, visual, or dramaturgical vehicles that transport us to the secondary world. But when "the spell" works and we are there, "inside," Tolkien calls this "literary belief." In the same passage where Coleridge speaks of a "suspension of disbelief," he also calls it "poetic faith."

This brings us to some of the positive aspects of a definition of fantasy. Gary K. Wolfe inventories historical definitions of fantasy, and besides the "impossible" a number of other terms recur: "strangeness," "wonder," "astonishment," "desirability," "the marvelous," "the pararational," "the numinous," and "the supernatural."[10] The fantasy story in these cases engages the reader in an imaginative story that may be pure illusion or elaborate symbol, mere whimsy or profound mysticism. But as it creates these listed effects, fantasy turns itself in three directions, the "three faces" of fantasy, according to Tolkien: "the Mystical towards the Supernatural; the Magical towards Nature; and the Mirror of scorn and pity towards Man" (1947, 53). Besides these three incarnations of fantasy and their characteristic interests—the mystical, transcendental, and satirical—we might add other categories, like the ludic and recreational, the monitory and ideal, the wonderland and *Gedankenexperiment*, and others. Across these forms fantasy can connect with nature or the divine, it might play, or it might be the only ready means to certain kinds of knowledge. In this latter case, Shakespeare speaks of the poetic powers of fantasy to figure forth the "forms of things unknown" and Patricia McKillip of the "Wonders of the Invisible World."[11]

Clearly, by broaching these subjects, fantasy literature provides this important service to culture that realism had otherwise discredited or rendered irrelevant. In this way, fantasy literature picks up and concentrates elements from many earlier forms of literature, including ancient epic, medieval romance, religious allegory, folk tale, fairy story, gothic tale, nineteenth-century Romanticism, medieval revivalism, and perhaps other influences as well. Fantasy commences by rejecting the dogmatic realism embodied in the witch from Lewis's *The Silver Chair*, who intones again and again to the children she has imprisoned, "There never was any world but mine" (1953, 154). By freeing readers from the tyranny of received assumptions that may or may not be true, fantasy literature shifts the ground, reorients the frame of reference, and seeks the insight available from new perspectives. All that brings us to a provisional definition: fantasy worlds are literary worlds that are ontologically other than the reader's world of familiar experience, positioned at some degree of proximity or remoteness from that world, that evoke a sense of strangeness, wonder, and the numinous as its figures produce insight, knowledge, and pure diversion. To model those worlds—and how readers reach them and what they find there—requires a theory of possible worlds.

A "Wood between the Worlds": Possible Worlds and Fantasy

Possible worlds theory allows us to move beyond the metaphors of "world" and "otherworld" that fantasy critics sometimes use simply to denote other images of our world. Possible worlds theory emerges in Western poetics when the idea of world that art was said to mirror becomes problematic in light of early modern discoveries. Classical mimesis and medieval allegory were both grounded in the idea that art reflects reality, the reality of this world below or the one above. But as new discoveries led to new pictures of nature, a new poetics developed with them. A fascination arose over the ways the mind could have been mistaken for so long, and a new emphasis arose on the methods of obtaining knowledge and the creative powers of the mind. Cartographers mapped new lands in this world, astronomers mapped new regions of the night sky, and poets, according to Philip Sidney, created altogether new natures he christens "golden worlds." In these developments, artists made use of this greater grasp of both mind and world, as well as of many other worlds artists conceive. Spenser, Marvell, and Traherne all spoke of "other worlds." Renaissance poetics in this way coordinated developments in ontology and epistemology with aesthetic theory.

Those developments were relatively short-lived, however, as the succeeding age found free-form imagination a source of intolerable ambiguity rather than insight and play in the face of a plenitudinous creation. Such inventions were dismissed as mere "fancy"—or "fantasy" in its full form from the Greek. Let this line from Samuel Johnson's *Rambler* 4 suffice for capturing the new attitude: "Why this wild strain of imagination found reception so long in polite and learned ages, it is not easy to conceive" (1750, 21). Mimetic doctrine returns with a vengeance, but imagination not to be repressed returns again with the Romantic period, only to be abandoned again when modern realism doubles down on its positivist aesthetics.

We reach the twentieth century, when aesthetics were naturalized and made scientific, when art was reduced to an observable phenomenon called aesthetic response, and when that response was reduced to something even more observable in the objective form of the text. This new textualism led to a self-referential poetics that not only was unsatisfying for some critics but also, when its scientific pretensions were pierced, led to the nihilism of deconstruction. In his history, Doležel identifies this as the point when the idea of possible worlds reentered literary theory (1990, 52). It happened around the time the philosophy of logic and language were undergoing their own version of the realism-fantasy debate. At one great moment of that debate, Bertrand Russell affirmed that "logic . . . must no more admit a unicorn than zoology can" (1919, 168), and Jaakko Hintikka answered that logic is not about this world alone but all possible worlds.[12] Since the time of Hintikka, Saul Kripke, and Nicholas Rescher, the idea of possible worlds opened up the strictures of a purely realist approach and enriched the philosophy of logic and language, philosophical and lexical semantics, model theory and game theory. In the hands of such theorists as Doležel, Thomas Pavel, and Marie-Laure Ryan, it has enriched other fields in the humanities—from art theory, to narratology, to historiography—and even fields in the sciences—from cognitive science, to particle physics, to cosmology.[13]

In its own way, fantasy literature has been up to this sort of thing for a long time, albeit informally and imaginatively, coaxing readers beyond familiar assumptions to consider all manner of new possibilities. Like Edwin Abbott's *Flatland*, possible worlds theory offers a kind of hypergeometry in which familiar coordinates and dimensions are seen from a wider frame of reference. The match between the theory and the literature is, what we might say, a natural one. Despite this, developments in fantasy theory still linger behind those in science fiction studies. Whether that is due to the uncertainty critics feel about the fitness of theory to fantasy, or because science fiction is largely explicable through scientific rules extrapolated from this world, while fantasy's impulses and ultimate meanings remain elusive to the theoretical mind, is unclear. What is clear is that a robust theory of fantasy is needed that does not falsify the literature, and a number of attempts at theorizing fantasy seem in this regard to fall distinctly short.[14]

A possible worlds theory of fantasy must begin by acknowledging the ontology of fictional worlds. Fantasy texts are about worlds that may or may not be our world. As such, they can be both possible and compelling in their own right. Readers approaching one such novel encounter this first line: "Gormenghast . . . tower, patched unevenly with black ivy, arose like a mutilated finger from among the fists of knuckled masonry and pointed blasphemously at heaven" (Peake [1946] 1992, 9). As they process the narrative, readers relocate their awareness to and ascertain what makes up this other place. The more developed the subcreation, the more they might even lose sight of their own world. Lewis remarked of *The Lord of the Rings*, "Our own world, except at certain rare moments, hardly seems so heavy with its past" (1966, 86). Ryan describes readers' acts of reorienting themselves to the literary text and its own system of actuality and possibility as "fictional recentering" (1991, 18, 21ff.). Rabbits might talk there, rings might possess great powers, and new creatures might roam about governed by laws utterly strange to us. The space of possibility the artist as subcreator shapes in a world of fantasy is the broadest we find in all narrative art. No small task to the creative mind, the form readily separates lesser artists from greater. Tolkien spent some fifty years creating Middle-earth.

That does not necessarily mean that fantasy worlds float in sealed containers over the reader's experiential world and bear no relation to it. Of course, to concede that would be to side with those long-standing objectors who say that fantasy is mere escape. Logically and ontologically, the fantasy world occupies its own space, taking no restraints except what its author and readers give it; but practically, it partakes of the reader's world and all sorts of other relations, with other scenarios and possible offshoots. The world of the reader and the world of the fantasy—as with any literary world—always stand in a two-way relation of comparison, influence, and exchange. Doležel's term for this is "bidirectional exchange": "In one direction, in constructing fictional worlds, the poetic imagination works with 'material' drawn from actuality; in the opposite direction, fictional constructs deeply influence our imaging and understanding of reality" (1998, x). Those relations can be variously theorized in our critical accounts. They are also highlighted in the literature of fantasy itself in many ways as characters pass over thresholds, enter and return through portals, and cross world boundaries inside and outside of their stories.

Pavel (1986) offers a formal account of these interactions he calls "salient structures." Drawing from the work of Kendall Walton, Pavel explains that these structures can be seen from simple games of make-believe to the most sophisticated kind of theatrical representation, where objects in the viewer's immediate surroundings are transformed into objects in a fictional world. So a mud-ball becomes a pie, a stick a sword, a character onstage King Lear, and the like. Elements in the primary world become a gateway to the other world, and the more these elements depart from a one-to-one correspondence with the primary world, the less they are manifestly "dual structures" and the more they become "salient structures." Developing like this, imagined worlds take on a life of their own with their own distinct reality. Pavel remarks that this pattern is also analogous to how religious consciousness relates natural realms to supernatural ones. Salient structures are one important way to think about the interactions between the real world and the worlds of fantasy.

The major study of fantasy from the vantage point of possible worlds theory is Nancy Traill's *Possible Worlds of the Fantastic: The Rise of the Paranormal in Fiction* (1996). As her title indicates, most of her book is devoted to the paranormal, one of the forms of the fantastic, though the principles she articulates shed light on other forms as well. On the way to her typology of fantasy modes, she dismisses the thematic, psychological, and pragmatic accounts as inadequate on their own without a fundamental reckoning of the order of worlds these stories present. The idea of possible worlds orients her account of fantasy.

Another limited approach Traill discusses is the structuralist one of Tzvetan Todorov, whose *The Fantastic* is a major study of one aspect of fantasy literature broadly conceived. Todorov's (1973, 7) is a "generic" approach to the fantastic in which ambiguity plays a key role. Ambiguity manifests itself in what Todorov calls a "hesitation" between natural and supernatural explanations. As soon as a work resolves into either the uncanny or the marvelous, it ceases to be fantastic in Todorov's sense, settling into one of these neighboring genres. This neither-fish-nor-fowl approach of Todorov—rejected by most scholars of the fantastic today—shows at once Todorov's fundamental commitment to structuralism and its limitations. If the fantastic cannot be defined in binary terms, then it must be some halting of the binary process as it generates literary meaning as a matter of course. Always on the cusp of a binary, neither A nor B, the fantastic must maintain its fundamental ambiguity to the last line of the story. While some stories might fit the description, many more do not. While *The Turn of the Screw* makes the cut, clearly the fantasies of Rabelais, Swift, Coleridge, and Tolkien do not.

Moving beyond Todorov, Traill argues that the fantastic is not a genre but a *"universal aesthetic category"* evident over many different forms and media: "It cuts across genres. It may be a play, short story, novel, ballad; we may find it in the form of a painting or a statue, or perhaps a symphony or an opera" (1996, 7). As a universal aesthetic category, its artistic expressions might also involve elements of philosophy and religion. This is where Traill's argument for a theory of possible worlds comes to the fore. She accommodates the kinds of literary worlds she gathers under this universal category, linking them all in the manner they relate a supernatural realm to a natural one. She posits six classes of relation among these domains: "central or peripheral, functional or auxiliary, dominant or subordinate" (8). As they combine, these relations make for four broad kinds of fantasy world, including a fifth as a subtype.

First is the *ambiguous* mode, which is the kind of fantasy Todorov describes. In it "the supernatural domain is constructed as a potentiality" that the narrator never "fully authenticate[s]" alongside the story's natural events (Traill 1996, 13). Here is *The Turn of the Screw* as exemplar of the form. The second mode she calls the *supernatural naturalized*. In this second kind of fantasy the supernatural is presented plausibly throughout the story but then suddenly evaporates, typically at the end. This is the moment when, as she says, "it was all a dream, a hallucination, a drug-induced illusion, or the effect of fear, madness, hysteria" (16). Here she places *Alice's Adventures in Wonderland*.

The third mode is the *disjunctive*, whose name is perhaps a bit misleading and might as well have been called the *conjunctive*, because in it both natural and supernatural realms are authenticated by the narrator to the very end. Traill adds a requirement: "Entities of both domains interact, but a supernatural entity is never absorbed into the natural domain, and a supernatural event is not naturalized" (1996, 137). Her example of this natural-supernatural, disjunctive-conjunctive mode is Dickens's "The Bagman's Story" from *The Pickwick Papers*.

The fourth mode, which she calls the *paranormal*, occurs in those stories that absorb the supernatural into the natural without explaining them away. These are the stories that enlarge the natural domain by incorporating the supernatural as fringe phenomena—"clairvoyance, telepathy, and precognition, for instance" (Traill 1996, 17). Traill argues that by means of the innovations of this new mode, fantasy literature undergoes a "radical modernization that helped it to endure in the nineteenth and on into the twentieth century" (138). The example she gives is Maupassant's "Le Horla."

Traill adds a fifth form, a "subtype" of the third or disjunctive-conjunctive mode, leaving her with a total of four main types. This subtype she calls *fantasy* proper. In it, the supernatural dominates in such a way that "either the natural domain is not represented at all or it is part of an enframing narrative" (Traill 1996, 137). William Beckford's *Vathek* and Swift's *Gulliver's Travels* are examples. Her mention of these two works is welcome. And while I understand that the primary focus of her book is the paranormal, I wish there had been more discussion of how traditional literature might or might not fit her categories. Then the absence of what some call "genre fantasy" and such authors as Dunsany, Tolkien, and Le Guin is a serious disappointment: at least some mention of them in the typology would have been warranted. Still, the study is valuable for the way it applies insights from possible worlds theory to the study of fantasy, for its sustained discussion of the paranormal, and especially for its typology.

Another study that goes beyond the mimetic approach and similarly describes four modes of fantasy is Farah Mendlesohn's *Rhetorics of Fantasy*. While there is no robust theory of possible worlds in what she calls her descriptive "taxonomy" of the modes, and though she never surmounts the limitations of her decidedly generic approach, her distinction between the two domains she calls "the narrated world" and "the fantastic" underlies her classification system (Mendlesohn 2008, xiv). To the extent that distinction allows her to explore ways these disparate realms interact, it is useful to set her study next to Traill's, though Mendlesohn never mentions Traill's book.

While both authors offer four modes of fantasy, Mendlesohn's modes never quite align with Traill's. Mendlesohn is concerned with more than just the interaction of two domains and includes in her discussion the experience of the reader "ideal and implied." Her account shades from a formal narratological analysis to a rhetorical and poetic one. Mendlesohn's focus on the reader—who is issued "an invitation to construct a fictionalized self"—allows her to examine the ways protagonists and readers experience the merging of the fantastic with the natural (2008, xviii). These movements in and out of worlds, in an admittedly limited sense, are important to Mendlesohn and to this extent allow her to give a more dynamic account of fantasy worlds than the one formulated by Traill.

Mendlesohn's first mode is the *portal* fantasy, in which the protagonist passes through some gateway from a natural to a fantastic order. The portal fantasy is perhaps her clearest example of a possible worlds journey, where a gateway is opened up and a link established between our world and another world. For her, the portal is the hallmark of the quest. For obvious reasons, the classic example is *The Lion, the Witch and the Wardrobe*, though perhaps less obviously she also includes in this category *The Lord of the Rings*. Even though it has a "reputation as a 'full secondary world,'" she says, Tolkien's tale follows the portal-quest pattern. Thus, she separates the two: "Frodo moves from a small, safe, and understood world into the wild, unfamiliar world of Middle-Earth" (2008, 2).

Mendlesohn's second mode is *immersive* fantasy. This is the kind of fantasy one might have expected *The Lord of the Rings* to epitomize because it is the most developed of secondary worlds, but her category of immersive fantasy is again as much about the experience as it is about the fictional locale, so her literary pragmatics tend to overshadow her semantics in this mode. Here the characters "take for granted" the fantastic world, given "without comment" to characters and readers alike, who are all "assumed to be of it" (2008, xx–xxi). An example she gives is China Miéville's *Perdido Street Station*. Perhaps a bit unintuitively, the immersive is the place where the fantastic is so domesticated that no magic occurs at all.

Mendlesohn's third mode is the *intrusive*, and it is as straightforward as its name suggests. In this form, "the world is ruptured by the intrusion, which disrupts normality and has to be negotiated with or defeated" (2008, 115). Readers of this literature react in shock or horror as they follow the limited points of view of protagonists. An example is Stevenson's *Strange Case of Dr. Jekyll and Mr. Hyde*, and horror literature in general resides here. Her fourth mode is the *liminal*, which completes her taxonomy and returns us to Todorov. Perhaps her name for this fourth kind of fantasy is also unfortunate, since liminality is evident anytime the fantastic manifests itself in a natural order. Here the key is not crossing a threshold, as in the portal story, but remaining stuck on its transitional point throughout the tale. She takes the reaction to this state of affairs as important: "The tone of the liminal fantasy could be described as blasé" (2008, xxiii). Mendlesohn considers John Crowley's *Little, Big* liminal in this sense.

Both studies are important and advance our understanding of fantasy. Mendlesohn's terms appear more descriptive of what happens in fantasy as a genre, while Traill's types reach deeper into the kinds of worlds that make up those forms. Mendlesohn's approach is based more on reader position and textual tone, while Traill's is based more on world authentication and world resolution. Mendlesohn's modes appear more fluid as they move with readers' experiences when they encounter the fantastic, while Traill's modes appear to stake out the ways the fantastic interacts with natural phenomena. Mendlesohn's approach is more inductive, as she adduces an impressive number of examples, while Traill's approach is more deductive, as she clarifies top-down distinctions. In short, Mendlesohn sets out to create a taxonomy, Traill a typology.

All this is useful for both theorists and practical critics. One interesting outcome is that of all categories employed by both authors, the two realms said to interact with one another—Traill's natural and supernatural, Mendlesohn's narrated world and fantastic—may end up merging as a single world. At the philosophical level of Traill and the rhetorical level of Mendlesohn, the reader encountering these two discontinuous orders of reality may find they ultimately resolve in a single ontological domain. This may happen within the text or even outside as the fantasy realm expands or the reader's understanding is augmented. But what these observations speak to the most is the need for a detailed account of the idea of world in the context of fantasy, the domains that make up fantasy worlds, the objects and their relations across those worlds, how characters' actions and interactions affect the constitution of those worlds, and how the words of fantasy texts conjure those worlds.

As I outline in my *Poiesis and Possible Worlds*, a world is any local course of events that holds together in our ordinary language, in historical counterfactuals, in philosophical scenarios, in scientific thought experiments, in engineering simulations, and in a host of other places, including our fictions. To be in any state of information at all is to have some grasp of possible worlds, and our language and minds and imaginations cannot do without them. Every object in this semantics carries with it relations and identity conditions that designate it over an unlimited set of worlds. That is true for real-world objects like you and me, and it is also true for fictional ones like Sherlock Holmes and Gandalf the Grey. What Leibniz calls an object's "compossibility" interacts with the compossibility of other objects. Before the literary text appears, those relations suggest alternative ways the world might be, the fundamental elements of this world might suggest different objects, and the fecund imagination might suggest entirely different elements and laws by which they are bound. For a possible worlds theorist, a world is indeed in a grain of sand.

From the granular level to the broadly philosophical, possible worlds are intimately bound up with our understanding of language, logic, ontology, epistemology, deontology, and aesthetics. We can see fantasy terms in this chapter distribute across philosophical categories that possible worlds theorists regularly discuss and therefore deserve further treatment (see fig. 8.2).[15]

That does not mean we need an atomic theory of fantasy in which we identify the standard objects of this literature—mirrors, portals, amulets, and so on—as much as it means that every object of our common experience and all objects utterly imagined have the potential to be transformed by fantasy across those categories. Fantasy writers change ordinary desks, doors, shoes, pens, and an untold number of other objects that apparently have no limit outside of our imaginations into the stuff of this literature. We truly are the stuff that dreams are made on.

Hence, nonporous worlds without relations to either the actual or other possible worlds are to be rejected as much as atomized objects in this theory. Fantasy stories are, as we saw, ontologically other worlds that challenge and expand our understanding, producing with their discontinuous realities our responses of astonishment, shock, and horror. These wonder stories show once again how speakers work to model the statements of their language, both literary and nonliterary, whose relations reach outward in countless suggestive ways. The ancient sees Aeolus playing invisible strings in the music of the wind, and the modern scientist sees infinitesimal strings deep within the eleven dimensions singing the song of the world. Fantasy works on the fringes of possibility, ahead

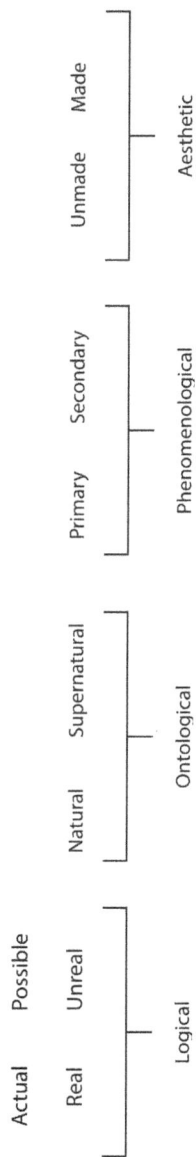

Fig. 8.2. World distinctions and fantasy theory terms across philosophical categories.

of reason, teasing us out of familiar assumptions as we try our hypotheses in the realm of the imagination, if only because the resources of the actual world are so limited.

Conclusion

Fantasy forces us to consider new information in small- and large-scale ways. Taken as a whole, it is a kind of ontological metaphor in which discontinuous tracts of reality come into contact with one another—where they interact, repel, and fuse. Worlds of dream, desire, terror, and pure literary invention connect with accepted ways of understanding to provoke a response in readers. That response can range from the enjoyment of playful diversion to the profound reshaping of readers' minds as they confront often the remotest of truths. This mention of metaphor takes us again from the macro- to the microcosmic. Tolkien talked about the power of the adjective to uncouple the green from grass and blue from sky to create "blue grass," and our imagination runs ahead of the verbal conjuring beyond the trees and surrounding rocks that live there to see what might come next in that fairy glade. Little formal work has been done since Tolkien's insight on how metaphor manages possibilities and creates worlds.[16] If fantasy literature was ever about impossibilities, then it must be about how what was reckoned impossible is made possible by its authors. Instead of impossibilities, we might as readily talk of "imp possibilities," as tiny creatures run from the end of our pens to find their own local habitations and names in their own tales.

Such is the game of the fantastic when the reader's imagination meets the transformative creativity of its authors in this apparently boundless medium. Not all verbal fantasies in this literature or beyond will resolve themselves in models, of course.[17] Some, like Alice's, topple at the end of their own excesses, and others, like Vane's in MacDonald's *Lilith*, approach so near to greater realities that at the end language fails. And sometimes worlds will seek a language all their own to speak them, as the most imaginative authors take up the challenge. The best of these writers capture Pope's definition of true wit, showing they are true poets not only in Shelley's sense above but also, as Sidney reminds us, poets in the classical senses of maker and seer.

Insofar as these principles hold, fantasy literature will remain at the outer limits of an expanding literary universe. Readers of fantasy thus stand in a veritable Lewisian "Wood between the Worlds." From there, they venture forth to explore what might be. The best of these stories add to our understanding, all the while giving the lie to reductive accounts of literary imagination. Is literary imagination an important instrument of reason, or is that the other way around? Let us pick up another story and think more on the question, recalling Gandalf's closing words to Bilbo, that he is "a little fellow in a wide world after all."

Notes

1. Tom Shippey makes a convincing case that Tolkien's work should head that list in his book *Author of the Century*.
2. For cites and the rest of this history, see Timmons (2000, 1ff.).
3. Notable among them are Harold Bloom's "inflated, over-written, tendentious, and moralistic in the extreme" (2008, 1) and Michael Moorcock's "*Winnie-the-Pooh* posing as an epic" (quoted in Timmons 2000, 1).
4. Compare this 1984 statement by Ann Swinfen: "The attitude of the majority of contemporary critics . . . suggests that the so-called 'realist' mode of writing is somehow more profound, more morally committed, more involved with 'real' human concerns" (10–11). Bill Senior also reminded me of an International Conference of the Fantastic in the Arts meeting at which Doris Lessing spoke and repeated how "astonished" she was at the prohibitions against fantasy by the first-world literary establishment. Many thanks to him for this anecdote and many suggestions for improving this chapter.
5. See Kathryn Hume's *Fantasy and Mimesis*.
6. Perhaps they are influenced by early critics who often repeat the "impossibility thesis" or even by Irwin's apparently influential *Game of the Impossible*. My purpose is by no means to replace Clute and Grant's indispensable work but to reorient its best insights within a possible worlds framework.
7. Modern science contradicts perception but does not qualify as "impossible" under this definition. Nor are dominant worldviews exclusive worldviews, and that is never more true than for modern readers. From the perspective of one worldview, another worldview might be wrong, but it need not be impossible. Impossibility is quite another matter and might be quite difficult beyond this tenuous definition to clarify. Is it physical impossibility or logical impossibility? In terms of sensory experience, scientists may tell us as many impossible things as the fantasists. The White Witch who says in *Through the Looking Glass* "sometimes I've believed as many as six impossible things before breakfast" no doubt has some scientific or theoretical analogues in the Oxford mathematician's mind (Carroll 2015, 226).

8. See Lewis Carroll's *Annotated Alice*, edited by Martin Gardner et al.

9. See also Doležel, *Heterocosmica*, and Ryan, *Possible Worlds*, for the development of a typology of literary worlds based on possible worlds theory. For a discussion of world creation across media and an impressive historical catalog of created worlds, see Mark Wolf's media-based study *Building Imaginary Worlds*.

10. All of these are from Wolfe's list (1986, 38–40), except "astonishment," which is Rabkin's (1976, 5); "numinous," which is from Brian Attebury, *Stories about Stories* (2014); and "desirability," which is Tolkien's (1947, 62).

11. Of course, from his *Midsummer Night's Dream* and the title of her late collection of stories reclaimed from Cotton Mather.

12. For more of this history, see chapters 3 and 4 of my *Poiesis and Possible Worlds*, where I surmise that "the real world itself has undergone such changes in the meantime that Russell's language might no longer refer even to it: zoology will soon be able to create its own fantasy creatures!" (2004, 61).

13. See, for example, Allén's Nobel Symposium and Marie Laure-Ryan's "Parallel Universes."

14. For a perspective other than the one developed here, a materialist account of fantasy based squarely in the one-world or mimetic tradition, one might see classic studies by Rosemary Jackson (1981) and Jack Zipes (2002).

15. None of the terms is mine, and none is without problems absent accompanying context. But as the terms emerge naturally from theorists and their discussions of fantasy, we can see they do so at the site of the logical, ontological, phenomenological, and aesthetic categories. Even in this passing observation, we can see that distinctions that normally denote fantasy cut across all these divisions in formal philosophy. So perhaps a case might be made that fantasy is a fundamental feature in human inquiry and evident across human consciousness. Such a case would delve deeply into the relationship of the imagination to reason and both to the nature of possibility. I have begun such a project and hope to bring it to print in the future.

16. For a discussion on metaphor and possible worlds semantics, see Martin (2004, chap. 5).

17. See the argument regarding satisfiability in Martin (2004, chap. 4).

References

Allén, Sture. 1989. *Possible Worlds in Humanities, Arts and Sciences: Proceedings of Nobel Symposium 65*. Research in Text Theory 14. Berlin: de Gruyter.

Attebury, Brian. 2014. *Stories about Stories: Fantasy and the Remaking of Myth*. Oxford: Oxford University Press.

Auden, W. H. 1956. "At the End of the Quest, Victory." Rev. of *The Return of the King* by J. R. R. Tolkien. *New York Times*, January 22. https://www.nytimes.com/books/ 01/02/11/specials/tolkien-return.html.

Bloom, Harold. 2008. *J. R. R. Tolkien's "The Lord of the Rings": New Edition*. New York: Bloom's Literary Criticism.

Carroll, Lewis. 2015. *The Annotated Alice: 150th Anniversary Deluxe Edition*. Edited by Martin Gardner et al. New York: Norton.

Charbonnier, G. 1973. *Conversations with Claude Lévi-Strauss*. London: Jonathan Cape.

Clute, John, and John Grant, eds. 1997. *The Encyclopedia of Fantasy*. New York: St. Martin's.

Coyle, William. 1986. *Aspects of Fantasy: Selected Essays from the Second International Conference on the Fantastic in Literature and Film*. Westport CT: Greenwood.

Doležel, Lubomír. 1990. *Occidental Poetics: Tradition and Progress*. Lincoln: University of Nebraska Press.

———. 1998. *Heterocosmica: Fiction and Possible Worlds*. Baltimore MD: Johns Hopkins University Press.

Eco, Umberto. (1988) 2008. *Foucault's Pendulum*. Translated by Richard Weaver. New York: Houghton Mifflin Harcourt.

Hume, Kathryn. 1984. *Fantasy and Mimesis: Responses to Reality in Western Literature*. New York: Methuen.

Irwin, W. R. 1976. *The Game of the Impossible*. Urbana: University of Illinois Press.

Jackson, Rosemary. 1981. *Fantasy: The Literature of Subversion*. London: Methuen.

Johnson, Samuel. 1750. *The Works of Samuel Johnson*, vol. 4. London: Longman.

Lewis, C. S. 1953. *The Silver Chair*. New York: Collier.

———. 1966. "Tolkien's *Lord of the Rings*." In *On Stories: And Other Essays on Literature*, edited by Walter Hooper, 83–90. Grand Rapids: Eerdmans.

Martin, Thomas L. 2004. *Poiesis and Possible Worlds: A Study in Modality and Literary Theory*. Toronto: University of Toronto Press.

McKillip, Patricia A. 2012. *Wonders of the Invisible World*. San Francisco: Tachyon.

Mendlesohn, Farah. 2008. *Rhetorics of Fantasy*. Middletown CT: Wesleyan University Press.

Mendlesohn, Farah, and Edward James. 2009. *A Short History of Fantasy*. London: Middlesex University Press.

Pavel, Thomas G. 1986. *Fictional Worlds*. Cambridge MA: Harvard University Press.

Peake, Mervyn. (1946) 1992. *Titus Groan*. Woodstock: Overlook.

Proust, Marcel. 1948. *The Maxims of Marcel Proust*. New York: Columbia University Press.

Rabkin, Eric S. 1976. *The Fantastic in Literature*. Princeton NJ: Princeton University Press.

Russell, Bertrand. 1919. *Introduction to Mathematical Philosophy*. London: Allen.

Ryan, Marie-Laure. 1991. *Possible Worlds, Artificial Intelligence, and Narrative Theory*. Bloomington: Indiana University Press.

———. 2006. "From Parallel Universes to Possible Worlds: Ontological Pluralism in Physics, Narratology, and Narrative." *Poetics Today* 27 (4): 633–74.

Shelley, Percy Bysshe. (1840) 1891. *A Defense of Poetry*. Edited by Albert S. Cook. Boston: Ginn.

Shippey, Tom. 2000. *J. R. R. Tolkien: Author of the Century*. New York: Houghton Mifflin.

Swinfen, Ann. 1984. *In Defense of Fantasy: A Study of the Genre in English and American Literature since 1945*. London: Routledge.

Timmons, Daniel. 2000. *J. R. R. Tolkien and His Literary Resonances: Views of Middle-Earth*. Westport CT: Greenwood.

Todorov, Tzvetan. 1973. *The Fantastic: A Structural Approach to a Literary Genre*. Translated by Richard Howard. Ithaca NY: Cornell University Press.

Tolkien, J. R. R. 1947. "On Fairy-Stories." In *Essays Presented to Charles Williams*, edited by C. S. Lewis, 38–89. Grand Rapids: Eerdmans.

Traill, Nancy. 1996. *Possible Worlds of the Fantastic: The Rise of the Paranormal in Fiction*. Toronto: University of Toronto Press.

Wolf, Mark J. P. 2012. *Building Imaginary Worlds: The Theory and History of Subcreation*. New York: Routledge.

Wolfe, Gary K. 1986. *Critical Terms for Science Fiction and Fantasy: A Glossary and Guide to Scholarship*. New York: Greenwood.

Zipes, Jack. 2002. *Breaking the Magic Spell: Radical Theories of Folk and Fairy Tales*. Rev. ed. Lexington: University Press of Kentucky.

9 The Best/Worst of All Possible Worlds?

Utopia, Dystopia, and Possible Worlds Theory

MATTISON SCHUKNECHT

As one of the most diverse and interdisciplinary fields in the humanities and social sciences, utopian studies often attract researchers from a variety of intellectual backgrounds.[1] *Utopian Studies*, the leading journal on utopias and utopian literature, even boasts that its contributors come from fields as diverse as "American studies, architecture, the arts, classics, cultural studies, economics, engineering, environmental studies, gender studies, history, languages and literatures, philosophy, political science, psychology, sociology and urban planning" (Penn State University Press 2016). Given this "big tent" approach to utopian texts, one could reasonably assume that such diversity has led to a quantifiable increase in the variety of interpretations of literary utopias. Although such an assumption seems reasonable in theory, this interdisciplinary method often fails to produce anything more than a critical echo chamber, especially in regard to the ontological status of the imaginary worlds discussed. In this chapter I explore the feasibility of applying several concepts and models developed in possible worlds semantics to utopian and dystopian literature. In contrast to popular methods to theorizing utopias and dystopias, I promote an approach that begins with an examination of the fictional world in question and not the sociopolitical status of our actual world. In turn, I offer a formal and narratological alternative to the political and sociological models that have increasingly dominated utopian studies in recent years. Scholars of utopian and dystopian literature should, at the very least, be offered a choice of interpretive frameworks.

Utopian critics have looked to theories deeply concerned with conditions in the actual world—Marxist political theory, feminism, various genetic theories, cultural studies, and contemporary sociology—and applied these real-world themes and interests to utopian texts. In essence, the critic who understands the nature of our real world can understand the utopian worlds that appear across various fictions. Whatever benefits may originate with this putatively interdisciplinary approach, too much is needlessly lost in their united adherence to a one-world framework. All such approaches tether the fictional creation too closely to real-world events and real-world principles. An approach that would truly be "interdisciplinary" would incorporate a broader philosophical framework and account for world-to-world relations across utopian and dystopian worlds as they depart from the real world. What I mean to suggest through this chapter is that our understanding of utopias as fictional worlds is not predicated on our knowledge of the actual world but on any number of departures therefrom, brought into play by what possible worlds theorists call "accessibility relations." The utopian field is in desperate need of a broader interpretive framework that better reflects the status of fictional utopias as autonomous ontological entities. An approach based on developments in possible worlds semantics could enrich the study of the utopian/dystopian genre, shedding significant light on this important literary art form.

Lyman Tower Sargent, one of the most influential utopian scholars, has defined "utopianism" as "social dreaming" (1994, 1). Grounding this idea, he has rooted his definition of utopian literature firmly in the realm of a one-world semantic framework: "There is a general form for the term utopia as a literary genre. It refers to works which describe an imaginary society in some detail. Obviously the completeness will vary. Some centuries stressed certain aspects of society and neglected others, and some authors are concerned with certain parts of society more than others. But it must be a society—a condition in which there is human (or some equivalent) interaction in a number of different forms and in which human beings (or their equivalent) express themselves in a variety of ways" (7).

In other words, utopian fiction must depict a society that can be evaluated as any other human society in the real world. Does Sargent's principle undergirding his critical project restrict either the creative artist of utopias and dystopias or the readers who encounter them? Under his definition, sociological and political theories play a central role in evaluating these unique fictional narratives.[2] Must a utopia always be a society, as Sargent specifies, and must it always resonate with political sensibilities we can readily identify in the reader's world? Possible worlds theorist Lubomír

Doležel describes a one-person fictional world in which "one and only one person is admitted into this world" (1998, 37). A society, in the purest sense, cannot exist without two or more people. Might a one-person fictional world then be considered a utopia? Despite being "an artificial and precarious structure," Doležel notes that the "theoretical importance of this primitive narrative world is much greater than its rarity in literary fiction would warrant" (37). Thus a one-person world is of particular interest to the utopian scholar: the very existence of such a structure would from the outset challenge Sargent's definition of utopia as a society.

Doležel selects Daniel Defoe's *Robinson Crusoe* as a text that exemplifies a one-person world for the vast majority of its narrative: from his shipwreck to the discovery of the solitary human footprint in the sand, Robinson resides in such a world. Defoe's novel is particularly relevant because many scholars single out the text as one of the exemplary literary utopias.[3] Sargent acknowledges that an influential critical tradition considers *Crusoe* and similar fictions as utopian texts under the mantle of the "Robinsonaden" (1994, 13), but he doubles down on his thesis that utopias must construct societies.[4] Although Sargent admits that "solitary eutopias are possible, . . . they are rare and, with these few exceptions, social interaction is fundamental to the utopian form" (13). In this way, he refuses to consider *Crusoe* as a nonsociological and apolitical utopia.

Yet despite its apparent lack of sociological relevance, *Crusoe* exhibits all of the hallmarks of a utopia: Robinson, once stranded on the island, works tirelessly to actualize the utopian project he envisions within the private world of his mind. It is not until the arrival of the cannibals on his island that this utopian world collapses. Sociality devours his utopia. *Crusoe* proves that a one-person utopia is possible, and to that extent we must reject Sargent's insistence that utopias/dystopias must depict societies. A broader framework is needed and, given the room to expand, might open up further insights into the utopian genre.

To that end, I begin with an assessment of previous attempts to apply possible worlds theory to literary utopias/dystopias, the successes and failures of such studies, and the lines along which possible worlds readings of utopia/dystopia may proceed in the future. Drawing on the work of scholars such as Marie-Laure Ryan, Thomas Pavel, and Lubomír Doležel, I outline both a transuniversal and an intrauniversal possible worlds approach to utopian and dystopian fiction. By "transuniversal," I mean a possible worlds approach that focuses on the relations between our actual world and the many possible worlds depicted in works of fiction; by "intrauniversal," I mean an approach that focuses solely on the properties and internal configurations of fictional worlds themselves. The chapter ends with a few concluding remarks about the widespread decline of literary utopia and the subsequent rise of dystopia as an art form. I utilize the possible worlds approach developed in this chapter to provide a formal and narratological, as opposed to a cultural and causal, explanation to this recent literary phenomenon.

Possible Worlds in Utopian/Dystopian Criticism

Darko Suvin, noted science fiction and utopian critic, was the first scholar to recognize the potential behind possible worlds theory to enrich the study of utopian and dystopian literature. In an essay titled "Locus, Horizon, and Orientation: The Concept of Possible Worlds as a Key to Utopian Studies," Suvin crafts a theoretical approach informed by research developments in analytic philosophy, semantics, and modal logic. His central thesis is that "utopias exist as a gamut of Possible Worlds in the imagination of readers, not as a pseudo-object on the page" (Suvin 1990, 76). Introducing the concept of the "locus" and the "horizon" as keys to understanding utopian texts, Suvin defines the first as "the place of the agent who is moving" in an imaginary space and the second as the place "toward which that agent is moving" (77). Already we sense the wide-open theoretical space such an approach affords the critic over an approach like Sargent's. Suvin explains that narratives where the locus moves toward the horizon but, for whatever reason, never reaches it are "dynamic, or open" utopias (79). He includes texts such as Ursula K. Le Guin's *The Dispossessed* under this description.[5] These works present a clear utopian vision, but this vision is never achieved within the pages of the text. Robert Heinlein's *The Moon Is a Harsh Mistress* provides another example. The success of the Lunar Revolution at the novel's end seems to suggest the formation of a libertarian utopia, but Heinlein is quick to curb this overly optimistic expectation: "But Prof underrated yammerheads. They never adopted any of his ideas. Seems to be deep instinct in human beings for making everything compulsory that isn't forbidden" ([1966] 1996, 382). At the end of Heinlein's narrative, not much has changed: the Professor's libertarian utopian vision, still unrealized, hangs tantalizingly on the utopian horizon just out of reach. In contrast to open utopias, texts where the locus meets or surpasses the horizon are "dogmatic, static, or closed" utopias, a category that includes most literary utopias and dystopias. In other words, the utopian vision has been actualized in these worlds. Suvin's "locus" and "horizon" are useful terms to an interpreter of literary and fictional utopias; I employ them in the following section of this chapter.

Given Suvin's perpetual popularity among science fiction and utopian theorists, it is unsurprising that some scholars have latched on to his conception of possible worlds as key to utopian studies. Yet these individuals who follow his example frequently fail to engage with current critical conversations occurring in possible worlds theory. Moreover, they tend to utilize the concept of possible worlds in such a simplistic and nonformal manner that it is not useful to the discerning reader. Lacking Suvin's familiarity with analytic philosophy and the applications of insights of possible worlds semantics to linguistics and narratology,[6] these critics tend to reduce the concept of possible worlds to a metaphor for physical or historical probability. The central misconception made by such theorists is that possible worlds must posit distinct and "possible" future states for our actual world. Phillip Wegner, one such critic who employs Suvin's "play of Possible Worlds," makes this critical error. Writing on the dystopian novel *We*, he declares, "Zamyatin's text offers a vision of multiple competing 'possible worlds' or historical trajectories for modernity" (Wegner 2002, xxiv).[7] In terms of modal logic, possible worlds are generally stipulated to uphold the logical rules of the excluded middle and noncontradiction, even if they depart from the actual world in other aspects. A fictional world would only become impossible if it violates either of these two principles. In other words, for most logicians working with possible worlds, a world is possible if it maintains an adherence to a set of internal logical laws. For Wegner, a world is possible if, and only if, it fashions a possible future for the actual world. *Fahrenheit 451* and *A Clockwork Orange* present possible worlds as they are set in the near future, but *Star Wars* ("A long time ago in a galaxy far, far away") and various fairy tales ("Once upon a time") do not register possible worlds. Wegner thus advocates a definition of possibility in fiction even stricter than the dominant view in modal logic. Moreover, critics such as Ryan have gone further to suggest that this traditional view of possibility is itself too restrictive for use in fictional studies, especially in regard to postmodern and experimental literary texts.[8] Wegner additionally fails to respect the ontological sovereignty of possible worlds, in principle rendering them subservient to the demands of the actual world.[9] Those familiar with the critical history of possible worlds semantics will recall that most theorists who utilize insights from this study have reached conclusions opposite to those of Wegner and like-minded scholars.[10]

On the other hand, critics attuned to the history of philosophical debates surrounding the idea of possible worlds have significantly extended our understanding of the semantics of fictional narrative. Due in part to the antirealistic outlook of possible worlds semantics, these critics have explored possible worlds in relation to a number of literary genres that blatantly depart from the actual world. Peter Stockwell provides a remarkable application of possible worlds theory to the genre of science fiction, George Sefler utilizes science fiction texts to criticize the idea of science as a universal language across all possible worlds, and Matt Hills examines "transfictional" (or "counterfictional" in his terms) retellings of several Gothic science fiction stories.[11] R. B. Gill acknowledges the similarities between possible worlds and speculative fiction but rightly cautions against hastily conflating the two terms.

Although not as popular as science fiction or speculative fiction, utopian/dystopian fiction has attracted considerable interest from possible worlds scholars. Joaquín Martínez Lorente provides a tentative possible worlds reading of Thomas More's *Utopia,* while Jaqueline Wernimont assesses the world of René Descartes's writings in light of possible worlds theory.[12] Martínez Lorente's and Wernimont's new applications of possible worlds theory are welcome, though their scope is narrow: the first focuses on a single text and the second on the select works of a single author rather than on the utopian genre as a whole. Calin Andrei Mihailescu offers a wider picture of the potential of possible worlds theory for utopia and dystopia. Attending to issues of completeness and incompleteness for fictional worlds, he suggests that many dystopian novels "present 'shrinking' worlds where nothing escapes the 'hallucinatorily' intense force of attraction of the center" in an attempt to appear more ontologically complete (Mihailescu 1991, 217). Although Mihailescu's contributions are noteworthy and necessary, he remains focused solely on issues of ontological completeness in dystopian texts, fails to address completeness in utopian works, and overlooks any of the other concepts developed in possible worlds semantics such as modality, accessibility, transfictional-ity, plot typology, world structure and typology, and so forth. His analysis remains a focused examination of one of possible worlds theory's criti-cal issues in a single, specified literary subgenre. Despite the widespread interest in utopia and dystopia from a possible worlds standpoint, a more comprehensive treatment of the genre is needed.

A Transuniversal Approach to Utopian/
Dystopian Possible Worlds

I begin with a transuniversal approach to utopian possible worlds. As mentioned, this approach looks outside the fictional world in question by highlighting how a textual actual world (TAW) created in a work of fiction departs from and conforms to the many rules of the actual world (AW). While this section of the chapter focuses on the transuniverse domain of relations between utopian/dystopian TAWs and the AW, the following one analyzes the intrauniverse domain of utopian/dystopian textual universes. Central to my transuniversal approach is Ryan's system of accessibility rela-tions. Summarized briefly, accessibility relations detail points of departure (or connection) between the AW and its many possible alternatives. From the nine relations she formulates, Ryan successfully constructs a typology of literary genres based on how the fictional worlds of literary texts depart from or conform to the actual world. The accessibility relations suggested by Ryan are as follows: identity of properties (A/properties), identity of inventory (B/same inventory), compatibility of inventory (C/expanded inventory), chronological compatibility (D/chronology), physical com-patibility (E/natural laws), taxonomic compatibility (F/taxonomy), logical compatibility (G/logic), analytic compatibility (H/analytical), and linguis-tic compatibility (I/linguistic) (1991, 32–33; see Ryan 1991 for a more com-prehensive explanation of these terms). In the following pages, I attempt to incorporate utopian/dystopian literature into her typology.

As the model currently stands, Ryan's accessibility relations and their associated typology of genres offer no specified place for utopian litera-ture. The closest analogue seems to be the genre of anticipation novels. Anticipation novels maintain most accessibility relations but sever identity of inventory and chronological compatibility. Ryan illustrates the genre using the unambiguously dystopian *1984*.[13] Yet as *1984* is unquestionably a dystopian novel, we must question if anticipation is the best genre to house literary utopia and dystopia. Many utopian texts certainly fit under the parameters required by the anticipation genre: works such as Francis Bacon's *New Atlantis* and Aldous Huxley's *Brave New World* certainly come to mind as texts that "predict" the future of our world, but can this assessment be reached about all utopian or dystopian fiction? Such a conclusion would imply that the creator of a utopian or dystopian text must always recenter the system of reality around a world similar to the AW in all ways except in being furnished by the exact same objects and being set in a past or present time. To put it as simply as possible, must all utopian and dystopian texts anticipate the future?

I offer Kazuo Ishiguro's *Never Let Me Go* as a sample text to determine utopia's compatibility with the anticipation genre. *Never Let Me Go* is a dystopian work ostensibly about the horrors of human cloning. In the novel, scores of human clones are genetically engineered for the sole purpose of "donating" their vital organs to sickly noncloned humans. Diseases such as cancer are effectively eliminated, but this medical progress comes at the cost of the lives of the sentient human clones who supply the healthy organs. Ishiguro's novel is unquestionably dystopian, but does it exemplify the qualities associated with anticipation novels as described by Ryan? As previously stated, anticipation novels maintain all accessibility relations except for identity of inventory (B/same inventory), a violation true for all works of fiction (excepting "true fiction"), and chronological compatibility (D/chronology). *Never Let Me Go* keeps the identity of properties (A/properties), meaning objects have the same properties that they do in the actual world (horses have four legs, a circle contains 360 degrees, a square has four sides, and so forth). The novel, like all fiction, violates B/same inventory as it introduces objects that cannot be found in the actual world (fictional characters, places, etc.). Similarly to anticipation novels, *Never Let Me Go* maintains C/expanded inventory by including "all members of the AW, as well as some native members" (Ryan 1991, 32). London is a very real place in *Never Let Me Go,* and the world of the novel once contained a person named Napoleon.[14] But the text also introduces nonactualized objects such as the fictional Hailsham boarding school, where a number of the cloned children grow up.

It is not until we reach the fourth accessibility relation, D/chronology, that Ishiguro's text deviates from the form of the anticipation novel. Works of anticipation do not maintain chronological compatibility, for, in the words of Ryan, the "point of anticipation novels is to show what may become of the actual world given its present state and past history" (1991, 36). In order for a work to uphold chronological compatibility, the TAW must not be located posterior to the AW. In other words, a text must be set in the present (at the time of its writing) or the past; works that describe future events (a quality quintessential to the anticipation genre) violate this relation. Even though *Never Let Me Go* deals specifically with human cloning, a scientific possibility unrealized in our AW, the novel is not set in the future. Instead, the novel's setting is one clearly recognizable to most readers: 1980s England. No temporal relocation is necessary for readers to imagine the history of *Never Let Me Go*'s TAW. As a result, we cannot classify all utopian/dystopian works as anticipation novels.

Although utopia and dystopia need not be anticipation from a literal standpoint, many of these texts contain didactic warnings against possible futures. In this metaphoric sense, one could argue that these texts still "anticipate" the future and warn against possible developments in the actual world. *Never Let Me Go* may not "anticipate" a literal future world, but it "anticipates" a possible scientific advancement in the real world: human cloning. Yet we must remind ourselves that accessibility relations function on a purely literal level. In order for a world to violate the chronology relation it must be set in the future. Although this could be viewed as a limitation of accessibility relations, metaphorical anticipation nevertheless does not signify a true anticipation novel. Other famous utopian texts, unlike anticipation novels, similarly maintain chronological compatibility. In More's *Utopia*, the eponymous nation exists contemporaneous with More's present time. The civilization has gone unnoticed only because it is located in the Western Hemisphere, previously inaccessible until European exploration of the New World. While many utopian fictions are set in the future, they can just as readily be located in the past or present. In such cases, even if the text offers some metaphorical didactic or anticipative value, D/chronology holds, thereby making such texts incapable of being classified as anticipation novels.

Let us now discuss another genre closely related to utopia: science fiction. Is science fiction, as opposed to anticipation, the best of Ryan's genres to house utopian texts? Suvin has argued that, "strictly and precisely speaking, utopia is not a genre but the *sociopolitical subgenre of science fiction*" (1979, 61, emphasis original). I have already refuted the supposed sociopolitical requirements of utopian fiction in the introduction to this chapter. I will presently address the second part of Suvin's claim: utopia as a subgenre of science fiction. Although it is certainly true that many utopian texts have science fiction elements, not all utopian works qualify as science fiction based on Ryan's accessibility relations model. Plato's *Republic* and the previously mentioned *Utopia* contain no science fiction elements as described in Ryan's typology. Unlike those works of science fiction that sever D/chronology and F/taxonomy, both of these utopian texts maintain these accessibility relations: neither *Republic* nor *Utopia* presents future societies or introduces new manufactured objects, frequently called the "novum" in science fiction theory. The classification of science fiction, like that of the anticipation novel, is inadequate for utopian and dystopian literature.

Regardless of the difficulties in placing utopian and dystopian texts within her typology, Ryan's model remains too rich a form to abandon without an attempt at some adjustments. Ryan, foreseeing the need for additional accessibility relations to be added to her typological model over time, proposes three tentative additions: historical coherence, psychological credibility, and socioeconomic compatibility (1991, 45). The relation of most interest to the utopian scholar is socioeconomic compatibility; however, as my earlier slotting of *Robinson Crusoe* as utopian text highlights, socioeconomic compatibility is not a universal requirement of utopian texts. Historical coherence and psychological credibility, while important to historical fiction or the psychological novel, also offer little of value to distinguish utopian fiction from the anticipation novel or science fiction. Left with no other choice, we must posit an entirely new accessibility relation that can distinguish utopian/dystopian texts from science fiction and anticipation novels. This proposed relation would maintain if the possible world presented through the fictional text does not systemically ameliorate or deteriorate the state or conditions of our actual world. I argue that utopian and dystopian texts must necessarily abandon this rule, while all other texts uphold it. In other words, utopian and dystopian worlds represent possible worlds that are significantly better or worse than the reader's AW. I designate this relation the principle of non-a/melioration (J/non-a/meliorate).[15] Figure 9.1 provides an illustration of the utopian genre in terms of a revised version of Ryan's accessibility relations typology.

	A	B	C	D	E	F/F'	G	H	I	J
Utopia/Dystopia	+/-/*	-	+/-	+/-	+	+/-	+	+	+	-
Anticipation	+	-	+	-	+	+	+	+	+	+
Science Fiction	+/*	-	+/-	-	+	F+F'-	+	+	+	+

*: nonapplicable because of a – on C

A = identity of properties

B = identity of inventory

C = compatibility of inventory

D = chronological compatibility

E = physical compatibility

F = taxonomic compatibility
(natural species only)

F' = taxonomic compatibility
(for both natural species
and manufactured objects)

G = logical compatibility

H = analytical compatibility

I = linguistic compatibility

J = non-a/meliorative compatibility

Fig. 9.1. Revised accessibility relations.

The following thought experiment further elucidates my proposed addition to Ryan's model. Suppose that sometime in the future humanity is severed from the physical world and unknowingly forced to live inside a virtual environment. The entities who created the machine responsible for maintaining this virtual reality must work to ensure that humanity does not realize the digital nature of their existence and regain access to the physical world. The machine's creators first fashion a virtual world more perfect than the physical world. This world is so much better than the original that many of the humans reject it as unbelievable. As a result, they awake from their virtual slumbers. The creators of the machine quickly revise their virtual world to accommodate human incredulity. They now produce a virtual world much worse than the original, physical world. Once again, humans in the machine reject this world as unbelievable because of its dissimilarity to the original world. The machine's creators realize that humankind will only accept a virtual environment that is similar in state to their original world. Those familiar with science fiction will recognize this scenario as a slightly modified version of the plot premise of *The Matrix*.

Of course, literary fiction provides a form of cognitive engagement that is fundamentally different from complete virtual immersion. Readers of dystopian and utopian fiction do not suffer the same adverse effects as those living in a purely virtual utopian or dystopian environment. Consumers of fiction always remain cognizant, at least subconsciously, of the ephemeral nature of the form: the game of make-believe only lasts for a finite period of time. Regardless of the entrancing nature of the theatrical performance occurring before them, spectators may choose to look away and reenter reality. The virtually enslaved humans in my analogy are never granted this luxury. Nevertheless, my point is that each time readers consume a work of fiction, they implicitly compare the state of this fictional world to their opinion of the state of affairs in the actual world. Astute readers of my model may have noticed that utopian and dystopian fiction is marked by an extreme flexibility in terms of its corresponding accessibility relations. Authors of utopias and dystopias are thus granted extreme freedom when it comes to crafting a fictional world: science fiction utopias, anticipation utopias, and even fairy tale or fantastic utopias are all commonly produced forms of this type of fiction.

At this point we can proceed to outline a tentative theory for the creation of literary utopias and dystopias. Building on the work of Suvin, we can identify his locus as "the actual world of [a] textual universe created by [a] fictional text" reached by readers through the process of "fictional recentering" as proposed by Ryan (1991, 22–23). In other words, the locus functions as the present center (the textual reference world or TRW) of a system of reality. In contrast, the horizon serves as an alternative possible world within that system of reality that the locus may or may not move toward and realize. Thus, the horizon operates as just one of the many satellite possible worlds that encircle the center world (either our actual world or a TRW) of a system of reality. This world on the horizon aims to replace the locus as the central world of the system. More often than not, this possible world begins as a private, nonactualized world in the thoughts of one or more persons in a narrative.[16] The utopian world of *Crusoe* originates as a desirable private world in Robinson's head; Robinson attempts to reframe his entire system of reality around this private world. Pavel's suggestion that "utopia devours actuality in various ways" (1986, 111) gains new life and significance under this context. When the locus meets the horizon, the private wish-world (W-world) of the horizon annihilates the central world of the locus. The original system of reality is effectively destroyed, and a new system forms with the formerly private wish-world as the new central world. Although I have focused primarily on the formation of utopias in fictional narratives, this "devouring" of actuality could conceivably occur in our own system of reality. In practice, however, this process remains exclusive to fiction—I am aware of no utopian project that has succeeded in reshaping our own world to the degree required of utopian worlds.

My transuniversal approach to utopian and dystopian possible worlds unfortunately highlights one of the most consistent problems faced by utopian scholars: the inability to formally distinguish utopias from dystopias. Obviously, utopias represent worlds better than the actual world and dystopias worse ones,[17] but employing this distinction in practice is often more difficult than it may first appear. This issue crystalizes when we examine older works of utopia, such as Plato's *Republic* and More's *Utopia*. To modern readers, the worlds of these texts appear totalitarian and antidemocratic; in fact, many readers could reasonably claim that each constructs a dystopia. In a phrase: one person's utopia is often another's dystopia.

The current transuniversal possible worlds model I have offered provides no true solution to this problem that does not rely on either the interpretation of the reader or what scholars often term "the intentional fallacy."

Sargent notes that while many literary scholars are perturbed by the utilization of authorial intent in utopian criticism, the method should be considered permissible based on the status of utopian studies as an interdisciplinary field: "But since other methodologies in North America and dominant methodologies in other parts of the world and in other disciplines (utopian studies is, after all, an interdisciplinary field) accept that authorial intention is important if difficult, it is possible, and, I believe, essential to use it when and where it is possible" (1994, 6). Although I am not as eager as some in completely removing authorial intention from literary discussion, I must reiterate that authorial intent by itself is not a sufficient reason to classify a text as definitively utopian or dystopian, at least on a formal level. Moreover, relation J/non-a/meliorate offers no inherent way to differentiate between utopian and dystopian texts. Violation of the relation merely suggests that the possible world in question is either better or worse than the actual world of the reader; the reader must then decide if this world is better or worse. Unable to distinguish utopian worlds from dystopian worlds on a transuniversal level, we must approach these possible worlds from within.

An Intrauniversal Approach to Utopian/ Dystopian Possible Worlds

In the previous section, I explored a transuniversal possible worlds approach (AW to TAW) to utopian/dystopian fictional worlds, yet this transuniversal method failed to distinguish adequately between utopian and dystopian texts without relying on the expressed opinion of the author or reader. In order to resolve this dilemma, we can formulate a complementary intrauniversal possible worlds approach that examines utopian fictional worlds from the internal perspective of the utopian textual universe in question. Crucial to the intrauniversal method developed in the remainder of this section is Doležel's system of four narrative modalities: alethic, deontic, axiological, and epistemic.

Doležel's system is useful because it allows the literary critic to associate certain genres with the different modal systems. For example, the epistemic system (incorporating such categories as known, unknown, and believed) generates everything from detective stories, to murder mysteries, to the German Bildungsroman. A combination of the alethic (possible, impossible, and necessary) and epistemic systems generates science fiction and speculative fiction texts; such works frequently ask what may be possible in the future given the current understanding of the actual world's scientific principles (scientific extrapolation) or what could be possible if such principles were fundamentally altered. Fairy stories combine both the axiological (good, bad, and indifferent) and the alethic modalities. The quest narrative, a trademark of the axiological system, dominates fantastic texts, while mythical beasts and supernatural forces stretch the boundary between the possible and impossible. While not as complete a system of semantic classification as Ryan's accessibility relation typology, Doležel's modalities remain a useful way to analyze the various worlds of fiction.

Where then do utopia and dystopia fall in Doležel's system? I propose that most utopian and dystopian texts engage with the deontic system (permitted, prohibited, and obligatory). Specifically, dystopian texts contain extensive conflict between the modalities of the deontic system, while utopian texts contain a substantial degree of harmony between the same modalities. To put it simply, utopian worlds minimize deontic conflict, while dystopian worlds maximize it. If we combine the transuniversal approach developed in the previous section, we can now readily distinguish utopian worlds from dystopian worlds on a formal level.

I must stress that not all texts with deontic conflict can be classified as utopian or dystopian. As Doležel identifies, the "deontic marking of actions is the richest source of narrativity" (1998, 121). Most stories feature some form of deontic conflict, but what distinguishes utopian/dystopian texts from other, nonutopian deontic works is the degree and scale of such conflict. Utopian and dystopian worlds frequently have "codexal norms [that] are valid for an entire world" spelled out as "explicitly promulgated rules, regulations, and laws" as opposed to "tacitly accepted conventions" (120). For example, Fyodor Dostoyevsky's *The Brothers Karamazov* features deontic conflict between father and son over shared romantic interest in the same woman, but the novel fails to qualify as dystopian because this conflict is limited to two members of the same family unit. Deontic conflict between members of a single family does not imply deontic conflict across the entire fictional world. Contrast this situation to a dystopian hero such as Winston Smith, who almost single-handedly attempts to battle the obligations and prohibitions of Big Brother's Party in *1984*. Deontic conflict in dystopia frequently occurs on a world level where the stakes are at an all-time high: the actions of one or more individual could decide the future modal structure of the entire fictional universe. The same cannot be said about traditional deontic texts: after the events of Dimitri's trial in *The Brothers Karamazov*, the many villagers return to the rote of their ordinary lives, mostly unaffected by Dimitri's criminal sentence.

We often characterize conflict in dystopia as a clash between one man and the entire dystopian state: Winston Smith battles Big Brother and his representatives in George Orwell's *1984*, Prometheus strikes out against the collectivist society in Ayn Rand's *Anthem*, and Guy Montag turns against the bibliophobic culture of Ray Bradbury's *Fahrenheit 451*. Yet dystopias do not always depict totalitarian states: anarchy can similarly generate large-scale deontic conflict. In such cases, deontic conflict occurs not between one or more person and a totalitarian government but between one or more character and the void of governing authority created after its collapse. Margaret Atwood's *Oryx and Crake* fashions a dystopian world where capitalism and genetic engineering have gone unchecked. These two forces taken together have caused the complete annihilation of government and society. Octavia Butler's *Parable of the Sower* similarly details deontic conflict caused by the dangerous void of power left after the collapse of the U.S. government. Only by banding together in tightly knit communities can characters in the novels fight against dystopia.

Conclusion: The Death of Utopia?

The heading to this section may sound unnecessarily apocalyptic, but such concern for the genre is not unwarranted when we consider the recent eclipse of utopian fiction by dystopian stories across a variety of fictional mediums. It is difficult to think of a utopian work in the past couple of decades that has gathered as much critical or commercial interest as contemporary dystopias. I am not the first to acknowledge this recent development in aesthetic taste: critics such as Krishan Kumar have gone as far as to suggest that the present cultural environment might not be hospitable for literary utopia.[18] What is to blame for the fall of this once esteemed genre? Did the collapse of the Soviet Union obliterate any remaining hope for the Marxist dream of "Heaven on Earth"? Has postmodern skepticism of "metanarratives" and the uncertainty of societal and political progress eroded any remaining optimism for a better tomorrow? Alternatively, perhaps we have simply exhausted the possibilities of a literary form developed over two thousand years ago? Whatever cultural or historic particulars might be responsible for the downfall of utopia, I would like to posit a formal explanation for the decline of literary utopia. Is there something about utopian narratives that makes them less "tellable" than dystopian ones?

Central to my examination of the decline of utopia is the concept of tellability, an approach developed in narratology to explain the intrinsic "noteworthiness" of certain plots over others. Ryan writes that "not all plots are created equal. Some configurations of facts present an intrinsic 'tellability' which precedes their textualization. This is why some stories exist in numerous versions, survive translation, and transcend cultural boundaries" (1991, 148). The potential tellability of a plot is deeply entwined with narrative conflict. Ryan reminds us that "conflicts are necessary to narrative action and that conflicts arise from incompatibilities between TAW and the private worlds of characters" (156). In essence, plot and narrative cannot exist without some form of conflict. Recall the definition of utopian and dystopian worlds developed in the previous section of this chapter: utopias minimize deontic conflict, while dystopias maximize it. Utopias, as a narrative form, possess limited tellability, as they construct fictional worlds containing minimized levels of conflict. On the other hand, dystopias and other highly tellable narratives "seek the diversification of possible worlds in the narrative universe" (156). This formal difference between literary utopia and dystopia, as opposed to cultural or historical factors, could provide an explanation for the decline of utopia as an art form.

Compare our conceptualization of utopian fiction to what Ryan refers to as the "best of all possible states of affairs for a system of reality": "The best of all possible states of affairs for a system of reality is one in which the constitutive propositions of all private worlds are satisfied in the central world. In such a system, everybody's desires are fulfilled, all laws are respected, there is consensus as to what is good for the group; what is good for the group is also good for every individual, everybody's actions respect these ideals, and everybody has epistemic access to all worlds of the system" (1991, 120). Although utopian worlds are not necessarily perfect systems of reality, they provide the closest representation of a perfect system of reality available in fiction. Conflict does indeed occur in most utopian worlds, but this conflict is necessarily short-lived: the utopian structures operating in these worlds quickly resolve any conflict, lest these disputes lead to the collapse of the entire utopian system.

Due to the limited conflict present in utopian worlds, tellability remains significantly inhibited in such narratives to the degree that most utopian stories reflect one of three standard plot archetypes: (1) the struggle to build a utopia as frequently depicted in "critical" or "open utopias," (2) the mostly uneventful existence of "static utopias," and (3) the potential or actual collapse of the utopian state. For a substantial portion of literary history, most utopian narratives fell into the second category. Plato's *Republic* and More's *Utopia* do not exist primarily for the purpose of entertainment; what these texts lack in tellability, they make up for in the philosophical and moral information they dispense to their readers. On the other hand, the richest source of tellability for utopian fiction comes from the first and third plot types: the rise and possible fall of utopian states. The first plot type thrived in the critical utopias of the 1960s and 1970s. The third plot arrangement found new life in television programs such as *Star Trek*. Nearly all narrative conflict in *Star Trek* originates from internal or external threats to the utopian United Federation of Planets. Yet even *Star Trek* ultimately could not overcome the limited tellability inherent to the genre: too often did the show's writers have to retreat to the virtual environment of the *Enterprise*'s holodeck to provide entertaining plot paths. Dystopia, with its maximized levels of conflict, is not limited to these three basic plot structures.

Whatever historical or cultural explanations may be responsible for utopia's decline, the formal narratological shortcomings of the genre are at least partially to blame. Although utopia's discernible slide into obscurity is certainly regrettable, the rise of dystopia holds great promise for the future of the genre. With a propensity for conflict and the imaginative power granted to the author, it is easy to understand why this highly tellable genre has succeeded in utopia's place. Dystopia offers authors the same imaginative possibilities of utopian worlds with few of the narratological shortcomings in terms of narrative tellability. Thus, we need not mourn the end of utopia: these utopian worlds will always exist in the collective minds of their authors and numerous readers.

Notes

I would like to thank Thomas L. Martin for his comments on this chapter and suggestions for improvement.

1. See Fitting (2009) for a history of utopian studies as a field.

2. See Sargent's (1994) discussion of "intentional societies" in the real world and their relation to fictional utopias.

3. *The Encyclopedia of Utopian Literature* contains an entry for *Robinson Crusoe* (Snodgrass 1995, 449–52).

4. Sargent, unwilling to consider the Robinsonaden as utopian fiction proper, nevertheless keeps it in his utopian taxonomy out of respect for the longstanding critical tradition.

5. Suvin's open/dynamic utopia is analogous to what some scholars have termed the "critical utopia." See Sargent (1994) for a taxonomy that makes use of the critical utopia as a utopian subgenre. Peter Stockwell (2000, 208) has additionally referred to critical utopias as "heterotopias," following Samuel Delany's appropriation of the term from its original usage by Foucault.

6. Suvin, unlike his numerous followers, shows remarkable familiarity with possible worlds theory and scholarship (especially with the criticism of possible worlds theorist Umberto Eco). See Suvin (1985) for a rigorous application of possible worlds theory to the realm of theater and live performance.

7. This mistake is not exclusive to interpreters of literature. Warren Buckland, a film critic, argues that Steven Spielberg's *Jurassic Park* films constitute possible worlds for the sole reason that such a scenario, based on our present scientific understanding, could reasonably occur in the actual world. He argues that Spielberg's dinosaur films "do not operate in the realm of pure fantasy, imagination or fiction, but present a possible world, by drawing out extreme consequences from a nonfictional state of affairs in the actual world" (1999, 181). In essence, Spielberg's films are "possible worlds" because they depict a world state that is scientifically plausible. C. Paul Sellors has correctly criticized Buckland for his ideas, even going as far as to point out his blatant misuse of the philosophy informing possible worlds theory. See Sellors (2000) for this critique and Buckland (2001) for Buckland's response.

8. Ryan writes, "Texts such as nonsense rhymes, surrealist poems, theater of the absurd, or postmodernist fiction may liberate their universe from the principle of noncontradiction" (1991, 32). There is little universal agreement on where (or how precisely) the line should be drawn between possible and impossible fictional worlds. Nevertheless, it is clear that Wegner's view of possibility is too restrictive for fictional analysis. See Ashline (1995) for a discussion of the differing views of fictional impossibility among possible worlds scholars.

9. As Pavel says, "In this precise sense, one can say that literary works are autonomous," and although this "does not mean that a comparison between art and reality is illegitimate, . . . any such comparison is logically second-

ary to the exploration of the unique ontological perspective posited by the work" (1975, 175). Compare to Eco: "A fictional text has an ontology of its own that must be respected" (1994, 72). Mark A. Tabone makes errors similar to Wegner in his "possible worlds" analysis of Delany's "We, in Some Strange Power's Employ, Move on a Rigorous Line." Tabone argues "the text's 'play of Possible Worlds' reorients and amplifies analytical scrutiny of the 'actual' historical present from which it emerged, thus opening a critical space outside the text and outside the binary of culture/counterculture from which a latent, unrepresentable 'impossible'—a something-yet-again-other—might possibly be imagined" (2013, 188). Tabone's application of possible worlds incorrectly asserts that these fictional worlds, never truly autonomous or existing on their own, exist primarily to give readers a better understanding of conditions in the actual world.

10. See Pavel's criticism of "naïve realism" (1975, 169–70), Doležel's critique of mimesis (1998, 5–10), and Ryan's comments on "the referential theory of fiction" (1991, 13–16).

11. Despite the validity of his response, I must criticize Hills's tendency to reinvent the wheel when it comes to several concepts in possible worlds theory. Suggesting that we need a fictional counterpart to counterfactuals, Hills advocates for the idea of "counterfictionals" (2003, 439) but remains unaware of previous possible worlds scholarship on the issue of transfictionality. See Doležel's (1998, 199–226) discussion of "postmodern rewrites" and "transduction."

12. See also Corin Braga's (2014) useful discussion of utopia, science fiction, and fantasy as three contemporary genres particularly well suited to possible worlds analysis. Braga correctly notes that scholars have a tendency to conflate utopia with science fiction or fantasy; many critics do not give utopia the attention it deserves as its own literary genre.

13. Ryan notes that from today's viewpoint, "*1984* is no longer anticipation, but a strange breed of imaginary history," as the future proposed by *1984* has now passed (1991, 36). Nevertheless, Ryan recommends that we base the genre of a text on its original status and not its standing in the present. Therefore, "*1984* will forever remain a novel of anticipation" (41).

14. Doležel reminds us that "Tolstoy's fictional Napoleon or Dickens's fictional London are not identical with the historical Napoleon or the geographic London" (1998, 16).

15. My new accessibility relation would technically require a relabeling of some of Ryan's accessibility relations, as Ryan lists her accessibility relations in terms of decreasing stringency. For instance, A/properties rule is the most stringent relation and I/linguistic is the least stringent. My new rela-

tion should come after rule F/taxonomy but before G/logic because worlds that violate G, H, and I are considered logically incoherent. Utopian or dystopian worlds that do not maintain non-a/meliorative compatibility do not necessarily create logically incoherent worlds. However, for the sake of clarity and consistency with Ryan's system, I keep the original notation for her original accessibility relations and name the non-a/meliorative principle J, even though this relation should fall between relations F and G in terms of stringency. Figure 9.1 also follows this pattern.

16. The germ of a utopian possible world is often the wish-world (W-world) of a particular character or group of characters. Ryan notes that "characters may aim successively at various layers of their W-world, settling for lower levels as higher ones become unattainable" (1991, 118).

17. I agree with Sargent's insistence that although "some authors insist that utopian society must be perfect and *therefore* unrealizable," such critics maintain a misconstrued notion of utopia (1994, 6).

18. Kumar has suggested that "while it is true that the dystopia uses many of the same literary devices as the utopia, the unwillingness to essay the literary utopia suggests a distinct lack of confidence in its capacity to be effective, as well perhaps as a failure of the utopian imagination" (2010, 550).

References

Ashline, William L. 1995. "The Problem of Impossible Fictions." *Style* 29 (2): 215–34.

Braga, Corin. 2014. "Fictional Worlds: Utopia, Science-Fiction, Fantasy." *Caietele Echinox* 26:38–48.

Buckland, Warren. 1999. "Between Science Fact and Science Fiction: Spielberg's Digital Dinosaurs, Possible Worlds, and the New Realism." *Screen* 40 (2): 177–92.

———. 2001. "A Reply to Sellors's 'Mindless' Approach to Possible Worlds." *Screen* 42 (2): 222–26.

Doležel, Lubomír. 1998. *Heterocosmica: Fiction and Possible Worlds*. Baltimore MD: Johns Hopkins University Press.

Eco, Umberto. 1994. *The Limits of Interpretation*. Bloomington: Indiana University Press.

Fitting, Peter. 2009. "A Short History of Utopian Studies." *Science Fiction Studies* 36 (1): 121–32.

Gill, R. B. 2013. "The Uses of Genre and the Classification of Speculative Fiction." *Mosaic* 46 (2): 71–85.

Heinlein, Robert A. (1966) 1996. *The Moon Is a Harsh Mistress*. New York: Tom Doherty Associates.

Hills, Matt. 2003. "Counterfictions in the Works of Kim Newman: Rewriting Gothic SF as 'Alternate-Story Stories.'" *Science Fiction Studies* 30 (3): 436–55.

Kumar, Krishan. 2010. "The Ends of Utopia." *New Literary History* 41 (3): 549–69.

Martínez Lorente, Joaquín. 1996. "Possible-World Theories and the Two Fictional Worlds of More's Utopia: How Much (and How) Can We Apply?" *Sederi* 6:117–23.

Mihailescu, Calin Andrei. 1991. "Mind the Gap: Dystopia as Fiction." *Style* 25 (2): 211–22.

Pavel, Thomas G. 1975. "'Possible Worlds' in Literary Semantics." *Journal of Aesthetics and Art Criticism* 34 (2): 165–76.

———. 1986. *Fictional Worlds*. Cambridge MA: Harvard University Press.

Penn State University Press. 2016. "Utopian Studies Journal." Accessed August 20. http://www.psupress.org/journals/jnls_utopian_studies.html.

Ryan, Marie-Laure. 1991. *Possible Worlds, Artificial Intelligence, and Narrative Theory*. Bloomington: Indiana University Press.

Sargent, Lyman Tower. 1994. "The Three Faces of Utopianism Revisited." *Utopian Studies* 5 (1): 1–37.

Sefler, George F. 1986. "Science, Science Fiction, and Possible World Semantics." In *Aspects of Fantasy: Selected Essays from the Second International Conference on the Fantastic in Literature and Film*, edited by William Coyle, 213–19. Westport CT: Greenwood Press.

Sellors, C. Paul. 2000. "The Impossibility of Science Fiction: Against Buckland's Possible Worlds." *Screen* 41 (2): 203–16.

Snodgrass, Mary Ellen. 1995. *The Encyclopedia of Utopian Literature*. Santa Barbara CA: ABC-CLIO.

Stockwell, Peter. 2000. *The Poetics of Science Fiction*. Harlow: Longman.

Suvin, Darko. 1979. *Metamorphoses of Science Fiction*. New Haven CT: Yale University Press.

———. 1985. "The Performance Text as Audience-Stage Dialog Inducing a Possible World." *Versus* 42:3–20.

———. 1990. "Locus, Horizon, and Orientation: The Concept of Possible Worlds as a Key to Utopian Studies." *Utopian Studies* 1 (2): 69–83.

Tabone, Mark A. 2013. "Beyond *Triton*: Samuel R. Delany's Critical Utopianism and the Colliding Worlds in 'We, in Some Strange Power's Employ, Move on a Rigorous Line.'" *Utopian Studies* 24 (2): 184–215.

Wegner, Phillip E. 2002. *Imaginary Communities: Utopia, the Nation, and the Spatial Histories of Modernity*. Berkeley: University of California Press.

Wernimont, Jacqueline. 2011. "Discovery in the World: The Case of Descartes." In *The Invention of Discovery, 1500–1700*, edited by James Dougal Fleming, 109–24. Abingdon: Ashgate.

PART 4   *Possible Worlds and*
          Digital Media

10 Digital Fictionality

Possible Worlds Theory, Ontology, and Hyperlinks

ALICE BELL

Digital technology has allowed narrative experimentation to expand beyond the page and into an entire network of linked media. Hypertext provides a structure within which chunks of text can be connected in both linear and multilinear configurations; the web, as an ever-expanding hypertext system, allows digital texts to be linked to other digital texts, both fictional and nonfictional. In this chapter I explore recent experiments with hyperlinks in digital fiction and argue that hyperlinks offer authors a medium-specific (Hayles 2004) means of playing with the ontological boundary between fiction and reality. I propose a method for analyzing the ontological function of external hyperlinks in web-based fiction by developing possible worlds theory for its application to digital literary fiction. Rather than offering a purely philosophical or abstract account of fictionality (e.g., Lewis 1978) or a transmedia approach to fictionality (e.g., Zipfel 2014; Ryan 2006, 31–58), this chapter contributes to the development of possible worlds theory as a transmedial approach to fiction, fictionality, individual fictional texts, and, in this case, digital fiction. I propose that some texts use hyperlinks to create flickers between worlds that require the reader to recenter into two different modal universes simultaneously or else rapidly toggle between them, a process that I define here as double-deictic (cf. Herman 2002) recentering. I then show how external links can be used to create a denouement that relies on readers completely revising their perspective of the fictional world. Finally, I show how digital texts can use external links to cause unmarked ontological merges between the actual and textual worlds so as to create an emotionally immersive experience. I thus provide a typology of ontologically playful hyperlinks. I end by suggesting that the use of hyperlinks in digital fiction is part of a more general artistic trend in postmillennial fiction, that of "Remix" (Navas 2012), and that the texts also embody post-postmodern (McLaughlin 2012) thematic concerns.

Digital Fiction, Links, and the Boundaries of the "Text"

Digital fiction is "fiction that is written for and read on a computer screen, that pursues its verbal, discursive and/or conceptual complexity through the digital medium, and that would lose something of its aesthetic function if it were removed from that medium" (Bell et al. 2010). Digital fiction is therefore "born digital" and created for and through digital media rather than being converted from print. It includes hypertext fiction, kinetic poetry, Flash fiction, and some videogames. Digital fictions are often multimodal, so that in addition to text, they may use images, film, sound, or animation to depict the textual actual world (TAW). Further, in almost all digital fictions, the reader has an overt role in constructing the narrative (e.g., by selecting hyperlinks or by responding to textual cues) so that the reader must interact with the narrative throughout the reading experience.

Digital fiction emerged in the late 1980s with CD-ROM-based hypertext fiction. Since the advent of the web in the 1990s, digital fiction has also been published online, meaning that writers and programmers can utilize and experiment with the tools that web technology affords. For example, in addition to the more sophisticated aesthetic qualities that the web offers over CD-ROM-based work (the use of animation, the embedding of film, etc.), the web also facilitates different kinds of interaction, including user-generated content and, as will form the focus of this chapter, different forms and uses of hyperlinking. Hyperlinks in web-based hypertext fiction can be, as in self-contained CD-ROM-based hypertext, "internal," leading to a destination within another part of the same fiction, but they can also be "external," leading to an external website that already exists beyond the boundaries of the hypertext fiction.

The use of external links to external websites means that content from the wider web on which the digital fiction is housed but that has been created independently of the fiction can be materially linked to the text. This is significant for two reasons. First, external hyperlinks lead to external websites that, though they lie beyond the physical boundaries of the text, contain information that is used to construct the fictional world.

The TAW is thus partially constructed not only by content written specifically for the fiction but also by extratextual sources that are linked to the fictional text. Second, because the web houses both fictional and nonfictional content, the external websites may be used as a fictional or nonfictional source relative to the actual world (AW) and, depending on how they are used in the digital fiction, fictional or nonfictional source relative to the TAW. The reader cannot rely on the ontological status of the extratextual sources in the abstract but has to decide how to categorize them relative to both the actual and textual actual worlds. The ontological status of these extratextual sources is therefore flexible and relative, and it ultimately depends on their existence on the web as a network of interconnected documents. These two interrelated issues mean that the model that we apply in the analysis of links in fictional texts must be able to account for the ontological mechanics of these extratextual sources in digital fiction, and the theory we apply must be able to model the way that digital fiction readers process them.

It is important to note that the use of sources that originate in the AW is not something that is exclusively afforded by the digital medium, and it occurs in other forms of (mainly postmodern print) fiction. As Marie-Laure Ryan notes, "In the past few decades, the border between fiction and nonfiction has been the site of numerous violations" (2006, 42), in which she includes "new journalism," "autobiographical writing," "fiction imitating biography," and other texts that "borrow elements from both sides of the divide and . . . link them together in a deliberately heterogeneous collage of individually identifiable fragments" (45), including digital hypertext. For example, in print, W. G. Sebald's novels contain photographs that can be regarded as depictions of the fictional world, AW, or both. Counterfactual historical novels, such as Robert Harris's *Fatherland*, use quotations from actual historical figures to construct the fictional world. In both cases, the artifacts are indexical; they are fictional or nonfictional relative to which world they are read against.

Yet while all media can play materially with ontology, the intertextual collage technique we find in digital fiction is different from the aforementioned devices in print because rather than artifacts being incorporated and printed within the physical boundaries of the text, in web-based fiction the external links provide access to information that lies beyond the physical borders of the text (i.e., the digital fiction website). Thus while, according to Gerard Genette, "a fictional text declares itself to be such by *paratextual* marks that protect the reader from any misunderstanding" (1993, 79), the external websites in digital fiction problematize this way of determining the fictional status of an appropriated source because they reach outside of the digital fiction to other documents. In web-based digital fiction, as in print, paratextual attributes signal the boundaries of the text. These attributes include a URL that indicates that we are viewing a particular website. They might also include a homepage with an author's name on it, a description of the work, and possibly instructions as to how to view and interact with the text. However, when readers follow external hyperlinks, they access information that lies outside of those medium-specific paratextual markers. As Dorothee Birke and Birte Christ conjecture about web-based fiction, "The concept of paratext loses its analytic value at the moment when, on the World Wide Web, context (or the universe of texts) moves so close to the text that 'thresholds,' paratextual elements that negotiate the space between text and context, become increasingly difficult to isolate and identify" (2013, 72).

As the preceding discussion suggests, external links represent a medium-specific device that problematizes the distinction between inside and outside the text and potentially between fictional and nonfictional domains. While hypertext theory has long recognized the epistemological function of the link (e.g., Harpold 1991; Landow 2006) and the cognitive processes that readers apply to understand links in digital fiction (e.g., Ciccoricco 2007; Bell 2014), the ontological function of links and the destinations to which they lead has yet to be addressed. Outside of hypertext theory, as will be shown below, possible worlds theory offers a means of conceptualizing and analyzing fictional ontology. However, theories that have been developed largely in relation to print fiction and that have not had to take this digital intertextual device into account must be modified for their application to digital fiction.

Possible Worlds Theory and Fictionality

Since possible worlds theory is fundamentally concerned with ontology, it is a suitable framework for analyzing the way that texts play with fictionality and, for the purpose of this chapter, the ambiguous ontological games that some digital fictions create with external hyperlinks. Some possible worlds theorists see ontological play as incompatible with the theory because of the impossibilities that digital fictions result in. Doležel, in discussing what he calls "self-disclosing narrative" (1998, 162), in which "fiction-making procedures are overtly exposed" (162), draws on speech act theory to suggest that "the authenticating act is voided by being 'laid bare'" (162) so that these texts "cannot bestow fictional existence" (163). He suggests that while these texts exist as artifacts in the AW, their ontological games undermine their performative force and thus their existence as a fictional world.

Yet while metafictional texts might compromise the logical foundations of possible worlds theory, as Doležel also recognizes, literary texts can and do play with ontology; he later acknowledges that "when it comes to feats of the imagination, nothing is more attractive than impossible worlds" (2010, 35). Indeed, fictional worlds may compromise possible worlds logic to some extent because the concerns of fiction and the aims of associated literary analysis are not those of possible worlds logic. While some fictional texts may compromise possible worlds theory's logical foundations, from a cognitive point of view, readers are adept at conceptualizing ontological configurations that do not necessarily obey the logic laws of the AW. Thus, ontological peculiarities, while impossible according to AW logic, can form part of a fictional reading experience and are not necessarily problematic to process.

Ryan's (1991) possible worlds framework emphasizes the reader's role in cocreating fictional worlds, and it therefore offers a suitable cognitive model for analyzing all kinds of fictional texts, irrespective of the relative (im)possibility of the scenarios that they construct. Her approach begins with the premise that when readers read a fictional text, they deictically relocate or, to use her terminology, "recenter" into a different, fictional modal system. Crucially, therefore, she distinguishes between two systems of modality: the "system of reality" (vii), which is the system in which we live and for which the "actual world" forms the center, and the "textual universe" (viii), which is a modal system created by a text. The textual universe is, like our system of reality, comprised of a "sphere which the narrator presents as the actual world . . . [and] a variety of APWs [alternative possible worlds] revolving around it" (22) that are created by the mental processes of the characters. That is, just as our system of reality is comprised of an AW surrounded by possible worlds that are caused by the dreams, wishes, hypotheticals, and so on of its inhabitants, so too is the textual universe conceptualized as having a central TAW surrounded by alternative textual possible worlds that are created by the dreams, wishes, hypotheticals, and so on of its inhabitants—in this case, the characters.

Ryan suggests that "through their act of make-believe, readers, spectators, or players transport themselves in imagination from the world they regard as actual toward an alternative possible world—a virtual reality—which they regard as actual for the duration of their involvement in the text, game, or spectacle. . . . I call this projection into a virtual body an imaginative recentering" (2008, 251; cf. Ryan 1991, 21–23). Recentering is therefore a cognitive process by which readers imagine and pretend or make-believe and thus, for the duration of their reading, recenter into that TAW. As Ryan acknowledges above, recentering occurs whenever readers encounter a fictional narrative of any kind—they can be "readers, spectators, or players"—and thus the concept of recentering can apply to and also be analyzed in a range of media (e.g., Van Looy 2005). Regardless of which medium is experienced and which modes are used to construct fictional worlds, however, "we know that the textual universe, as a whole, is an imaginary alternative to our system of reality; but for the duration of the game, as we step into it, we behave as if the actual world of the textual universe were *the* actual world" (Ryan 1991, 23).

When reading any fictional narrative, readers rely on their knowledge of the AW to construct the TAW because a text cannot specify absolutely every detail about a TAW. TAWs are thus, strictly speaking, incomplete, and readers have to fill in the gaps by making inferences and speculations about that domain from their knowledge of the AW. In possible worlds theory, the principle of minimal departure (Ryan 1991) is used to explain this process by proposing that readers assume that the TAW resembles the AW until the text describes it otherwise. The use of external hyperlinks in digital fiction can be seen to literalize the principle of minimal departure by making it explicit that information from the AW is being used within the TAW. Hyperlinks thus highlight the process that readers go through when they read fiction because hyperlinks import information very overtly and make what might otherwise be an implicit process very explicit. The ontological boundary between the TAW and AW is thus foregrounded by hyperlinks because they draw attention to the constructed nature of the narrative; the hyperlinks point to another text—one that belongs outside the boundaries of the TAW.

Yet while external links are self-reflexive, they do not completely block the process of recentering or the associated state of immersion. While Ryan claims that recentering is "the basic condition for immersive reading" (2016, 73), which might suggest that readers are in a permanent state of immersion in a TAW, she also acknowledges that different kinds of texts maneuver readers differently. Texts can spatially, temporally, and/or emotionally immerse readers by employing particular stylistic (e.g., immersive forms of narration) and/or plotting (e.g., suspense) structures, or texts can stifle immersion, as she reports postmodern texts do, by "shuttling the reader back and forth between worlds" (2001, 199). The consequence of this kind of interruption to immersion is that readers become aware of their ontological status in the AW and thus aware of the inherent fictionality of the TAW, but that does not mean that they are not recentered or at least partially immersed.

The relationship between immersion and the reader's awareness of the text's fictionality is important for this chapter because external links can affect both. Of course, in any text, irrespective of the modes at work that recenter the reader cognitively, the reader of any text is corporeally and ontologically situated in the AW and therefore external to the TAW. However, this external position can be emphasized or hidden depending on how the text behaves. In any type of text, readers must interact physically with the technology used to display the work. Reading digital fiction is almost always a very physical experience, however, because in order to advance the narrative, readers must click or hold the mouse button, move the mouse across a surface, or type text with a keyboard. web-based digital fictions, which use external links to the (external) AW, can use this interactive, intertextual technique to consistently or intermittently accentuate or minimize the reader's awareness of her ontological position. Links can be self-reflexive or immersive depending on how they are used in a particular text.

In what follows, I analyze the stylistic, multimodal, and interactive features on which external links rely in three digital fictions and propose three new ontological effects—flickering, refreshment, and merging—that are caused by external hyperlinks in digital fiction. I show that possible worlds theory can account for these forms of ontological ambiguity but that Ryan's theory of recentering requires some modification. I address the question of how and why external links, and the medium-specific ontological configurations they facilitate, are used in each text. Not only does this avoid making unsubstantiated conclusions about how external links work in digital fiction in general, it also allows us to see what each text says about the AW to which it electronically, ontologically, and epistemologically connects.

Ontological Flickering: *10:01*

10:01 by Lance Olsen and Tim Guthrie (2005) is a web-based fiction set in a movie theater in the Mall of America in Bloomington, Minnesota, and documents the ten minutes and one second running up to the beginning of the main feature. It is narrated by an omniscient third-person narrator who has access to the thoughts and feelings of the characters. The narrative style thus often drifts into free-indirect discourse. Accordingly, the narrative is primarily concerned with the internal musings, memories, and speculations of the movie theater audience members and ends, chronologically at least, when the movie begins. Olsen and Guthrie's *10:01* is a digital version of Olsen's print novel *10:01*. What the digital platform allows the text to do is to use medium-specific devices to construct the fictional world.

As shown in figure 10.1, visually, readers see a darkened movie theater in which the perspective suggests they are standing at the back with the projection screen; audience members are in front of readers in silhouette.[1] Occasionally, sound effects can be heard, including the heartbeats and heavy breathing of characters. Thus, readers are recentered multimodally in this TAW by being shown a visual image of the movie theater, by hearing noises that originate from it, and by reading about it.

Rather than employing a hypertextual configuration that causes disorientation—a common characteristic of early Storyspace hypertext fiction (see Ryan 2016; Bell 2010)—*10:01* has a very explicit and thus easily navigable structure. Readers can follow internal links on a timeline at the bottom of the screen to experience the narrative in chronological order, or they can click on silhouettes of characters in the movie theater to reveal the parts of the narrative that focus on that particular character. In addition to internal links, *10:01* also uses external links that lead to websites that exist outside of the *10:01* website on the wider web. Notably, while all of the internal links in *10:01* are located either on a character or on a temporal marker on the timeline and thus on a visual anchor, all of the exter-

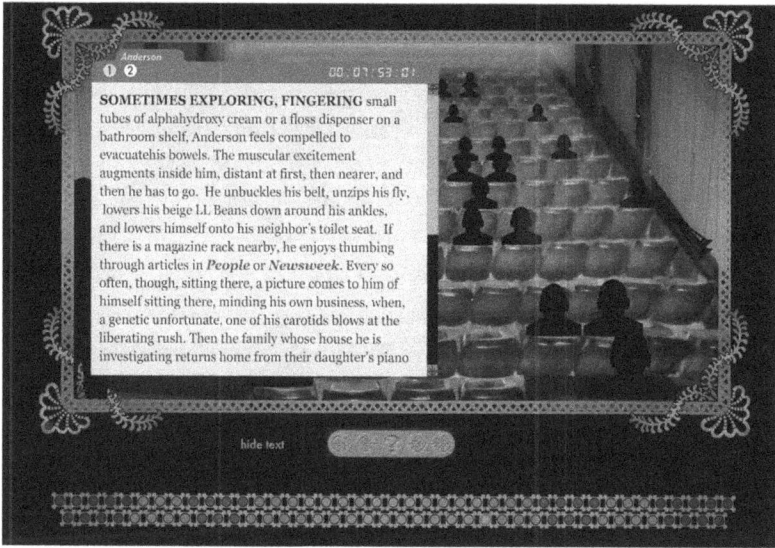

Fig. 10.1. Screenshot of the 00:07:53:01 lexia in *10:01*. Text and concept by Lance Olsen; layout and coding by Tim Guthrie. Reproduced courtesy of Lance Olsen.

nal links are located on words or phrases, meaning that the ontological switch to another domain is initiated via a linguistic marker.

On the one hand, this transparent configuration means that readers know what to expect from each lexia (i.e., a snippet about a particular character), and they can thus read the text according to their own curiosity and without being distracted from the content by being lost in an opaque narrative structure; it is easier for them to be immersed. On the other hand, the interactive function that the reader must perform does still highlight the fictionality of the TAW to some extent because the reader is aware that she is responsible for constructing the fiction. As Ryan notes, in hypertext reading, "every time the reader is called upon to make a decision, she must detach himself from the narrative 'here and now' and adopt a point of view from which she can contemplate several alternatives" (2016, 202; cf. Bell 2010). Thus while the reader can be recentered into the TAW to some extent, her spatial immersion in *10:01* is somewhat limited by the interactive function she has outside of the TAW. Moreover, while materially, the hyperlinks in *10:01* lead to a range of external websites, including commercial, tourist, religious, and literary webpages, in terms of their epistemological function, they are used for three key reasons: to locate the narrative within its geographical setting, to explore the characters' views on life, and to transmit the text's thematic concerns medium-specifically.

Locations such as the Mall of America (in which the narrative is set), Beaver Bay (from which we are told two characters have just returned), and Lake Superior (which Josh Hartnett, a Hollywood actor, intends to visit) lead to their respective official websites. In what Jeff Parker (2001) defines as a "blatant link" that "tells the reader exactly what information will be revealed when activated" (cf. Ryan 2006, 110–11), these hyperlinks act to spatially anchor the narrative in AW locations, but they also show how those particular entities are marketed. The Mall of America website, for example, has the high-production feel of a well-resourced commercial business, with good-quality animation, sleek photo images, and an intuitive navigational structure. The Lake Superior website has more of an amateur feel and signifies a less prosperous enterprise. In these examples, the TAW is populated via information located in the AW, and the link here literalizes the process readers go through according to the principle of minimal departure. Whereas readers usually unconsciously fill in the gaps by, for example, imagining what the Mall of America or Beaver Bay might look like based on their knowledge of AW malls and/or tourist destinations, *10:01* overrides this process by taking the reader to a very particular representation of that space directly. These links thus give the reader a specific sense of the locations, one that, crucially, is based on how those entities are represented in the AW.

Other links give a further sense of the TAW, but from the characters' perspective. We learn that "fastidious . . . contract layer" (04:07:09) Anderson breaks into his neighbors' empty houses to rifle through their belongings. He "envisions himself as an anthropologist" (04:07:09) and, while using their toilet, "enjoys thumbing through articles in *People* or *Newsweek*" (07:53:01). While the description of Anderson gives an impression of an intense and creepy character, the links to the *People* and *Newsweek* sensationalist news magazine websites give some sense of flippancy to his behavior while also showing readers an example of popular American culture.

In both location and character hyperlinks, while readers are initially recentered in the TAW, the external links temporarily expel readers from that domain and recenter them into the AW. However, while readers know that the websites that they are accessing are located in the AW, readers are also required to use this information in the TAW; they are meant to imagine that the characters are sitting in the Mall of America or that Anderson has read the same magazines to which readers have access. The information that they access must therefore be integrated back into the TAW, and the websites must be used as a reference to both the actual and the TAW.

Ryan (2006) offers a means of conceptualizing the ontology of this maneuver. While her modal structure and associated concept of recentering rely on a sharp distinction between the AW and the TAW, she also notes that some texts play with that boundary, making it more difficult for readers to unambiguously determine where the boundary between them falls. In order to conceptualize the ontological status of texts that play with fictionality, she invokes a metaphor of transmission signals. Fictionality can be conceptualized as existing on a continuum of fictional and nonfictional (what she calls the "analogue approach"), or it can be conceptualized in terms of fiction and nonfiction, with a boundary between the two across which elements can be borrowed (what she calls the "digital approach").[2]

The digital approach is the more appropriate metaphor with which to explain the ontological mechanics of links in *10:01*, but it requires modification for it to more accurately account for the way that external links work in this text, as well as the way the reader processes them. Ryan suggests that the digital approach "allow[s] texts to borrow elements from the other side of the border . . . [and] the reader makes separate judgements of fictionality on the local and global level" (2006, 53). Globally, in a general sense as entities in the AW, the Beaver Bay, Lake Superior, and News-week websites are nonfictional. Locally, in the context of *10:01*, however, they depict parts of the TAW, and they therefore become fictional locations or artifacts. That the hyperlink moves the reader from the TAW to the AW spatially while those two spaces are united epistemologically means that the ontological disparity between them is also accentuated. Situated in the AW, the reader uses and evaluates the extratextual source relative to both the TAW and AW. These external websites are thus ontologically indexical and cause flickering (cf. McHale 1997) between the two ontological domains. It is not a static process but one that I would like to define as double-deictic (cf. Herman 2002) recentering, in which readers perceive the external website as relevant to both sides of the ontological boundary, if not at the same time, then in very quick succession.

While I have focused on blatant links to locations and popular culture in this analysis, readers access a range of links in *10:01*, and the connection between the linguistic anchor and the destination website is not always as immediately obvious (see Bell 2014). However, the frequency with which readers visit commercial websites in particular throughout the text makes the TAW seem dominated by capital and consumerism. As well as providing information about the TAW of *10:01*, the links also encourage readers to reflect on the world in which they live, because all of the websites to which the links lead are authentic—that is, they preexisted on the web rather than being constructed for the purposes of the fiction. The print version of *10:01* clearly cannot play the same ontological tricks as the digital *10:01*. In fact, the print *10:01* does not utilize any media or mode aside from printed text. What the links add to the digital *10:01* is a very specific and literal representation of the TAW and, by implication, the AW. There is a risk in using external links to construct the TAW because links are ultimately ephemeral and can be broken. The locations in particular are not described anywhere else in *10:01*, meaning that readers are given all of the information about them by following links to websites. If they are broken, readers will not be able to directly access the impression of, for example, the Beaver Bay that the text wants to give them via the links. However, broken links can also be seen to demonstrate the temporary nature of commercial culture; when the websites are no longer required for capital gain, they are neglected and thus disappear. The same bombardment of the reader by popular culture is not achieved if the links are broken, but the commercialized sense of the world still remains.

With the links functioning, however, I suggest that *10:01* represents a digital example of "Avant-Pop," which, according to its proponents, is a form of art that "combines Pop Art's focus on consumer goods and mass media with the avant-garde's spirit of subversion and emphasis on radical formal innovation" (McCaffery 1995, xvii–xviii, quoted in Olsen 2012, 200). Relying on metafictional devices associated with postmodernist fiction, Avant-Pop works do not just call attention to the artificiality of narratives; instead, Olsen suggests, they seek to "better capture how it feels to exist now" (2012, 206) and thus comment on contemporary Western society. Using a fragmented, hypertextual structure that links directly to the world on which it is commenting, *10:01* embodies the Avant-Pop by directly appropriating artifacts from the AW, paralleling the way that individuals are bombarded with mediated versions and endorsements of people, places, services, and entertainment and thus mimetically using hyperlinks to show the vulgarity of Western (hyper)reality. The ontological flickering and associated double-deictic recentering is thus used thematically as a means of materially and literally representing the AW on which the fiction is based. *10:01* may use playful, self-reflexive devices, but its message is somewhat more serious.

Ontological Refreshment: *Clearance*

While ontological flickers cause a switch back and forth between the actual and textual actual worlds, hyperlinks can also be used to cause a more stable, if not unanticipated, ontological realignment. *Clearance* by Andy Campbell and Judi Alston (2008) is a first-person web-based digital fiction that uses text, film, and sound effects to present an unnerving TAW in which readers are unsure as to what is fictionally real and what is only imagined by the protagonist. On the opening screen, readers witness information being generated from a digital database about protagonist Iggi, his parents, and his wife; Iggi lives in Britain, but the others are dead. Readers experience a car journey down a British country lane, as though they are sitting in the passenger seat before the image is scrambled. Readers then see a British countryside scene that is overlaid in parts with fragments of text and occasionally accompanied by sound. Readers explore the fictional world of *Clearance* using the mouse rather than employing the hypertextual structure of *10:01*. *Clearance* thus utilizes what Jan-Noël Thon, in relation to videogames, calls a "subjective point of view" in which readers experience the fictional world from both "the spatial and perceptual perspective of the player's avatar" (2009, 282). From the first-person perspective we cannot see our avatar, but in terms of navigation, when we move the mouse the screen pans accordingly, thus determining the spatial point of view.

As shown in figure 10.2, in what we are led to believe is the current TAW, the landscape looks desolate. The visuals show a rural setting, but objects such as a dumpster and piles of trash make it appear deprived and neglected or else abandoned. The reader's exploratory function means that she or he is given partial responsibility for the visual perspective, but the visual perspective is partially focalized through Iggy or equipment he might be using. Visuals are sometimes distorted as though a transmission

Fig. 10.2. Screenshot of *Clearance* by Andy Campbell and Judi Alston.
Reproduced courtesy of One-to-One Development Trust—Dreaming Methods.

is being interrupted, and the background sound is a dull rumbling interspersed with crackles that get louder and softer intermittently. Occasionally, we hear the sound of fighter jets flying overhead, and a voice-over
with an American accent warns of an impending military attack. Some
visuals also appear to depict Iggy's memories; as shown in figure 10.2, an
aesthetically grainy scene of young children playing on their retro-style
bicycles is superimposed onto the countryside and suggests a bygone era
rather than the present day that the rest of the narrative depicts. Readers
therefore share Iggy's current point of view with some of his memories.

In the penultimate scene, we see files being deleted from a database,
suggesting that someone in addition to ourselves has been observing Iggy's
behavior and, as a consequence, destroying the data that contain the con-
spiracies that Iggi knows about. Audio recordings taken from news broad-
casts and speeches warn that "everything you have been told about . . .
what was going on was a total lie" and that "they can see everything and
hear everything." Thus, many of the messages we experience are connected
to surveillance and suggest a point of view from someone in psychological distress. Much of Iggy's first-person narrative, often directed at an

unnamed intradiegetic addressee, appears to be paranoid: "I've been seeing new things since you disappeared." This internal perspective allows the
reader then to see the TAW through both the protagonist's and the reader's
own eyes, creating a cofocalized visual and psychological perspective. The
reader is thus recentered, if not spatially immersed, within the TAW via
film, static images, moving visuals, sound, and text. However, throughout, we are unsure whether the verbal accounts and the visual perspective given in the text represent the reality of the TAW or whether they are
Iggy's delusions and thus his private worlds only.

The ontological ambiguity exhibited via Iggy's verbal narrative and
visual perspective is heightened further at the very end of the text via
an external link. As can be seen in figure 10.2, throughout the text large
stone carvings in the shape of human heads appear as though scattered
throughout the TAW in, for example, country fields or inside the garden
shed that forms the last scene. They look incongruous and anachronous
with the landscape because their ancient style conflicts with the modern
temporal setting of the rest of the space. We assume, therefore, that the
stone heads are a product of Iggy's distorted view of the world, that they
are hallucinations along with the other constructions of the world that
we can categorize as paranoid. At the end of the text, the reader is automatically directed via an external link to a Sky News webpage that reports
that twelve "mystery stone sculptures have turned up outside a number
of properties in Yorkshire—but no-one knows why or where they have
come from" (Sky 2007). The effect of this extratextual document for me
was that I tried to determine whether this was an authentic Sky News
website or whether it was a contrived version created specifically for the
text. Once the reader confirms that the report is real and exists on the
actual world Sky News website, the reader is recentered from the TAW to
the AW because the article is about the AW. However, because the article
refers to the stone heads that we see also in the TAW, the content of the
article is retrospectively applied to the TAW. The implication is that if the
stone heads are not a delusion, then perhaps the rest of Iggy's account
also has some truth to it.

This use of an actual world source in *Clearance*, like the external links
in *10:01*, means that an element from the AW is materially appropriated
across the ontological boundary with the TAW. However, because this
occurs at the end of the text and adds a fresh perspective on the narra-

tive, it does not involve a flicker but rather a retrospective realignment of the reader's take on the ontological status of Iggy's tale in the TAW. The external link is used to refresh the ontological status of some elements in the TAW: what we might initially conclude to be a nonactual state of affairs in the form of paranoid delusions in the TAW ultimately materializes to be based on truth.[3]

In terms of conceptualizing this device, the analogue approach to fictionality, which "welcomes every new combination of fact and invention" (Ryan 2006, 52), is more appropriate than the digital analogy. After the denouement, *Clearance* moves from being a purely fictional narrative to a fictionalized and embellished account of an actual world event and becomes a fictional text based on factual events. On a scale, it would sit toward the fictional end, but with a nonfictional base. Thematically, this ontological device is used in *Clearance* to foreground the nature of surveillance. While the postapocalyptic scenario depicted in the text presents a near future possibility that is not yet realized in the AW, we do, like Iggy, live in a world in which we are under some degree of surveillance. Once Iggy's apparent visual delusions of stone heads are reframed as being based on reality, therefore, we question what else in Iggy's narrative can be reframed in the same way. The ontological status of the database with intricate details of citizens' lives, the surveillance voices, and the sounds of military attacks are all problematized. The ontological refreshments that take place in *Clearance* can occur in other media; a novel may end with a declaration that what we thought were purely fictional events are actually based on historical happenings. However, the link to independently published material that exists beyond the boundary of the *Clearance* website, of whose ontological status we might not be immediately sure, is unique to fiction published on the web.

Ontological Merging: *We Are Angry*

We Are Angry by Lyndee Prickitt is described on the homepage as "a piece of multimedia fiction including photos, videos, audio and artwork, but . . . also bolstered by real reports, statistics and editorials." It thus announces itself paratextually as an ontological mix at the outset. The use of the verb "bolstered" is significant because it implies that sources are used to increase the authenticity of, as opposed to undermining or "voiding" (Doležel 1998), the ontological status of the events in the TAW. This is not surprising, given the content of the work. *We Are Angry* is inspired by

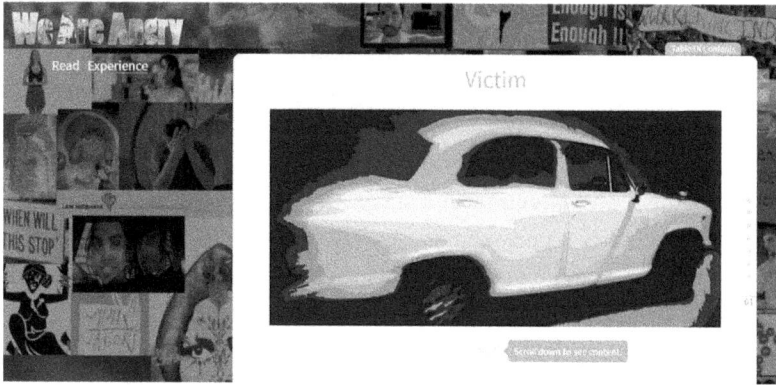

Fig. 10.3. Screenshot of "Episode 1: Victim" in *We Are Angry* by Lyndee Prickitt. Reproduced courtesy of Lyndee Prickitt.

and written as a response to the actual world case of a medical student, Jyoti Singh, who was raped in India and subsequently mistreated by the authorities (Baddeley 2015).

Split into nineteen short sections, the story is told in the first-person mode by an unnamed narrator. As shown in figure 10.3, it opens with a graphically designed image of a white car accompanied by the following text: "This is the car it happened in. A repurposed government car, can you believe?" The proximal demonstrative, "this," recenters the reader within the TAW by deictically aligning his or her spatial point of view within it; the image of the car also works to anchor the narrator's account within that space by offering a visual depiction to accompany her verbal narrative. While the initial image looks artificially constructed, the authenticity of the narrator's tale is more firmly established by a subsequent slideshow of photographs that show the inside and outside of a white car, with blood stains shown on the back seat. The photographic images are shocking; they are used to depict the aftermath of the rape. The narrator presses the reader: "You're not looking at the pictures of the car. Did you look? You wanna see inside?" The use of the second person here acts as an intimate form of address, pulling the reader into an apparent dialogue with the narrator in the TAW. Stylistically and multimodally, therefore, the reader is communicatively connected to and emotionally invested in the narrator's account from the very beginning.

The motives behind the multimodal and multimedia nature of the text are implied via the narrator's early invitation to readers to examine their own attitude to her account. She tells them, "OK, you don't have to look at the photos. You can just read my words and rely solely on my description," before adding, "Only, how do you know I'm telling the truth?" Here the narrator draws attention to the fact that many rape victims are not believed when they report their abuses. This narrator is therefore forced to use all the tools at her disposal to convince her audience that she is telling the truth. In addition to photographs and videos, external hyperlinks are also utilized alongside the first-person narrative. For example, in episode 4 she describes the responses of the police to the rape. She tells us, "Some of them are no better than the brutes they're meant to be protecting the public from" with "Some of them" hyperlinked. The hyperlink takes the reader to four different online newspaper articles from, for example, the *Times of India* and the *Kashmir Observer* about police officers who have been accused of and/or committed rape. That these articles are accessed alongside a fictionalized account of an actual world event adds a further layer of authenticity to the victim's account.

Hyperlinks in *We Are Angry* are not used playfully and therefore flippantly but rather very seriously to enhance the faithfulness of the narrative and the reader's subsequent emotional immersion with the TAW. Ontologically, hyperlinks allow the border between the TAW and AW to be breached so that we see the TAW not just based upon but a feasible version of the AW. In this sense, the TAW merges with the AW. As the examples from *10:01* and *Clearance* analyzed above show, hyperlinks can draw attention to the reading experience and, in some cases, the ontological status of the text. In *We Are Angry*, the links do not self-reflexively highlight the ontological boundary in order to highlight the fictionality of the text. Rather, this fictionalized account of a real-world event is enhanced by the incorporation of extratextual sources. It is as though the reader is reading a hypertextual news report; all sources are there to build a case, but using a mixture of evidence. The reader's emotional immersion is therefore enhanced, and the authenticity of the narrator's account is underlined.

Like *Clearance*, *We Are Angry* suits the analogue approach to fictionality. Since the narrator's tale is a fictionalized version of an actual world event, it represents a digital example of "nonfiction novel" in which "narratives depict actual contemporary events . . . using the styles and techniques of fictional discourse, [but] [u]nlike historical novels, non-fiction novels focus on contemporary themes and dispense with fictive story elements" (Zipfel 2005, 397). It thus exists somewhere in between the nonfictional and fictional poles. In using a first-person account that is verified with a combination of fictional and authentic documents, the reader is asked to accept the narrator's account as viable. Rather than this text upholding the "doctrine of panfictionality" (Ryan 1997), in which fiction and nonfiction are seen as indistinguishable because of their reliance on the same modes of representation, *We Are Angry* is committed to truth in the AW. A rape happened. This text thus relies on a self-reflexive intertextual device—hyperlinks to extratextual sources—but rather than this causing a simply playful ontological self-consciousness, it emotionally immerses readers in and asks them to take a critical stance on this world. That the TAW is based on events from the AW makes the hyperlinks even more powerful in showing the reader the brutality and injustice expressed in the narrator's account.

Conclusion

"As we extend the notion of fictionality to more and more art forms and to more and more media," argues Ryan, we should not "try to fit all media into a rigid mold inherited from language based narrative" nor "completely re-design criteria of fictionality, as we adapt to new media" (2011, 25). In tailoring possible worlds theory for its application to digital fiction and, in particular, modifying Ryan's framework for its application to hyperlinks, this chapter balances medium-specific and transmedial concerns. Theoretically, I have proposed three new ontological effects— flickering, refreshment, and merging—that are caused by external hyperlinks in digital fiction and that can be used to increase immersion and/ or self-reflexivity. While I have shown how these effects are caused via a medium-specific device in digital fiction, the analysis of other media would establish the transmedial existence of these effects, as well as the devices on which they rely. I mention the use of quotations and photographs in print fiction, but there are others.

Indeed, while this chapter has focused on the hyperlink and thus a medium-specific device, I would like to end this chapter by arguing that the use of preexisting sources in web-based fiction is not an esoteric device found only in experimental digital writing but rather is part of a wider cultural trend. In particular, I suggest that external hyperlinks in digital fiction belong to what Eduardo Navas (2012) defines as "Remix." Different from remix culture (Lessig 2009), Remix is a *cultural variable* that is able to move and inform art, music, and media in ways not always obvious as discussed in remix culture" (2012, 3). Remix has its roots in music production but, Navas argues, is the defining aesthetic of the beginning of the twenty-first century. He suggests that remix, "the activity of taking samples from pre-existing materials to combine them into new forms" (65), is a central part of contemporary culture because "new media depends on sampling, (cut/copy and paste)" (74) and "online activities rely on copying . . . information from one point to another" (75). Navas argues, therefore, that while remix as a process has existed since the mid-twentieth century, our current means of communication intrinsically rely on it.

Navas does not consider hyperlinks in his analysis of Remix, but, as the examples above show, the incorporation of sources via hyperlinks depends on reusing—or remixing—preexisting content in a new context. External links in digital fiction thus represent a medium-specific form of Remix, resulting in what Navas would define as a "mashup." As my analyses have also shown, these remix narratives use preexisting AW elements to encourage readers to think about the AW in which they live and/or add authenticity to the narrative. Rather than playing postmodern games that simply foreground the artificiality of the fictional world, therefore, these texts use a postmodern device—ontological self-reflexivity—but for a more sincere purpose. Robert McLaughlin argues that in post-postmodern literature, authors inherit "the postmodern fascination with representation" but that they do so in order to "reconnect with something beyond representation, something extralinguistic, something real" (2012, 213). While the very idea of "post"-postmodern is currently being debated (e.g., Toth 2010), I would argue that the web-based digital fictions analyzed in this chapter represent something different from and thus beyond postmodernist fiction because they use self-reflexive devices to comment on sociopolitical issues in the world beyond the text. As McLaughlin defines the post-postmodern, they "break through the cycle of self-reference, to represent the world constructively, to connect with others" (2012, 215). However, while they may be examples of the current artistic milieu, they also offer something different to print. More specifically, their digital form means that their engagement with the actual world is not just cognitive, conceptual, or thematic but also, via external hyperlinks, material.

Notes

1. The lexia titles track the narrative chronologically in terms of hours, minutes, seconds, and milliseconds. Thus 00:07:53:01 represents seven minutes, fifty-three seconds, and one millisecond into the ten minutes and one second of the title.
2. Digital here does not refer to the medium of the fiction but is used metaphorically.
3. As another nod to the ontological games played in *Clearance*, authorship of the text is attributed to Andy Campbell, Judi Alston, and Billy Johnson. Further exploration of the stone heads reveals that an artist named Billy Johnson was responsible for distributing the stones around Yorkshire (Wainwright 2007).

References

Baddeley, Anna. 2015. "Outrage in India: Rape and Misogyny Exposed—New Ebooks." *Guardian*, March 15. http://www.theguardian.com/books/2015/mar/15/ebooks-the-new-reading-we-are-angry-lyndee-prickitt-jyoti-singh.

Bell, Alice. 2010. *The Possible Worlds of Hypertext Fiction*. Basingstoke: Palgrave Macmillan.

———. 2014. "Schema Theory, Links and Hypertext Fiction." *Style* 48 (1): 140–61.

Bell, Alice, Astrid Ensslin, Dave Ciccoricco, Jess Laccetti, Jessica Pressman, and Hans Rustad. 2010. "A [S]creed for Digital Fiction." *Electronic Book Review*. http://www.electronicbookreview.com/thread/electropoetics/DFINative.

Birke, Dorothee, and Birte Christ. 2013. "Paratext and Digitized Narrative: Mapping the Field." *Narrative* 21 (1): 65–87.

Campbell, Andy, Judi Alston, and Billy Johnson. 2008. *Clearance*. Dreaming Methods. http://dreamingmethods.com/clearance/.

Ciccoricco, David. 2007. *Reading Network Fiction*. Tuscaloosa: University of Alabama Press.

Doležel, Lubomír. 1998. *Heterocosmica: Fiction and Possible Worlds*. Baltimore MD: Johns Hopkins University Press.

———. 2010. *Possible Worlds of Fiction and History*. Baltimore MD: Johns Hopkins University Press.

Genette, Gerard. 1993. *Fiction and Diction*. Cornell NY: Cornell University Press.

Harpold, Terrance. 1991. "The Contingencies of the Hypertext Link." *Writing on the Edge* 2 (2): 126–38.

Hayles, N. Katherine. 2004. "Print Is Flat, Code Is Deep: The Importance of Media-Specific Analysis." *Poetics Today* 25 (1): 67–90.

Herman, David. 2002. *Story Logic: Problems and Possibilities of Narrative.* Lincoln: University of Nebraska Press.

Landow, George. P. 2006. *Hypertext 3.0: Critical Theory and New Media in an Era of Globalization.* Baltimore MD: Johns Hopkins University Press.

Lessig, Lawrence. 2009. *Remix: Making Art and Commerce Thrive in the Hybrid Economy.* New York: Penguin.

Lewis, David. 1978. "Truth in Fiction." *American Philosophical Quarterly* 15 (1): 37–46.

McHale, Brian. 1987. *Postmodernist Fiction.* London: Routledge.

McLaughlin, Robert. 2012. "Post-postmodernism." In *The Routledge Companion to Experimental Literature,* edited by Joe Bray, Alison Gibbons, and Brian McHale, 212–23. London: Routledge.

Navas, Eduardo. 2012. *Remix Theory: The Aesthetics of Sampling.* Vienna: Springer.

Olsen, Lance. n.d. "avant pop." lanceolsen.com. http://www.lanceolsen.com /AP.html.

———. 2012. "Avant-Pop." In *The Routledge Companion to Experimental Literature,* edited by Joe Bray, Alison Gibbons, and Brian McHale, 199–211. London: Routledge.

Olsen, Lance, and Tim Guthrie. 2005. *10:01.* http://www.lanceolsen.com/1001.html.

Parker, Jeff. 2001. "A Poetics of the Link." *electronic book review* 12. http://www .altx.com/ebr/ebr12/park/park.htm.

Prickitt, Lyndee. 2014. *We Are Angry.* Digital Fables. http://www.weareangry.net/.

Ryan, Marie-Laure. 1991. *Possible Worlds, Artificial Intelligence and Narrative Theory.* Bloomington: Indiana University Press.

———. 1997. "Postmodernism and the Doctrine of Panfictionality." *Narrative* 5 (2): 165–87.

———. 2006. *Avatars of Story.* Minneapolis: University of Minnesota Press.

———. 2008. "Fictional Worlds in the Digital Age." In *A Companion to Digital Literary Studies,* edited by Susan Schreibman and Ray Siemens, 250–66. Oxford: Blackwell.

———. 2010. "Fiction, Cognition, and Non-verbal Media." In *Intermediality and Storytelling,* edited by Marina Grishakova and Marie-Laure Ryan, 8–26. Berlin: de Gruyter.

———. 2016. *Narrative as Virtual Reality 2: Revisiting Immersion and Interactivity in Literature and Electronic Media.* Baltimore MD: Johns Hopkins University Press.

Sky. 2007. "Heads Turning over Mystery Sculptures." SkyNews.com, October 1. http://news.sky.com/story/542889/heads-turning-over-mystery-sculptures.

Thon, Jan-Noël. 2009. "Perspective in Contemporary Computer Games." In *Point of View, Perspective, and Focalization: Modeling Mediation in Narrative*, edited by Peter Hühn, Wolf Schmid, and Jörg Schönert, 279–99. Berlin: de Gruyter.

Toth, Josh. 2010. *The Passing of Postmodernism: A Spectroanalysis of the Contemporary*. New York: State University of New York Press.

Van Looy, Jan. 2005. "Virtual Recentering: Computer Games and Possible Worlds Theory." *Image and Narrative* 12. http://www.imageandnarrative.be/tulseluper/vanlooy.htm.

Wainwright, Martin. 2007. "Yorkshire Stone Heads Artist Unmasked." *Guardian*, October 3. http://www.theguardian.com/uk/2007/oct/03/artnews.art.

Zipfel, Frank. 2005. "Non-fiction." In *Routledge Encyclopedia of Narrative Theory*, edited by David Herman, Manfred Jahn, and Marie-Laure Ryan, 397–98. New York: Routledge.

———. 2014. "Fiction across Media: Toward a Transmedial Concept of Fictionality." In *Storyworlds across Media: Toward a Media-Conscious Narratology*, edited by Marie-Laure Ryan and Jan-Noël Thon, 103–25. Lincoln: University of Nebraska Press.

11 : Possible Worlds, Virtual Worlds

FRANÇOISE LAVOCAT

The affinity between the imaginary character of possible worlds and of cyberculture is so obvious that until recently it has barely attracted scholarly interest. Several well-known specialists of online gaming (e.g., Caïra 2007, 2011; Besson 2015) have explicitly rejected the adoption of a logical or ontological perspective in favor of a pragmatic sociological approach or one inspired by cultural studies. When a point of view inspired by literary studies is adopted to treat digital artifacts, it is chiefly narratology that is called upon in order, for example, to examine whether the sources of narrative tension are also at work in video games.[1] When issues concerning the theory of fictionality are used to look at synthetic game environments (Juul 2011; Ryan 2014), often in order to compare them with other narrative media such as literature, drama, and film (character vs. avatar, immersion vs. interaction), these issues usually do not raise the question of possible worlds.[2]

Yet the link between the virtual and the possible (however these terms are understood) is intuitive. The pyramid imagined by Leibniz in Theodore's dream suggests an intermedial framework that combines properties of the theater and the library.[3] The unrepresentable multiplicity of the versions, the moving back and forth between a restricted or expanded representation of how things are, the numbering of Sextus's counterparts, all point to a digital environment that could be implemented through interactive tools such as a hypertext or a touch screen. As anachronistic as this association might be, it seems to fulfil the potential of Leibniz's theory of possible worlds and the imaginary associated with it.

The notion of world is so central in cyberculture that some scholars suggest that terms like "world" and "universe," which in their opinion are only being used metaphorically and abusively in literary theory, should be reserved for digital artifacts (Caïra 2011). One does not have to be an aficionado of video games to recognize the founding role that Tolkien's work played for them by providing the fauna, flora, maps, geography, language, and history of an exceptionally rich imaginary country. Also well known is the crucial role of experiences such as creating objects, traveling, and passing from one world to another, as well as of notions such as space and habitat, for the visualization, development, and use of digital artifacts. *Second Life*, the very name of the persistent universe that proved itself to be the most durable (together with *World of Warcraft* in the category of video games), suggests the possibility of offering an alternative existence to its users. (At the time of this writing, this meant about a million people.) As the interface of Apple products suggests, the cosmological imaginary is consubstantial with the digital medium: every Apple user sees a galaxy on the start-up screen.

The association of worlds with digital technology may seem too obvious to be worth developing. Although the algorithms necessary for the visualization of these pixelated worlds are invisible and their functioning is beyond the competence of users, "building a world" has a very literal meaning in a synthetic environment. Under these conditions, isn't the somewhat ponderous apparatus of possible world theory superfluous? And what would a possible world be like in a synthetic environment? Would it be a game space presented as a world, that is, a mimetic space with its towns, its flora and fauna, it inhabitants, and its laws? Would it be the world created by one particular game session? Could every possible development of the game, as determined by the choice of a player, be regarded as a distinct possible world?[4] The first option seems the most compatible with our project of accounting for the diversity of games through modal categories. The other options would be adequate for an approach more interested in narrativity and hypertext, but this is not the concern of this chapter. Alternatively, one could consider cyberspace in general as a giant possible world inhabited by pixelated creatures. This option is tempting (we shall see below that the marketing strategy of some games, such as *Second Life*, plays on the global appeal of the virtual as world), but it is not very useful for our approach because it does not allow sufficient distinctions. We will therefore associate possible worlds with particular games without forgetting that their ontology is strongly conditioned by the fact that they belong to digital media.

The difficulty is increased by the fact that "possibility" can have very different meanings. It is sorely tempting to restrict the "possible" to the Aristotelian meaning of the term: the "possible" is whatever can be produced by virtue of antecedents, laws of causality, and observance of the laws of physics in a given world. It should be remembered that from a logical point of view, a "world" is only an abstraction and "possibility" is an accessibility relation, that is, a relation between possible worlds and a particular world serving as point of reference or between possible worlds themselves. In logic, a possible world is a set of modalized propositions (Kripke 1963). This set must be consistent, maximal, and complete.[5]

In the literary domain, a possible world (which is not necessarily noncontradictory) is generally understood, in the broadest terms, as an alternate state of affairs with respect to the world of reference.[6] Other possible worlds are accessible from literary possible worlds, whether they are textually actualized (e.g., as variants, versions, adaptations) or not (as conceivable but undeveloped possible plots, as mental projections of the characters, etc.). The possible worlds of the actual world and those of fictional worlds do not have quite the same status: an inhabitant of the actual world only has a single life tethered to this world (disregarding potential postmortem survivals in supernatural worlds, according to certain belief systems), whereas alternate versions of the life of a fictional character are potentially infinite. Another version of the actual world cannot be actualized, whereas in the fictional universe the cohabitation of several noncompossible states of this world can occur (Woody Allen's 2004 film *Melissa and Melissa* is an example).[7] The real world is surrounded by a myriad of nonactualized possible worlds (dreams, hypotheses, all the possibles that never come to be), all of which develop fictional other versions of the real world. On the other hand, literary or cinematic fictions, in their rough drafts, their adaptations, their translations, their sequels, are surrounded by a multitude of actualized possible worlds. Insofar as they function as actual worlds within a world system, the real world and traditional fictional worlds have different statuses.

The application of possible world theory to the fictional worlds of literature and film reveals quite easily the ontological characteristics of these worlds. The connection between the virtual worlds of digital technology and possible worlds presents greater difficulties. First, in online game worlds, the same characters return every time the game is played, but a new state of affairs is generated that is a variant of the state of affairs of the preceding game session. One could say that a video game is less a possible world in relation to the real world than it is a collection of possible worlds drawn from elements of both fictional (characters, setting, theme) and real (the rules of the game) (Juul 2011).

But the most fundamental difficulty arises from the ontological status of the virtual. Should we consider virtual worlds to be actualized possible worlds, as the inventors and developers of certain online worlds would have us believe? According to them, the attractiveness of these games resides in great part in their supposed ontological status. The exact nature of this status will be the first question that I will address; it will be examined through some of the practices found in cyberculture and synthetic environments like *Second Life*. I will then look at the comparison between actual worlds, fictional worlds in literature and film, and online worlds from the perspective of modalities (alethic, epistemic, deontic, and axiological), and I will show that these worlds differ radically from each other from a modal point of view. Finally, I will ask what the theory of possible worlds might contribute to the understanding of video games compared with what it offers for other media. Does the main advantage of applying possible worlds theory to online worlds go beyond allowing us to discern their ontological properties? In other words, does the virtuality of digital worlds condition their modal characteristics?

In the discussion to come I will distinguish metaverses, or massively multiplayer online games (MMOGs), such as *Second Life*, from massively multiplayer online role-playing games (MMORPGS), such as *World of Warcraft*, and from single-player video games, such as *Grand Theft Auto*.[8] Metaverses are empty playgrounds that users fill with objects and avatars of their own design, while most video games have a built-in narrative that gives players specific roles and tasks to accomplish. Metaverses are dominated by the kind of play that Roger Caillois called *paidia* (more specifically, mimicry, i.e., imitation) and games of the kind that he called *ludus* (more specifically, *agôn*, i.e., competition).

Metaverses: Actualized Possible Worlds?

In the wake of the creation of *Second Life* (2003, henceforth *SL*) numerous online worlds, more or less ephemeral, have been created (Lavocat 2016, 316). I will nevertheless take *SL* as my example, despite its being dated, given that it is still the best-known world of its kind. Although the appearance of the virtual environments and the rules governing the movement and abilities of the different avatars might differ, most of the observations I make about *SL* are applicable to the rest of these worlds.

A persistent world like *SL* can be thought of as a possible world in two ways: in a broad, affective sense, as a habitat (a conception used strategically by creators and developers of Linden Lab, the proprietary owner of *SL*), and in a somewhat more precise way: this world can be envisaged as a collection of states of affairs that can be expressed in propositions, susceptible to being analyzed in terms of modalities, and compared with the modalities governing the real world. *SL* is therefore "accessible" via the real world in the sense that relations can be established between the two worlds conceptually. But "access" to the virtual worlds is generally understood in a far more literal fashion because it requires specific active procedures. Access (to another world) is moreover often highly thematized: many online worlds and video games (like *Minecraft*) require the construction or the discovery of "portals" that represent and dramatize the passage from one "world" to another. This is clearly the case in "Better Life" with Robbie Dingo (the name of the avatar of the author, Rob Wright), one of the machiminas contained in the CD that comes with the official guide for *SL* (Rymaszewski et al. 2006).[9] This short promotional film shows a man sitting at a desk in front of a computer in a room that is empty except for a scale model of an old airplane, a sort of vintage children's toy. After a few minutes, we see that the man, who looks strangely like an avatar, is in a wheelchair. Illegible numbers scroll by on the screen and end up coming out of the screen that the man is looking at to form a gaseous planet, which looks like the earth. The man plunges his head into this spherical mass, a gesture reminiscent of Thomas Anderson's dive into the mirror in the film *Matrix* (1999) (see fig. 11.1).

The man's literal dive into the planet (which is as explicit a visualization of immersing oneself in a world as one could hope for!) is transformed into the image of this man flying, floating, falling, and pirouetting in a cloudy sky. He is wearing a light parachute, which, once open, swells above his head into an orange corolla in harmony with the sunset (see fig. 11.2).

The feet of the man finally land on the ground. At that moment, a rain of stars surrounds the legs of the avatar, suggesting a miracle: this is

Fig. 11.1. Immersion in a new world. From "Better Life" by Rob Wright.

Fig. 11.2. The flight of the disabled man. From "Better Life" by Rob Wright.

expressed both in the recovered agility of the man in the wheelchair and in the gentle landing on a magical earth.

There follows for the spectator a return to the initial world, showing the man in his wheelchair asleep on his keyboard. Then the same sequence of fall, flight, and landing is repeated. The video underlines the compensatory dimension of a voyage about which it is suggested that it extends or replaces an airplane ride from a childhood dream. What is impossible for a man in the real world, and even more so for someone in a wheelchair, is possible in another world: on this globe that bursts out of the computer as the counterpart of our real world.[10] In reality, of course, *SL* does not breach the barrier of the screen (despite the best efforts of those who dress up in real life as their avatars in *SL*!). This metalepsis is precisely the object of desire. In the Rob Wright video, the oneiric version of *SL* presents the flight of the Robbie avatar in a way that is never presented in *SL*. The script is paradoxical and rather ingenious: the relation actual world (AW) / virtual world (VW, or *SL*) is represented by a present virtual world that can be called virtual actual world (VAW), the present-world-in-the-fiction, here the fiction in a digital environment (therefore virtual, because it already belongs to the universe of *SL*: the "real" man is an avatar).[11]

The animation shows a world "real in the digital fiction," the world inhabited by the disabled man (let's call it VAW) and a possible alternative of VAW: the world of the dream that comes out of the computer (let's call it virtual possible world, VPW). VAW perhaps belongs to the world of *SL*, since the supposedly real man looks like an avatar, but (and here lies the paradox) in VAW, *SL* does not exist: the pixelated planet (PVW) is the dream of the disabled man. It must be understood that in life, in AW (or, according to the users' jargon, "in real life," or IRL), *SL* is analogous to this dream, or better still, *SL* fulfils this dream, which makes the desire of the user and that of the avatar coincide. It is in this sense that *SL* presents itself, with a suspicious insistence, as an actualized possible world: a world where our avatars would have desires that are ours and where virtuality and reality would be indiscernible. This, of course, is not the case.

The objection will perhaps be made that traditional fictional worlds also present themselves as desirable possible worlds and are no less capable of being actualized by the imagination by means of fictional immersion. So what is the difference? A long series of literary characters have been represented in a situation of fictional immersion, from Don Quixote to Thursday Next.[12] A critical attitude and humor are never absent from the story of their adventures. By contrast, one of the characteristics of *SL*'s promotional machimina is its seriousness, not devoid of pathos, which annuls the distance that would be created in traditional fictional worlds (at least in principle) by a metafictional dimension. This deliberate naïveté is perhaps inherent to the novelty of the medium. What is more, virtual worlds such as *SL* are, in contrast to traditional fictional worlds, devoid of scripted plots and system-created characters. In these empty spaces, the desiring projection of the users can be freely fulfilled via the ambiguous alter egos that are the avatars.[13]

Finally, virtual worlds differ from fictional worlds in that they become present-for-us through interactivity, rather than through the imaginative and purely subjective operation that Marie-Laure Ryan has called "recentering." The supposed actualization of this possible world comes from the fact that the avatars and their activities are the product of a series of actions and operations carried out, IRL, by the user. Nothing prevents an imaginary shift in point of view, but this shift is inseparable from a presence, admittedly mediated but concrete, of the user in the virtual world. The illusion of the actualization of a desirable possible world thanks to a digital environment depends on real gestures executed by the user. It rests also largely on the ambiguous nature of the avatars, which can be considered both as the expression of the user's identity and as fictional characters (even if this nature is less and less enigmatic as digital natives become dominant among the users of video games; see Besson 2015). The difference between an avatar and a character derives from the difference between a virtual world and a traditional fictional world. Envisaging these worlds in terms of modalities enables us to measure this divergence.

Virtual Possible Worlds and Modalities

As Lubomír Doležel (1998) sees it, the manipulation of the domain of application of modalities is a basic aesthetic resource for the creation of the fictional possible worlds of literature. This is equally true for online worlds. The play of modalities is quite different in online worlds from the play in other media. Let's observe, however, that the modification of the domains of the possible and the impossible (which depend on the alethic modality) in digital environments is not without a passing resemblance to the universe of fairy tales. The predominance of the magical in everything related to the digital is evident to any observer, even though realistic and fantastic worlds coexist within *SL*. (The most recent trend in contemporary video games seems indeed to be a move toward realism, as the game *Arma 3 Altis Life* [see below] suggests.) The revival of the fantasy genre and of its magic is paired historically with the emergence of digital media. This coincidence derives in my opinion from the profound affinity of digital media and the fantasy genre in their treatment of modalities (in particular the alethic and, to a lesser degree, the axiological).

The domain of application of the alethic modality in *SL* is indeed both expanded and restricted by comparison with the real world. First, it affects avatars: if the avatar is conceived as an alter ego, a counterpart of the user (in this regard there are as many debates as there are practices), it can undergo a change of sex or of species; it can be rejuvenated, embellished; and it can survive its user if somebody else activates it. Avatars are potentially eternal and will live as long as the game operates, provided Linden Lab does not cancel the user's account following an infraction of the (few) rules of the game. Avatars' abilities are at once more extensive than those of human beings (some of them can fly) and infinitely more reduced (they are not autonomous).[14] In addition to the avatars' stereotypical character, the ease and rapidity with which they can act on their environment, construct it, destroy it, and fill it with objects is reminiscent of the universe of fairy tales. With a couple of demiurgic clicks, as if the mouse were a magic wand, blocks pile up, walls go up, vegetation grows, mountains rise up, seas dry up. Yet despite a few aesthetic successes, which are often highly publicized, these worlds are not only unstable (because their accelerated construction and destruction follow one another without a pause), they are extremely incomplete, compared to the real world: in *SL* virtual Paris or Venice only comprises a few streets. It is true in this regard (it is also a characteristic of novels, as Thomas Pavel [1983] has noted) that video games are able to maximize or minimize incompleteness. But their degree of completeness has no impact on their success. A game like *Minecraft* offers us a world made of an assemblage of cubes that represent small flora and fauna (the latter is limited to sheep and pigs). The obviously primitive character of this world's components has not stopped it from reaching a total of about one million users. In contrast, *Arma 3 Altis Life* takes place in a realistic setting, a counterpart of the island of Lemnos based on photographs of its map, streets, houses, and lesser-known spots. Several internet users who post their mods for educational purposes claim that this realism is one of the attractive features of the game. But even in this kind of realistic environment, the ease with which one can acquire money and weapons (the game revolves around a confrontation of "civilians," criminals, terrorists, and the police) has something magical about it.

If the modification of the domain of application of alethic modality, which involves principally the elimination of certain material and physical constraints, is inherent to all virtual ludic universes, then the modification of epistemic modality is no less crucial. Access to ludic virtual worlds requires knowledge and know-how. In the case of video games, these competences allow users to fulfill quests (in general, killing monsters) that lead to the acquisition of merit points; in the case of online worlds such as *SL*, they determine the appearance of the avatar, its ability to act, its social status vis-à-vis other avatars, all factors that contribute to the enjoyment of the virtual world. Users can potentially make up for their insufficiencies by paying in Linden dollars (bought with a currency in circulation IRL) for the acquisition of objects or competences that they cannot obtain by their own means.[15] It could be said that this is no different from the real world. But the resemblance is deceptive: in a video game killing a monster, building a house, or making clothes are all the visible manifestations of one and the same ability that underlies all activities in all virtual worlds, namely, the ability to master computer technology and the interface of the game. Aptitudes as diverse as foresight, motor and cognitive agility, a sense of organization, and many other qualities are admittedly mobilized depending on the game, whether it is one of combat, strategy, or simulation (those who want to integrate video games within pedagogy insist on the innumerable cognitive benefits afforded by these games), but the primary ability required by computer games, the one that gives access, in the literal sense of the word, to their world, the one that makes it possible to earn money, the one that is taught, the one that creates a gulf between generations and genders,[16] the one that, all things considered, makes it impossible to assimilate digital artifacts with any other artistic or cultural product, is computer competence. This is even more evident for universes (such as *SL*) that are not organized primarily as *agôn* games. It could therefore be said that the defining characteristic of virtual worlds with respect to the epistemic modality resides in the importance of digital literacy.[17]

What about the two other modalities, the axiological and deontic? The domain of application of the deontic modality (which concerns the permitted, the obligatory, and the forbidden) is totally different depending on whether one is speaking of online universes like *SL* or of video games in the narrow sense of the term. These cases must consequently be treated separately.

From a legal point of view, to enter *SL* implies the contractual acceptance of rules and policies (or terms of agreement), which are defined in a charter known as "Community Standards." Linden Lab stipulates six rules: (1) tolerance, (2) nonharassment, (3) nonaggression (users are absolutely not in a competitive game), (4) protection of private life (it is forbidden to divulge any information about users IRL), (5) division of *SL* into different regions and groups, and (6) peace (it is forbidden to interfere with the normal functioning of the game, e.g., by pirating the server). The first three rules, which concern relations with other people, are common in the real world and in the virtual world, with the important exception of sanctions: insulting, humiliating, raping, torturing, or threatening an avatar will entail no worse punishment than the suspension of the account of the user of the trouble-making avatar. Notably, nobody has ever been jailed for having their avatar murder other avatars. So we are only dealing here with a partial homology. Rules 4, 5, and 6 are specific to the virtual world. The purpose of the fourth and fifth rules is to provide this world with a form of autonomy: the fourth aims at preventing interference from real-world information that would threaten users' privacy; the fifth territorializes the domain of application of rules that are implicitly in force in the real world: dividing the *SL* universe into sectors ("general," "moderate," "adult") amounts to allowing various degrees of permissiveness concerning the representation of sexual acts. There are also numerous reserved spaces in the general domain of *SL*, such as private properties surrounded by an invisible barrier that stops unwelcome avatars. In the "Adult" part or in reserved spaces, avatars can participate in activities that are difficult or impossible to do IRL, provided their users have bought them the necessary competences and attributes. Pedophilia is generally prohibited, whether the user is a minor, which is hard to verify, or whether he is an adult but his avatar has a childlike appearance.[18] Also forbidden is slavery. It is, however, difficult for the company to prevent anyone from receiving money IRL for selling his avatar to a slave-master avatar! *SL*, like other virtual worlds, is a permissive world with a high level of criminality. Because control is largely nonexistent and because sanctions are only virtual, a number of criminal practices not covered by the charter are rampant in it, such as blackmail, extortion, and money laundering (Cornelius and Hermann 2011; Castronova 2005; Pfeiffer, Wang, and Beau 2007, 198–220).

From a deontic perspective, the most paradoxical aspect of virtual worlds comes from the status of the body. Even though much has been written on this subject, how to define an avatar and, above all, the relation linking it to its user remains extremely problematic.[19] The extreme permissiveness that reigns in *SL*, at least from the point of view of representing sex, can be explained by the fact that the avatars are nothing but an assemblage of pixels and a few lines of code. One wonders why the charter forbids physically mistreating other avatars, such as shooting, pushing, or shoving, since this is physically impossible. The charter relies on the idea that the relation between the user and his or her avatar involves the subjectivity of the user, otherwise it would not be forbidden to insult another avatar. Other difficulties arise, of course, all of which refer back to the difficulty of working out the status of the virtual world. A marriage in *SL* (of which there are many) has no validity of any kind, and a user will never be found guilty of bigamy because he has a real wife and one or several virtual wives. This, obviously, cannot stop the real-life partner of the user from regarding this virtual relationship as a cause for divorce. But how should one treat the case of the multiple enclaves within *SL* that have referential ties to the real world? A grade given to the avatar of a student in one of the numerous universities that have an annex in *SL* will be valid, in contrast to a marriage performed in Pixel City Hall. It is also fair to suppose that students who, in the form of an avatar, insult the professorial avatar could be punished IRL. Moreover, if a lot of money circulates in online worlds, the status of virtual goods fluctuates: it is difficult to file a complaint IRL for the theft of virtual goods (although it does happen).[20] If Linden Lab, accidentally or intentionally, destroyed a virtual life or virtual possessions, no recourse would be possible against the company, even if these properties were acquired at great expense (Castronova 2005).

From a deontic point of view, the world of video games is much more coherent than the world of metaverses of the MMOG type such as *SL*. In these games, a relation of identification of the player to the game-playing character and to his or her multiple "lives" is not expected, and for digital native players, sentimentality in this regard is not called for. The charters of good conduct that regulate (not without contradictions) social behavior in the heart of the virtual community are replaced by the rules of the game, which function less as conventions that one might potentially infringe than as the laws of nature that govern the world and that one is forced to accept to gain entrance. As Juul has so aptly observed, this fundamental characteristic of game rules makes the modalities of single user video games (this is even truer for MMORPGS) completely different in relation to those of MMOGS.

The axiological system also differs in the persistent online worlds of the *SL* type and the MMORPGS, just as it differs in these cases from the system governing the moral values that reigns in the real world, as well as in fairy tales and many novels (even though it would be risky to treat "novels" as a unified world from the axiological point of view).

In a world like *SL*, the deontic system and the axiological system are linked. To be aggressive in words as in acts is evaluated negatively from a moral point of view, as we see from the first three articles of the charter. For the rest, the world of *SL* is indifferent to deviant behavior, which leads to liberal morality. Since a myriad of microworlds exists in *SL*, nothing can prevent a community from imposing its rules and its morality in its territory. But on the level of the microworld, the domain of application for axiological modality is reduced and focalized on one aspect alone: relations to another person. We have already noted a comparable limitation concerning epistemic modality practically reduced to computer competence. The rules of a world like *SL* still depend on the rules in force in the real world, even if only a very reduced and simplified part of the normative system of (Western) societies is retained.[21] In the case of video games, independence with regard to the norms and laws of the real world is much greater. This independence is, however, not total, especially if we take into account current debates and the widely accepted belief that video games promote a taste for violence and immorality. When a game distributor declares, the day after an attack, that it will suspend its ad campaign "for the sake of decency," it is because it acknowledges the public's opinion concerning the supposed porosity between the virtual world and reality.[22] It could be objected that this accusation has been made about every fictional universe, whatever their medium. However, games are not traditionally concerned with questions of morality. From the axiological point of view, games in general are indeed characterized by their neutrality, as we will see later. This is not exclusive to MMORPGs. Someone playing Battleship with pen and paper never asks himself or herself whether it is good or bad to sink a ship. In games of Cops and Robbers, it would never occur to anyone to make the children aware of the immorality of identifying with one role or the other. In a game of checkers or chess, the fact that White or Black wins has no importance on the political or moral level. For most users, the same applies to video games.[23] Even if certain users complain about what they call the "Manichaeism" of the games, that accusation stems, according to them, from the fact that their avatar must always kill the dragon. Nobody seriously thinks that the dragon is the incarnation of evil or that eliminating it provides ethical benefit, beyond the fact that it is good for the player, since he can earn some points that way.

But video games are often mixed universes. Insofar as they are possible worlds, their status is ambivalent: they are both games and, most of the time, fictions that share some features with traditional literary or cinematic fictions. Now fictions, to use Thomas Pavel's insightful definition, are "worlds of norms and goods" ("Univers de fiction: un parcours personnel," 2003, 312). Insofar as fictions are operators of empathy, the modal system pertaining to games thus conflicts with that of fiction. If the detractors of games regard them as particularly dangerous, it could be because the moral qualities inherent to fiction (especially literary and cinematic) risk being neutralized by games. Interestingly, realism seems to be an aggravating factor; remember that the same thing was said about the novel (cf. the accusation of immorality of *Madame Bovary*, which resulted in a court case).

A game like *Arma 3 Altis Life* takes place in a very realistic setting: the fullness of this possible world has been maximized, since almost all the houses and streets of the two real islands, Lemnos and Agios Efstràtios, are reproduced in a photographic form in the virtual universe. The game inspires, on the part of certain players, frequent clarifications. In the sequence "taking hostages," available on YouTube, the player reminds us on numerous occasions not to take the game "to the first degree," as if he felt the need to remind us that in the real world he was not a robber or a terrorist (another sequence, also available on YouTube, is called "suicide vest").[24]

This explicit distancing on the part of a player who is about to share his ludic exploits with a very large audience reveals an uneasiness that, to my knowledge, has never been expressed by players of a game like *World of Warcraft*. In this massively multiplayer game, the designers have cunningly distributed strengths between the Horde and the Alliance so that there is not too great an imbalance between these opposing forces on the battlefield. Axiological neutrality is a condition of playability. But how does this work in the many games based on history, particularly in those games that pit against each other the Allies and the Axis instead of the Horde and the Alliance?[25] The game *Arma 3* (in the 2013 version) opposes NATO at the end of its mandate and groups of guerrillas made of former allies who are seeking to overthrow the government in power while fighting the American occupier. Even though the action is slightly displaced temporally and spatially (the game takes place in 2053 on some islands in the Mediterranean), it is easy to read into it an oblique reference to current wars. In such a case, is axiological neutrality possible? Is it desirable? We can see that the problem raised by the reference to the real world is, to some degree, similar for video games and traditional fiction: it is clearly this kind of reference that defines, in a great number of cases, the threshold of acceptability for a cultural artifact. But it makes a difference, once again, when fiction is combined with a game. The question of the favorable presentation of a morally reprehensible individual or party is not as important in games as in traditional fictions. Nor is the question of the player's possible identification with these negative models. The relevant question centers rather on the possible and even necessary neutralization of moral evaluations required in order to play.

The modal specificity of the possible worlds constituted by video games also operates when empathy is the issue. In principle empathy is not one of the attitudes required in competitive games. If the hero of a combat game must pass as many tests as possible and react as fast as possible to achieve his goal, he cannot afford any compassion or sympathy for the enemies he encounters on his way. Yet empathy, an essential resource in fiction, is a dimension that certain ludic worlds would like to harness. In order to avoid slowing down the hero or annoying the player, some games limit altruistic attitudes to secondary characters, companions, or auxiliaries, such as doctors, who can stand at the hero's side; it also happens, more and more frequently, that the decision to act altruistically on the part of the hero is rewarded by extra points. But if it is a matter of earning a reward, can we properly speak of a moral action, or should we expect moral actions to be totally disinterested? Advocates of serious games (e.g., Krebs 2013) argue that certain games (like *Heavy Rain* in 2010 and *Catch 22* in 2012) confront players with sophisticated moral dilemmas that test their critical faculties and their aptitudes for moral reasoning.[26] But it is still questionable whether ethical conflict really constitutes the most powerful source of appeal of these games.

There are, however, some games meant to attract women (who are supposedly more sensitive to ethical questions) in which the rules of the game reward a morally positive attitude, an inclination to care. This could be the case when the game goal is a matter of developing a community in a given environment. But, here again, are we really dealing with moral issues? A certain number players of *The Sims*, instead of building a prosperous and harmonious community, subvert the game goal and seek on the contrary to destroy their family of avatars as fast as possible (Suler and Wende 1998; Meadow 2008). Should we consider it immoral to exterminate a *Sims* family? Is it any more or less so than for a child to drown a doll or for an author to kill a character? If exterminating a *Sims* family is not immoral, it would be difficult to consider that the inverse action, namely, making your avatars prosper, is an authentically moral action. However, the Japanese parents who, since 1996, have given their children Tamagotchi (virtual pets) consider undoubtedly that the care shown to a pixelated creature is conducive to the development of their children's moral and social qualities and constitutes an educational experience. To let your virtual horse die from neglect is certainly not praiseworthy and may elicit a guilt feeling. However, now that the development of virtual animals has progressed considerably, allowing people to raise penguins, earthworms, dinosaurs, and virtual dragons, the young breeders probably become indifferent to them, just as people become jaded with respect to video game avatars. The importance of the axiological modality in the different categories of video games is decidedly weak.

Conclusion

The virtuality of digital worlds conditions their ontological status, as well as their modal characteristics. Virtuality, which can be defined as a form of presence deprived of corporality and summoned by interacting with the computer, causes an extension of the domain of the possible, a concentration of the domain of knowledge, a specialization of the domain of rules, and an extreme reduction of the domain of ethics. It is evidently the absence of body and of physical matter that explains this dissymmetry between the enlargement of the domain of the possible and the reduction of that of morality: experienced differently depending on the nature of the worlds and of the games, the lack of embodiment leads to permissiveness in the representation of sexuality, to indifference with respect to the elimination of avatars, and to reluctance on the part of the law to prosecute infractions concerning virtual property and to punish its theft or illegal sale.

We might ask why a work of literary or cinematic fiction whose characters are certainly no more physically present (with the exception of the theater) than the avatars in a digital environment inspires far greater emotions and stronger moral judgments than digital worlds. One reason for this is that fictions, at least novelistic ones, construct situations that present interesting ethical choices, while ethical matters are not a concern of online worlds and rarely one of video games. Video games often take place (although the current tendency favors realism) in fantasy universes: dragons and elves are less likely to arouse empathy than more anthropomorphic creatures. In addition, the reader's imagination bestows on the paper creatures of literary fiction the full range of human attributes (and even more on the characters of films or theater who are represented in the flesh by human beings), whereas a pixelated entity is often incomplete to begin with: it must develop abilities, attributes, even organs that can be purchased or won by playing the game. While none of these characteristics totally prevent the experience of an emotional relation to the artifact, they do not encourage it. Finally and above all, the more important the ludic dimension, the more autonomous the modal, deontic, and axiological values become in relation to the real world; and the more the deontic dimension, which is assimilable to the rules of the game, neutralizes the axiological dimension. This is why games and traditional fiction (fiction being understood here as any artifact produced by the imagination that induces immersion and empathy) produce different and in many respects incompatible possible worlds: it is the examination of video games as possible worlds that enables us to understand their difference.

Notes

1. Among the most recent contributions on this question, see in particular Walsh (2011); Caracciolo (2015).

2. For an intermedial perspective about video games, see especially Ryan (1994); Chaouli (2005); Caracciolo (2015); Caïra (2016). On the issue of virtual worlds and PW theory, see, however, the work of Ryan (2001b); Van Looy (2005); Punday (2005); and Bell (2010). Punday focuses exclusively on the first generation of multiplayer games (*Dungeons and Dragons*, 1974), which he sees as a way for users to reenact literary genres and characters: "Role-playing games, then, are fundamentally a way for players to engage in favorite books and popular subgenres, to make beloved texts into a place where one can play" (2005, 121). He is only interested in possible worlds theory to the extent that it brings to light phenomena of hybridization and recycling. He does not develop the issue of modalities but observes instead that the rules of games are based on intertextuality with respect to fantastic texts. It is doubtful, however, that this observation is still accurate for recent games, which tend to move away from the fantastic. Van Looy applies to virtual worlds Ryan's notions of recentering and minimal departure. He demonstrates in particular how the game *Myst* comments on its own status as virtual world.

3. "Thereupon the Goddess led Theodorus into one of the halls of the palace: when he was within, it was no longer a hall, it was a world, *Solemque suum, sua sidera norat*. At the command of Pallas there came within view Dodona with the temple of Jupiter, and Sextus issuing thence; he could be heard saying that he would obey the God. And lo! he goes to a city lying between two seas, resembling Corinth. He buys there a small garden; cultivating it, he finds a treasure; he becomes a rich man, enjoying affection and esteem; he dies at a great age, beloved of the whole city. Theodorus saw the whole life of Sextus as at one glance, and as in a stage presentation. There was a great volume of writings in this hall: Theodorus could not refrain from asking what that meant. It is the history of this world which we are now visiting, the Goddess told him; it is the book of its fates. You have seen a number on the forehead of Sextus. Look in this book for the place which it indicates. Theodorus looked for it, and found there the history of Sextus in a form more ample than the outline he had seen. Put your finger on any line you please, Pallas said to him, and you will see represented actually in all its detail that which the line broadly indicates. He obeyed, and he saw coming into view all the characteristics of a portion of the life of that Sextus. They passed into another hall, and lo! another world, another Sextus. who, issuing from the temple, and having resolved to obey Jupiter, goes to Thrace.

There he marries the daughter of the king, who had no other children; he succeeds him, and he is adored by his subjects. They went into other rooms, and always they saw new scenes" (Leibniz [1710] 1996, 213–14).

4. This is the option defended by Van Looy (2005).

5. Naturally, the actual world is, for its part, also "possible." However, in the following exposition, I will call "actual world" the real world, and "possible worlds" imaginary constructions (whether realized or not in the form of cultural artifacts), which can be thought of as alternatives or variants of a referential world (the real world or another fictional world).

6. For the discussion on this subject, I allow myself to refer to Lavocat (2013).

7. We could also cite Haruki Murakami's *iq84*, which, like so many other of this author's novels, depicts a parallel world coexisting on the margins of the real world.

8. The term "metaverse" is borrowed from Neal Stephenson, who uses it in his novel *Snow Crash* (1991) to describe persistent virtual universes.

9. See https://www.youtube.com/watch?v=8_4dW1rZBhI.

10. Cameron's film *Avatar* (2007) relies on exactly the same idea, since the hero, Jack Sully, a paraplegic, agrees to infiltrate the Na'vi people in the form of a particularly agile and athletic avatar.

11. This terminology follows that proposed by Marie-Laure Ryan while adapting it for the virtual worlds. She uses TAW (textual actual world) to designate what passes as real or as fact within a fiction.

12. Thursday Next is the heroine of series of novels by Jasper Fforde, who has the power to enter books and interact with the characters. In the first novel of the series, *The Eyre Affair*, the heroine introduces herself into the *Jane Eyre* world (this title designates a novel different from the one of the real world). She modifies it and so produces a version identical to the one we are familiar with through Charlotte Brontë's novel (Fforde 2001). The version produced by Thursday Next is a fictional alternative to a fictional version of Jane Eyre in which Rochester does not marry Jane Eyre.

13. There is an abundance of literature on this point. The first generation of users naturally tended to dramatize the relation to avatars patterned on the model of absolute identification (Ludlow and Wallace 2007). Now people distinguish far more diversified relations to avatars (Meadows 2008; Di Fillipo 2012; Georges 2012). Digital natives have a far more ludic and distanced relation to the avatars than their elders (Besson 2015).

14. However, some people are predicting the coming automation of avatars (Geser 2007) and the introduction of random processes to determine the behavior of certain avatars (*The Sims*, beginning with version 3) as an op-

tion: while this of course does not mean any real autonomy, some degree of randomness may give the illusion that avatars are acting on their own.

15. There exist sweatshops in China (but also in Rumania, Indonesia, Tijuana) where "goldfarmers," playing twelve hours a day, sell avatars whose appearance and performance they have improved, as well as virtual arms or rare objects (Pfeiffer, Wang, and Beau 2007, 210–13).

16. There has been an unending stream of articles in the media proclaiming the disappearance of the gulf separating boys and girls with respect to video games (e.g., Jayanth 2013; Frum 2013). However, all you have to do is walk around a video game convention hall (e.g., the Paris Games Week in 2016) to confirm the overwhelming majority of boys making up the attendees and YouTubers.

17. It is often said that people learn a lot from games, especially in the area of history (Caïra and Larré 2009). Weighty volumes and numerous maps can provide the information the players need, and this information is not always fictional. But this learning is always subordinated to the game itself, whose main goal is pleasure and not education, even if the promoters of "serious games" disagree.

18. As for virtual pedopornography, I permit myself to refer to Lavocat (2016, 297–302).

19. A good example is the famous case of "rape in cyberspace" reported by Julian Dibbell in 1993 (see Dibbell 1998).

20. There are recent cases, however, where the theft of virtual objects has been punished either by ordering the restitution of the objects or by a fine (Beau 2007, 221–25, 229–44).

21. Users of *SL*, like the enthusiasts of MMORPGs, are in the great majority American, European, and Asian (Japan, China).

22. This was the case after the terrorist attack on November 13, 2015. The launch campaigns of Ubisoft's *Rainbow Six Siege* (France) and Activision's *Call of Duty: Black Ops III* (United States) were postponed.

23. As a twelve-year-old female player pointed out (heard at the Paris Games Week in 2016), "In *Arma 3*, you have the choice of being either a policeman or a rebel; everyone wants to be a rebel because there is more to do. It is not like a novel where you always want to be on the good side."

24. https://www.youtube.com/watch?v=LMJDOCRO9x8.

25. See the excellent discussion of this subject by Caïra (Caïra and Larré 2007, 5–8).

26. *Heavy Rain* highlights this dimension with this catchphrase: "Make choices. Face the consequences."

References

Arma 3 Altis Life. 2013. Bohemia Interactive (Czech Republic).

Beau, Frank, ed. 2007. *Culture d'univers: Jeux en réseau, mondes virtuels; Le nouvel âge de la société numérique*. Limoges: Éditions FYP.

Bell, Alice. 2010. *The Possible Worlds of Hypertext Fiction*. Basingstoke: Palgrave Macmillan UK.

Besson, Anne. 2015. *Constellations: Des mondes fictionnels dans l'imaginaire contemporain*. Paris: CNRS Éditions.

Caillois, Roger. 1967. *Les jeux et les hommes: Le masque et le vertige*. 2nd ed. Paris: Gallimard.

Caïra, Olivier. 2007. *Jeux de rôles: Les forges de la fiction*. Paris: CNRS Éditions.

——— . 2011. *Définir la fiction: Du roman au jeu d'échecs*. Paris: Éditions de l'EHESS.

——— . 2016. "Mondes numériques, écosystèmes et zookeeping." In *Mondes fictionnels, mondes numériques, mondes possibles: Adolescence et culture médiatique*, edited by Anne Besson, Nathalie Prine, and Laurent Bazin, 143–58. Rennes: Presses Universitaires de Rennes.

Caïra, Olivier, and Jérôme Larré, eds. 2009. *Jouer avec l'histoire*. Villecresnes: Pinkerton Press.

Cameron, James. 2009. *Avatar*. Twentieth Century Fox, Dune Entertainment, Giant Studios, Lightstorm Entertainment, Ingenious Film Partners.

Caracciolo, Marco. 2015. "Playing Home: Videogame Experiences between Narrative and Ludic Interest." *Narrative* 23 (3): 231–51.

Castronova, Edward. 2005. *Synthetic Worlds: The Business and Culture of Online Games*. Chicago: University of Chicago Press.

Catch 22. 2012. Mango Down.

Chaouli, Michel. 2005. "How Interactive Can Fiction Be?" *Critical Inquiry* 31 (3): 599–617.

Cornelius, Kai, and Dieter Hermann, eds. 2011. *Virtual Worlds and Criminality*. Berlin: Springer Verlag.

Dibbell, Julian. 1998. "A Rape in Cyberspace." In *My Tiny Life. Crime and Passion in a Virtual World*. New York: Henry Holt & Company. http://www.juliandibbell.com/articles/a-rape-in-cyberspace/.

Di Fillipo, Laurent. 2012. "Les notions de personnage: Joueur et Roleplay pour l'étude de l'identité dans les MMORPG." *Revue ¿ Interrogations ?* 15. http://www.revue-interrogations.org/Les-notions-de-personnage-joueur.

Doležel, Lubomír. 1998. *Heterocosmica: Fiction and Possible Worlds*. Baltimore MD: Johns Hopkins University Press.

Fforde, Jasper. 2001. *The Eyre Affair*. New York: Penguin Books.

Frum, Larry. 2013. "Nearly Half of All Video-Gamers Are Women." CNN, August 11.

Gensollen, Michel. 2007. "Vers une propriété virtuelle? L'économie réelle des univers persistants." In *Cultures d'univers: Jeux en réseau, mondes virtuels; Le nouvel âge de la société numérique*, edited by Frank Beau, 229–44. Limoges: Éditions FYP.

Georges, Fanny. 2012. "Avatars et identité dans le jeu video." *Hermès: La Revue* 1 (62): 33–47. http://hdl.handle.net/2042/48274.

Geser, Hans. 2007. "Me, My Self and My Avatar: Some Microsociological Reflections on *Second Life.*" In *Towards Cybersociety and "Vireal" Social Relations*. Zürich. http://socio.ch/intcom/t_hgeser17.htm.

Heavy Rain. 2010. David Cage, Sony Computer Entertainment.

Jayanth, Meg. 2013. "52% of Gamers Are Women—but the Industry Doesn't Know It." *Guardian*, September 18.

Juul, Jasper. 2011. *Half-Real: Video Games between Real Rules and Fictional World*. Cambridge MA: MIT Press.

Krebs, Jacqueline. 2013. "Moral Dilemmas in Serious Games." Conference paper, August. https://www.researchgate.net/publication/261947749.

Kripke, Saul A. 1963. "Semantical Considerations on Modal Logic." *Acta Philosophica Fennica* 16:83–94.

Lavocat, Françoise. 2013. "Impossible Possible Worlds." *Zeitschrift für französiche Sprache und Literatur* 123 (2): 113–29.

———. 2016. *Fait et fiction, pour une frontière*. Paris: Éditions du Seuil.

Leibniz, Gottfried. (1710) 1996. *Theodicy*. Translated by E. M. Huggard, edited by Austin Farrar. La Salle IL: Open Court.

Ludlow, Peter, and Mark Wallace. 2007. *The Second Life Herald: The Virtual Tabloid That Witnessed the Dawn of the Metaverse*. Cambridge MA: MIT Press.

The Matrix. 1999. The Wachowskis, Warner Bros., Village Roadshow Pictures, Groucho II Film Partnership, and Silver Pictures.

Meadows, Mark Stephen. 2008. *I, Avatar: The Culture and Consequences of Having a Second Life*. Berkeley: New Riders.

Meiller, Éric. 2007. "La cession des biens virtuels." In *Cultures d'univers: Jeux en réseau, mondes virtuels; Le nouvel âge de la société numérique*, edited by Frank Beau, 221–28. Limoges: Éditions FYP.

Milon, Alain. 2005. *La réalité virtuelle: Avec ou sans le corps?* Paris: Éditions Autrement.

Minecraft. 2011. Markus Persson, Jens Bergensten, Mojang Microsoft Studios, Sony Computer Entertainment.

Murakami, Haruki. 2009–10. *iq84*, vols. 1–3. Translated by Jay Rubin and Philip Gabriel. New York: Vintage International.

Neitzell, Britta. 2014. "Narrativity of Computer Games." In *The Living Handbook of Narratology*. Hamburg: Hamburg University. http://www.lhn .uni-hamburg.de/article/narrativity-computer-games.

Pavel, Thomas. 1983. "Incomplete Worlds, Ritual Emotions." *Philosophy and Literature* 7 (2): 48–58.

———. 2003. "Fiction et perplexité morale." Paper presented at the XXVe conférence Marc Bloch, EHESS, June 10. http://cmb.ehess.fr/59.

Pfeiffer, Aurélien, Lingyun Wang, and Franck Beau. 2007. "Goldfarmers, mythes et réalités." In *Cultures d'univers: Jeux en réseau, mondes virtuels; Le nouvel âge de la société numérique*, edited by Frank Beau, 210–13. Limoges: Éditions FYP.

Punday, Daniel. 2005. "Creative Accounting: Role-Playing Games, Possible-World Theory and the Agency of Imagination." *Poetics Today* 26 (1): 113–39.

Ryan, Marie-Laure. 1991. *Possible Worlds, Artificial Intelligence, and Narrative Theory*. Bloomington: Indiana University Press.

———. 1994. "Immersion vs. Interactivity: Virtual Reality and Literary Theory." *Postmodern Culture* 5 (1): 447–57.

———. 2001a. "Beyond Myth and Metaphor: The Case of Narrative in Digital Media." *Game Studies* 1 (1). http://www.gamestudies.org/0101/ryan/.

———. 2001b. *Narrative as Virtual Reality: Immersion and Interactivity in Literature and Electronic Media*. Baltimore MD: Johns Hopkins University Press.

———, ed. 2004. *Narrative across the Media: The Languages of Storytelling*. Lincoln: University of Nebraska Press.

———. 2009. "From Narrative Games to Playable Stories: Toward a Poetics of Interactive Narrative." *Storyworlds* 1:43–59.

———. 2014. "L'expérience de l'espace dans les jeux vidéo et les récits numériques." *Cahiers de Narratologie* 27. http://journals.openedition.org /narratologie/6997.

Rymaszewski, Michael, James Au Wagner, Mark Wallace, Catherine Winters, Cory Ondrejka, and Benjamin Batstone-Cunningham. 2006. *Second Life: The Official Guide*. Hoboken NJ: John Wiley & Sons, Inc.

Second Life. 2003. Philip Rosedale, Linden Lab.

Stephenson, Neal. 1991. *Snow Crash*. New York: Bantam Books.

Suler, John R., and Wende L. Phillips. 2008. "The Bad Boys of Cyberspace: Deviant Behavior in Multimedia Chat Communities." *CyberPsychology and Behaviour* 1:275–94.

Van Looy, Jan. 2005. "Visual Recentering: Computer Games and Possible World Theory." *Image & Narrative*. http://www.imageandnarrative.be /inarchive/tulseluper/vanlooy.htm.

Walsh, Richard. 2011. "Emergent Narrative in Interactive Media." *Narrative* 19 (1): 72–85.

World of Warcraft. 2001. Chris Metzen, Ayman Adham, Robert Pardo. Irvine CA: Blizzard Entertainment.

Wright, Rob / Robbie Dingo. 2006. "Better Life." *In Your Time.* https://archive.org/details/BetterLife_HighQuality.

12 : Rereading Manovich's Algorithm

Genre and Use in Possible Worlds Theory

DANIEL PUNDAY

Digital computation and possible worlds theory have a surprisingly inter-twined history. Marie-Laure Ryan's 1991 *Possible Worlds, Artificial Intelli-gence, and Narrative Theory* stands as an especially explicit early exploration of the links between the computer and possible worlds theory, but a shared interest in the philosophy of language means that the fields are far more alike than might initially seem. Amichai Kronfeld's 1990 *Reference and Computation: An Essay in Applied Philosophy of Language* explicitly artic-ulates a shared interest in reference. Although the modern philosophi-cal roots of possible worlds theory can be traced back to Meinong and Russell at the beginning of the twentieth century, seminal work by How-ell, Putnam, Donnellan, and Kripke was all published in the 1970s—the same time when programing languages like Pascal, Smalltalk, and C were developed. In *The Cultural Logic of Computation* (2009) David Golumbia associates functionalist theories of the mind with a computationalist ori-entation common through the latter part of the twentieth century. Ruth Ronen (1994, 5) has argued that possible worlds theory is by its nature interdisciplinary, but this history suggests an especially close relation-ship with digital media.

In this chapter I will explore the database central to digital media and its relationship to possible worlds theory's account of the ontology of the fictional world. My frame for doing this is the discussion of database, nar-rative, and algorithm in Lev Manovich's influential *The Language of New Media* (2001). Ultimately, I will argue that Manovich's account of the data-base and algorithm reveals commonly overlooked features of the fictional world as it appears in more traditional media.

Possible Worlds Theory and the Database

Many critics have noted the relevance of possible worlds theory to digital media. Alice Bell's 2010 *The Possible Worlds of Hypertext Fiction* is the most extensive and direct investigation of these two fields, but many others have noted how what David Ciccoricco calls "network fiction" challenges traditional ways of structuring narrative. This term does not designate fiction disseminated through the internet but rather fiction that challenges traditional ways of structuring narrative, whether in print or in digital media: "Network narratives have boundaries and limits, but they do not offer a reliable way to analyze a structural whole: in an obvious sense readers may or may not encounter all of the nodes that exist in the textual database, but less obvious is the fact that even if they do, it is unlikely that all of the possible permutations of the text will be realized" (Ciccoricco 2007, 28–29). Bell treats the challenges raised by the "database" structure of digital narrative extensively, looking at the way that we can grasp the often inconsistent worlds projected by these narratives: "In response to the ontological shift, readers must reconsider where the characters and the worlds sit in relation to each other, causing disorientation or confusion if only temporarily. This creates a feeling of uneasiness because the reader's original relationship to the text is disturbed" (2010, 45). As Bell's and Ciccoricco's comments suggest, analysis of possible worlds in digital narrative has largely focused on how readers can make sense of stories that depend on variable events, outcomes, and reading order.

I would like to argue, however, that there is a more fundamental question about the way that this database structure generates a fictional world that has been largely overlooked. I would like to turn to Manovich's discussion of database and narrative forms, which is a central part of *The Language of New Media*. Manovich argues that the database is an underappreciated but crucial element of contemporary structures of meaning that has been neglected in favor of the more traditional interest in narrative: "Database and narrative are natural enemies. Competing for the same territory of human culture, each claims an exclusive right to make meaning out of the world" (2001, 225). Narrative is embodied in the traditional media forms with which we are most familiar—such as the novel or cinema—and it is Manovich's goal to define the database and articulate what its prominence in contemporary culture means: "Many new media objects do not tell stories; they do not have a beginning or end; in fact, they do not have any development, thematically, formally, or otherwise that would organize their elements into a sequence. Instead, they are collections of individual items, with every item possessing the same significance as any other" (218).

Writing at the end of the 1990s, it is unsurprising that Manovich's main examples of the database are the internet and CD-ROM. He sees the shift away from narrative toward the database as itself an element of the postmodern loss of narrative described by Lyotard. Manovich says that since "the world appears to us as an endless and unstructured collection of images, texts, and other data records, it is only appropriate that we will be moved to model it as a database," and he sets out to offer "a poetics, aesthetics, and ethics of this database" (2001, 219).

It is clear that Manovich is exaggerating the conflict here, in large part to keep the emerging database logic from being subordinated to more established forms. Ciccoricco notes that "'narrative' and 'network' are not opposing cultural forms. Networks redistribute narrative—both in shifting the delivery model from *one-to-many* to *many-to-many* and in the sense that networks redistribute narrative elements into self-contained semantic units" (2007, 8).[1] Manovich recognizes that we can have a narrative experience of the database as we navigate through it. In fact, the 1990s forms that he has in mind would sometimes mimic narrative structures. He notes the case of a CD-ROM that might "simulate the traditional museum experience of moving from room to room in a continuous trajectory" but warns, of course, that "this narrative method of access does not have any special status in comparison to other access methods" (Manovich 2001, 220). It is clear that Manovich sees such narrative modes of access as an artificial and even nostalgic structure being imposed on the new database form and that his emphasis on a fundamental opposition between narrative and database is designed to help move away from these nostalgic modes.

In thinking about the database/narrative relationship, Manovich offers the concept of interface as a way to understand their fundamental similarities and differences. In new media like the CD-ROM or the internet, "the content of the work and the interface are separated" (Manovich 2001, 227). We might access a particular website through one of many browsers or even use a mobile app to pull that same information and organize it differently. In this regard, he suggests, traditional media with their narrative structure might be seen as simply one instance of what could be a more variable experience: "An interactive narrative (which can also be called a *hypernarrative* in an analogy with hypertext) can then be understood as the sum of multiple trajectories through a database. A traditional linear narrative is one among many other possible trajectories, that is, a particular choice made within a hypernarrative" (227).

This separation of interface from data source is why I feel that Manovich's theory of the database is so relevant to possible worlds theories as they are applied to literary texts. Possible worlds theory grows out of an interest in the problems of accounting for how references to nonexistent entities can be meaningful. Although some philosophers maintain that the best way to address the problem of such references is by appealing to a speech-act theory of language and claiming that such references are merely pretended, possible worlds theory emerged as a more compelling explanation.[2] Ryan's 1991 book is in many ways a magisterial synthesis that brings together the work in the field as it emerged in the 1970s and 1980s. The core of her account of fictionality is the idea of a textual universe organized by modal worlds that surround an actual world of the story:

> If we regard the actual world as the center of a modal system, and APWS [alternative possible worlds] as satellites revolving around it, then the global universe can be *recentered* around any of its planets. From the point of view of an APW, what we regard as the actual world becomes an alternative. We can make conjectures about what things would be like if Hitler had won the war; conversely, the inhabitants of the world in which Hitler won the war may wonder what would have happened if the Allies had triumphed—just as they have in actuality. (Ryan 1991, 18)

Once we adopt this model of possible worlds that surround the actual world and whose perspective we can adopt as a kind of mental exercise, it is easy to account for our experience of fictionality: "For the duration of our immersion in a work of fiction, the realm of possibilities is thus recentered around the sphere which the narrator presents as the actual world" (Ryan 1991, 22).[3]

By putting the status of entities at the center of their accounts of fictionality, these philosophers and literary theorists look at texts in a way that will remind us of Manovich's database logic, which is defined by distinct objects. Ronen describes possible worlds in this way: "A world of any ontological status contains a set of entities (objects, persons) organized and interrelated in specific ways (through situations, events, and space-time). A world as a system of entities and relations, is an autonomous domain in the sense that it can be distinguished from other domains identified with other sets of entities and relations" (1994, 8). Other critics adopt the slightly broader phrasing of "state of affairs," such as Lubomír Doležel: "*Fictional worlds are ensembles of nonactualized possible states of affairs.* Fictional worlds and their constituents, fictional particulars, are granted a definite ontological status, the status of nonactualized possibles" (1998, 16). Doležel makes clear that for him, as for Ronen, the fictional world is constituted by fictional "particulars." These particulars include objects and persons along with their states. Overall, these objects are independent of how the "interface" presents them. Thomas Pavel notes that these states of affairs are "distinct from the statements describing those states" (1986, 50). Although it might initially seem strange to refer to the written text as simply one "interface" on the fictional world, this separation of text and world is particularly important for explaining narrative worlds that encompass multiple books or even multiple media. This is especially the case in popular media franchises like *Star Wars* and *The Lord of the Rings,* in which characters, events, and settings constitute a world that reappears in multiple individual works, but it is equally the case when we speak of Sherlock Holmes and his London being represented in many different, relatively independent novels by Arthur Conan Doyle.

Fictional worlds, in this sense, are fundamentally a matter of entities. Indeed, possible worlds accounts of fictionality actually deemphasize the narrativity to which Manovich contrasts the database. Consider how Ryan's emphasis on modality as the center of fictional worlds redefines narrativity. For Ryan, a fictional text creates a "textual actual world," which we adopt as our temporary point of view while reading. Our experience of the fictional text is a matter of exploring the possibilities that open out from this textual actual world. This can involve a variety of ways of projecting these modal worlds: "If possible worlds are constructs of the mind, we can classify them according to the mental process to which they owe their existence. . . . A convenient point of departure for this classification is what James McCawley calls 'world-creating predicates': verbs such as to dream, to intend, to believe, to consider, to fantasize, to hypothesize"

(Ryan 1991, 19). From this perspective, then, any story actually creates a "narrative universe" made up of multiple worlds with modal relationships that are different from what we take to be the actual world projected by the story. As Ryan writes, "Within the semantic domain, the text may outline a system of reality: an actual world, surrounded by APWs. I regard this semantic dimension as constitutive of the narrative text. Narrativity resides in a text's ability to bring a world to life, to populate it with individuals through singular existential statements, to place this world in history through statements of events affecting its members, and to convey the feeling of its actuality, thus opposing it implicitly or explicitly to a set of merely possible worlds" (112).

When reading a fictional text, we are invited to consider the hopes and dreams of characters, what they believe to be true, what they plan for the future, what they imagine could have happened in the past, and so on. In fact, Ryan makes a compelling case that it is precisely the complexity of these projected worlds that makes some stories better than others: "I propose the following principle: *seek the diversification of possible worlds in the narrative universe.* We have seen [earlier] that conflicts are necessary to narrative action and that conflicts arise from the incompatibilities between TAW [textual actual world] and the private worlds of characters. The diversification of the narrative universe thus constitutes the most basic condition of tellability" (1991, 156).

In other words, texts that project more complex and varied possible worlds make the best stories: stories in which some characters are plotting their actions, other characters are fantasizing about the future, and others are imagining how life would be different had they made other choices in the past. What strikes me as especially important in the context of Manovich's distinction between the database and narrative is that this modal theory is a way of transforming the narrative temporality that we associate with storytelling into a structure of states connected to different possible worlds. From this point of view, Ryan's theory could be seen as a way of making the objects of the text central and treating events as largely secondary, associated with the various worlds that surround the textual actual world.

I am arguing, then, that possible worlds theory represents the application of a database logic focusing on entities to narrative texts that have traditionally been discussed in terms of plot, surprise, and resolution—of temporality, in other words. Although I am not arguing for a straightforwardly causal relationship between possible worlds theory and this database logic, it is clear that both emerge from a computational mindset that came to prominence during the 1970s.[4]

The Algorithm and Possible Worlds

Having shown the similarities between the database and possible worlds thinking, I would like now to begin to answer the question that my title poses: How might recognizing this database logic produce insight into the dynamics of possible worlds theory as it is applied to literary texts? In particular, I would like to focus on Manovich's discussion of the algorithm and its relationship to the text that is our interface to this narrative world.

I want to start with a discussion of the idea of structure in the database and possible worlds theory. Manovich notes that in computer science, "*database* is defined as a structured collection of data" (2001, 218). Such structures can take many forms: "Different types of databases—hierarchical, network, relational, object-oriented—use different models to organize data. For instance, the records in hierarchical databases are organized in a treelike structure. Object-oriented databases store complex data structures, called 'objects,' which are organized into hierarchical classes that may inherit properties from classes higher in the chain" (218).

Manovich is quick to point out that the databases of new media need not "employ these highly structured database models" (2001, 219). Websites, he notes, are usually "collections of separate elements—texts, images, links to other pages, or sites" (220). Manovich tends to treat new media database forms as largely unstructured and to see our experience of these objects as being shaped by the way that we encounter them—such as his example of the museum CD-ROM mentioned earlier.

This issue of encounter adds complexity to the role of the database in new media. When Manovich first introduces the idea of structure in the database, he does so by treating it as a quality of the object; in an object-oriented database, for example, child objects inherit qualities from their parents. When he talks about databases in new media, however, he emphasizes the way that we can act on them: "From the point of view of the user's experience, a large proportion of them are databases in a more basic sense. They appear as collections of items on which the user can perform various operations—view, navigate, search" (Manovich 2001, 219). Manovich doesn't pursue the potential tension between the database's structure and the operations that we can perform on it, but it is easy to see that they are related without quite being the same thing.

A crucial element of database structures in new media for Manovich is their relationship to algorithms. Manovich describes this relationship as "symbiotic" (2001, 223), but the exact way that the structure provided by the database interacts with that of the algorithm is somewhat murky. An algorithm is, of course, simply a step-by-step set of operations to be performed. Manovich introduces the concept into his discussion by using the example of the video game: "As the player proceeds through the game, she gradually discovers the rules that operate in the universe constructed by this game. She learns its hidden logic—in short, its algorithm" (222). Learning to play the game, he argues, involves "trying to build a mental model of the computer model" that will allow the player to execute the algorithm (223). Anticipating Golumbia, Manovich argues that within contemporary computing culture the world is translated into the database and algorithm: "The world is reduced to two kinds of software objects that are complementary to each other—data structures and algorithms. Any process or task is reduced to an algorithm, a final sequence of simple operations that a computer can execute to accomplish a given task. And any object in the world—be it the population of a city, the weather over the course of a century, or a chair, or a human brain—is modeled as a data structure, that is, data organized in a particular way for efficient search and retrieval" (223).

According to Manovich, database and algorithm work together to model the world. It seems clear as well that the kinds of actions that we can perform on the database are generally related to the algorithm. For example, knowing that file systems depend on nested directories of some sort means that before we can do a search we need to know that we are using the proper path. But knowing the structure of the files doesn't tell us everything about how to act on them, such as the availability of a wild-card operator or the degree to which the search system can use Boolean logic.

Of particular interest is Manovich's somewhat surprising turn to equate algorithm and narrative. I have already noted that many later theorists have criticized Manovich's categorical opposition between narrative and database, and this move only seems to confirm that the two are more intertwined than he will initially admit. Reading a narrative does not require us to adopt "algorithm-like behavior"—we can get to the end of a novel merely by knowing how to read and turn the pages of the book, in contrast to a video game that may require a complex understanding of movement and combat to progress. Nonetheless, he argues, "narrative and games are similar in that the user must uncover their underlying logic while proceeding through them—their algorithm. Just like the game player, the reader of a novel gradually reconstructs the algorithm (here I am using the term metaphorically) that the writer used to create the settings, and the events" (Manovich 2001, 225).

This is a provocative suggestion, even though Manovich backs off from its implications somewhat by suggesting that the equation of narrative and algorithm is merely metaphorical. Although it might initially seem strange to apply the idea of an algorithm to the novel, it helps to make sense of a common phenomenon: when confronted with a new type of writing, readers must learn how to read these stories before they can fully enjoy them. This insight is the foundation of Peter Rabinowitz's explanation of the "rules of reading" in *Before Reading*: "These rules govern operations or activities that, from the author's perspective, it is appropriate for the reader to perform when transforming [i.e., interpreting] texts" (1987, 43).

Manovich is describing, then, a level of organization in the database that is more than just an enumeration of its objects. In possible worlds theory, Doležel describes a similarly intermediary structure when he distinguishes what he calls extensional and intensional narrative worlds. Doležel offers this contrast as a reformulation of the difference between reference and sense. He cites Kirkham, "The extension of an expression is the object or set of objects referred to, pointed to, or indicated by, the expression" (1992, 4, cited in Doležel 1998, 136). Intention, in contrast, is defined in various ways by the philosophers and literary critics who use the term. Doležel specifically treats the texture as a quality that reveals the implied structure of values embodied in the intensional world: "Literary texts thrive on exploiting the semantic differences of expressions with the same informational content, revealing the vacuity of the notion of intensional equivalence (synonymy). They demonstrate that intension is necessarily linked to texture, to the form (structuring) of the expression; it is constituted by those meanings, which the verbal sign acquires through and in texture" (137–38).

Doležel's example of texture is the way a narrative might refer to characters differently: by a proper name (Odysseus) or a definite description (the king of Ithaca) (1998, 139–40). From an extensional point of view the inventory of objects in the world is the same regardless of how they are referenced. However, it is easy to see how different styles of reference would subtly color the work. He gives the example of Robinson Crusoe: "Three persons of its world are given proper names—'Robinson,' 'Xury,' and 'Friday'—while all the other inhabitants are named by definite descriptions only—'my father,' 'the Portuguese captain,' 'the English captain's widow,' 'Friday's father,' and so on" (140). This textural difference reveals an intensional world that supplements its extensional one.

I find Doležel's concept of extensional and intensional narrative worlds to be powerful precisely because it gets at aesthetic patterns in the writing of the story that can sometimes get neglected in possible worlds theory's focus on entities and modalities. However, it is clear from this summary that Doležel's theory still makes entities and their states of affairs the basis of the work. He summarizes the interconnection between the intensional and extensional: "Although extensions and intentions can and must be differentiated in semantic theory, they are by definition complementary in the production of literary meaning. Extensions are available only through intensions and, conversely, intensions are fixed by extensions" (Doležel 1998, 142). Indeed, Doležel suggests that "authors conceive the fictional world first as an extensional structure, inventing the story, individuating the acting persons in their properties and relationships, setting them in landscapes and cityscapes" (143). This summary nicely captures the fact that possible worlds theory imagines narrative primarily in terms of the entities that populate the world. This is clear when Doležel explains how readers reconstruct these worlds: "The readers are presented first with the intensional structuring, since they access the fictional world through the text's texture; by information or formalized paraphrasing they translate the texture into extensional representations and thus reconstruct the extensional world structure and its parts—story, character portraits, landscapes, and cityscapes" (143).

Like Manovich, Doležel sees reading as a matter of gradually building a model of the fictional world (its database of extensional objects and the values that structure them intensionally). Precisely how the algorithm contributes to this model is somewhat vague. After all, writing a novel is hardly a step-by-step process. If we return to the example of video games, we can think of learning about its regularities, not only the mechanics that allow a player avatar to move but also the implicit rules of enemy behavior, the types of jumps that are successful, and so on. In a novel, the equivalent of these implicit rules includes the sort of values that Doležel associates with the intensional world, but these regularities would also involve other things like patterns in character behavior, the kinds of situations in which they tend to find themselves, and so on. The metaphorical algorithm Manovich associates with fiction, then, seems to be a structure that exceeds that provided by the intensional world. In comparison, the intensional world is much closer to the way that a database might be given structure, since both concern the ordering of low-level components.

Genre and the Use of Possible Worlds

I have focused so much on Manovich's discussion of the algorithm because it gets at something that has intuitive relevance to narrative fiction: our sense of the inherent logic of the world. Manovich's claim that readers (or players in a video game) intuitively grasp the logic of the narrative world strikes me as a step beyond this possible worlds description and gets at higher-level concerns that we might describe as the "style" of the world. The concept of *style* has always been both intuitive and yet problematic within possible worlds theory. Doležel is quite explicit in associating literary style with the texture: "The concept of style in general, and of literary style in particular, is hardly a rigorous concept. However, it has been useful in literary study and beyond by expressing the intuition of an organized, regulated, consistent individuality or specificity. I am tempted to define literary style in terms which, at first glance, appear almost contradictory: *Literary style is an ordered set of global regularities of texture, determining conjointly the idiosyncrasy of the literary text*" (1985, 195).

Doležel makes clear that texture helps us to recognize a characteristic ordering of the textual world. He introduces this concept carefully because the idea of *style* in a fictional world might seem contradictory: worlds seem to be independent of the phrasing of the story, but we also know that we can get clues about the underlying logic of those worlds from the way that texts describe them. To take a simple example, we know that historical specificity is going to be unimportant to the fairy tale, and thus not part of the style of its world, in many ways: we can observe the lack of geographical names or precise dates, but we can also intuit this value from the fairy tale's classic opening line: "Once upon a time . . ."

Although Doležel's account of literary style is important, we should recognize that there are many other aspects of the style of a fictional world. I have always found one of the most compelling sections of Ryan's *Possible Worlds* her struggle with the limitations of what she calls "the principle of minimal departure," the rule that "we reconstrue the alternate world of a textual universe in the same way we reconstrue the alternate possible worlds of nonfactual statements: as conforming as far as possible to our representation of" the actual world (1991, 51). In other words, when we read a novel set in modern Paris, we assume the existence of the Seine and Eiffel Tower even if they are never mentioned in the book; likewise, we don't wonder how characters get around the city, because we assume the existence of taxis and the Metro. Although the concept of minimal departure is well-known, Ryan's attention to its limitations has gotten less attention than it deserves. She gives the example of the problematic implication that the writings of Aquinas are part of the world of "Little Red Riding Hood" and offers the observation that "the principle of minimal departure may be too powerful for most fictional genres" (53). Ryan goes on to suggest that we learn these principles through intertextuality, rejecting "the view that textual universes are created *ex nihilo*, and that textual meaning is the product of a self-enclosed system" (55). Like Rabinowitz, Ryan recognizes that stories depend on materials and forms that can be shared across different texts.

Ryan's observation about the way that genres influence the nature of the fictional worlds points us to a number of textual qualities that create the impression that a particular world has a style. In *On Literary Worlds*, Eric Hayot offers a suggestive listing of the stylistic features of what he calls "worldedness." Initially, Hayot's characterization of literary worlds accords with what we have seen in Ryan and others according to what I have been describing as a kind of database logic: "The world of a Balzac novel, for instance, is located in a time (the early nineteenth century) and a place (mostly Paris); includes certain kinds of people (the bourgeoisie; the aristocracy, their servants) and largely excludes others (the noncriminal working class); is organized around certain types of plots and social units (the family, particularly the extended family); and so on" (2012, 43).

Hayot's summary of Balzac's world could easily be described using a language of inventories (what spaces and characters are in the world and how these objects are organized into modalized alternative worlds) and modalities (what kinds of actions are possible, required, etc.). As his discussion develops, however, Hayot becomes increasingly focused on what we might describe as matters of style. His first of six "aspects of worldedness," for example, is drawn from Auerbach's famous discussion of the stylistic difference between *The Odyssey* and the Bible, which of course emphasizes the degree to which each work provides detail about the world. Even more suggestive is Hayot's focus on the nature of time in Bakhtin, which he sees as describing a degree to which the world is dynamic.[5]

Although Hayot doesn't emphasize the term *chronotope* specifically, it is clear that Bakhtin's concept is precisely the matter of style that seems to be a problematic part of possible worlds theory. Bakhtin's theory describes how at different historical moments the novel imagines time and space and how that in turn produces very different ways of representing human life. The Greek adventure novel relies on an abstract space of random events whose characters do not change or progress, for example, while the chivalric romance describes a miraculous world that puts the hero at its center and makes him "at home" and "every bit as miraculous as his world" (Bakhtin 1981, 154). At the very beginning of his essay, Bakhtin associates the chronotope and genre: "The chronotope in literature has an intrinsic *generic* significance. It can even be said that it is precisely the chronotope that defines genre and generic distinctions, for in literature the primary category in the chronotope is time. The chronotope as a formally constitutive category determines to a significant degree the image of man in literature as well. The image of man is always intrinsically chronotopic" (84–85).

Bakhtin's focus on genre resonates nicely with Ryan's observation about the way that genre defines the limits of minimal departure. In both of these cases, genre is a feature more general than the particular text and helps to create in the reader a set of expectations about the way to build a world out of the particular objects and events represented explicitly. In other words, genre describes a style of our access to the represented world that cannot be equated either with the catalog of entities or the values associated with them—Doležel's extensional and intensional worlds. Ryan is actually quite explicit in discussing how genre helps to guide us when we imagine fictional worlds. Genre, she argues, provides three factors: thematic focus (such as psychological, historical, or detective), stylistic filtering (which features of the worlds objects are represented, such as the idyllic), and probabilistic emphasis (the degree to which unlikely events are the focus of the story) (Ryan 1991, 43–44). When we pick up a detective novel, we know that it will generally be about crime and guilt (thematic focus), a mixture of often densely populated public and private spaces is likely to be the focus of events (stylistic filtering), and events will be resolved logically and without appeal to extraordinary or supernatural forces (probabilistic emphasis).

Although the role of genre has gotten relatively little attention in possible worlds theory outside of Ryan's work, I think that it allows us to describe a crucial feature of the "style" of these worlds that is related to but ultimately independent of the style of writing in the text itself. As I have already argued, the most obvious case of this is how we know to fill in gaps differently according to genre—we expect to apply the principle of minimal departure rigorously in realist fiction and loosely in fairy tales. To appreciate the difference between the style of the text and the style of its world, we might think of postmodern reworkings of the fairy tale. In a novel like Donald Barthelme's *The Dead Father* or a story like Robert Coover's "The Magic Poker" we encounter narratives that share the fairy tale world style but whose sentence-level writing is frequently more sophisticated or explicitly sexual than would be conventional in such stories. We might likewise think of the way that some genres encourage us to use them in different ways: some stories are clearly intended to develop realistic worlds (such as in science fiction), while others are designed to teach a moral lesson (such as a fable), and still others are designed to serve as thought experiments ("If one twin travels in a spaceship near the speed of light while the other remains back on earth . . ."). Pavel touches on this element of the use of worlds: "Semantically, tragedy can be characterized in contrast with mythical ontologies and epic sequences of events. Myths, being narratives, are composed of chains of events; by virtue of their privileged ontology, they serve as models of intelligibility for events in the profane world" (1986, 131). In other words, the features of the fictional world lend themselves to different uses—even if the worlds themselves happen to contain the same objects and values. In this regard, Manovich's choice of the term *algorithm* is especially appropriate, since that term describes what is *to be done* with the objects in the database. Genre, I argue, helps readers to build particular types of worlds from the texture of the work and to know to what use to put that world.

Conclusion

I hope to have shown that the four-part model that Manovich offers—of object, data structure, algorithm, and interface—can serve as a useful model for thinking about the structure of possible worlds in fiction. Objects and their modalities form the base of the world, and the data structure is similar to the intensional world that Doležel describes—a system by which the objects in the world are valued and given shape. The interface, obviously, is the highest level of the work, the place where we encounter the story from which we reconstruct this world. It is the equivalent of the algorithm that has largely escaped notice in possible worlds theory. I have argued that the algorithm is roughly equivalent to genre and defines the way that a world can be imagined and used. It is the metaphorical algorithm and its relationship to genre that Manovich helps us to recognize.

This emphasis on genre and the uses to which a world can be put is what Manovich allows us to recognize. My understanding of genre departs from more conventional theories that see genre simply as a form of classification—what Tzvetan Todorov describes as "discursive properties" that may appear either natural or conventional (1976, 163) and that are codified historically according to the values and ideology of a particular society (164). Instead, I have followed John Frow's account of genre as a means "to mediate between a social situation and the text which realizes certain features of this situation, or which responds strategically to its demands. Genre shapes strategies for occasions; it gets a certain kind of work done" (2015, 14–15). Carolyn Miller's rhetorical account of genre particularly embodies this equation of genre and action: "Genre refers to a conventional category of discourse based in large-scale typification of rhetorical action; as action, it acquires meaning from situation and from the social context in which that situation arose" (1984, 163). I have argued that one aspect of that social context is the actions that readers are supposed to take in building a fictional world. In this sense, genres provide guidance about what to *do* with the story, which is independent of the surface-level writing of the text itself—although one hopes as a reader that these two features of the story ultimately work together.

I would suggest that this emphasis on genre and the algorithm-like task of building a fictional work has been somewhat overlooked in more recent transmedia narratology. In their introduction to *Storyworlds across Media*,

Jan-Noël Thon and Ryan address the transtextual media franchises that I mentioned early in this essay as a particularly compelling instance of the independence of the world from the particular textual "interface" through which we encounter it: "Each of the sequels, prequels, adaptations, transpositions, or modifications that make up the body of these franchises spins a story that provides instant immersion, because the recipient is spared the cognitive effort of building a world and its inhabitants from a largely blank state" (Ryan and Thon 2014, 1). In his subsequent book *Transmedial Narratology and Contemporary Media Culture*, Thon frames the issue of how we fill in the gaps as a central concern for the concept of storyworld as it moves across media. He describes the concept of the storyworld as a "transmedial concept" even though this "does not necessarily mean that storyworlds across media are all alike" (Thon 2016, 46). In discussing storyworlds across media, he focuses on two particular qualities:

> Both narrative representations of storyworlds and these storyworlds themselves are necessarily incomplete, but recipients use their (actual as well as fictional) world knowledge to "fill in the gaps," to infer aspects of the storyworld that are only implicitly represented. This also leads us . . . to the observation that storyworlds—as worlds populated with characters and situated in space and time—consist not only of existents, events, and characters but also of the spatial, temporal, and causal relations between them, which are essential for understanding the various locally represented situations as part of a more global storyworld. (46)

Thon's discussion of storyworlds leads him to a focus on two of the qualities that I have associated with intermediary structuring concepts: the process of filling in gaps, and the style of spaces and time. My discussion of the algorithm suggests that we can add to this list the uses to which the world is put and reframe the whole set as a matter of an intermediary structure that shapes how we imagine the world that is represented in the particular media "interface."

To Thon's account of transmedia narratives, then, I am reintroducing genre and the way that it guides our use of those worlds.[6] Use is also especially relevant as we think about cross-media franchises, which so often depend on varying genre in order to give readers or game players a different experience of the same narrative world. Just as different video games set in the *Star Wars* universe allow players to do different things (fly space-ships, fight with lightsabers), so too do we expect a young-adult novel and a mainstream movie set in the same world to allow the audience to do different things. No doubt different media impose different constraints and provide different affordances on narratives in these franchises, but genre also helps to guide our sense of what we can do with these different stories set within the same world.[7] Genre and the way that it supports the imagination and use of worlds is the feature of possible worlds theory that Manovich's algorithm reveals.

Notes

1. Katherine Hayles offers a more extensive articulation of this relationship, describing narrative and database as different ways of using the syntagmatic and paradigmatic: "This insight opens onto further explorations of how databases and narratives interface together, especially in electronic literature and the more general question of literariness" (2005, 53).

2. This is particularly the case in literary criticism and more pragmatic narrative theory focused on describing the features and strategies of particular texts and less so in philosophy. In 1988 Peter J. McCormick defined the speech act model as the "standard view of fictionality" because it "remains one of the few comprehensive and influential accounts on record which continues to solicit sympathetic critical qualifications" (39).

3. In this essay I am largely treating possible worlds and fictional worlds as equivalent. As many critics have noted, fictional worlds have unique qualities that are not the case for possible worlds as applied to the actual world. Most notably, fictional worlds are necessarily incomplete.

4. I discuss a parallel focus on entities in role-playing games in *Five Strands of Fictionality*. It is easy to see this similarity as part of Golumbia's larger "culture of computation," especially since the earliest role-playing game, *Dungeons & Dragons*, was created during the same time under discussion here—the 1970s.

5. Other aspects include the completeness of the world (Hayot 2012, 60), its metadiegetic structure (67), the connectedness of the parts of the world (73), and the nature of its character system (78).

6. Media theories have, of course, tried to address this issue of use. In her introduction to *Narrative across Media*, Ryan includes "cultural role and the methods of production/distribution" to explain why the physically similar media of newspaper and novel are different (2004, 19). Lars Elleström includes "context" and "operation" as two "qualifying aspects" of media in his

theory (2010, 24–25). Both accounts try to capture something of the issue of media use, but *genre* is the broader term that describes variation even within the same medium and the same distribution system.

7. In fact, at the outset of this book Thon cites Ansgar Nünning's interest in "transgeneric and transmedial applications and elaborations of narratology" (2016, 1), but for the remainder of the book genre is clearly subordinate to media, missing an opportunity to explore how our expectations of generic use influence or experience of these works.

References

Bakhtin, M. M. 1981. *The Dialogic Imagination: Four Essays*. Translated by Caryl Emerson and Michael Holquist. Austin: University of Texas Press.

Barthelme, Donald. 1975. *The Dead Father*. New York: Farrar, Straus and Giroux.

Bell, Alice. 2010. *The Possible Worlds of Hypertext Fiction*. Basingstoke: Palgrave.

Ciccoricco, David. 2007. *Reading Network Fiction*. Tuscaloosa: University of Alabama Press.

Coover, Robert. 1969. *Pricksongs & Descants*. New York: Grove.

Doležel, Lubomír. 1985. "Literary Text, Its World and Its Style." In *Identity of the Literary Text*, edited by Mario J. Valdés and Owen Miller, 189–203. Toronto: University of Toronto Press.

———. 1998. *Heterocosmica: Fiction and Possible Worlds*. Baltimore MD: Johns Hopkins University Press.

Elleström, Lars. 2010. "The Modalities of Media: A Model for Understanding Intermedial Relations." In *Media Borders, Multimodality and Intermediality*, edited by Lars Elleström, 11–48. Basingstoke: Palgrave.

Frow, John. 2015. *Genre*. 2nd ed. New York: Routledge.

Golumbia, David. 2009. *The Cultural Logic of Computation*. Cambridge MA: Harvard University Press.

Hayles, N. Katherine. 2005. *My Mother Was a Computer: Digital Subjects and Literary Texts*. Chicago: University of Chicago Press.

Hayot, Eric. 2012. *On Literary Worlds*. New York: Oxford University Press.

Kirkham, Richard L. 1992. *Theories of Truth: A Critical Introduction*. Cambridge MA: MIT Press.

Kronfeld, Amichai. 1990. *Reference and Computation: An Essay in Applied Philosophy of Language*. Cambridge: Cambridge University Press.

Manovich, Lev. 2001. *The Language of New Media*. Cambridge MA: MIT Press.

McCormick, Peter J. 1988. *Fictions, Philosophies, and the Problems of Poetics*. Ithaca NY: Cornell University Press.

Miller, Carolyn R. 1984. "Genre as Social Action." *Quarterly Journal of Speech* 70 (2): 151–67.

Pavel, Thomas G. 1986. *Fictional Worlds*. Cambridge MA: Harvard University Press.

Punday, Daniel. 2010. *Five Strands of Fictionality: The Institutional Construction of Contemporary American Fiction*. Columbus: Ohio State University Press.

Rabinowitz, Peter J. 1987. *Before Reading: Narrative Conventions and the Politics of Interpretation*. Ithaca NY: Cornell University Press.

Ronen, Ruth. 1994. *Possible Worlds in Literary Theory*. Cambridge: Cambridge University Press.

Ryan, Marie-Laure. 1991. *Possible Worlds, Artificial Intelligence, and Narrative Theory*. Bloomington: Indiana University Press.

———, ed. 2004. *Narrative across Media: The Languages of Storytelling*. Lincoln: University of Nebraska Press.

Ryan, Marie-Laure, and Jan-Noël Thon, eds. 2014. *Storyworlds across Media: Toward a Media-Conscious Narratology*. Lincoln: University of Nebraska Press.

Thon, Jan-Noël. 2016. *Transmedial Narratology and Contemporary Media Culture*. Lincoln: University of Nebraska Press.

Todorov, Tzvetan. 1976. "The Origin of Genres." *New Literary History* 8 (1): 159–70.

Postface

THOMAS G. PAVEL

At the very beginning of their illuminating introduction to this volume, Alice Bell and Marie-Laure Ryan reflect on a distinction made by Jaakko Hintikka (1988) concerning the two ways of understanding the relationship between us human beings and our language. One option considers that natural language is a universal medium that governs our links to, and only to, the actual world. By shaping, determining, and limiting this relationship, it confines us, as the striking expression of Fredric Jameson (1972) puts it so well, to a "prison-house of language." The alternative view consists in seeing natural language as a "calculus," in Hintikka's terms, namely, as a flexible means to describe the world. Language, according to this view, allows us to reflect on the adequacy of these descriptions and of the particular idiom that conveys them, as well as to imagine and build other kinds of languages. This view, therefore, emphasizes the plasticity of languages—both natural and formal—and our aptitude to evaluate their adequacy.

In twentieth-century literary studies, as Thomas L. Martin, discussed in the introduction, showed, these two views on language had a strong impact, the first leading to several trends that put the linguistic structure of literary text in the center of critical attention and dismissed the referential power of literature, its links with political and cultural history, and its ability to generate interesting hypotheses about human life. When, by contrast, language is considered as a "calculus," that is, as a tool for proposing more or less reliable descriptions of the world, literary studies have the ability to go beyond formal considerations and examine the topics treated by literary works; the way they stage their characters, actions, and feelings; and their degree of closeness and relevance compared to the writers' and the public's actual environment. This approach thus allows us to express the conviction that, both at an ontological level and historically and culturally, "things could be different from what they are," as David Lewis put it. This view would even enable us to say, in a slightly more charged formulation, that "the existing world is not the last word."

In other terms, the distinction between, on the one hand, language as a "prison-house" and, on the other hand, language as a flexible instrument for describing what there is in the world and inside us, as well as imagining a variety of possible alternatives, offered literary studies the option of moving from a formalist approach—be it closer to behaviorism, as was the case with structuralism, or linked with aestheticism, as was the case with New Criticism and poststructuralism—to a more realist, world- and person-sensitive attitude. As we know, this change did in fact happen a generation ago and took two complementary directions. One was the energetic rise of politically inspired criticism, the most conspicuous being gender, LGBT, and race studies, interested in examining the presence of concrete, well-defined, and politically topical issues in literature. The other was the development of a more general, theoretical study of what literature focuses on, depicts, and presents to its public.

The logic of possible worlds, its vocabulary and its specific interests, as developed in the 1960s and 1970s by a group of analytical philosophers, provided the initial impulse of this more general approach. Its advantage consisted in its ability to provide a clear vocabulary, a couple of important new areas of research, and a nonnegligible promise of rigor. After a period when the referential power of literature had been neglected, it became again possible to say that literary works were *about* something, about a story—in epic poems, novels, novellas, and plays—or about feelings, based or not on a story, in lyrical poems. Being able to distinguish in these literary works between, first, the actual world in which writers and readers live, second, the slightly or drastically modified fictional one represented in this work, and third, the various possible paths—or even worlds—that the latter includes was also a great improvement. One could, for instance, evaluate the distances at which these worlds dwell from each other, their similarities and dissimilarities, the sober or playful way in which these distances and dissimilarities were meant to be received by the public. From the mere sequence of sentences examined by structuralist analyses, *Madame Bovary* turned back into the artistic report on a set of imaginary situations. From a linguistic creature, Emma Bovary became again a fictional character worthy of being admired, blamed, or pitied for her passions, actions, and tragic fate. It made sense again to argue that some of the novel's passages refer to elements belonging to our own actual world: nineteenth-century French Normandy, its social and professional groups, its daily life, the place assigned to women, their dreams and their discontent. In this novel, these latter features of the *actual* world, that is, social roles, dreams, discontent, are presented as belonging to *fictional* characters: Emma Bovary, her husband, her lovers. By perceiving these features and recognizing them as plausible, perhaps even as strikingly real, readers acknowledge that the world of this novel resembles the factual one due to a multiplicity of factors that are located beyond individual objects, landscapes, individuals, and events. Even though the human beings that act in this novel are fictional, their feelings and behavior are borrowed from our own real world. The possible world approach thus confirms Aristotle's old insight that literature represents its topics at a more general level than history, given that its *invented* characters and situations depict *real* general features of human life.

Yet precisely because it contains a promise of clarity and precision, the notion of possible (or fictional) *world* was accused of inserting yet another elusive metaphor in the traditionally vague, often inaccurate field of literary terminology. How can one call the rather narrow theater of a novel or a play its *world*? Why would we need to replace the term "fiction" by "fictional *worlds*"? How *possible* are these possible literary worlds? Jean-Marie Schaeffer ([1999] 2010) and Ruth Ronen (1994), who criticized these terms quite early, saw that, indeed, fictional *world* and *possible* literary world are metaphors. Yet, I'd suggest, there is nothing wrong about it. We should not forget, first, that scientific and humanist terminology often uses metaphors (e.g., *atoms*, genetic *code*, the *organic* unity of an artwork) and, second, that in most of these cases the meaning of the term is quite clear. Some scholars provided excellent definitions of possible literary worlds and of storyworlds, but even for scholars who didn't, inspired perhaps by Wittgenstein's interest in the *use* of a word rather than its definition, a possible literary world is a simple, clear way of pointing to the location, period, culture, and context in which the story narrated and the emotions disclosed by a literary work are taking place. One might have selected the term "setting" if it didn't exclude the characters and their actions; by contrast, a "world" is full of people, their interests, feelings, actions, and interactions. Lubomír Doležel's beautiful essay examines in detail the philosophical debates around this notion and concludes by defending a flexible view of existence according to which the worlds of fiction are quite close to the alternative versions of our actual world as postulated by philosophical or scientific hypotheses.

Concerning the important distinction between fact and fiction, highlighted so effectively by Françoise Lavocat (2016), one needs to distinguish between the "internal" experience of readers immersed in the world of a literary work and the "external" position of those who reflect on the same work. When Napoleon Bonaparte appears in a novel by Balzac, the internal approach need not distinguish between actual historical characters and fictional ones, just as when reading a novel whose main character is a contemporary public figure, one does not feel the fictional inner thoughts of the protagonist to be strikingly distinct from the correct factual details. Things obviously change when, after finishing the novel, the reader reflects on it "externally" or a critic writes a study about it. By multiplying the fictional layers within a literary work, playful postmodern stories can change this situation to some extent, yet, generally speaking, each layer of fiction in these works tends to be homogeneous and, at that particular level, to integrate elements of fact and fiction.

Brought about by the fictional worlds approach, the realization that literary works shouldn't be reduced to the language conveying them does not mean that within this new theoretical framework the study of *diegesis*, the art of telling stories, is less crucial. The work of the Ohio School (e.g., James Phelan, Brian McHale, David Herman, Peter J. Rabinowitz, Brian Richardson, Robyn Warhol) is particularly attentive to the ways in which narrative technique conveys important traits of the worlds described by fiction, for example, their social aspects, gender attitudes, and ethical significance. Sensitivity to diegetic nuances, always present in Marie-Laure Ryan's work, shapes the remarkable taxonomies proposed by Marina Grishakova of the virtual narrative voices embedded in the narratives of other speakers. As Grishakova shows, embedded, hypothetical, impersonal, fictive, metaleptic, and alternative voices serve the contemporary predilection for elusive, opaque, hybrid kinds of diegesis. Possible worlds theory also has political implications, as shown by Mattison Schuknecht's reflections on utopian and dystopian novels that fictionally magnify features of actual forms of government.

Equally interesting and equally difficult to describe if attention were only paid to the linguistic layers of literary fiction are the postmodern unnatural narratives examined by Jan Alber, narratives that excite the reader's imagination by presenting utterly impossible worlds, as well as those, analyzed by Christoph Bartsch, that play with time in ever surprising ways. Typically postmodern, these techniques highlight the playfulness of literature and art in an unprecedentedly vivid fashion. Both W. Michelle Wang's and Françoise Lavocat's articles refer to Roger Caillois's ([1958] 1961) classification of games, which distinguishes between games of mimicry or imitation, clearly related to the artistic games of make-believe, competitive games, games of chance, and games of vertigo (ilinx), the latter targeting the stability of perception and triggering a special kind of mental panic. Whereas the games of make-believe were always central for literary fiction and remain so in most lowbrow and middlebrow contemporary narratives and films, the games of chance and the games of vertigo were much less frequent in past literary works. Twentieth-century literary avant-garde, however, changed this state of affairs. Oulipo, a French literary school founded in the 1960s, promoted playful chance as the starting point of literary invention. Earlier surrealist poetry and prose works like James Joyce's *Finnegans Wake* could be seen as early examples of the literary games of vertigo that contemporary postmodern prose and narrative games use frequently and, in the case of cyberculture, as Lavocat shows, together with games of competition.

Games of make-believe being still the most frequent and most popular, they provide excellent examples for scholars who reject poststructuralist dogmas. Thus, Thomas L. Martin shows that twentieth-century fantasy-literature decisively refutes the idea that literature is first of all *écriture* (writing), as Jacques Derrida and his disciples argued in the second half of the past century. The immense success of *The Lord of the Rings* (1937-49), by J. R. R. Tolkien, is not the result of stylistic glamor—for in fact, as many critics agree, Tolkien's style is rather muddy—but it rewards the extraordinary capacity for *invention*, which gave fictional life to the universe that includes the hobbits; the Dark Lord, Sauron; and the wars to conquer or defend Middle-earth. To dismiss this argument one certainly could maintain that *The Lord of the Rings* is nothing but popular literature, "kitsch" in the terminology of the art critic Clement Greenberg, who in the mid-twentieth century held in contempt figurative art and readable literature and reserved praise for avant-garde nonfigurative art and highly sophisticated, barely comprehensible literature. Whatever side one prefers in the rivalry between the latter kind of artistic productions and the mainstream, successful works, the possible worlds approach allows one to avoid excluding the other side: instead of an "either . . . or" attitude one can adopt an "and . . . and" position that accepts and values, say, both *Finnegans Wake* and *The Lord of the Rings*, each for its own kind of success, be it an elitist ilinx or a popular fantasy fable.

Notably, by paying attention to the effects of literary invention, some of the literary scholars interested in the possible/fictional worlds approach feel close to the ecological approach to literature, as well as to the "embodied mind" psychology. To briefly go back to the critique of the *world* notion in literary studies, Richard Walsh (2007) raised a notable objection to its powerful generalization as *storyworlds* in David Herman's (e.g., 2002) theoretical works. Walsh's critique descends from the venerable tradition opened by Gotthold Ephraim Lessing's *Laokoon or the Limits of Poetry and Painting* ([1767] 1836), which distinguishes the spatial nature of visual arts from the temporality of literature. Likewise, according to Walsh's argument, since *stories* are temporal artifacts, while *worlds* are organized as spaces, the term "storyworlds" is contradictory. In his contribution to this volume, however, Marco Caracciolo convincingly argues that reality *unfolds* itself to us as *beings-in-the-world* (Martin Heidegger's expression), that time is part of this world-inhabiting experience, and that as embodied creatures we fully belong to the *Umwelt* (Jakob von Uexküll's [1909] term for the world that surrounds us) and learn/act according to the *affordances* (James J. Gibson's [1979] term), that is, according to the opportunities for action and interaction nature offers us. We experience possible/fictional worlds, Caracciolo submits, in a similar way, as unfolding themselves to us and offering us a wide range of vicarious (my term) affordances.

Narrative experimentation made possible by digital technology is the topic of Alice Bell's cutting-edge reflections on the ontological effects of external hyperlinks in digital fiction. These effects, labeled by Bell "flickering" (a disorienting presentation of a variety of links), "refreshment" (by allusion to the actual world), and "merging" (between fact and fiction), are digital forms of the games of clues and discovery, for example, finding a hidden object by following various hints. New and exciting versions of possible worlds are thus offered to our imagination. Daniel Punday's essay on narratives as databases (possible worlds) accompanied by algorithms (rules governing their use) provides the volume with an insightful finale.

To conclude, I would suggest, first, that because we live in a time when stimulating experiments and innovations abound, we shouldn't be tempted to neglect the *history* of fiction. It is important to remember that virtually all human groups, be they organized as hunter-gatherer, agricultural, or warrior societies, need myths, legends, and daily life stories that both widen and limit their access to the world. What is deemed to be fictional or actual varies to some extent along history, as does the distance at which mythical and fictional worlds are located. But this variation is not necessarily uniform, and it makes little sense to argue, say, that fiction as such appeared at this or that time and place in human history. True, myths tend with time to turn into fictions (pleasant or horrible), but myth as a category of human imagination is remarkably stable (nowadays being satisfied by economic, sociological, or neuropsychological stories), as are legends (nowadays created by politicians, historians, and journalists) and fiction (still favored by literary narratives).

Second, contemporary narratology and possible worlds theory offer a remarkably advanced knowledge of the artistic means of the literary craft, concerning both narrative techniques and ways of imaginary world building. Next, possible/fictional worlds theory might want to examine the reasons why this literary craft has always existed and continues to prosper. We could, in other words, turn our attention to questions like "why fiction?" and "why the need to invent worlds of make-believe, of chance, of vertigo?"—questions to which the possible/fictional worlds approach could offer new and convincing answers. These answers would most probably include the venerable—and incredibly durable—notions of delight (*delectare*), becoming aware (*docere*), and being moved (*movere*). They would also tell us more about the ways in which fiction "transports" its public away from daily life, makes it *cross the distance*, minimal or maximal, between actual and fictional worlds, and, after the *detour* through fiction—after the visit to the worlds of *Hamlet*, of *Madame Bovary*, or of *The Lord of the Rings*—invites this public to recognize and evaluate its own world. These answers might remind us that because each work of fiction shows us a set of situations involving human actions, their motives and goals, as well as the values and inner powers that guide characters through a labyrinth of life-paths, the vicarious reality, distance, and detours offered by these works delight us; the examples they propose, each case with its own individual solution, make us aware of the complexity of the moral order; the moving fear, joy, empathy, and catharsis they provide resonate deeply within us.

References

Caillois, Roger. (1958) 1961. *Man, Play, and Games.* Translated by Meyer Barash. New York: Free Press.

Gibson, James J. 1979. *The Ecological Approach to Visual Perception.* Boston: Houghton Mifflin.

Herman, David. 2002. *Story Logic: Problems and Possibilities of Narrative.* Lincoln: University of Nebraska Press.

Hintikka, Jaakko. 1988. "Exploring Possible Worlds." In *Possible Worlds in Humanities, Arts and Sciences: Proceedings of Nobel Symposium 65,* edited by Sture Allén, 52–73. Berlin: de Gruyter.

Jameson, Fredric. 1972. *The Prison-House of Language: A Critical Account of Structuralism and Russian Formalism.* Princeton NJ: Princeton University Press.

Lavocat, Françoise. 2016. *Fait et fiction: Pour une frontière.* Paris: Seuil.

Lessing, Gotthold Ephraim. (1767) 1836. *Laokoon or the Limits of Poetry and Painting.* Translated by William Ross. London: Ridgeway.

Martin, Thomas L. 2004. *Poiesis and Possible Worlds: A Study in Modality and Literary Theory.* Toronto: University of Toronto Press.

Ronen, Ruth. 1994. *Possible Worlds in Literary Theory.* Cambridge: Cambridge University Press.

Schaeffer, Jean-Marie. (1999) 2010. *Why Fiction?* Lincoln: University of Nebraska Press.

Uexküll, Jakob von. 1909. *Umwelt und Innenwelt der Tiere.* Berlin: J. Springer.

Walsh, Richard. 2007. *The Rhetoric of Fictionality: Narrative Theory and the Idea of Fiction.* Columbus: Ohio State University Press.

Contributors

Jan Alber is professor of English literature and cognition at RWTH Aachen University and president of the International Society for the Study of Narrative (ISSN). He is the author of *Narrating the Prison* (2007) and *Unnatural Narrative: Impossible Worlds in Fiction and Drama* (2016). Alber received fellowships and research grants from the British Academy, the German Research Foundation, and the Humboldt Foundation. In 2013 the German Association of University Teachers of English awarded him the prize for the best *Habilitation* (2011–13). Between 2014 and 2016 he worked as a COFUND (Marie-Curie) Fellow at the Aarhus Institute of Advanced Studies.

Christoph Bartsch was a research assistant and lecturer in German literature at the University of Wuppertal, Germany. Bartsch has published various book chapters and reviews in the fields of possible worlds theory, cognitive narratology, and psychoanalytic narrative theories. Most recently he has authored a contribution to *Ordnungen des Unheimlichen* (Könighausen & Neumann, 2016) dealing with the Freudian uncanny as a concept for narrative analysis. He is coediting the forthcoming collection *Welt(en) erzählen: Paradigmen und Perspektiven*, which focuses on several approaches exploring narrative worlds. In 2012 he organized a graduate conference called "Welten erzählen: Narrative Evokation des (Un-)Möglichen."

Alice Bell is professor of English language and literature at Sheffield Hallam University, UK. Her research specialisms are cognitive stylistics, narratology, empirical approaches to literature, and digital fiction. Bell is author of *The Possible Worlds of Hypertext Fiction* (Palgrave, 2010) and coeditor of *Analyzing Digital Fiction* (with Astrid Ensslin and Hans K. Rustad; Routledge, 2014). She has published articles in journals such as *Narrative, Journal of Narrative Theory, Storyworlds, Style,* and the *International Journal of Literary Linguistics,* as well as essays in collections, including *World Building: Discourse in the Mind* (Bloomsbury, 2016) and *A Poetics of Unnatural Narrative* (Ohio State University Press, 2013).

Marco Caracciolo is associate professor of English and literary theory at Ghent University in Belgium, where he leads the ERC Starting Grant project "Narrating the Mesh." Marco's work explores the phenomenology of narrative, or the structure of the experiences afforded by literary fiction and other narrative media. He is the author of three books: *The Experientiality of Narrative: An Enactivist Approach* (De Gruyter, 2014); *Strange Narrators in Contemporary Fiction: Explorations in Readers' Engagement with Characters* (University of Nebraska Press, 2016); and *A Passion for Specificity: Confronting Inner Experience in Literature and Science* (coauthored with psychologist Russell Hurlburt; Ohio State University Press, 2016).

Lubomír Doležel, fellow of the Royal Society of Canada and honorary doctor of the Masaryk University in Brno and the Palacký University in Olomouc, was professor emeritus of Toronto University. He was selected for the 2016 Wayne C. Booth Lifetime Achievement Award. He published widely and internationally on stylistics, poetics, semiotics, linguistics, narratology, and literary theory. Among his book publications are *Narrative Modes in Czech Literature* (1973) and *Occidental Poetics: Tradition and Progress* (1990). He contributed substantially to the formation of fictional worlds semantics in *Heterocosmica: Fiction and Possible Worlds* (1997), *Possible Worlds of Fiction and History: The Postmodern Stage* (2010), and *Heterocosmica II: Fictional Worlds of Postmodern Czech Prose* (2014, in Czech). Professor Doležel passed away on January 28, 2017.

Marina Grishakova is professor of literary theory and comparative literature at the Institute of Cultural Research, University of Tartu, Estonia. She is the author of *The Models of Space, Time and Vision in V. Nabokov's Fiction: Narrative Strategies and Cultural Frames* (2nd ed., 2012) and a coeditor of *Intermediality and Storytelling* (with Marie-Laure Ryan, 2010) and *Theoretical Schools and Circles in the Twentieth-Century Humanities: Literary Theory, History, Philosophy* (with Silvi Salupere, 2015). Her articles have appeared in *Narrative*, *Sign Systems Studies*, and *Revue de littérature comparée*. She has contributed chapters to international volumes such as *Strange Voices in Narrative Fiction* (2011); *Literature, History and Cognition* (2014); *Intersections, Interfer-*

ences, Interdisciplines: Literature with Other Arts (2014); and *Blackwell Companion to Literary Theory* (2017).

Françoise Lavocat is professor of comparative literature at the University Sorbonne nouvelle—Paris 3. She specializes in theories of fiction (fact and fiction, possible worlds, characters), early modern literature, and the narrative of catastrophes. She was formerly a fellow at the Wissenschaftkolleg zu Berlin (2014–15), and she is currently a member of the Institut Universitaire de France (2015–20) and of the Academia Europaea (2017–). She has published *Arcadies malheureuses: Aux origines du roman moderne* (Champion, 1997); *La Syrinx au bûcher: Pan et les satyres à la renaissance et à l'âge baroque* (Droz, 2005); *Usages et théories de la fiction: La théorie contemporaine à l'épreuve des textes anciens* (Presses Universitaires de Rennes, 2004); *La théorie littéraire des mondes possibles* (CNRS, 2010); and *Fait et fiction: Pour une frontière* (Seuil, 2016).

Thomas L. Martin is associate professor of English at Florida Atlantic University, where he teaches literary theory, Renaissance literature, and literature of the fantastic. He is the author of *Poiesis and Possible Worlds* (University of Toronto Press, 2004), coauthor of *The Renaissance and the Postmodern* (with Duke Pesta; Routledge, 2016), and editor of *Reading the Classics with C. S. Lewis* (Baker Academic, 2000). He is also author of various articles on Renaissance literature, literary theory, and fantasy literature. He is currently working on an introductory textbook for literature classes using possible worlds theory with the title "Dwelling in Possibility: A New Introduction to Literature."

Thomas G. Pavel was born in Bucharest, Romania. Educated in his native country and in France, he pursued an academic career in Canada and the United States. A lover of literature, he reflected on the nature of fictional worlds, their puzzling distance from the actual world, and their inexhaustible diversity. His recent work *The Lives of the Novel* (2013) is a history of the novel as a genre, from its ancient Greek origins to the present. Having taught at the University of Quebec in Montreal, the University of California, Santa Cruz, and Princeton University, he now serves as the Gordon J. Laird Distinguished Service Professor in Comparative Literature, Romance Languages and Literatures, and Social Thought at the University of Chicago. His books, written in English and French, have been translated into Italian, Spanish, Portuguese, Romanian, Czech, and Japanese.

Daniel Punday is professor in and head of the Department of English at Mississippi State University. He works in narrative theory, contemporary U.S. literature, and digital media. His most recent book is *Computing as Writing* (Minnesota, 2015).

Marie-Laure Ryan is an independent scholar working in the areas of narrative theory, media theory, digital textuality, and representations of space. She is the author of *Possible Worlds, Artificial Intelligence and Narrative Theory* (1991), *Narrative as Virtual Reality: Immersion and Interactivity in Literature and Electronic Media* (2001, 2nd ed., 2015), and *Avatars of Story* (2006), and she is the coauthor of *Narrating Space / Spatializing Narrative* (2016). She has been scholar in residence at the University of Colorado, Boulder, and Johannes Gutenberg Fellow at the University of Mainz, Germany, and she is the recipient of the 2017 lifetime achievement award from the International Society for the Study of Narrative. Her website is www.marilaur.info.

Mattison Schuknecht is a graduate student of English at Pennsylvania State University. His main areas of research include British Renaissance literature, especially the work of Edmund Spenser, the literature of the fantastic, and narrative theory. His work has appeared in the journals *The Explicator* and *Mythlore*. He is presently writing on the long /ī/ vowel sound in Ayn Rand's *Anthem*.

W. Michelle Wang is a postdoctoral scholar at Queen Mary University of London and a research fellow at Nanyang Technological University, Singapore. Her major field is in postmodern and contemporary fiction, with a scholarly interest in East Asian popular culture. She has published articles in the *Review of Contemporary Fiction* and the *Journal of Narrative Theory*. Her latest article is published in *Narrative* and is titled "Hearing the Unsaid: Musical Narration in *The Journey of Flower* and *Nirvana in Fire*" (January 2018).

Index

Page numbers in italics refer to figures and tables.

Mann, Thomas, 99

Manovich, Lev, 36–37, 296–312

Margolin, Uri, 94–95

Márquez, Gabriel García, 95, 204

Martin, Thomas L., 1, 13–14, 33–34, 201–24, 315, 319

Marvell, Andrew, 210

Marxism, 22, 225, 240

The Matrix, 236, 276

Maupassant, Guy de, 215

maximal departure, 31–32, 134, 136, 141–42, 144, 147

maximality, 74, 274

McCawley, James, 300

McCormick, Peter J., 312n2

McHale, Brian, 25, 98, 136–38, 318

McIntyre, Dan, 97

McKillip, Patricia, 209

McLaughlin, Robert, 268

mediacy, 120–21

Meinong, Alexius, 58, 296

Melia, Joseph, 54

Melissa and Melissa (Allen), 274

Melville, Herman, 99

Mendlesohn, Farah, 204, 215–17

metafiction, 28, 67, 96, 142, 149, 253, 260, 279

metalepsis, 25–26, 66, 95, 100, 137, 278, 318

metanarrative, 67, 240

metaphor, 115, 117, 118, 127, 210, 220, 229, 233, 259, 272, 304, 306, 310, 317

metaverses, 36, 275–79, 283, 290n8. See also *Second Life*

microfiction, 68–70

Miéville, China, 216

Mihailescu, Calin Andrei, 230–31

Miller, Carolyn, 310

mimesis, 53, 75, 76–77, 80–81, 98, 126–27, 142, 206, 210–11, 215, 261, 273

Minecraft, 276, 280

minimal departure, 29, 31, 72, 80, 127, 134, 136, 141–42, 181–82, 188–89, 254, 258, 307–9

Mitchell, David, 65

MMOGs, 275, 283–84. See also *Second Life*

MMORPGs, 36, 275, 284–85, 291n21. See also *World of Warcraft*

Moby Dick (Melville), 99

modal logic, 4, 8, 11, 13, 35, 47, 54–55, 62, 89, 126–27, 179–80, 182–83, 185–86, 228, 229, 231, 238–40, 274–75, 279–88, 299–301, 305, 307–8, 310; accessibility in, 4, 8, 12, 14–15, 20–22, 31, 65, 126, 134–36, 145, 147, 148, 157, 170, 188, 193, 226, 231–34, 235, 236, 239, 244n15, 274, 276. *See also* Kripke, Saul; Ryan, Marie-Laure

modal realism, 6, 7–8, 15, 50–51, 96. *See also* Lewis, David

model theory, 211

modernist fiction, 91–92, 94, 203

Modern Library, 203

Molloy (Beckett), 17

"Les mondes possibles du texte" (Vaina), 11. *See also* Eco, Umberto; Ryan, Marie-Laure

monstrosity, 88

The Moon Is a Harsh Mistress (Heinlein), 228–29

More, Thomas, 35, 230, 233–34, 237, 242

Morrell, Edward H., 188, 192

Morris, Charles, 50

Morris, William, 203

Morrison, Toni, 96

Morson, Gary Saul, 89

motor resonance, 124, 128. *See also* Taylor, Lawrence J.; Zwaan, Rolf A.

Mulligan Stew (Sorrentino), 25

multiple endings, 164–65, 170

Phelan, James, 318
phenomenology, 117, 118, 128, 161–65, 170, *219*
Phillips, Elizabeth, 100
The Pickwick Papers (Dickens), 215
Pirandello, Luigi, 25
Planck, Max, 202
Plantinga, Alvin, 3
Plato, 35, 53, 234, 237, 242
play, 120–21, 132, 136, 141–44, 147, 148, 165, 170, 209, 220, 249, 252–53, 261, 319
plot, 115, 123, 125, 181–82, 185–86, 194, 231, 241–42, 255, 274, 279, 301, 307
The Plot against America (Roth), 23
Plunkett, Edward. *See* Dunsany, Eighteenth Baron of (Edward Plunkett)
Poe, Edgar Allan, 100
Poetics (Aristotle), 62
Pohl, Frederik, 24
Poiesis and Possible Worlds (Martin), 13–14, 217–18
point of view, 257–58, 261–63, 265, 279, 300
Point Omega (DeLillo), 102–3
Pope, Alexander, 220
Popova, Yanna, 120–21, 122, 126
Porfyry's tree, 48, *49*, 56
possibilism, 54–55, 201
The Possible and the Actual (Jacob), 88
Possible Worlds, Artificial Intelligence and Narrative Theory (Ryan), 12, 19, 21–22, 75, 96–97, 127, 296, 299, 307
"Possible Worlds in Humanities, Arts and Sciences" Nobel symposium (1986), 8, 54
"Possible Worlds in Literary Semantics" (Pavel), 9, 47
Possible Worlds in Literary Theory (Ronen), 13

Possible Worlds of Fiction and History (Doležel), 13, 22
The Possible Worlds of Hypertext Fiction (Bell), 13, 27–28, 297, 315, 320
Possible Worlds of the Fantastic (Traill), 13, 213–17
possible worlds theory, 1–39, 53–57, 67, 88–91, 96–97, 113, 157–76, 182, 205–15, 217–18, 225–31, 252–56, 267, 274–75, 296–313, 315–22
postmodernism, 168–69, 240, 268, 298, 309, 319
postmodernist fiction, 24–26, 27, 30, 31, 35–36, 66, 71, 75, 91, 132–38, 142, 147, 148–49, 158, 170n1, 204, 229–30, 251, 255, 260, 268, 318–19
post-postmodernism, 250, 268
"Postscript to 'Truth in Fiction'" (Lewis), 17
poststructuralism, 1, 3, 48, 81, 316, 319
pragmatics, 48–50, 57, 216, 253, 299
Pratchett, Terry, 204
Pratt, Mary Louise, 69
prehension, 90. *See also* Whitehead, Alfred North
Prickitt, Lyndee, 264–67, *265*
Pride and Prejudice (Austen), 71, 73
Pride and Prejudice and Zombies (Grahame-Smith), 71
Priest, Graham, 158, 169
Prince, Gerald, 69
principle of amelioration, 234, *235*, 236–38, 244n15
principle of maximal departure. *See* maximal departure
principle of minimal departure. *See* minimal departure
Problems of Dostoevsky's Poetics (Bakhtin), 92
protointerpretation, 161, 170

Wittgenstein, Ludwig, 1, 317
Wittig, Monique, 95
Wolf, Mark, 222n9
Wolfe, Gary K., 209
Wolterstorff, Nicholas, 49, 74, 75
world. *See* actual world (aw); alternate possible world (apw); doxastic worlds; fantasy world; fictional world; impossible world; narrated world; nonporous worlds; possible worlds theory; secondary world; small worlds; storyworld; subworld; textual actual world (taw); total worlds; virtual world (vw)

World of Warcraft, 36, 273, 275, 286
Wright, Rob, 276, *277*, 278
Wyndham, John, 24

Yagisawa, Takashi, 55
Yakobi, Tamar, 99
YouTube, 285

Zamyatin, Yevgeny, 229
Zipes, Jack, 222n14
Zuleika Dobson (Beerbohm), 203
Zunshine, Lisa, 162
Zwaan, Rolf A., 124, 128. *See also* motor resonance

9 780803 294998